Black Dixie

NUMBER FORTY-ONE
*The Centennial Series
of the Association of Former Students,
Texas A&M University*

BLACK DIXIE

Afro-Texan History and Culture in Houston

Edited by Howard Beeth and Cary D. Wintz

Texas A&M University Press
College Station

Copyright © 1992 by Howard Beeth and Cary D. Wintz
Manufactured in the United States of America
All rights reserved
First Paperback Edition

The paper used in this book meets the minimum requirements of the
American National Standard for Permanence of Paper for
Printed Library Materials, Z39.48-1984. Binding materials
have been chosen for durability. ∞

Library of Congress Cataloging-in-Publication Data
Black Dixie : Afro-Texan history and culture in Houston / edited by
Howard Beeth and Cary D. Wintz. — 1st ed.
p. cm. — (Centennial series of the Association of Former
Students, Texas A&M University ; no. 41)
ISBN 0-89096-494-7 (alk. paper) ISBN 0-89096-976-0 (pbk.)
1. Afro-Americans — Texas — Houston — History.   2. Houston
(Tex.) — History.   I. Beeth, Howard.   II. Wintz, Cary D., 1943-   .
III. Series.
F394.H89N418   1992
976.4'235 — dc20   91-39257
                                                                  CIP

To Alexis and Jason
and to the memory of our colleagues
Lorenzo J. Greene (1899-1988)
F. Kenneth Jensen (1943-88)

Contents

List of Illustrations *page* ix
List of Tables xi
Acknowledgments xiii

Part I. Historians, Houston, and History
    Historians, Houston, and History
        Howard Beeth 3

Part II. Slavery and Freedom: Blacks in Nineteenth-Century Houston
    Introduction 13
    Use and Distribution of Slave Labor in Harris County, Texas, 1836–60
        Tamara Miner Haygood 32
    Seeking Equality: Houston Black Women during Reconstruction
        Barry A. Crouch 54
    Richard Allen: The Chequered Career of Houston's First Black State Legislator
        Merline Pitre 74

Part III. Economic and Social Development in Black Houston during the Era of Segregation
    Introduction 87
    The Emergence of Black Business in Houston, Texas: A Study of Race and Ideology, 1919–45
        James M. SoRelle 103
    "Yes, We Have No Jitneys!": Transportation Issues in Houston's Black Community, 1914–24
        Frances Dressman 116
    Houston's Colored Citizens: Activities and Conditions among the Negro Population in the 1920s
        Clifton F. Richardson, Sr. 128

    Sidelights on Houston Negroes as Seen by an Associate
    of Dr. Carter G. Woodson in 1930
      Lorenzo J. Greene   134

Part IV. Segregation, Violence, and Civil Rights: Race Relations
in Twentieth-Century Houston
    Introduction   157
    Race Relations in "Heavenly Houston," 1919–45
      James M. SoRelle   175
    Black Houstonians and the White Democratic Primary,
    1920–45
      Robert V. Haynes   192
    The Houston Sit-In Movement of 1960–61
      F. Kenneth Jensen   211
    Operation Breadbasket in Houston, 1966–78
      Cecile E. Harrison and Alice K. Laine   223
    Housing Problems and Prospects in Contemporary Houston
      Robert D. Bullard   236
    Organizing in the Private City: The Case of Houston, Texas
      Robert Fisher   253

About the Contributors   278
Index   281

Illustrations

Rev. Jack Yates	*page* 26
African-American longshoremen, 1922	93
Alpha Kappa Omega chapter of Alpha Kappa Alpha, circa 1942	95
Mollie Brown at Douglass Elementary School in Houston's Third Ward, circa 1906–11	97
Martha Yates Jones and Pinkie Yates in Juneteenth parade buggy, 1908	99
Houston Negro Chamber of Commerce headquarters	110
Pinkie Yates with class at Colored High School in Houston's Fourth Ward, circa 1910	132
Black businessmen, circa 1910	150
Helen Glover Perry conducting voter registration drive, circa 1961	159
Members of Third Battalion of Twenty-fourth U.S. Infantry	162
Artist John Biggers, 1983	166
African Americans participating in Democratic Harris County Rump Convention, 1948	207
Louie Welch campaigning, 1966	225
Houston's Fourth Ward, mid-1980s	246
Texas Southern University students demonstrating, 1967	263

Tables

1. Houston's Black Population by Ward, 1870–1910 page 23
2. 1840 Size of Slaveholdings, Harris County 36
3. 1850 Size of Slaveholdings, Harris County 39
4. Age-Sex Distribution of Slaves in Houston, 1850; Age-Sex Distribution of Slaves in Harris County outside Houston, 1850 40
5. 1850 Agricultural Slavery, Harris County 41
6. 1860 Size of Slaveholdings, Harris County; 1860 Number of Slaves per Household, Harris County 46
7. Black Population in Houston, 1850–1980 89
8. Comparison of Black Neighborhoods, 1970 and 1980 167
9. Black Occupations, 1920–80 169
10. Number of Public Housing Units in the Ten Largest U.S. Cities, 1982 240
11. Houston Housing Authority Developments, 1983 241
12. Ethnic Composition of Houston Housing Authority Developments, 1976 243
13. Ethnic Composition of Houston Housing Authority Developments, 1984 244
14. Ethnic Composition of Allen Parkway Village for Selected Years 245
15. Housing Discrimination Complaint Activity in Houston, 1975–82 247
16. Disposition of Housing Discrimination Complaints in Houston, 1979–82 248
17. Geographic Location of Housing Discrimination Complaints in Houston, 1979–82 249
18. Type of Alleged Housing Discrimination by Percent Minority in Complaint Census Tracts, Houston, 1979–80 249

Acknowledgments

All works of scholarship are deeply collaborative in a way that no title page by itself can suggest. To begin with, projects such as this build squarely upon the work of earlier generations of scholars, without which current scholarship could scarcely be imagined, let alone achieved. The editors of *Black Dixie* acknowledge with thanks their predecessors whose legacy is such a rich and varied one. In addition, most scholarship could not be accomplished without the valuable material housed in archives and the equally valuable archivists who work in them. The editors are pleased to acknowledge with gratitude the help of several archives whose personnel made our visits to them so worthwhile. In Houston, the director of the Houston Public Library's Metropolitan Research Center, Louis J. Marchiafava, as well as his able assistants, Nancy Hadley and Chuck Hamilton, extended courtesies above and beyond the call of duty. In Austin, the director of the Eugene C. Barker Texas History Center at the University of Texas, Don E. Carleton, and his colleague, Ralph Elder, likewise shared their expertise. We also wish to thank all of our friends and associates who, through numerous conversations and interactions, contributed to this work in ways in which they probably were not even aware, especially Wolde Michael Akalou and our colleagues in the Department of History and Geography at Texas Southern University. Finally, we wish to acknowledge the women in our lives, Melodie Andrews and Celia Janet Wintz, who endured the days when our preoccupation with this project detracted from our time with them, and whose love, caring, and patience sustained us throughout the long months occupied by this endeavor.

The following publishers had the good sense to publish the following works that they were kind enough to allow us to reprint in this volume:

Merline Pitre, "Richard Allen: The Chequered Career of Houston's First Black State Legislator," *Houston Review* 7 (1986): 2, 79-88.

Frances Dressman, "'Yes, We Have No Jitneys!': Transportation Issues in Houston's Black Community, 1914-1924," *Houston Review* 9 (1987): 2, 69-81.

Robert V. Haynes, "Black Houstonians and the White Democratic Primary, 1920–1945," in Francisco A. Rosales and Barry J. Kaplan, eds., *Houston: A Twentieth Century Urban Frontier* (Port Washington, N.Y.: National University Publications/Associated Faculty Press, 1983), pp. 115–38.

These pieces appear essentially in the form in which they were first published. Minor errors that do not alter substance or meaning have been corrected.

Part I

Historians, Houston, and History

Historians, Houston, and History

Howard Beeth

The historical profession in the United States traditionally has been overwhelmingly staffed and thoroughly dominated by white, middle-class males whose teaching, research, and writing have been marked by their prejudice towards groups of people unlike themselves. In an important new study, *Black History and the Historical Profession, 1915-1980,* August Meier and the late Elliott M. Rudwick offer ample evidence that few white historians paid much attention to black history, and that most of what they wrote was seriously flawed by their racism. The ability of black historians to correct the historical record was, as Rudwick and Meier demonstrate, severely limited. Denied appointments at white institutions that promoted scholarship and faculty development, African-American scholars were forced to spend their careers being overworked in the classroom and woefully underpaid by poor, small, black church or public schools that had little, if any, funds for faculty travel and research. Blacks who attempted to overcome these disadvantages often were not welcomed at white-controlled research facilities. The occasional exceptions to these patterns, as Rudwick and Meier indicate, serve only to underscore the general rule. The direct consequence of these developments for the history of black America has been a disturbing combination of neglect and distortion. This has also been the consequence for the history of black Houston. As one scholar recently observed, "Texas and Houston have a sordid racial past and unpromising racial future, but no collective racial memory."[1]

These, however, are not the only reasons why so little of Houston's rich, multicultural history is known. Other factors, although less evident, have not only shrouded the history of black Houston but indeed have kept veiled much of the larger history of the city. At first glance, this historical amnesia is puzzling and difficult to explain. Houston is, after all, now the largest city in Texas and the fourth largest in the nation. In earlier years it played a prominent role in the timber, cotton, rail, and shipping industries; currently it is a center in oil, gas, and petrochemical production and processing as well as medical technology and space exploration. Indeed,

Houston's impressive size, legendary prosperity, and considerable influence have earned it the well-deserved sobriquet as the Buckle of the Sunbelt.[2] What, then, accounts for the wanton neglect of a city whose characteristics should have commanded it to the attention of scholars—particularly in a state well known for promoting its history ad nauseam?[3] A brief examination of the relationship between events, time, and memory in Houston might suggest a similar relationship in other southern cities.

Houston's growth pattern has done little to foster either cultural development or an inclination toward thoughtful reflection. From its founding in 1836 by a pair of New York real estate promoters until the beginning of this century, when its population reached 44,000, Houston lacked the required "critical mass" of residents and capital necessary to sustain expensive cultural institutions. Hence, the settlement on Buffalo Bayou remained a busy but nondescript and undistinguished town in the nineteenth century. The tempo of its evolution, however, changed dramatically thereafter; by 1920 the city's population more than tripled to 138,000, and within the next two decades it almost tripled again to over 400,000. By the middle of the century, Houston numbered almost three quarters of a million people, and in 1986, the year of its 150th anniversary, it was approaching the two-million mark.

This frenetic rate of growth—essentially the city has been a residential construction site for decades—has whetted more of an appetite for profit than for circumspection. Indeed, according to two contemporary historians, Houston has come to symbolize the ethos of "liberated capitalism"— that is, "the belief in the superiority and sacredness of the individual's right to promote, speculate, build, buy, and sell without outside restraint or control." This ethic, the historians conclude, "has shaped and defined nearly every aspect of Houston's development. It has created a city whose history is characterized by rapid growth, boosterism, and . . . 'men on the make.'"[4] Traditionally, Houstonians thus have been far more concerned with tomorrow's possibilities than by yesterday's accomplishments.

Paradoxically, Houston's history also has suffered because of the popularity of Texas history—or at least selected portions of the state's history. Despite J. R. Ewing and company on the television program "Dallas," the Hollywood stereotype of Texas still does not include freeways and skyscrapers. Instead, Texas is almost invariably associated with the Alamo, the independence struggle with Mexico, the Texas Rangers, and the Indian-Anglo wars of the frontier period. The attention lavished on these and a few other celebrated aspects of Texas history, such as the Civil War and Reconstruction, has resulted in a corresponding neglect of the rest of the state's history, including the growth and contributions of urban areas.[5]

The biases and priorities of professional historians likewise have deflected attention from the study and appreciation of Houston's history.

Two of the more significant and now generally acknowledged prejudices of earlier generations of historians were their bias against local history and their equally pronounced bias against urban history. For years most professional historians seldom assigned any real value to local studies, and they were content to leave such work to amateurs, antiquarians, and genealogists. Grass-roots history was widely regarded as history with the brains taken out — that is, not really history at all but something that, intellectually speaking, fell between mumbling and speaking in tongues. As for urban history, the *Journal of Urban History* did not appear until 1974, decades after cities had achieved obvious importance to everybody — except to the majority of historians.[6]

Another important cause of the neglect of Houston's history was the absence in the city for many years of universities whose faculties and graduate students might have taken a scholarly interest in their surroundings. Rice University, although founded in 1912, awarded no doctoral degree in American history until 1933 and none in local history for many more years. The University of Houston did not confer its first doctorate in U.S. history until 1974. The historians who taught at these schools in earlier years were predominantly products of Ivy League and other elite schools. Almost without exception, their biases against local and urban history were the same as those of the professors who trained them and of the profession at large. As well, many of them disdained Houston and Texas as provincial, and they regarded their stay in the state as a temporary way station to better postings in civilized places. Hence, these early scholars had no incentive to write about local, urban topics, which their mentors and peers regarded as trivial and unimportant, which were not easy to publish in the better journals, and which were not likely to mark the trajectory of a successful career. Nor did they encourage their graduate students to undertake local projects. Consequently, the first modern, scholarly, general history of Houston — David McComb's *Houston: The Bayou City* — did not appear until 1969. It was based on a doctoral dissertation submitted not at the University of Houston or Rice University, but at the University of Texas in Austin, located some 160 miles from Houston.[7]

A final and major consideration that inhibited the exploration of Houston's history was the lack, until recently, of any policy to collect and preserve a data base of local, historical records. Over the years, individuals and families as well as institutions and organizations maintained a variety of records favored by scholars, such as diaries, letters, photographs, scrapbooks, and administrative paperwork. Often these records were kept scrupulously for decades — until they were burned up, thrown out, ruined by moisture, devoured by insects or animals, loaned out and never returned, misplaced, or otherwise abused and often destroyed. Paper is, after all, fragile, and its mortality rate in Houston has been high. The city's heat and humidity, combined with a prevalence of fire-prone, wooden buildings and a generally casual attitude toward the preservation of records, have resulted in an appalling loss of vital documents. Since much of this material is one of a kind, once it is gone, it is gone forever. Needless to say, scholars will hardly be able to see or use records that no longer exist. The absence of record preservation in Houston will continue to stunt knowledge of its past long into the future.

Fortunately, in recent years there have been changes in the physical and attitudinal conditions that for so long discouraged interest in Houston's history. There is, for example, now a consensus that Houston's reputation in coming years depends on significant cultural development as well as economic vitality. Hence a new convention center has been built, and plans are afoot for a multi-million-dollar historical museum. In 1975 the University of Houston hired an urban historian and subsequently founded an Institute of Public History. There also has been a noticeable trend toward studying local history by faculty and graduate students alike at Texas Southern University, which is the second largest predominantly black educational institution in the United States, as well as at Rice University and the University of Houston. Furthermore, each of these institutions has made at least a modest commitment to collect documents relating to the city's history.[8]

These and related developments paved the way for the creation of the Houston Metropolitan Research Center in 1975. The center is a division of the Houston Public Library and is housed in the original main library building in downtown Houston, adjacent to city hall. It is wholly funded by the city, and it is dedicated to locating, acquiring, preserving, and making available to the interested public documents relating to the history and culture of Houston, Galveston, and the surrounding Gulf Coast area.[9]

The center has already proven its worth. It is the official depository of the city of Houston and its voluminous municipal records alone would qualify the center as an important urban archive. The center's popular photographic component has over one and a half million images, most of them identified as to place, date, and content. An oral history collection includes over five hundred interviews with representative as well as extraordinary people who have participated in community life. An architectural component emphasizes the built environment of the city. Manuscript holdings, now in excess of twelve thousand linear feet and steadily expanding, include papers of individuals, families, organizations, and institutions. The *Houston Review,* sponsored by the center and published three times annually, is a quality scholarly journal that features a montage of academic articles, photo essays, edited oral history interviews, and book reviews pertaining to the Houston-Galveston metroplex. In 1978 the center inaugurated a Mexican-American component, followed by an African-American component in 1981.[10]

Changes in Houston have been paralleled by developments in the nation's scholarly community. Racism among historians has not wholly vanished but it is both less blatant and much diminished. The bias against local and urban history has receded. This book is a direct result of all these changes and would not have been possible without them. Most of the essays that follow were written by younger scholars within the last decade, many written within the last few years. Collectively they help redress the historical imbalance between black and white, between local and national, and between the city and the countryside. For Texas, it is hoped that the book will contribute to filling a gaping hole in the historiography of the Lone Star State. For the South, it is intended to be part of the continuing and exciting process of reexamination whereby the complexity and multifarious elements of southern history are being recognized and brought, sometimes painfully, into a focused relationship with one another. As this process continues, the South surely will rise again—if not approaching wholeness for the first time, then at least expanded and greatly different from earlier versions and visions.

Notes

1. August Meier and Elliott M. Rudwick, *Black History and the Historical Profession* 1915-1980 (Urbana, Ill., 1986). For an earlier examination of this problem, see Michael R. Winston, "Through the Back Door: Academic Racism and the Negro Scholar in Historical Perspective," *Daedalus* 100 (Summer, 1971) 3:678-719. For more about racial discrimination within academe, and the consequences of this discrimination, see two articles by John H. Stanfield, "The Cracked Back Door: Foundations and Black Social Scientists between the World Wars," *American Sociologist* 17 (1982): 193-204, and "Race Relations Research and Black Americans between the Two World Wars," *Journal of Ethnic Studies* 11 (Fall, 1983) 3: 61-94. Also see Jacqueline Goggin, "Countering White Racist Scholarship: Carter G. Woodson and the *Journal of Negro History*," *Journal of Negro History* 48 (Fall, 1983) 4:355-75, as well as Francille R. Wilson, "The Segregated Scholars: Black Labor Historians, 1895-1950" (Ph.D. diss., University of Pennsylvania, 1988). Concerning Houston, see Michael A. Olivas, "Houston Pride and Prejudice," *Texas Journal of Ideas, History and Culture* 10 (Spring/Summer, 1988): 23-24, quote from p. 23.
2. The names of Houston's baseball (Astros), basketball (Rockets), and football (Oilers) teams nicely reflect some of the city's leading economic interests.
3. For a corrective to the usual historical hype about Texas, see the fine short essay by George Lipsitz, "Goin' On: Afro-American Imagery in Texas Film and

Folklore," *Southwest Media Review* 3 (Spring, 1985): 42–45. Especially pertinent is a passage on p. 43:

> For black Texans, questions of myth and history command especially great importance. Like all Afro-Americans they face the dilemma of trying to enter a society that does not want them or of attempting to separate from a society that makes too much profit from racism to let them go. Texas myths provide an additional layer of oppression through an idealized portrait of the past which inverts the real historical experience of blacks in the state. In these myths, slaveholders appear as freedom fighters, the pathology of white racism masquerades as individualism, and the cowardly sadism of conquest appears as valor. At the same time, the historical accomplishments of Afro-Americans disappear and the black struggle for citizenship and opportunity becomes transformed into folklore that presents black people as either fools or villains.

4. These extracts are from a well-conceived historical pamphlet by Don E. Carleton and Thomas H. Kreneck, "Houston: Back Where We Started" (Houston, n.d.), 1.

5. On the battle at the Alamo, for instance, see Susan Prendergast Schoelwer with Tom W. Glaser, *Alamo Images: Changing Perceptions of a Texas Experience* (Dallas, 1985) and Don Graham, "Remembering the Alamo: The Story of the Texas Revolution in Popular Culture," *Southwestern Historical Quarterly* 89 (July, 1985): 35–66, as well as Brian Huberman and Ed Hugetz, "Fabled Facade: Filmic Treatments of the Battle of the Alamo," *Southwest Media Review* 3 (Spring, 1985): 30–41. For a broader look at how the film industry has presented the history of Texas, consult Don Graham, *Cowboys and Cadillacs: How Hollywood Looks at Texas* (Austin, 1983). For another aspect of Texas ignored by Hollywood, see Don Graham, "The Displacement of East Texas in Movies about Texas," *East Texas Historical Journal*, 25 (1987) 1:18–22.

6. A significant exception concerning urban history in Texas was the appearance of Kenneth W. Wheeler's *To Wear a City's Crown: The Beginnings of Urban Growth in Texas, 1836–1865* (Cambridge, Mass., 1968). Mention should also be made of the activities and publications of the Texas Gulf Coast Historical Association, whose records are now housed at the Houston Public Library's Metropolitan Research Center. "History with the brains taken out" is a paraphrasing of Asa Briggs cited in Alexander B. Callow, Jr., ed., *American Urban History* (New York, 1969), p. 638.

7. David G. McComb, *Houston: The Bayou City* (Austin, 1969). A second and improved edition of McComb's book appeared in 1981. Useful companions to McComb's volume are Fred R. von der Mehden, ed., *The Ethnic Groups of Houston* (Houston, 1984) and Joe R. Feagin, *Free Enterprise City: Houston in Political and Economic Perspective* (New Brunswick, N.J., 1988). McComb now teaches in Colorado. In 1986 he published a companion to the Houston volume entitled *Galveston: A History* (Austin, 1986).

8. At Texas Southern University, the Heartman Collection contains some published material pertaining to local blacks. See also the voluminous Barbara Jordan Collection, which documents the career of a successful Houston politician and

educator, as well as material, reports, and programs associated with the Center for Urban Programs. The recently inaugurated Mickey Leland Center for World Hunger and Peace at Texas Southern University contains the papers of the popular activist and congressman whose untimely death in a 1989 airplane accident in Africa stunned the city. Local material is also housed in the Special Collections Department of the University of Houston library and the Woodson Research Center at Rice University.

9. The center had an earlier life of several years at Rice University, where it began as a grant largely developed and administered by Rice historian Harold M. Hyman. For more about this, see Don E. Carleton, "A Cooperative Urban Archives Program: The Houston Metropolitan Research Center," *Midwestern Archivist* 4 (1982): 177-95.

10. For the evolution and scope of the Mexican-American component, see Thomas H. Kreneck, "Documenting a Mexican American Community: The Houston Example," *American Archivist* 3 (1985): 272-85.

Part II

Slavery and Freedom:
   Blacks in Nineteenth-Century Houston

Introduction

Historical Overview

Houston, which often strikes both visitors and residents as a city with no history, actually dates back to the 1830s. This was the era of city building that saw communities like Chicago, Detroit, Cleveland, and scores of less successful urban ventures either founded or first establishing themselves as urban areas. The initial exploration and European settlement of the Houston area, like most of the other cities of this period, predated the founding of the city by a considerable period. Blacks participated in the initial explorations and settlement of both Texas and the Houston area.

Estaban, an African who was one of the four survivors of the Cabeza de Vaca expedition that shipwrecked on the Texas coast in 1528, established the pattern of black involvement in Spanish Texas. Blacks accompanied most Spanish expeditions into Texas in the sixteenth and seventeenth centuries, and they were part of the population of most Spanish garrisons and settlements in Texas in the eighteenth century. Blacks probably comprised between fifteen and twenty-five percent of the population of Spanish Texas in the late eighteenth century. Furthermore, although the Spanish introduced slavery into Texas, the majority of blacks residing in the province were free. For example, in the San Antonio area in 1778, 151 of 759 male residents were black or mulatto, and only 4 of these were slaves. Free blacks in Spanish Texas faced few, if any, restrictions on their freedom. They were accepted socially and followed whatever trade or profession that they chose. Census data lists blacks or mulattos as farmers, merchants, teachers, shoemakers, carpenters, miners, teamsters, laborers, and domestic servants. Several of them owned land and cattle.[1]

Most of the blacks who resided in Spanish Texas were born there or even further south in what is present-day Mexico. However, beginning in the early nineteenth century, an increasing number came from the United States. This migration increased after 1821, when Mexico won its independence from Spain. Free blacks came to Texas because there was greater opportunity and much less racial prejudice under Spanish and Mexican governments than in the United States. Texas also attracted its share of runaway slaves, especially from neighboring Louisiana. Under Mexican rule, conditions that blacks faced in Texas were hospitable enough for abolitionist Benjamin Lundy to seek official permission to establish a colony of free American blacks there in the early 1830s. The Mexican government endorsed Lundy's proposal, but the project was dropped after Texas achieved its independence.[2]

Despite the generally enlightened racial attitude of the Mexican government, the situation for blacks in Texas began to deteriorate under Mexican rule, especially when the government opened Texas' borders to colonists from the United States. When Moses Austin rode into San Antonio in 1820 seeking permission to establish a colony in Texas, he brought a black servant with him. Nearly all of the white settlers who followed Austin into Texas either brought slaves with them or strongly supported slavery. Mexican law prohibited slavery, and the Mexican government periodically attempted to apply this law. Enforcement was never effective, however, and Texas settlers rather easily circumvented the law. Consequently, slavery flourished in most Anglo communities in Texas. In 1825, for example, 69 of 1,347 residents of the Austin colony were slave holders who owned 443 slaves. As more Anglos migrated from the United States, slavery grew; as a result, by the late 1820s slaves outnumbered free blacks in Texas for the first time. The number of slaves in the Austin colony grew to approximately 1,000 in 1835; in that year there were an estimated 5,000 slaves in all of Texas. After independence the slave population increased from 11,323 in 1840 to 58,161 in 1850 and then to 182,556 in 1860. Due to restrictions imposed by the Texas government, the free black population in the state dwindled to less than 500 by the eve of the Civil War.

Blacks in Antebellum Houston

The first blacks living in the Houston area were slaves who arrived several decades before the city itself was founded. Between 1816 and 1821, first Louis de Aury and later the pirate Jean Lafitte used Galveston Island and the bayous around Galveston Bay to warehouse slaves prior to smuggling them into the United States. In 1819 and 1820 several blacks accompanied Dr. James Long on his ill-fated filibustering expeditions into Texas. When Jane Long accompanied her husband into Texas, she brought with her Kiamata, a young slave girl, as a companion for her two young daughters. After the collapse of Dr. Long's expedition, Jane Long, her two daughters, and Kiamata were stranded at a makeshift fort at Point Bolivar on Galveston Bay. The four survived severe weather, hostile Indians, and the birth of a third daughter. They subsisted largely on oysters that Kiamata dug up from the bay as they waited in vain for the return of Dr. Long—unbeknownst to them, he had been captured and killed in Mexico. Finally they were rescued by settlers on their way to Austin's colony, which they later joined. They lived first in Harris County; then they were in Brazoria county, where Kiamata helped Jane Long run a boarding house; finally they lived in Richmond, southwest of Houston, where the two women ran a prosperous plantation. Kiamata married and had four children. One of her sons became an overseer on the Long plantation, and one of her grandsons, Henry C. Breed, became a Houston police officer.[3]

In the city of Houston, many of the initial white settlers brought slaves with them. Early accounts mention that blacks and Mexican prisoners of war cleared the land for the original townsite in the summer of 1836.[4] From the beginning, slaves made up a significant portion of the community. In the censuses of both 1850 and 1860, slaves constituted 22 percent of the city's population. In the plantation areas that surrounded the city, slaves accounted for 49 percent of the 1860 population.

Most of the plantation slaves in the Houston area raised cotton or sugar cane on the rich lands south and southwest of the city along the Brazos River. While life on these plantations varied greatly from place to place, records from the Peach Point Plantation, owned by James Perry in Brazoria County about forty miles south of Houston, detail the conditions that at least some slaves experienced in the Houston area in the years preceding the Civil War. In 1848 and 1849 Peach Point slaves began preparing the fields for planting in early February. They grew cotton along with corn, potatoes, vegetables, and a little tobacco; they also raised these same crops for themselves on small plots of land that Perry allowed each slave to work. In addition, they cleared new land, split rails, cut board timber and basket timber, tore down and rebuilt fences, hauled wood, shelled corn, slaughtered hogs and beef, and kept birds out of the corn fields; they worked on the roads, dug drainage ditches, built a chimney, and cared for a brood of sows and piglets. They worked from sunrise to sunset (from "can see to can't see") and had time off Saturday afternoons and all day Sunday. In the 1850s when sugar cane replaced cotton as the chief cash crop of the plantation, slaves worked seven days a week during the sugar-refining season.[5]

Slave life in the cities differed greatly from that on the plantations. Urban slaves generally had more freedom and a somewhat easier, more rewarding life than their counterparts on the plantations. Many slaves in Houston worked as house servants or worked on the farms and plantations on the edge of town. Their lives differed little from those of plantation slaves. Others, however, found employment as cooks and waiters in hotels, as teamsters, or as laborers on the docks and in warehouses. Black labor helped build the plank roads and railroads by which the produce of the plantations flowed into the city, and they helped erect the buildings that housed the city's merchant activity. While most slaves performed unskilled labor, there were enough skilled black workers in the city to alarm white workers. One objective of the early workingmen's associations and trade unions in Houston was to limit the employment of black craftsmen.[6]

The great advantage that the urban slave experienced was the relative freedom of city life — especially for slaves who avoided the close daily supervision of their owners by participating in the practice of "hiring out." This system, while technically illegal, was both widespread and popular because it enabled the slaveholders to gain a significant profit from the labor of their slaves, especially in the 1850s, when the rapidly rising cost of slaves pushed wages upward. In addition, hiring out enabled slaveholders to transfer part or all of the cost of a slave's upkeep to the party who contracted for the slave's labor. It also eliminated the need for slaveholders to house all of their slaves on their property, which was a significant advantage in urban areas. Some holders even allowed their slaves to hire out their own time. Under this system bondsmen found their own employment, gave their masters a specified sum each month, and kept the rest of their wages for their own use and support. Most slaves in this position enjoyed a great deal of freedom — especially if they rented housing away from their holder's dwelling.[7]

As a consequence of the hiring-out system and the presence of a handful of free blacks, Houston had a significant number of black residents who, at least to a casual observer, seemed fairly prosperous and who did not appear to be under anyone's supervision. One visitor to antebellum Houston recorded that he witnessed numerous well-dressed blacks, some of whom had the privilege of using their holders' carriages for pleasure drives.[8] In 1849 another visitor reported that he met a free black man and woman who dressed in the latest Parisian fashions and ran a dancing school for wealthy whites in Houston and Galveston. This visitor also noted the presence of a black-owned restaurant that by all appearances was doing an excellent business providing both food and entertainment for the city's black population.[9]

Slaves clearly recognized the advantages of urban life, and most resisted any attempt to be transferred to a plantation. This fact was so widely known that most plantation owners were reluctant to purchase urban slaves because they considered them to have been spoiled by city life. Usually before a planter acquired a city slave he insisted upon a trial period to determine whether the slave could adjust to plantation life; in most cases urban slaves failed this test and were returned to their city holders.[10] Few slaves wanted to surrender the advantages of urban life for the regimen of the plantation, and some took extreme measures to avoid it. Illustrating this is the case of a slave known only as Dave, who belonged to William Ballinger, an attorney in Galveston and Houston. During the Civil War Ballinger tried to send Dave to work on Aaron Coffee's plantation, but the effort failed. As Coffee reported, Dave was deeply attracted to urban life and "has sworned not to work on any plantation and says he will not live out of a city or town." Dave held fast to these views. After eight months of plantation life, he escaped and returned to the Ballinger household in Houston. Every time the bondsman was returned to Coffee, he ran away again—always returning to Houston. Dave did not insist on total freedom. He was willing to remain a slave, but only in an urban setting. Ultimately his efforts prevailed, and he was allowed to return to Houston, where he worked as a domestic for the Ballingers and occasionally hired out as a day laborer.[11]

While most of the white residents of Houston supported the institution of slavery, some expressed concern about the presence and demeanor of the city's sizable black population. Newspapers regularly complained about the freedom of movement and the rowdy behavior of blacks in the city. Both the city and the state attempted to control this situation through legislation. Slaves were prohibited by law from gambling, carrying weapons, buying liquor, or selling anything without their holders' permission. They were required to treat whites with respect, were subject to a curfew, and could not appear on the streets without a written pass from their owners. They could not gather in groups of more than four, unless one of their holders or another responsible citizen was present. Finally, slaves who were convicted of crimes received harsher punishment than whites convicted of similar acts. In addition to the controls placed on slaves, legal restrictions also limited the freedom of free blacks. State law, in fact, attempted to prevent the migration of free blacks to Texas, while the Houston City Council passed an ordinance in 1839 requiring all free blacks to leave the city within thirty days.[12]

There is some question about how effectively these laws were enforced. Though it was illegal, many slaveholders hired out their slaves to other employers, and some even allowed slaves to hire out their own time. Slaves who hired out often lived away from their owners, and consequently they were not closely supervised. Laws attempting to restrict the movement of slaves or to prohibit slave gatherings, drinking, and gambling were also rarely enforced. Visitors to the city noted that blacks were always visible on the streets; newspapers confirmed this, complaining that blacks went wherever they pleased without supervision or passes and frequently congregated at loud and unruly parties and gatherings.

Much of the hostility toward free blacks developed because of fears that their presence in Houston made it even more difficult to control the city's slave population. A grand jury in 1839 accused the free black population of corrupting slaves by presenting an example of laziness and by introducing them to vice and petty crime.[13] For a time following that accusation, city authorities enforced the laws against free blacks somewhat more stringently; some free blacks left the city. In 1839 there were approximately twenty free blacks in Houston; the census of 1860 counted only eight, seven of whom were women working as laundresses, seamstresses, or housekeepers and who enjoyed the support of several prominent citizens. Some free blacks apparently ignored the restrictions placed on them—Peter Allen, a barber, moved to Houston in 1846 but did not bother seeking legal permission to reside in Texas until 1863. In all probability others did likewise and lived in the city and state for years in spite of laws prohibiting it.

Free blacks occupied a curious legal status in Houston. They could not become citizens, and, like slaves, they faced restrictions on their freedoms. One law discouraged them from gathering in saloons, another required them to obtain permission from the mayor before they could legally hold a dance, and in 1855 a local ordinance required them to post bond and receive permission from the city council in order to rent a house within the city limits. On the other hand, free blacks were guaranteed a trial by jury, and, in most cases, their punishment if convicted of a crime was the same as it was for whites.[14]

One of the advantages of urban life for both free blacks and slaves was that it gave them the opportunity to establish the rudiments of their own community and to establish a social life relatively free from outside interference. For example, the origins of the first black church in Houston can be traced back to the antebellum period. In 1841 Houston Methodists organized their first church, located above a store on Capital Avenue between Milam and Louisiana in the Fourth Ward. The original sixty-eight members included thirty-two blacks, both free and slave. In 1843 the congregation, still including blacks, built their own church at that same site. By the early 1850s, however, the black members of the congregation began worshiping in a separate building (with a white pastor) on the Milam side of the property. In 1867 the white members of the congregation gave the black members the title to the building on the Milam side, which they moved to a lot they purchased at the corner of Travis and Bell, further south in the Fourth Ward. This church, now with a black pastor, became Trinity Methodist Episcopal Church, the first black church in the city.[15]

The origins of black education can be traced to the same period and to the black Methodist church. Although it was never against the law to educate slaves in Texas, neither whites nor blacks made any real effort to establish a public school system for blacks before emancipation. Indeed, there was not even a public school system for whites until after the Civil War.[16] Nevertheless there is evidence that a private school for blacks operated, at least for a time, in the black Methodist church during the late

1850s. In November, 1858, the *Tri-Weekly Telegraph* noted that "Mrs. M. L. Capshaw will resume her school in the African Methodist Episcopal Church on Monday the 22."[17] Since the 1860 census counted only eight free blacks in the city, and only one of these was of school age, we must assume that either slave children, adult slaves, or both made up the student body of this early black school. These institutions and the handful of small black businesses that appeared during slavery, along with the experience of living away from their holders, making their own economic decisions, and acquiring marketable labor skills, provided Houston slaves with an embryonic black community and left them relatively well prepared for emancipation.

White Houston had mixed feelings about the activities of urban slaves. Apparently the city tolerated church services, an occasional dance, and even the school. Other social gatherings created more concern. Newspapers worried about the eating, drinking, singing, dancing, and card playing that commonly occurred at the frequent illicit black gatherings in town. On the other hand, slaves were a vital element of the work force and made a significant contribution to the development and even the safety of the city. For example, nearly everyone praised the role that blacks played during the Civil War, when, due to the shortage of white workers, they took over and operated the fire department. Years later one Houstonian recalled that they were "splendid firemen" who threw their "whole souls into the work."[18]

Emancipation and the Beginning of the Free Black Community

In the late spring of 1865, a cloud of uncertainty hung over Houston. In nearly every issue of the newspapers, there were reported rumors, still unconfirmed, that the South had suffered major military setbacks. If the war continued, Houston newspapers estimated that 200,000 black troops would be needed by summer to keep Confederate armies in the field.[19] Some whites even suggested emancipation as the prerequisite to the effective utilization of black troops. Instead, emancipation was achieved in another way. All Confederate resistance collapsed in May of 1865, and the war ended. On June 19, 1865, Gen. Gordon Granger landed at Galveston with the first units of United States occupying forces and immediately announced that all Texas slaves were free. Houston officials were apprehensive about the effect that this change in status would have, urging strict enforcement of the municipal vagrancy law to prevent idleness and vagrancy among the city's newly freed black population.[20]

City officials totally failed to anticipate the most immediate effect of emancipation—the rapid increase in black population that occurred within a few weeks of the end of slavery. Houston's slave population had increased steadily during the war, first as slaveholders from other parts of the Confederacy shipped some of their slaves to Texas for safety, and then as slaves were transferred inland from Galveston and other coastal points to protect them from a feared northern invasion. As the news of emancipation spread and slavery collapsed, hundreds of freed slaves poured into Houston from Peach Point and plantations in Brazoria, Fort Bend, and other neighboring counties. A witness to this migration described it vividly: "They travel mostly on foot, bearing heavy burdens of clothing, blankets, etc., on their heads — a long and weary journey, they arrive tired, foot sore, and hungry."[21] Most came to the city hoping to make a better life for themselves. Rumors that federal officials in Houston would provide assistance and protection attracted many. Some had heard that the Union Army would provide them with food, housing, and jobs, while still others believed that they would not have to work at all.[22] Reality, of course, was quite different. The sheer number of refugees totally overwhelmed federal officials. Colonel Clark, for a time commander of Union troops in Houston, put some blacks to work repairing streets and cleaning out ditches in the city, and to the best of his ability, he provided food and shelter.[23] But the government could not accommodate all of the newcomers. Local newspapers began to urge blacks to remain on the plantations for their own good.[24]

Neither city officials nor most white Houstonians welcomed this flood of blacks into the city. Many problems, some imagined and some real, were associated with this migration. Many residents feared that the city could not absorb the influx and worried about the expected rise in vagrancy and crime. By July, 1865, almost every issue of the Houston *Tri-Weekly Telegraph* remarked on the growing number of robberies and petty crimes, which they attributed to black vagrants in the city. A more serious problem was the shortage of adequate housing for blacks, the overcrowding that resulted, and the potential public health crisis that these conditions portended. With more and more blacks crowding into old, dilapidated, vacant buildings, especially warehouses and stables, officials grew concerned about the danger of fire, disease, and poor sanitation. Some observers noted that much of this housing was not fit for human occupation, and wondered how blacks would manage when winter came.[25] White workers, on the other hand, were apprehensive that blacks might take their jobs. A few years earlier they had protested against the practice of hiring out, and now they sought to protect their jobs from the former slaves. In July of 1865, white mechanics officially protested the hiring of black mechanics, while white teamsters tried to block the employment of blacks as wagon and omnibus drivers.[26] The editors of the *Tri-Weekly Telegraph,* as well as other business leaders, suggested that European immigrants be recruited to replace blacks as the city's labor force, and recommended again and again that blacks leave Houston and return to the "comfortable homes" that they had left behind on the plantations. Not all reports about blacks were negative, however. The Houston press acknowledged that many blacks had taken jobs to pay for the food they were buying from the army, and they also recognized that the newcomers who were working on the streets and ditches had made great strides in cleaning up the city.[27] Blacks continued to come to Houston—the migration of blacks that began in the summer of 1865 has never ended.

There can be no accurate count of the number of blacks who migrated to Houston in the months following emancipation. Efforts to estimate this figure are complicated by not knowing how many blacks were shipped to the city during the war; it is complicated further by not knowing how many who came to Houston at the end of the war remained only briefly and then returned "home" as the press and city authorities urged them to do. Houston could not immediately absorb all those who came to the city, and there was a strong demand for labor on the old plantations. However, many came and stayed. The black population of Houston grew from 1,077 in 1860 to 3,691 in 1870; this increased the proportion of blacks in the city's population to 39.3 percent. Those who remained would confront and solve most of the problems they encountered there. In the process they gave birth to the black community in Houston.

Union troops arrived in Houston on June 20, 1865. Initially the provost marshal's office assisted blacks who migrated to the city. However, since the city experienced little social unrest, the provost marshal's office closed the following November. At that point the Freedmen's Bureau assumed the responsibility of helping Houston's blacks adjust to emancipation. In the summer of 1865 the pressing need to provide food and shelter for destitute blacks, and to put as many as possible to work on the roads and ditches under city supervision, occupied the time and energies of the provost marshal's office. Due to the lack of sufficient resources, however, most blacks had to fend for themselves when they arrived in the city. When officials of the Freedmen's Bureau reached Houston in the fall of 1865, they focused their efforts on providing legal protection for blacks, helping them negotiate fair labor contracts, and opening schools to begin the process of educating the largely illiterate black population. Again, lack of resources prevented the Freedmen's Bureau from substantially addressing the ex-slaves' more basic and immediate needs of food and shelter. For these essentials, blacks largely had to develop their own solutions.

The general inability of federal authorities to provide for the immediate needs of the hundreds of blacks who came to the city after the war forced the members of Houston's black community to turn inward, organize, and rely on themselves. Housing was the most immediate problem. Many sought shelter in empty warehouses, like the Hotel d'Afrique, a run-down building where a large number of homeless blacks slept each night. Others camped on the outskirts of town in gatherings like the one at Vinegar Hill, which soon became infamous for its polyglot population and its concentration of saloons, brothels, and gambling houses.[28] The housing problem could not be solved overnight. In the summer and fall of 1865, long-time black residents of the city held colored fairs in several parts of town to raise money to help newcomers.[29] Black churches provided assistance when they could, and one group of blacks organized a Freedmen's Aid Society.[30] Free blacks and former urban slaves, who already possessed the skills needed to survive in the city, provided the bulk of the aid, helped many of the new arrivals find jobs and shelter, and set up many of the early organizations and institutions in the black community.

As table 1 indicates, in the years following the Civil War, blacks were fairly evenly distributed throughout the city, although the largest number lived in Freedmantown and similar neighborhoods of the Fourth Ward. Other concentrations in the immediate postwar period were found in the Third Ward and in the Frosttown area of the Second Ward. Most blacks settled on the edge of the city, where vacant property was available, and often along the road that first brought them into the city. Bird's-eye maps of Houston in the early 1870s indicate that the most accessible empty land lay southwest and southeast of the city, on the fringes on the Third and Fourth Wards.[31]

Surprisingly, some blacks quickly acquired land and built their own homes. As early as the fall of 1865, several blacks had bought property in Freedmantown, and more did so during the next several years. By 1870, only five years after emancipation, one black out of twenty-five living in the Fourth Ward owned a home; by the end of the century the number had risen to about one in eight. The level of black home ownership was about the same in the other parts of the city.

It is not clear how blacks acquired property so quickly. Many whites seem to have been willing to sell land to blacks on credit, and the economic hardships that followed the disintegration of the Confederacy—the collapse of the economy and the loss of the agricultural labor supply—made farm land on the edge of the city cheap. White landowners, reacting rationally to new economic realities, profited by subdividing their land and either selling it to blacks or building rental property for them. Anecdotal accounts add to this picture and document the way that individual blacks acquired land. For example, Charles S. Longcope, who owned a large home in the city's Second Ward, was reported to have gathered his slaves around him in June of 1865. He stood in the doorway of his front door, read aloud the proclamation that gave them their freedom, and then offered each a building lot in the Fourth Ward.[32]

Contrary to popular perceptions, none of the areas where blacks settled

Table 1
Houston's Black Population by Ward, 1870-1910

Ward	Total Population	Black Population	Percent Black	Percent of Total Black Population
		1870		
1	738	250	33.9	6.8
2	1,638	474	28.9	12.8
3	2,812	1,075	38.2	29.1
4	3,055	1,314	43.0	35.6
5	1,319	578	43.8	15.7
TOTAL	9,562	3,691		
		1890		
1	1,980	777	39.2	7.5
2	3,341	1,262	37.8	12.2
3	7,366	2,661	36.1	25.6
4	8,761	3,682	42.0	35.5
5	6,109	1,997	32.7	19.2
TOTAL	27,557	10,379		
		1910		
1	6,954	1,390	20.0	5.8
2	7,572	2,335	30.8	9.8
3	24,705	7,662	31.0	32.0
4	16,772	6,366	38.0	26.6
5	16,854	4,967	29.5	20.8
6	5,943	1,209	20.3	5.1
TOTAL	78,800	23,929		

SOURCE: U.S. Department of the Interior, Bureau of the Census, *Ninth Census of the United States: 1870* (Washington: Government Printing Office, 1872), p. 272; *Eleventh Census of the United States: 1890* (Washington: Government Printing Office, 1897), p. 555; and *Thirteenth Census of the United States: 1910* (Washington: Government Printing Office, 1913), p. 859.

in the post–Civil War period were completely segregated. As Table 1 indicates, not only were blacks fairly evenly distributed throughout the city's wards in the late nineteenth century, but in every ward except the Second Ward the percentage of blacks in the population actually declined between 1870 and 1910. The ward, though, was too large a geographical unit to accurately reflect residential segregation. Most historians have assumed that residential patterns in Houston followed those in other southern cities, with small, segregated residential clusters of blacks scattered around the perimeter of the city.[33] A detailed analysis of written census lists, however, suggests a different residential pattern for late nineteenth-century Houston. A sample of households indicates that according to the 1870 census, 53.7 percent of black families in the Fourth Ward lived next door to whites. Typically, for several blocks black and white households would be completely intermixed, then there would be a cluster of five or ten black households followed by several white homes. The white families that lived in the areas with the most concentrated black population were frequently, but not always, German or English immigrants.[34] In the vice-filled streets of Vinegar Hill, north of Buffalo Bayou in the Sixth Ward, the races also mixed without restraint in the immediate postwar era.

By the end of the century, residential segregation was more widespread. In the downtown area, among the bars and brothels of Prairie Street and the boarding houses of McKinney, Bagby, Milam, Travis, Clay, and Pease, the races still rubbed shoulders — 47.8 percent of black families lived next door to whites. In the heart of the black areas of the Fourth Ward, along San Felipe and adjacent streets, segregation was becoming more widespread, and clusters of black homes were more common, but 24.7 percent of the black families still had white next-door neighbors.[35] As late as the 1920s most black families continued to have at least one white family living across the street or down the block.[36]

Jobs were the second major need of the former slaves. In the summer of 1865 many whites were concerned about vagrancy among blacks, while white workers worried about job competition. Before the Civil War, slave labor had been very important to Houston's economy, and emancipation did not end the city's need for black labor. The former hired-out slaves were most feared by white workers, who had objected to their employment as skilled labor before the war. As early as July, 1865, blacks operated blacksmith shops, shoemaking establishments, and several other small enterprises.[37] Most blacks, however, were not so fortunate. The former plantation slaves who flocked to the city after the war had few salable skills and had a difficult time finding suitable employment. Many whites in Houston advocated a contract labor system for these blacks.[38] Under this system, which closely resembled hiring out, blacks surrendered much of their freedom to their employers in exchange for guaranteed work. The potential for abuse was so great that the Freedmen's Bureau intervened to police labor contracts. While some blacks achieved economic success quickly, most did not. Instead, the typical freedman ended up as a low-paid, unskilled worker; in 1870, 82 percent of the city's blacks worked as domestic, unskilled, or semi-skilled labor. Ten years later the situation was even worse, with 84 percent falling into these bottom three job categories.[39]

At the center of the emerging black community was the black church. If Trinity Methodist Episcopal Church was the city's oldest black church, Antioch Baptist was the most prestigious. Antioch was established by a white missionary, William C. Crane, in 1866. Initially it held its services in white churches, first at the First Baptist Church, then at the German Baptist Church. In the summer of 1866 a black minister, I. S. Campbell, took charge of the church. After first holding services in a brush arbor erected on the banks of Buffalo Bayou, he built a frame structure in 1868 at Rusk and Bagby in the Fourth Ward. Jack Yates became pastor of Antioch in 1868 or early 1869. Under his leadership, Antioch enjoyed rapid growth and increasing prestige; in 1879 he moved the church to its present site on Robin Street, where he directed the erection of an impressive red brick structure.[40]

The influence of Houston's early black churches extended far beyond religious matters. In 1869 black churches, especially Antioch Baptist, participated in the organization of the Harris County Republican Club.[41] In 1872 Antioch and Trinity Methodist Episcopal worked together to raise money and purchase a park for blacks in Houston. Initially both churches had sponsored picnics and Emancipation Day celebrations on land north of San Felipe in the Fourth Ward; in 1872 they acquired a permanent park site, Emancipation Park, in the Third Ward.[42] Antioch also took the lead in promoting black higher education. After failing in his efforts to locate Bishop College in Houston, Yates worked with white missionaries to establish Houston College (also known as Houston Baptist Academy) in the Third Ward in 1885. In 1894 the school moved to its own three-acre site west of the city limits on San Felipe. The college's mission was to train black youth for the ministry as well as to provide general education. The institution was a college in name only, however. Virtually all of its students were enrolled in its primary school, secondary school, and industrial training programs.[43]

To a large degree, then, blacks took care of their own basic needs in post–Civil War Houston, especially in the areas of housing, employment, and spiritual sustenance. In the area of education, however, they depended more on government assistance. Although the roots of black education predate the war, and although black churches took the lead in attempting to bring higher education to Houston blacks, the real beginnings of education for most of the city's blacks came when the Freedmen's Bureau and the American Missionary Association opened three schools in black churches during Reconstruction. The Freedmen's Bureau funded and operated the schools, while the American Missionary Association staffed them with northern white missionaries. They concentrated their efforts on providing adult blacks with basic literacy and mathematical skills. Their success helped black politicians in 1870 convince the Texas legislature to create public schools for blacks in the cities. That year Gregory Institute opened in Houston's Fourth Ward under the supervision of a group of Houston's leading black citizens, including Richard Allen (a businessman and Repub-

In the years following the Civil War, many ex-slaves made their way to southern cities where their enlarged communities formed a "city-within-a-city." In Houston, Rev. Jack Yates (1828–97) was prominent both as an educational and a religious leader. *Courtesy Houston Public Library, Houston Metropolitan Research Center*

lican politician) and Elias Dibble (pastor of Trinity Methodist Episcopal). When the Freedmen's Bureau schools closed in 1872, most of the students and teachers transferred to Gregory. From the beginning, black education in Houston was segregated. In the early 1870s, after several public complaints, black teachers replaced white teachers at the school. When the city of Houston opened its public school system in the 1870s, black teachers taught black students in black schools.⁴⁴

Black Houstonians played a surprisingly active role in local politics during the years following the Civil War. Immediately after emancipation, the Texas legislature prohibited black suffrage. However, in 1866, emboldened by Congressional approval of the Fourteenth Amendment, the city's blacks began to take a greater interest in politics. Initially blacks focused their political energies on the Democratic Party. In early 1868 a group of blacks founded the Colored Executive Committee to mobilize black votes in the city. That summer Henry Love and Calvin Bannister established the Colored Democratic Club. Meanwhile Republicans began an active campaign in the city to recruit black support. In March, 1869, blacks participated in the organization of the biracial Harris County Republican Club—one of the few truly integrated groups in the city at that time. Blacks served as vice-president and secretary of the organization and held two of the five seats on the executive committee. The club held several of its early meetings at Antioch Baptist Church.⁴⁵

The political success of Republicans in Houston as well as in Texas depended on registering all eligible blacks and ensuring that they voted. The only way to maintain the active interest and support of blacks was to involve them in the political process and to share with them the rewards of victory. Consequently when Republicans won control of the state government in 1869, they appointed a radical Republican, Thomas H. Scanlan, as mayor of Houston, and they named several blacks to the city council. This city council appointed a black, James Snowball, as street commissioner and hired several blacks in the police department. By 1870, due to the combination of restrictions on the suffrage of prominent former Confederates and a zealous effort to register all eligible blacks, black voters actually outnumbered white voters in Houston. In 1872 Scanlan and three black city council members won reelection, primarily because of the black vote. Nevertheless, black leaders were becoming increasingly frustrated with the low level of their influence on the Republican Party. In 1871 black leaders denounced white Republicans for blocking their efforts to nominate a black candidate for the legislature. In 1873, they noted bitterly that they received only five of twenty-five appointments to standing committees, although they held three of ten seats on the city council. Blacks did not hold on even to these positions in municipal government for very long. The victory of Democrats at the polls in 1874 effectively ended both Republican and black influence in municipal government. For the next twenty years blacks continued to vote and to play an important (and at times dominant) role in the local Republican Party, but their fairly even distribution among the city's wards prevented them from electing any of their number to city office.⁴⁶

In This Section...

In spite of the problems that persisted in black Houston in the late nineteenth century, this period clearly was central to the development of the black community in the Bayou City. Unfortunately, it has been the era least systematically investigated by historians. Until recently the studies of black life in nineteenth-century Houston suffered from a number of problems—problems arising from the inadequate availability of sources, poor research strategy and methodology, faulty conceptualization, and racism—as, indeed, has all of southern history.

The idea of a monolithic, solid South, a staple of antebellum abolitionist literature, survived the Civil War almost unscathed. It remained a popular and accepted idea following the conflict, and it dominated scholarly literature well into the post–World War II era. Although the idea even now remains widespread among the public, it has not fared as well among historians. Indeed, a leading dispute among scholars has focused on the very existence of the South itself. The late David M. Potter, who contributed more than his fair share to this important historical controversy, explained one key difficulty complicating the study of southern history. In 1968, he wrote that the southern historian has an anomalous job. His is the task of tracing the history "of a region that never possessed clearly defined limits and only for four years possessed an organizational identity as the Confederate States of America. For the rest of the time, he is dealing with an entity—the South—whose boundaries are indeterminate, whose degree of separateness has fluctuated historically over time, whose distinctiveness may be in some respects fictitious."[47]

In recent years an embracing compromise has emerged between those who argue for the existence of an enduring, identifiable South and those who enumerate too many regional differences to bind together and long sustain a common identity. This scholarly consensus suggests that a lasting South has existed despite a number of internal, intra-regional variations. It implies that insofar as the study of the southern experience is concerned, there are differences that do not really make a difference, and that the South all along has been several within one, a single tree of different fruits.

Texas might well serve as an example of the same-but-different hypothesis, for clearly the history of the Lone Star State both resembles as well as differs with patterns evident in other parts of Dixie. The similarities are striking. The black and white migrants who moved into Mexican Texas overwhelmingly arrived from the southern United States. White migrants from the South initiated a process of violent territorial transfer—involving penetration, settlement, agitation, subversion, armed revolt, separation, and independence—that proved very costly to Mexico in the mid-nineteenth century.

Resident southern slaveholders in Texas led the resistance to Mexican authority. This same landed elite dominated the Republic of Texas and, after 1845, the state. Accordingly, the laws throughout both periods sanctioned and buttressed slavery in every way until slavery itself was abolished by the Civil War and constitutional amendment. After the war, black women were among those throughout the South who quickly sought to locate family and loved ones while supporting themselves financially. In Houston, as described by Barry Crouch, these and other activities often brought them into contact with the Freedman's Bureau. The Bureau in Houston, as elsewhere, provided limited assistance to recently emancipated blacks until it was abolished in 1868. Ex-slaves also had recourse locally to blacks with political connections and influence. Although historians of the Burgess-Dunning school of thought unfairly and uniformly denigrated the behavior of these early race leaders in the South, it remains true that some prominent blacks compiled a decidedly mixed record of accomplishment. Merline Pitre's assessment of the career of one of them, Richard Allen, Houston's first black state legislator and prominent Republican party leader, reveals a man of complex motives and often self-serving behavior whose actions did not always benefit his black constituents.

While sharing most of the South's ways and means, Texas nevertheless has always had differences of varying degrees of magnitude that distinguished it from its southern neighbors. For example, South met West in Texas. The Lone Star State formed the westernmost frontier of the South and was separated from the rest of it by the Mississippi River. In addition, Texas alone had the experience of independence as a republic, an experience that left a lingering sense of separateness. Furthermore, of the southern states, only Texas has continuously shared an international border throughout its history and has contained a sizable Hispanic population — a third major ethnic group not characteristic of the dominant black-and-white composition of the rest of the South. These two facts make Texas one of the most culturally diverse parts of Dixie. Finally, Texas was the place where slavery effectively stopped. Texas did not promote or pass along the institution further into the southwest. Nor did slavery in Houston follow the patterns identified by Richard Wade in other southern cities. As Tamara Miner Haygood indicates in her essay, prior to 1850 slavery was still growing in the Houston area and differed markedly from the form it commonly took in the deep South states. In the Houston vicinity, more blacks lived and worked in town than in the countryside. Those who did live in the countryside were more often employed to work in ranching than in agriculture, as opposed to the usual case in the rest of the South.

In sum, the following studies on nineteenth-century black Houston reflect some important characteristics that the Lone Star State shared with Dixie as well as some of the differences that made Texas uniquely Texas.

Notes

1. Alwyn Barr, *Black Texans: A History of Negroes in Texas, 1528-1971* (Austin, 1973), p. 3; The Institute of Texan Cultures, *The Afro-American Texans* (San Antonio, 1975), pp. 2-3.
2. Barr, pp. 3-7.
3. *Afro-American Texans*, p. 4.
4. See Writers' Program of the Works Projects Administration, *Houston: A History and Guide* (Houston, 1942), p. 38 (hereafter cited as WPA). The source most often quoted as the basis of this claim was a nephew of Houston's founders, O. Fisher Allen, *The City of Houston from Wilderness to Wonder* (Temple, Tex., 1936), pp. 1-2.
5. Abigail Curlee provided a detailed study of the Peach Point regimen in "The History of a Texas Slave Plantation, 1831-1863" (master's thesis, University of Texas, 1922), and in "A Study of Texas Slave Plantations" (Ph.D. diss., The University of Texas, 1932). A more recent study is Marie Beth Jones, *Peach Point Plantation: The First 150 Years* (Waco, 1982).
6. Kenneth W. Wheeler, *To Wear a City's Crown: The Beginnings of Urban Growth in Texas, 1836-1865* (Cambridge, Mass., 1968), pp. 107-10; James Martin SoRelle, "The Darker Side of 'Heaven': The Black Community in Houston, Texas, 1917-1945" (Ph.D. diss., Kent State University, 1980), pp. 5-6.
7. SoRelle, p. 6.
8. Wheeler, p. 148.
9. Gilbert J. Jordan, trans. and ed., "W. Steinert's View of Texas in 1849," *Southwestern Historical Quarterly* 80 (Apr., 1977): 412.
10. Wheeler, p. 148.
11. Paul D. Lack, "Dave: A Rebellious Slave," in *Black Leaders: Texans for Their Times,* ed. Alwyn Barr and Robert A. Calvert (Austin, 1981), pp. 6-10.
12. SoRelle, pp. 8-13.
13. Andrew Forest Muir, "The Free Negro in Harris County, Texas," *Southwestern Historical Quarterly* 46 (Oct., 1943): 222.
14. SoRelle, pp. 15-17.
15. WPA, pp. 249-50. See also Jordan, p. 413, for a contemporary description of the origins of the black church.
16. SoRelle, p. 20; Mary Susan Jackson, "The People of Houston in the 1850s" (Ph.D. diss., Indiana University, 1974), p. 143.
17. *Tri-Weekly Telegraph,* Nov. 17, 1858.
18. S. O. Young, *True Stories of Old Houston and Houstonians: Historical and Personal Sketches* (Houston, 1974), p. 65.
19. *Tri-Weekly Telegraph,* Apr. 21, 1865.
20. Ibid., June 26, 1865.
21. Ibid., June 30, 1865.
22. Ibid., Aug. 15, 1865.
23. Ibid., June 30, 1865.
24. Ibid.
25. Ibid., July 7, 1865.

26. Ibid., July 10, 1865.
27. Ibid., July 20, 1865.
28. *Tri-Weekly Telegraph,* Aug. 25, 1865. See also Charles D. Green, *The Firefighters of Houston, 1830-1915* (Houston, 1915), pp. 137-41; Jesse A. Ziegler, *Wave of the Gulf* (San Antonio, 1938), pp. 56-58.
29. *Tri-Weekly Telegraph,* Sept. 25, 1865.
30. Ibid., Aug. 25, 1865.
31. *Bird's Eye View of the City of Houston,* 1873, Metropolitan Research Center, Houston Public Library (hereafter cited as MRC).
32. WPA, p. 288.
33. See John Kellogg, "Negro Urban Clusters in the Postbellum South," *Geographical Review* 67 (July, 1967): 310-21; and SoRelle, pp. 46-47.
34. This sample was based on every fourth black household. National Archives Microfilm Publications, *Population Schedules of the Ninth Census of the United States: 1870, Texas* vol. 9, *Guadalupe, Hamilton, Hardin, and Harris Counties* (Washington, D.C., 1965).
35. This sample consisted of every eighth page of census data and every third black household. Bureau of the Census Microfilm Laboratory, *Twelfth Census of the Population: 1900, Texas,* vol. 53, *Harris County.*
36. This situation was reported by a number of blacks interviewed in an oral history project. See, for example, Sylvia Harrison, interview with Shelly Jarmon, Houston, Tex., Apr. 3, 1981 (audio tape in possession of Cary D. Wintz).
37. *Tri-Weekly Telegraph,* July 10, 1865.
38. Ibid., July 3, 1865, July 4, 1865.
39. Robert E. Zeigler, "The Workingman in Houston, Texas, 1865-1914," (Ph.D. diss., Texas Tech University, 1972), pp. 36, 50.
40. Hunter O. Brooks, *Historic Highlights of the Antioch Missionary Baptist Church of Christ, Inc., 1866-1976* (Houston, 1976), pp. 1-2.
41. SoRelle, p. 41.
42. Rutherford B. H. Yates, Sr. and Paul L. Yates, *The Life and Efforts of Jack Yates* (Houston, 1985), pp. 31-35.
43. Ibid., pp. 44-45; Brooks, p. 3; *Catalog of Houston College, 1919-1920,* MRC.
44. SoRelle, pp. 21-23.
45. SoRelle, p. 40; Marion Mersenberger, "A Political History of Houston, Texas, during the Reconstruction Period as Recorded by the Press: 1868-1873" (master's thesis, Rice Institute, 1950), pp. 23-24, 29-31, 46, 51, 57-60.
46. See Mersenberger for a more detailed account.
47. David M. Potter, *The South and the Sectional Conflict* (Baton Rouge, 1968), p. 182.

Use and Distribution of Slave Labor in Harris County, Texas, 1836–60

Tamara Miner Haygood

Introduction

Harris County, Texas, constitutes a million acres of prairie straddling Buffalo Bayou at the head of Galveston Bay. Before 1836 the area's population was minimal; there was a tiny trading and shipping center called Harrisburg and a few farms, but nothing that could be called a city. Events of 1836, however, transformed the region dramatically. Texas declared independence from Mexico on March 2, 1836. This changed the Mexican municipality of Harrisburg into Harris County, Republic of Texas. It also led within a few months to the incineration of little Harrisburg by General Santa Anna. Shortly, however, residents established a new town to replace the burned-out village. A bold real estate venture named after the victorious Texas general of the Battle of San Jacinto, the settlement of Houston was to succeed far beyond the expectation of its founders, the brothers Augustus and John Kirby Allen.

Houston soon took advantage of its location on Buffalo Bayou to become a vital link in the import-export business of South Texas. The Bayou City connected the cotton planters of the Brazos and Colorado river bottoms with the shippers of Galveston Bay. Slow but dependable oxcarts burdened with cotton, some driven by slaves, made their tortuous way through prairie mud to the busy little town on the sluggish bayou. Sometimes these wagons, each hauled by sixteen or more oxen, traveled together in caravans of over a hundred. Their loads of cotton enriched planters, Houston merchants, and Houston itself. By 1860 the city was thriving and increasingly populous while its vast, expanding hinterland was dotted with lumber mills, plantations, and ranches.[1]

Much of the effort necessary to make this transformation was supplied by the black women and men of Harris County. Though not without protest, they performed numerous domestic chores, staffed cotton warehouses, and tended farm crops. As Harris County grew and labor needs changed, new slaves were brought in or the older ones were shifted to new jobs where their labor increased the county's wealth even more. This essay will discuss the growth and distribution of the county's slave population as both a reflection of and a contribution to its economic development between 1836 and 1860.

The Early Years — Prior to 1850

Slavery actually existed in Harris County, as in the rest of Texas, long before 1836. While Texas remained part of Mexico, however, the government's hostility towards slavery somewhat impeded the early development of the institution in the state.[2] Even so, clever and determined slaveholders were generally successful in evading government restrictions, as by bringing in black so-called indentured servants bound to them for life.[3] By the mid-1830s the influence of the Mexican government in Texas had so weakened that not only were immigrants importing slaves from the United States, but a vigorous slave trade developed between the Caribbean and Galveston Bay. This illicit trade offered fantastic profits to the successful participant. A slave could be bought in Cuba for three or four hundred dollars, then sold in Texas for fifteen hundred dollars. Considerable risks were involved, of course, since apprehension of a ship by Mexican authorities meant the loss of valuable cargo.[4]

Harris County's proximity to Galveston meant that it probably received its full share of illegally imported Caribbean slaves, while still others passed through the county en route to various other destinations. In February of 1834 a group of newly imported Africans, accompanied by three white men, stopped for a few days at the home of Dr. Pleasant W. Rose in Harris County. The party had become lost while traveling to the plantation of Benjamin Fort Smith in Brazoria County. By the time they stumbled upon the Rose farm they were hungry and exhausted, and the slaves were nearly naked. Provided with food, rest, and clothing, the Africans went up to the farmhouse, where they amused the Rose family's three children with their strange speech and habits.[5] In the mid-1830s Col. William F. Gray also encountered some newly imported slaves in or near Harris County. They had been brought from the West Indies but because they did not speak English, French, or Spanish, Gray supposed they were native Africans.[6]

Just how many slaves had been smuggled into Texas from the West Indies by 1836 is impossible to say. One historian of the Caribbean slave trade, however, estimated that about a thousand slaves arrived in Texas from the islands. In a total slave population of about five thousand, this represents a significant proportion of native Africans and Caribbeans among blacks in Texas.[7] The remainder of the slaves, of course, came from the United States, the majority of those in Harris County coming by ship to Galveston and then by boat up Buffalo Bayou.

In March, 1836, Mexico seemed on the verge of putting down the Texan bid for independence. The Texas army, pursued by Santa Anna's forces, was retreating towards San Jacinto, while white residents of Harris County and nearby areas fled with their slaves ahead of the armies. So many slaves were among the refugees that it seemed to one witness that there were more blacks than whites.[8]

Some of the slaves in the Runaway Scrape, as the refugee march was called, were singularly cooperative. Perhaps they had been told stories to make them as frightened of the Mexicans as were their owners. Uncle Ned, an elderly black man, particularly distinguished himself. After one fleeing group crossed to the east side of the Trinity River, the white men drove the livestock up onto the prairies leaving Ned to protect the women, children, and other slaves in the bottomland. He took charge and guarded the party until morning.[9] Initiative like that shown by Ned on the retreat later allowed many other Harris County slaves to gain positions of responsibility and a measure of independence. Some slaves ably administered their absent master's estate; others established themselves as semi-independent artisans or laborers in Houston.

Even in the late 1830s many slaves in Harris County already had a degree of independence and responsibility greater than any but a few privileged plantation slaves. They were ranch hands who often had to work cattle alone or under only loose supervision. They rounded up cattle, broke wild horses, and participated in cattle drives. Gustav Dresel, a German visitor to Texas from 1837 to 1841, encountered one of Harris County's black cowboys. When he bought a three-year-old bronc, a slave mounted the wildly plunging animal in an effort to subdue it. The horse threw its rider twice, however, and apparently emerged the victor from this particular contest.[10]

While early Harris County had an active and growing cattle business, cotton and sugar plantations were conspicuously absent. In neighboring regions, however, these staples were grown profusely along the fertile banks of the Brazos and Colorado rivers. The forested land along these rivers was better suited to cotton culture than most of Harris County. Stephen F. Austin had habitually settled his wealthier colonists on the best soil where, with their capital and slaves, they could begin cotton production. Harris County's wealth would come not by competing with these cotton planters but rather by serving them with storage, shipping, and credit. In the hinterlands away from the rivers, farmers in these counties, as in Harris, raised considerable herds of cattle as well as corn and hogs.[11]

Though spared the backbreaking work of a sugar or cotton plantation, many Harris County slaves performed an endless routine of domestic chores. For a year or so after the victory at San Jacinto, the duties of some may have been lightened by help from Mexican prisoners. Since the young republic was unable to care properly for soldiers captured at San Jacinto, officials entrusted them to responsible citizens who were to watch over them until their release. The Rose family guarded one of these captives. Their daughter later gave some insight into both the treatment of prisoners of war and the normal activities of slaves when she wrote that her family "treated the Mexican like a negro servant, and . . . made him work, churn, wash, and do all kinds of drudgery, besides working in the corn field."[12]

In addition to performing various household chores, slaves labored in Houston's new warehouses and waited on customers in the city's hotels. Matilda Houstoun, an Englishwoman visiting the Texas Gulf Coast in the late 1830s, stayed at the Houston House Hotel. There she was attended at her table by "Rosetta, a negress with rings on every finger," and by Jerry, a black porter.[13]

Tasks performed by early Harris County slaves did not generally require large, concentrated numbers of workers. The small scale of Houston's new commercial houses, many of which at this early time operated out of tents situated along the wharf and main streets, meant that only a few hands were needed at any one establishment. Indeed, throughout the antebellum South, urban slaves generally lived in small groups; the vast majority of their owners held only one or two slaves each.[14] On the ranches surrounding the city, the work of tending cattle, hogs, and corn also normally required few workers. A couple of riders on horseback could handle about a thousand head of cattle.[15] Given, therefore, a Harris County dominated by ranching and small-scale commerce, we would expect that many people did without black servants and that most of the remainder held only a few. This expectation is borne out fully by the evidence in Gifford White's *1840 Census of the Republic of Texas*. Since Texas did not conduct a census in 1840, White's work is a compilation of tax rolls for that year. The Harris County returns showed 388 slaves held by 95 individuals. Sixty-nine owners (73 percent) held only 1-5 slaves, 17 people had 6-10, and 7 held 11-15. Only 2 individuals, J. D. Andrue and James Scott, held more than 20 slaves. Neither of them appeared later on the 1850 census of Harris County.[16]

After 1840 Harris County grew rapidly in population and wealth. This growth was not limited to Harris County alone but occurred throughout Texas. Natural increase accounted for only a portion of the population growth. By 1850 the population of Texas, slave and free, had expanded so greatly through immigration that approximately two thirds of all Texans had been born outside the state.[17] Blacks, about a fourth of the total Texas population, came mostly from the United States. The Texas Constitution, promulgated in March of 1836, made the importation of slaves from

Table 2
1840 Size of Slaveholdings, Harris County

Number of Slaves Owned	Number of Owners	Percent of Total
1–5	69	72.6
6–10	17	17.9
11–15	7	7.4
16–20	0	0.0
over 20	2	2.1
TOTAL	95	100.0

any nation other than the United States illegal, declaring it piracy. Outlawing the Caribbean slave trade while opening the border to importations from the American South undoubtedly curtailed greatly the foreign traffic but did not end it entirely. While lying aboard ship just off Galveston Island in late 1839, Francis Sheridan, a British diplomat sent to provide Lord Palmerston with an eyewitness account of the Republic of Texas, saw two ships safely land cargos of slaves from Martinique. One vessel unloaded at Velasco, the other at the Sabine.[18]

This incident caused Sheridan to doubt the sincerity of Texas' condemnation of the overseas slave trade, but public opinion in Harris County at this time probably ran against slave smuggling. An editorial in May, 1839, in the Houston *Morning Star* expressed regret that several ships had been outfitted in New Orleans for transporting slaves from Cuba to Texas. The newspaper wished success to United States officials who planned to try to intercept the smugglers, and it urged that the law "be enforced with the utmost rigor and decision."[19]

Both in Texas as a whole and in Harris County, the largest contingent of free immigrants were southern whites. Of those who came to Harris and neighboring counties, more were from the Lower South than from the Upper South or the border states.[20] Accustomed to slave labor, the white population tried to make Harris County similar to much of the Lower South in both its social and economic life. To do so, they needed a slave population. Since it was much easier for whites to supervise blacks who spoke English, most Harris County whites probably did prefer slaves imported from the United States.

Once imported, slaves were carefully monitored. Efforts to control their movements and minimize the disruptive influence of the area's few free blacks reflected slavery's deep impact on the social life of the county. Many control measures were similar to those used in parts of the southern United States. By August, 1839, white Houstonians had tightened the reins on skilled black workers who had grown somewhat autonomous. The board of aldermen decreed that no slave should be able to make his or her own labor contract without written permission from his or her owner. Furthermore, such day laborers were always to spend their nights on their owner's premises.[21] Both of these provisions may have been aimed, in part, at preventing runaway slaves from posing as day laborers in Houston. Additional city ordinances made it illegal to give or sell liquor to slaves, enacted an eight o'clock curfew for them, and forbade blacks to hold dances inside the city's limits without the mayor's permission. Other southern cities made similar attempts to control urban slaves.[22] In 1846, complying with an order of Gov. James Pinckney Henderson, the Harris County Commissioners' Court established ten precincts and provided for their supervision by that ubiquitous southern institution, the slave patrol.[23] Patrol duties and other control measures necessarily restricted white people as well as blacks, yet most Harris County whites, even the nonslaveholders, were willing to tolerate them.

Concerned as they were to control their slaves, whites in early Harris County were even more worried about free blacks. Nearly hysterical outbursts against them occupied many pages of the Houston *Morning Star* throughout the spring of 1839. Free blacks were attacked for their alleged ignorance, dishonesty, indolence, and addiction to gambling and petty crime. Annoying as these supposed habits might be, the worst thing about free blacks was their potentially evil effect on slaves.[24] "Ours," one article said, "is emphatically a slave holding country and everyone, who has lived in the Southern States will bear testimony to the baneful influence which free blacks always exercise over the slaves."[25]

White Houston's hysteria over free blacks had little or nothing to do with reality. In the first place, even at the height of the free black panic in 1839, Houstonians admitted that there were probably only twenty or thirty free blacks in the city. Secondly, far from being the dregs of black society, free men and women were usually those who had been manumitted for faithful service or who had bought their freedom through hard work and industry. Though illogical, fear nevertheless remained, and whites expended much energy trying to keep slaves from mixing too often with free blacks. Gradually the concern lessened because state and municipal laws greatly limited the immigration and rights of "free" blacks. From at least February, 1845, it was illegal for any free black to remain in Texas without permission of the legislature—permission that was not given to any Harris County black.[26]

Just as a typical Lower South acceptance of slavery and some of the inconveniences associated with it shaped Harris County's social life, so did the practices of Lower South herders shape the cattle industry of southeast Texas. Southern herders led the frontier westward from South

Carolina, allowing their cattle and hogs to roam free on unfenced pasture or in the woods. As more people moved in after them and began fencing fields for crops, the herders either acquired land and became farmers or moved into marginal, piney-woods areas. Some pushed farther west with their animals. With its sparse population and large land area, Harris County in the 1830s and 1840s was a highly favorable place for them to establish cattle ranches. Fewer than fifty-five thousand of the county's one million acres were farmland in the antebellum period, and fewer than five thousand acres were fenced, thus leaving abundant public land available for grazing.[27]

Southerners were joined in Harris County by considerable numbers of foreigners, most of whom settled in Houston. At the time of the 1850 census there were 598 foreigners, composing 32 percent of the city's population of 1,870. By 1860 their numbers had increased so that 1,350 foreign-born made up 36 percent of a free population of 3,776. Historian Ralph Wooster has described slaveholding as being "commonplace among the wealthier aliens of major Texas towns," at least by 1860. In Houston, however, foreigners seem not to have accepted slavery very enthusiastically. In 1860 only about 13 percent of the city's slaveholders who could be located on both free and slave schedules of the census were non-American, despite a marked increase during the previous decade in property owned by Houston's aliens.[28] Because a large proportion of Houston's small shopowners and artisans were foreigners, their disapproval of slavery set limits on the possible expansion of the institution in the city and may have nurtured an environment in which a skilled black worker could ply a trade independently—which many, of course, did with relish.

The Later Years—After 1850

Immigration brought many people to Harris County; the census of 1850 found the county with 4,669 residents—905 slaves and 3,764 free. The free population was divided quite evenly between Houston and its environs, but, perhaps as a reflection of the low labor requirements of ranching, more slaves lived in the city than in the surrounding countryside. Slave ownership was restricted to a small, elite group. Only about 17 percent of Houston's free adult men—and therefore an even smaller percentage of the total population—held one or more slaves.[29] As in 1840 nearly three-quarters of the slaveholders had only a few slaves, the overall average being four.[30]

Houston's typical slaveholder of the 1850s was an American-born professional or merchant. The city's largest slaveholder was W. W. Stiles, a farmer and stockraiser from Mississippi who lived within the city limits and had eighteen slaves. Lawyer William J. Darden had seventeen slaves,

Table 3
1850 Size of Slaveholdings, Harris County

CITY OF HOUSTON			OUTSIDE HOUSTON		
Number of Slaves Owned	Number of Owners	Percent of Total	Number of Slaves Owned	Number of Owners	Percent of Total
1–5	97	74.0	1–5	64	72.7
6–10	21	16.0	6–10	17	19.3
11–15	10	7.6	11–15	5	5.7
16–20	3	2.3	16–20	0	0.0
over 20	0	0.0	over 20	2	2.3
TOTAL	131	99.9	TOTAL	88	100.0

1850 Number of Slaves per Household, Harris County

CITY OF HOUSTON			OUTSIDE HOUSTON		
Size of Household	Total Number of Slaves	Percent of Grand Total	Size of Household	Total Number of Slaves	Percent of Grand Total
1–5	185	35.1	1–5	131	34.7
6–10	157	29.8	6–10	132	35.0
11–15	133	25.2	11–15	58	15.4
16–20	52	9.9	16–20	0	0.0
over 20	0	0.0	over 20	56	14.9
TOTAL	527	100.0	TOTAL	377	100.0

and lawyer T. B. J. Hadley, physician H. C. Parker, and merchant W. B. Walker each held fifteen. C. B. Tucker, a woman who headed her household, also had fifteen blacks.[31]

Undoubtedly the majority of Houston's blacks, particularly women whose owners held only a few slaves, worked as household servants. The *Telegraph and Texas Register* carried occasional advertisements for slaves tucked in among the listings of patent medicines, potatoes, soapstone griddles, and the latest in ladies' and gentlemen's fashions. Typical notices in 1849 included Sampson and Company's attempt to sell "A Likely Negro Woman, Cook, Washer and Ironer, aged 28 years, and accustomed to the field."[32] Later that year the same company wished to purchase "A Negro Girl from 16 to 20 years of age, accustomed to house work, of good character and disposition."[33] Versatility was the order of the day, with emphasis put on domestic skills.

In the countryside, as in the city, most whites who had any slaves at all held only a few. Eighty-eight whites had a total of 377 slaves. The small number of slaves per household suggests that many of them probably com-

Table 4
Age-Sex Distribution of Slaves in Houston, 1850

	MALES		FEMALES	
Ages	Number	Percent	Number	Percent
0–9	62	12	72	14
10–14	25	5	52	10
15–49	115	22	166	32
50–64	10	2	13	3
65+	0	0	4	1
TOTAL	212		307	

Age-Sex Distribution of Slaves in Harris County outside Houston, 1850

	MALES		FEMALES	
Ages	Number	Percent	Number	Percent
0–9	63	16	63	16
10–14	24	6	24	6
15–49	77	20	100	26
50–64	14	4	9	2
65+	0	0	12	3
TOTAL	178		208	

bined domestic chores with working on the farm. Lucy Barnes, her brother, and her aged grandmother were the slaves of A. J. Burt of Houston. The grandmother cooked and Lucy milked the Burts' nine dairy cows. Mostly, though, she looked after her mistress's children.[34]

Of those slaveholders outside Houston whose occupations could be discerned from the census, 65 farmed or raised stock.[35] Combined with the farmers who lived inside Houston, 78 white farmers, or approximately one-fourth of all farmers, owned 377 blacks (see table 5). These figures underestimate the true number of slaves in agriculture, because it was common for people who listed a nonagricultural occupation on the free population schedule also to run a farm. Ownership of land conferred status in Texas as it did throughout the South. Frances Richard Lubbock, for example, gave his occupation as clerk of the District Court of Harris County, but in 1850 he already owned a four-hundred-acre ranch. There and on abundant public land his five slave cowboys tended some two thousand cattle. Also, fourteen slaveholders were women. While no occupations were listed for them, at least twelve were farmers or the wives, widows, or mothers of farmers.

As in 1840, most slaveowning farmers or ranchers held very few blacks. Only two slaveowners were planters, owing to the commonly accepted

Table 5
1850 Agricultural Slavery, Harris County

	Size of Ranchers' Slaveholdings	
Number of Slaves Owned	Number of Owners	Percent of Total
1–5	54	69
6–10	16	21
11–15	5	6
16–20	1	1
over 20	2	3
Total	78	100

	Number of Slaves per Household	
Size of Household	Total Number of Slaves	Percent of Grand Total
1–5	111	29
6–10	129	34
11–15	63	17
16–20	18	5
over 20	56	15
Total	377	100

convention that holding twenty slaves elevated a person to that celebrated status.[36] L. C. Stanley owned twenty-four, and Ashbel Smith, a prominent physician, soldier, statesman, and amateur scientist as well as planter, held thirty-two. While probably neither conformed to the image of a planter as one who raised plant crops, both fit the definition in the sense that the labor of their slaves largely freed them from field work. In fact, both Stanley and Smith were in the habit of leaving their farms, sometimes for extended periods, in the care of a black overseer. Such highly skilled agricultural slaves often played a major role in the efficient and profitable operation of a plantation or ranch. The slave family who ran Smith's plantation had a small house near Smith's own modest cabin.[37] Unlike Andrue and Scott, the two large slaveholders of 1840, both of whom had apparently moved on by 1850, Stanley and Smith established permanent residence in Harris County and were still living there in 1860.

Even ranchers with fewer slaves could increase the efficiency of their operation by choosing slaves carefully. For example, in 1850 James Morgan held only ten slaves, but all were between fourteen and forty-nine years of age and most of them were men. With their aid, he was very successful and became noted for his large herd of cattle as well as for his work in experimental agriculture.[38] Of course, such discriminating selection of slaves frequently meant breaking up families, so many farmers probably preferred the more haphazard method of natural increase and, trusting that happier slaves would work better, hoped to come out ahead in the long run.

Black and white farmers in Harris County produced cattle and hogs for markets in Houston, Galveston, New Orleans, and Natchez. In 1850 they raised some 23,500 beef cattle and almost 7,000 hogs. In their fields they grew 49,700 bushels of corn and about 20,000 bushels of sweet potatoes. Much of the corn and sweet potatoes was probably used to feed the county's numerous livestock as well as the slaves. Only three farmers in all of Harris County grew oats; the largest producer, with 100 bushels, was the aptly named James W. Oats. The county produced in 1850 virtually none of the South's usual staple crops. Two farmers grew a mere 11 bales of ginned cotton, two others raised a meager 5,000 pounds of sugar, and two together produced 2,300 pounds of tobacco. Very little truck farming showed up on the 1850 census, although peaches were commonly grown in the area.[39]

Slaveholding farmers were distinctly more successful than their slaveless neighbors. Partly because of the valuable help of their slaves and partly because of the same wealth that allowed them to buy slaves in the first place, the cash value of slaveholders' farms averaged over three times that of the farms of nonslaveholders. They likewise owned four times as many horses, three times as many dairy cows, and twice as many swine as those without slaves. But it was in their beef cattle holdings that the most startling difference appeared. Slaveholders, on average, had cattle herds nearly eight times larger than nonslaveholders. While tending these herds, black cowboys learned skills that some of them successfully used after being freed. One of Francis R. Lubbock's cattlemen, Willis, had his own brand and a good herd of cattle and horses. He bought his own freedom and was buying his wife and children when slavery was ended. Lubbock mentioned in his memoirs two other men, Osborn and William, whom he prized for "their honesty and intelligence" in working stock. After the Civil War, they drew high wages as cowboys.[40]

Though most rural slaves were held by ranchers and spent their time tending livestock, raising corn, or doing domestic tasks, a score or so were owned by sawmill operators and perhaps had a chance to learn their owners' trades. Two sawmill operators owned five slaves each, and a third held a dozen. Each lumberman had at least one adult man who probably helped run the mill. Two shipwrights also had slaves, and three merchants owned a few as well.[41]

From 1840 to 1850, the number of slaveholders and slaves in Harris

County had grown, especially in the city of Houston. The character of slavery had changed, too, because while most owners still had only a few slaves, a dozen or so large owners had appeared. Slaves worked in a wide variety of jobs, but especially as domestics, in warehouses, and in other commercial establishments.

For slavery to function efficiently in a rapidly growing area like Houston and Harris County, there had to be adequate means for the quick reallocation of labor, both on a permanent basis through the buying and selling of slaves as well as on a temporary basis by hiring or borrowing them. In Houston most slaves who changed hands permanently were put on the block and sold at auction. Until about 1865 Houston had a strong auction business, which enhanced the town's position as a commercial center. Slaves were among the merchandise commonly offered at auction by leading commercial firms in the Bayou City.[42]

Traveling through Texas in the mid-1850s, Frederick Law Olmsted stopped briefly in Houston. While there he noticed the town's "several neat churches, a theatre, . . . and a most remarkable number of showy bar-rooms and gambling saloons" as well as a "prominent slave-mart . . . which held a large lot of likely-looking negroes, waiting purchasers."[43] Perhaps he had noticed the establishment of Edward Riordan, who maintained slave depots both in Houston and in Galveston. While no other Harris County entrepreneur seems to have dealt exclusively with slaves for any length of time, many handled them occasionally.

The price of slaves varied considerably according to market conditions and the merits of the individual. Ferdinand Roemer gave the average price of a slave in this region as about $600 in the late 1840s. Historian Wesley Fornell estimated that during the prosperous 1850s, prices in Texas ranged up to $1,500 for men and $1,250 for women.[44]

Houston commercial companies sometimes bought and sold slaves on commission for their customers, accepted them in lieu of cash payment, or kept them as collateral on a loan or credit purchase.[45] Even in business agreements between private individuals, slaves were commonly used as security against money owed. Sometimes the arrangements amounted to nothing more than repossession by a slave's previous owner if payment was not forthcoming when the money was due.[46]

Houston's slave merchants and auctioneers made the city a local center for slave trading. Whites came from all over southeast Texas and western Louisiana to buy and sell blacks in the Bayou City. Thus slaves increased the wealth of Harris County actively, through their labor, as well as passively, by joining the cotton, sugar, and imported luxury items sold for a profit in Houston's stores or on the auction block. Eventually, as slave prices rose during the prosperous fifties, the slave trade became so economically important to Harris County that in the minds of many whites the desirability of a large supply of fresh slaves began to outweigh the humane impulses that had once turned public opinion against the foreign slave trade. Throughout the late 1850s, whites in Galveston and Houston debated the wisdom of reopening the African trade, and the question at times assumed a position of political importance.[47]

Slave-hiring was common in southern cities, and Houston was no exception. Those who chose this option could hope to have a servant for $120 per year in the 1840s, or $250 to $300 during the next decade. Room and board were generally provided by the employer. Hiring rates could vary a great deal. The historian David G. McComb noted an obviously highly skilled man hired for the fantastic price of $50 a month in 1839, while one woman was let out for a mere $12.50 a month in 1856.[48]

In 1860 the census taker carefully recorded both the owner and employer of each slave hired out. Out of a slave population of 2,040, 78 hired slaves were recorded.[49] These probably represent only those slaves who were hired to one individual long enough for the census taker to consider their permanent residence to be with their employer rather than their owner. Slaves who rented out for only a short time—those who made their own daily contracts as well as those who happened not to be employed when the census taker came by—were probably recorded simply as belonging to their owner, and their temporary employment was overlooked. If this guess is correct, then the 78 recorded hired-outs represent only a fraction of the actual total, and slave hiring was even more widespread in Harris County than these figures would indicate.

Hiring was a convenient way for some owners to obtain a profit from a temporarily idle slave, while other owners probably invested in slaves with the deliberate intention of renting them out. The attorney T. B. J. Hadley is a likely example of the latter case. By 1860 he held twenty-nine slaves, ten of whom he kept hired out to a local hotel proprietor.[50] For employers, hiring slaves was a way to acquire help for some particular project without incurring the expense of purchasing the slave. Hiring also meant employers could increase the ratio of productive to nonproductive personnel. While Harris County's slave population as a whole was very young and included more women than men, 59 percent of those recorded as hired out in 1860 were men in their most vigorous years—aged fifteen to forty-nine. Only six were young children, and two were over fifty-one. Sometimes, too, an employer was lucky enough to hire slaves who were already skilled. When in 1860 sawmill operator J. W. Bergin needed extra help, he hired a family of experienced slaves from Charles Spears, who also operated a sawmill.[51]

Hired blacks played a big role in building Harris County's railroads. In 1840 when work was to begin on the Harrisburg and Brazos Railroad, Andrew Brisco advertized in the Houston *Morning Star* for sixty black men to be hired for six months to two years. Some track was laid, but ultimately the project failed, and work on the line was abandoned in 1841. Eleven years later a new railway, the Buffalo Bayou, Brazos, and Colorado, began to push out from Harris County towards the plantation country of the Brazos River. Like Brisco's project, this railway originated not in Houston but in little Harrisburg. W. J. Kyle and Frank Terry, Fort Bend County planters who were later locally famous as Confederate officers of Terry's Rangers during the Civil War, contracted to grade the section between Harrisburg and the Brazos River. Many, if not all, of their laborers were slaves. When this section was completed in 1855, Houston merchants and Brazoria County planters decided to build a branch line connecting the B.B.B.&C. with Houston. Kyle and Terry were again the contractors, and their laborers were slaves provided by Brazoria County planters in payment for shares in the railway.[52] The completion of this railway in 1856 perhaps did more than any other single thing to ensure the continued growth of Harris County, and particularly Houston, in the years ahead.

Harris County's economic growth after 1850 is reflected in the increased size of both the white and black populations. According to the 1860 census, the white population increased from 3,754 in 1850 to 7,008 in 1860.[53] During the same decade the slave population more than doubled, from 905 to 2,040. As before there were slightly more slaves in the city of Houston than in its environs. Two hundred and four Houstonians held 1,060 blacks, while outside the city 161 whites held 980 slaves. These bare numbers alone clearly indicate a greater concentration of slaves in the hands of relatively fewer whites in 1860 than in 1850. In Houston, for example, the percentage of free adult men holding slaves dropped from about 17 percent in 1850 to just under 13 percent in 1860.[54]

How had this concentration been achieved? Most slaveholders in 1860, as in 1840 and 1850, still had ten or fewer slaves. Yet, while the total number of owners of 1–5 slaves increased steadily from 69 in 1840 to 161 in 1850 and finally to 257 in 1860, their proportion among all Harris County slaveholders dropped slightly from about 73 percent in 1840 and 1850 to 70 percent in 1860. The percentage of those owning 6–10 slaves also dropped by 1860. These small drops were reflected in proportionately large increases in the number of people controlling over 16 slaves.

Houston alone in 1860 had eleven owners of sixteen or more blacks. The occupations of these people indicate there was increased use of slaves in large-scale manufacturing and commerce. Two of these large slaveholders were merchants whose slaves probably labored in warehouses or on the wharf. There also was an attorney, a clerk, and a railroad executive, as well as T. S. Lubbock, a self-styled "gentleman of leisure." The rapid building then going on in Houston is suggested by the widespread use of slaves in manufacturing bricks. L. C. Stanley, owner of twenty-three blacks, perhaps still used some of them to work his ranch, but his principal occupa-

Table 6
1860 Size of Slaveholdings, Harris County

CITY OF HOUSTON			OUTSIDE HOUSTON		
Number of Slaves Owned	Number of Owners	Percent of Total	Number of Slaves Owned	Number of Owners	Percent of Total
1–5	147	72	1–5	110	68
6–10	32	16	6–10	27	17
11–15	14	7	11–15	11	7
16–20	4	2	16–20	3	2
over 20	7	3	over 20	10	6
TOTAL	204	100	TOTAL	161	100

1860 Number of Slaves per Household, Harris County

CITY OF HOUSTON			OUTSIDE HOUSTON		
Size of Household	Total Number of Slaves	Percent of Grand Total	Size of Household	Total Number of Slaves	Percent of Grand Total
1–5	369	35	1–5	222	23
6–10	232	22	6–10	212	22
11–15	188	18	11–15	141	14
16–20	106	10	16–20	93	9
over 20	165	16	over 20	312	32
TOTAL	1060	101	TOTAL	980	100

tion, and theirs too, had most likely become brickmaking. Another man, F. M. Anderson, owned Houston's biggest cotton warehouse as well as a brickmaking enterprise, and with forty-two slaves he was by far the largest slaveholder in the city. Several other brickmakers also used slave labor. Undoubtedly many slaves became skilled in the brickmaking and construction trades and were later able to use their skills to advantage. For example, one slave advertized for sale by Sampson and Company in 1850 was a "bricklayer and brick mason by profession."[55]

Between 1850 and 1860 the slave population of most southern cities did not grow as much as in Houston, where it actually exceeded in proportion the growth of the white population. Indeed, the trend throughout the older portions of the South was for urban slave populations to decrease gradually during the decade as tasks they formerly performed were assigned to free blacks or white laborers. In the southwestern cities of Austin, Galveston, Little Rock, and Shreveport, the slave population grew between 1850 and 1860, but only enough to maintain an approximately stable proportion of the city population as a whole.[56] That Houston's slave population increased both in absolute numbers and as a proportion of the total may have been due in part to the city's very tiny free black population, shrunken by 1860 to only eight persons or perhaps a few more. Another contributing factor may have been the absence of large-scale plantation agriculture in rural sections of Harris County, which meant that these immediately adjacent areas did not outbid the city for labor. This argument should not be given undue influence, however, for Houston was the hub of a slave-marketing area stretching throughout southeast Texas and including many rich plantation regions.

With the exception of C. T. Duer, a merchant, all of the largest slaveholders outside the Bayou City were farmers, planters, or stock raisers. In fact, when farmers are considered together as a statistical group, it is plain that in 1860 they demonstrated a great deal more concentration of slaves, and presumably of wealth, than they did in 1850. Eight men, compared to only two in 1850, now held over twenty slaves. One of them, Dr. J. C. Mapie, a newcomer to the county, had fifty-four slaves. Though a majority of farmers still held only a few blacks, more than half of all farm slaves lived and worked on farms or ranches with more than fifteen bondsmen, and 45 percent lived on plantations or large ranches holding twenty-one or more slaves.

If all slaveholders involved in agriculture were counted instead of only those found on the free census or who were actually identified as farmers or planters, then the concentration of farm slaves in large groups would probably be even more pronounced. There were a number of large slaveholders who were perhaps farmers, but for whom the relevant data are missing from the census records. T. S. Lubbock, the gentleman of leisure, for example, was also the owner of one of the largest cattle herds in Harris County. Many of his thirty-one slaves worked for him as ranch hands. A real enigma is William R. Baker. Though recorded to be the secretary of the "C" Railroad, he was also the owner of three hundred thousand dollars worth of real estate and held twenty-two blacks as slaves. It seems very likely that some of his real estate consisted of a farm or a ranch tended by his slaves.

Increased concentration of slaves reflected a modest shift away from ranching and towards a more diversified agriculture. Only some ten thousand cattle and four thousand hogs lived in Harris County in 1860. The horse and milk cow populations were also down from 1850. This may reflect a real reduction in the livestock holdings of Harris County ranches, or it may mean that as the population grew, ranchers simply shifted their livestock to the less populated central and southwest Texas plains where rustling was less of a problem. Other ranchers were doing the same, and by 1860 this area had become the new center of the ranching industry in Texas. Meanwhile, in Harris County sheep and wool production increased, and farmers continued to raise large quantities of corn and sweet potatoes. They also raised some hay, orchard products, peas, honey, and even a respectable amount of wine. Most significantly, cotton production increased from 11 bales in 1850 to 425 bales in 1860.[57]

Even taken together, the shift from livestock to plant crops did not represent a drastic break with the past. It becomes interesting, however, in light of the accompanying redistribution of the slave labor force. The increased concentration of slaves probably meant for many of them a more monotonous job and prolonged attention to fieldwork, although perhaps more companionship and a livelier social life compensated for more strenuous work. At the same time, the decrease in cattle herds meant that fewer slave ranch hands were needed. Some of them were probably sold or sent with their owners' cattle to the south or further west. Others no doubt had to exchange their spurs for a hoe.

Conclusion

The combination of Harris County's development of large commercial houses, a thriving brickmaking industry, and more diversified agriculture signals that a certain maturity had been reached in the twenty-four years between 1836 and 1860. The heady excitement of the years surrounding Houston's founding was settling into a pattern of stolid prosperity. Houstonians had confidence in their city's future, and every time they built a new house or laid down a railroad tie they gave visible proof of their faith. Each newly acquired slave was also a vote of confidence in continued prosperity, for at fifteen hundred dollars each, slaves were an expensive investment. By studying slaveholders and the distribution of the slave population, we may gain some insight into which sectors of the economy were growing most rapidly at any one time as well as which were stabilized and which were in decline.

In 1850 when most slaves lived in small groups and did domestic work or ranched, it seems that the major concern of ranchers and merchants in the county was to establish their small businesses on firm foundations that would later allow expansion or diversification. By 1860, however, commerce was firmly settled and white Houstonians were interested in improving the material resources of the city, so slaves were put to work in large numbers on railroad and building projects. Ranchers diversified, probably spread their cattle operations out into sparsely populated counties, and began using increased numbers of slaves to tend crops. By the measuring rod of slave ownership, merchants were clearly the dominant group in the county, followed by professionals and ranchers.

As patterns of slave ownership reflected the growth of Harris County, so the labor of slaves had a large part in causing this growth. Their role may be traced on two levels, for each black was at the same time both a piece of property and a person. As persons the slaves played an active role in Harris County life. Studying the uses made of their labor allows us to see some of the positive contributions they made towards increasing the wealth of their holders and all of Harris County. Unfortunately, direct evidence about the uses of slave labor is scanty. The accounts of travelers and other such anecdotal material often fails to differentiate between typical and atypical uses of slave labor, and it seldom even speculates on the number of slaves involved in particular activities. Cautious extrapolation from census records and from information on the use of slave labor in other areas of Texas or the South, however, indicates that most slaves in Houston worked as domestics. By 1860 they had become very important as laborers in warehouses and in construction. Many blacks also certainly worked as day laborers or artisans, although their existence often went unremarked except in laws providing for their regulation. In the countryside, most slaves also worked as domestics. However, black ranch hands were prominent throughout the period, although by 1860 many slaves had been shifted to farming.

Despite the change to free labor after 1865, the economic base of Harris County continued to rest for at least another twenty years upon foundations laid, largely by slave labor, between 1836 and 1860. The diverse ranching and farming practiced in the rural areas of the county began in the 1880s to be overshadowed by large-scale, highly mechanized rice production.[58] Houston's growth, however, continued to be fueled by cotton and sugar exportation until their primary position was gradually usurped by the twentieth-century development of the petroleum industry. This persistence of economic patterns established during slavery testifies to the importance of the institution in the development of the county. Indeed, because of the continued growth of the slave population and the relative absence of free blacks, slavery was at least as prominent a feature in antebellum Harris County and Houston as in other areas throughout the South.[59]

Notes

The author wishes to thank Professor John Boles of Rice University and the *Journal of Southern History* for encouragement and advice on both early and late drafts of this paper.

1. On the history of Harris County before 1836, consult C. Anson Jones, *Early History of Harris County, Texas* (Houston, 1928), pp. 1–5; Adele B. Looscan, "Harris

County, 1822-1845," *Southwestern Historical Quarterly* 18 (Oct., 1914): 195-207, and (Jan., 1915): 261-86; and Andrew Forest Muir, "The Buffalo Bayou, Brazos and Colorado Railway Company, 1850-1861, and Its Antecedents" (master's thesis, Rice Institute, 1942). For information on the extensive use of oxcart transportation in early Texas, see S. G. Reed, *A History of the Texas Railroads and of Transportation Conditions under Spain and Mexico and the Republic and the State* (Houston, 1941), pp. 43-46.

2. Fred Robbins, "The Origin and Development of the African Slave Trade in Galveston, Texas, and Surrounding Areas from 1816 to 1836," *East Texas Historical Journal* 9 (Oct., 1971): 157; Eugene C. Barker, "The Influence of Slavery in the Colonization of Texas," *Southwestern Historical Quarterly* 27 (July, 1924): 1-33; Randolph B. Campbell, *An Empire for Slavery: The Peculiar Institution in Texas, 1821-1865* (Baton Rouge, 1989), pp. 10-34.

3. This was the trick used by Harris County rancher James Morgan. Andrew Forest Muir, "James Morgan," in *The Handbook of Texas*, 2 vols., Walter Prescott Webb, ed. (Austin, 1952), 2, p. 234; Campbell, *Empire for Slavery*, pp. 23-24.

4. Robbins, "Slave Trade in Galveston," p. 157. Approximately half of the slaves that Benjamin Fort Smith attempted to import from Cuba during the winter of 1833-1834 were confiscated. May Wilson McBee, "Benjamin Fort Smith," *Handbook of Texas*, 2, p. 621.

5. McBee, "Benjamin Fort Smith," *Handbook of Texas*, 2, p. 621; "The Reminiscences of Mrs. Dilue Harris, I," Texas State Historical Association *Quarterly* 4 (Oct., 1900): 97-99.

6. William F. Gray, *From Virginia to Texas, 1835: Diary of Col. Wm. F. Gray Giving Details of his Journey to Texas and Return in 1835-1836 and Second Journey to Texas in 1837 . . .* (Houston, 1909), pp. 147, 158-59.

7. Robbins, "Slave Trade in Galveston," p. 153; Archie P. McDonald, "'Westward I Go Free': Some Aspects of Early East Texas Settlement," *East Texas Historical Journal* 4 (Oct., 1966): 77.

8. "Reminiscences of Mrs. Dilue Harris," p. 164.

9. Ibid., pp. 165-66.

10. Gustav Dresel, *Gustav Dresel's Houston Journal: Adventures in North America and Texas, 1837-1841*, Max Freund, ed. (Austin, 1954), pp. 92-93.

11. Muir, "Buffalo Bayou Railway Company," pp. 1-3; Terry G. Jordan, "The Origin of Anglo-American Cattle Ranching in Texas: A Documentation of Diffusion from the Lower South," *Economic Geography* 45 (Jan., 1969): 63-87.

12. W. P. A. Writers Program, *Houston: A History and Guide* (Houston, 1942), p. 42; Francis Richard Lubbock, *Six Decades in Texas or Memoirs of Francis Richard Lubbock, Governor of Texas in War-Time, 1861-63: A Personal Experience in Business, War, and Politics* (Austin, 1900), pp. 70, 94; see Reminiscences of Mrs. Dilue Harris," p. 181, for quote.

13. Matilda Houstoun, *Texas and the Gulf of Mexico; or, Yachting in the New World*, 2 vols. (London, 1844), 2, pp. 188-89.

14. Richard C. Wade, *Slavery in the Cities: The South, 1820-1860* (New York, 1964), pp. 20-23.

15. Jordan, "Cattle Ranching," p. 78.

16. Figures were derived from information in Gifford White, ed., *The 1840 Census of the Republic of Texas* (Austin, 1966). Andrue and Scott are not listed as slaveholders in Manuscript Census Returns, Seventh Census of the United States, 1850, Harris County, Schedule 2, Slave Population, National Archives Microfilm Series, Roll 317 (hereafter referred to as "Slave Population, 1850"). Historian Susan Jackson estimates that half of Houston's 1850 free population had moved elsewhere by 1860, so it is likely that Andrue and Scott were among those who left shortly after 1840. Jackson, "Movin' On: Mobility through Houston in the 1850s," *Southwestern Historical Quarterly* 81 (Jan., 1978): 251–82.

17. Terry G. Jordan, "Population Origins in Texas, 1850," *Geographical Review* 59 (Jan., 1969): 85.

18. *Declaration of Independence Made at Washington, on the Second of March, 1836, and the Constitution of the Republic of Texas, Adopted by the Convention, March 17, 1836* . . . (Houston, 1838), p. 20; Francis C. Sheridan, *Galveston Island or, a Few Months off the Coast of Texas: The Journal of Francis C. Sheridan, 1839–1840*, Willis W. Pratt, ed. (Austin, 1954), p. 89.

19. Furner Grober, comp., "Harris County Newspaper Excerpts, (1839–1911)," Allied Slave Material, Houston Metropolitan Research Center, Houston Public Library, Houston, Texas.

20. Jordan, "Population Origins," pp. 85–87.

21. Houston *Morning Star*, Sept. 19, 1839; Grober, "Newspaper Excerpts."

22. David G. McComb, *Houston, The Bayou City* (Austin, 1969), p. 82; Mary Susan Jackson, "The People of Houston in the 1850s" (Ph.D. diss., Indiana University, 1974), p. 114; James Smallwood, "Blacks in Antebellum Texas: A Reappraisal," *Red River Valley Historical Review* 2 (Winter, 1975): 463; Paul D. Lack, "Urban Slavery in the Southwest," *Red River Valley Historical Review* 6 (Spring, 1981): 15–17.

23. C. H. Smith, comp., "Harris County Commissioners' Court Minutes, (1846–1866) (Slave Patrols, etc.)," Allied Slave Material, Houston Metropolitan Research Center, Houston Public Library, Houston, Texas.

24. Andrew Forest Muir, "The Free Negro in Harris County, Texas," *Southwestern Historical Quarterly* 46 (Jan., 1943): 9–11.

25. Houston *Morning Star*, May 3, 1839; Grober, "Newspaper Excerpts."

26. Muir, "Free Negro"; Campbell, *Empire for Slavery*, pp. 110–12.

27. Forrest McDonald and Grady McWhiney, "The Antebellum Southern Herdsman: A Reinterpretation," *Journal of Southern History* 41 (May, 1975): 147–66; Grady McWhiney and Forrest McDonald, "Celtic Origins of Southern Herding Practices," *Journal of Southern History* 51 (May, 1985): 165–82; Jordan, "Cattle Ranching"; Terry G. Jordan, *Trails to Texas: Southern Roots of Western Cattle Ranching* (Lincoln, Neb., 1981), pp. 25–82; J. D. B. DeBow, *Statistical View of the United States, Embracing Its Territory, Population . . . ; Being a Compendium of the Seventh Census* (Washington, D.C., 1854), p. 316.

28. Ralph A. Wooster, "Foreigners in the Principal Towns of Ante-Bellum Texas," *Southwestern Historical Quarterly* 66 (Oct., 1962): 208–18, quotation on p. 218; Jordan, "Population Origins," pp. 87, 98; Jackson, "Movin' On," p. 260.

29. Jackson, "People of Houston," p. 101.

30. Unless otherwise indicated, information on the slave population for 1850 comes from "Slave Population, 1850," and information on the free population from Manuscript Census Returns, Seventh Census of the United States, 1850, Harris County, Texas, Schedule 1, Free Population, National Archives Microfilm Series, Roll 314 (hereafter referred to as "Free Population, 1850").

31. Jackson, "People of Houston," p. 101. J. N. Dupree, occupation unknown, also had seventeen slaves. Information about the occupation of slaveholders comes from correlating information in "Slave Population, 1850" and "Free Population, 1850."

32. *Telegraph and Texas Register,* Jan. 18, 1849.

33. *Telegraph and Texas Register,* May 10, 1849.

34. George P. Rawick, ed., *The American Slave, A Composite Autobiography,* (Supplement, Series 2), 10 vols. (Westport, Conn., 1979), 2, p. 178. Additional slave memoirs may be found in Ronnie C. Tyler and Lawrence R. Murphy, eds., *The Slave Narratives of Texas* (Austin, 1974). Unfortunately, the former slaves rarely stated their location.

35. Manuscript Census Returns, Seventh Census of the United States, 1850, Harris County, Texas, Schedule 4, Agricultural Productions, microfilmed by the Texas State Library, Roll 1 (hereafter referred to as "Agricultural Productions, 1850"). Information about the occupation of slaveholders was obtained by correlating data from "Free Population, 1850," "Slave Population, 1850," and "Agricultural Productions, 1850."

36. Ulrich Bonnell Phillips, *Life and Labor in the Old South* (Boston, 1929), p. 305, defines a plantation as a farm that had become so large that its owner had to devote full time to management. Common usage had it that this point was usually reached on a twenty-slave operation.

37. For a short treatment of Smith's career, see Harriet Smither, "Ashbel Smith," in *Handbook of Texas,* 2, p. 620. Also note Ferdinand Roemer, *Texas, with Particular Reference to German Immigration and the Physical Appearance of the Country,* trans. Oswald Mueller (San Antonio, 1935), p. 60; Dresel, *Houston Journal,* p. 106.

38. Muir, "James Morgan," p. 234.

39. Compiled census information from J. D. B. DeBow, *Statistical View of the United States,* pp. 315-19.

40. Lubbock, *Six Decades in Texas,* pp. 136-37. Smallwood, "Blacks in Ante-Bellum Texas," affirms that by 1850 a majority of Texas ranch hands were probably black. On the variety of positions filled by slaves, see John B. Boles, *Black Southerners, 1619-1869* (Lexington, Ky., 1983), pp. 108-14; Claudia Dale Goldin, *Urban Slavery in the American South, 1820-1860: A Quantitative History* (Chicago, 1976), pp. 42-46.

41. These data were obtained from the same source, using the same method, as described in note 35 above.

42. McComb, *Bayou City,* pp. 22-23, 83.

43. Frederick Law Olmsted, *A Journey through Texas; or, a Saddle-Trip on the Southwestern Frontier: with a Statistical Appendix* (New York, 1857), pp. 361, 363.

44. Smallwood, "Blacks in Antebellum Texas," p. 448; Roemer, *Texas,* p. 58;

Earl Wesley Fornell, *The Galveston Era: The Texas Crescent on the Eve of Secession* (Austin, 1961), p. 230; McComb, *Bayou City,* p. 83.

45. Jackson, "People of Houston," p. 115.

46. C. H. Smith, comp., "Harris County Deed Record Book A," Allied Slave Material, Houston Metropolitan Research Center, Houston Public Library, Houston, Texas.

47. Kenneth W. Wheeler, *To Wear a City's Crown: The Beginnings of Urban Growth in Texas, 1836-1865* (Cambridge, Mass., 1968), pp. 107-109.

48. Roemer, *Texas,* p. 58; Fornell, *Galveston Era,* p. 230; McComb, *Bayou City,* p. 83.

49. Manuscript Census Returns, Eighth Census of the United States, 1860, Harris County, Texas, Schedule 2, Slave Population, National Archives Microfilm Series, Roll 286 (hereafter referred to as "Slave Population, 1860"). Unless otherwise noted, all information on Harris County's slave population in 1860 comes from this source.

50. Information on the occupation of owners and employers of slaves was obtained by correlating "Slave Population, 1860" and Manuscript Census Returns, Eighth Census of the United States, 1860, Harris County, Texas, Schedule 1, Free Population, National Archives Microfilm Series, Roll 282 (hereafter referred to as "Free Population, 1860"). Unless otherwise noted, all information about Harris County's free population in 1860 comes from this source.

51. See Joseph C. G. Kennedy, *Population of the United States in 1860; Compiled from the Original Returns of the Eighth Census . . .* (Washington, D.C., 1864), pp. 480-81, for a detailed breakdown by age and sex of Harris County's slave population. Also see note 50 above.

52. Mar. 20, 1840; Grober, "Newspaper Excerpts"; Wheeler, *City's Crown,* pp. 97-100; Reed, *Texas Railroads,* pp. 34-37, 56-61, 81-83.

53. Kennedy, *Population in 1860,* p. 473.

54. Jackson, *People of Houston,* p. 101; Gavin Wright, *The Political Economy of the Cotton South: Households, Markets, and Wealth in the Nineteenth Century* (New York, 1978), pp. 29-37.

55. Houston *Telegraph and Texas Register,* Feb. 21, 1850.

56. Lack, "Urban Slavery," pp. 18-19.

57. Joseph C. G. Kennedy, *Agriculture of the United States in 1860; Compiled from the Original Returns of the Eighth Census . . .* (Washington, D.C., 1864), pp. 144-47.

58. Bell I. Wiley, "Salient Changes in Southern Agriculture since the Civil War," *Agricultural History* 13 (Apr., 1939): 66-67.

59. For an additional perspective on slavery in Houston, see Susan Jackson, "Slavery in Houston: The 1850s," *Houston Review* 2 (1980) 2:66-83. This essay and Jackson's article were derived at approximately the same time from independent research in the manuscript census records, which explains small discrepancies in numbers.

Seeking Equality:
Houston Black Women during Reconstruction

Barry A. Crouch

Contradictory perceptions surround the status and role of black women both in and out of bondage. "On the one hand," Suzanne Lebsock writes, "we have been told that black women, in slavery and afterward, were formidable people, 'matriarchs,' in fact." Yet nevertheless "all along, black women were dreadfully exploited." Rarely, she concludes, "has so much power been attributed to so vulnerable a group." A similar paradox embracing black women can be found in the works of America's most famous African-American historian. In his early writings, W. E. B. Du Bois described southern black women as tragic figures. In his later books, however, Du Bois noted that although black women suffered countless injustices during slavery and Reconstruction, their sacrifices produced "freedom and uplift" for themselves and their race.[1]

Within the past two decades feminist historians have rewritten women's history from the point of view of the women themselves. Still, only a handful of studies concentrates on the history of black women.[2] This essay will present a case study of Houston black women during the Reconstruction era. Its larger purpose is to inspire other local studies about black women so that we may fully document their history. Only after we have studied the role of black women through the use of primary source materials will we be able to resolve some of the paradoxes encountered by historians Lebsock and Du Bois.

The story of Houston's black women during the postwar years is based primarily upon information available in the records of the Bureau of Refugees, Freedmen, and Abandoned Lands (Freedmen's Bureau). Although the manuscripts vary in quantity for the former Confederate states, Texas does have a midsize collection of bureau papers.[3] Before examining them, it is appropriate briefly to explain the bureau's role.

The concept of a major social welfare agency resulted from the Emancipation Proclamation, and in early 1865 Congress established what eventually became the Freedmen's Bureau. The underlying premise of the bureau was that it would not serve southern blacks as a guardian but would attempt to ensure that they received a fair chance in their struggle for equality. Although the role of the bureau was originally viewed as a limited one, once Reconstruction commenced blacks quickly realized that they would not receive fair trials or justice in the South, and so the bureau established special tribunals to deal with black complaints. "Dissatisfied though blacks so frequently were at the bureau's feebleness and ambivalence," Michael Perman nevertheless concluded "they knew that without it they would have been far worse off."[4]

Bureau archives constitute a major source of information about what black women in Texas, and especially Houston, were doing in the immediate aftermath of war. Furthermore, these records catalogue some of the serious problems that women encountered in the first years of freedom.

Protecting the Family

It is impossible to know precisely how many blacks were in Houston when the Civil War ended in April, 1865, because slaveholders from other states transported blacks to Texas during the war for "safekeeping." By 1870, however, the city counted almost 9,400 residents — approximately 5,700 white and 3,700 black. Houston blacks made up 39 percent of the population.[5] Although the exact number of black women in Houston is not known, it is evident that they were active participants in postwar city life.

With the long and bloody conflict decided and slavery ended, blacks began to search for family members, move back to the vicinity of their old plantations, or locate the nearest bureau office. "While it is true that much of the traveling about that the Freedmen's Bureau paid for was inspired by the wish to try freedom out," historian Willie Lee Rose contends that "a great deal more of it is explained by the laudable urge to find out what had happened to relatives long gone to another part of the world." For the former slave, the "only way was to go and see, since the magic of writing was denied to him."[6]

The bureau generally investigated the "physical and pecuniary" condition of the individuals who applied for financial support to travel in order to determine whether they were "worthy objects of charity to the government or not." Thus, guided by local teachers, Rachel, an eighty-three-year-old Houstonian, turned to the bureau for assistance. The teachers had located and contacted Rachel's only daughter in Charleston, South Carolina, and both mother and daughter attempted to raise money so Rachel could journey to the distant state to "spend her remaining days." Rachel's health was tolerably good, and one of the teachers wrote that if she could "only get started right, she would be okay."[7] In a similar instance, the St. Louis relatives of Hannah Talbot and her children, all of whom lived in Lynchburg, requested that the Texas bureau provide Hannah and her children with the necessary aid to enable them to move to St. Louis.[8]

Another serious problem for freed blacks was that former masters sometimes tried to deny ex-slaves normal family rights. Some whites in postwar Texas "endeavored to prevent wives and children from joining their natural protectors, their husbands and fathers," a bureau agent noticed. Blacks appeared before the Houston bureau charging that former slaveholders were unlawfully detaining their wives and children. Thus Abraham received bureau assistance in retrieving his wife, Hannah, and their six children from a nearby Brazos River plantation. The bureau also gave blacks release orders to deliver to the white individuals holding their families, as they did to James, a freedman who sought his wife and three children. In "nearly every case" whites released ex-slaves upon receiving such orders from the bureau.[9]

Locating and gathering children back into the family became a compelling, exhausting task for many blacks after the war. From late 1865 until the demise of the bureau in 1868, black women and men appeared before the bureau courts claiming detention of their children by whites. When Mary Busby stated that her twelve-year-old daughter, Louisa, was being kept from her "by some party," this vagueness about the "detainer or detainees" provided the bureau an opportunity to formulate a policy that favored black women parents. "The Mother has the first claim to her child," the bureau stated, adding pointedly that "interference with this right will not be tolerated." Arrest and punishment were the mandated consequences for those who did. The intent of the policy was clear, and black women quickly used its provisions to their — and their children's — advantage.[10]

Black women sometimes used an intermediary to achieve reunification with their children. Lavinia Page enlisted a helper to wrest her daughters Lucy and Winnie from a white doctor in Danville. In another instance, John Lewis, a black Houston resident, also traveled to Danville to reclaim Mary, the daughter of a female acquaintance of his. Single black women who required help in reclaiming their children commonly relied upon other members of the community, often men, to provide it.[11]

The detention of children immediately after the cessation of hostilities but prior to the enactment of apprenticeship laws may have been a more serious problem for the southern black community than previously has been realized. This situation occurred before the Texas legislature met and had the opportunity to establish apprenticing statutes, which attempted economically to bind black children to whites against the wishes of the black community. It appears that whites detained young black girls more often than boys because it was easier to keep them in a state of semiservitude.[12] The institution of slavery cast many lingering shadows, and the forcible detention of children was one of them.

The Freedman's Bureau attempted to aid black women in their quest for their children, even if this developed into a lengthy or complicated process. Black women challenged even those of their own race who they felt unjustly retained children. Barbara Alfred complained that Jerry Gross, also black, was preventing her child from joining her. She won the case — and her daughter. In another incident, the bureau ordered Louisa, a Sandy Point resident, to turn over Rachel to her mother, Eliza. In a third instance, a Houston black woman claimed that a Galvestonian named Caroline Flash stole her child. The bureau stepped in and ordered the child returned to the Bayou City and her mother immediately. Although a bureau agent and an army officer were themselves accused of kidnapping a black girl in 1866, with the *Houston Telegraph* printing lurid headlines suggesting sexual improprieties, local black women continued to seek out the bureau, which became a central judicial agency for the Houston black community.[13]

Black women in Houston often protected children for whom they felt responsible, even if they were not strictly kin. Clara Parker, for example, charged that her "adopted child" was being kept by another black woman whom the bureau ordered to relinquish custody. In another case, Cynthia Ann Hickman found it necessary for reasons not recorded to arrange temporary care for her daughter Martha Allen, aged nine, with Alexander Pierce, a black man. However, she stipulated that while in his care nobody was to interfere with the child unless first getting Hickman's permission or contacting the bureau office. Black women monitored such arrangements closely. Even young women quickly learned the desirability of knowing the law and using it to their advantage. Rosa Johnson, a young black Houstonian, petitioned the authorities in order to have Dony Hamblin, who lived near the "old Government stables," appointed her guardian. All of her relatives were dead, and she wanted Hamblin to be "considered as if she were her mother."[14]

The bureau in Houston began to bind out black children starting as early as 1866. Its agents obtained required pledges from the white custodians who, in turn, agreed to a "faithful performance" of signed agreements. Sometimes agreements between the bureau and white people were struck over the apparent objection of black parents. In early 1866, for example, the father of two young black girls, Frances and Lucy, sought the bureau's aid in reclaiming them from a white man. Initially he was successful, for the bureau gave him a written order to the holder commanding their release. However, the very next day the bureau authorized the white man to keep the children in return for providing their care, culture, and education.[15] In another case, the Houston bureau administrators decided that a thirteen-year-old black girl, Harriet Carson, whose mother was deceased, should continue to live with Virginia Harris, a white resident of adjacent Harrisburg, as a house servant. Her stepfather, Edward Burlington, claiming to be "her next friend or nearest of kin," tried unsuccessfully to gain her custody. He stated that his stepdaughter had been Harris's slave and had been bound out to her without anyone's knowledge or consent. Nevertheless, young Harriet was obliged to serve as a domestic "in consideration of advantages guaranteed" until she was eighteen, after which she was free to leave. Harris, her white custodian, agreed to furnish her schooling and life necessities, as did other whites who the bureau allowed to retain black children. Burlington, her stepfather, like other blacks in similar situations, was specifically warned by the bureau not to interfere in any manner with the girl, or attempt to prejudice her against Harris.[16] Even when the parent was a mother, the bureau might rule that the child remain apprenticed to a white family.

But some black women forced a different resolution. When Ailsie Merrit supplied "satisfactory evidence of her respectability and [proof] that she is able to take care of her child," the bureau ordered a white woman to surrender the child to her mother forthwith.[17] The apprenticing law in Texas allowed the courts to bind out children if their parents were unable or unwilling to support them. It made no reference to race or color, but it was clear to most observers that it was aimed squarely at blacks. The bureau proctored such cases while the law was in effect from 1866 to its repeal in 1871.[18]

The residents of Houston were concerned about who would care for black orphans in the Bayou City after the war. There were a few instances of both blacks and whites claiming freedchildren, though this happened rarely, and it was up to the bureau to determine with whom they should be placed. In a typical case, the bureau authorized a white woman, O. A. Runnels, to retain two black girls. The bureau required Runnels to "instruct them in rudiments of English," and to supervise their "mental, moral, and physical culture." The same type of agreement applied to blacks when they applied for custody of orphaned children. Thus was Washington Brown, a Houston hack driver who lived on Congress Street, awarded custody of Annette. Although agreements such as these were often supposed to be temporary arrangements, they tended to become permanent.[19]

By 1867 the local government took charge of orphans, although it still relied upon the bureau for advice. In Houston that year the Harris County government had control of three orphan children. There were also several cases of indigent orphan children, too young to take care of themselves, whose relatives, according to the bureau, were too poor to support them. The civil authorities had no legal guidelines for providing care to such children who were under the age for apprenticing. Consequently they were normally assimilated into the black community on an ad hoc basis. One agent suggested the establishment of a home for destitute orphans to be supervised by a bureau employee, but his suggestion was not acted upon.[20] Subsequently an Orphan Society was established to raise funds for the care of these children. In a particularly distressing incident, Octavia Williams, an officer in the society, embezzled fifteen dollars from the proceeds of a fair held to benefit the needy youngsters, and then fled to Galveston. The Orphan Society brought charges against Williams, but the stolen money was evidently never recovered.[21]

Black Women, Black Men

While struggling to provide for their children and relatives, black women also began to assert their marital rights and privileges. When necessary, they used the bureau and local courts to pursue their objectives. They charged husbands with non-support, infidelity, and related offenses. For instance, when Milly Barnes asserted that Alfred Harroll had committed adultery, a Houston bureau agent negotiated a compromise and matters were "amicably adjusted," the couple returning home together. Another black Houstonian, Maria Flowers, had a more serious problem. Flowers contended that she bore Wash Sessuns two children, after which he threatened to leave his family and marry someone else. In mid-1866 Louisa Whiting's complaint echoed that of Flowers. After living with George Washington Holmes for two years, he had deserted Whiting and the children around Christmas in 1865, marrying another woman. Whiting believed he should be required to assist in supporting the children, especially since he was a housepainter with a steady income. The bureau sometimes came to the conclusion that it was best for couples to separate. Although it could not issue divorce decrees, it could and did issue orders for people to live apart. Such cases were common in Houston.[22]

It was not only black men who left the family. In one case, the bureau ordered a black woman named Anna Allen to return home to her husband and remain there. Allen's husband pledged to support her and, after studying the situation, a bureau agent concluded that he could "see no reason why you should live apart." Regardless of which partner lodged a complaint, the bureau served as a sort of marriage counseling agency, always hoping to compromise differences between spouses. When persuasion failed, as it sometimes did, bureau agents in Houston simply ordered couples to live together. However, when it became clear to them that a relationship could not be repaired, agents acquiesced and permitted couples to separate. Generally it was women who sought assistance against husbands who drove them away, ran off with younger women, or just left. When black men entered complaints, it was almost always because their wives were involved with other men.[23]

Whites and blacks in Houston had different perceptions of the behavior of black families. One Houston bureau agent, W. B. Pease, wrote that matrimonial problems among freedpeople had increased in early 1867. Pease claimed that blacks neither comprehended the "solemnity and binding force of the marriage ceremony" nor understood the duties they owed each other in marriage. He thought that the slave custom of "promiscuous intercourse" prevailed among many blacks and reported that infidelity was a common complaint. However, several black couples stated that whites had arbitrarily put slaves together as couples, so they were applying to the bureau for divorce in the mistaken belief that it could grant one.[24] Bureau agents were often in a position to see social practices from different points of view, even if they did not credit them equally.

Houston black women were not reticent about demanding child support from the fathers of their children. Emeline Anderson requested support for her child from George Gentry, whom she identified as the father. Gentry, adjudged the father, was ordered to support his offspring. Julianna Stevens fought a similar battle with Durke Woodall. Initially Woodall had refused Stevens's request for maintenance, but the court decided he should pay five dollars a month. In another instance, Rachel Neal not only testified in court but brought her child along as evidence. When couples separated and children were involved, authorities instructed both parents about their obligations to their offspring. The bureau thus reminded Martha and Jacob that if they separated, they were nevertheless "charged morally and legally to assist each other in supporting your children." Part of the bureau's concern was that these children never became part of the public dole, but bureau officials also generally evidenced a strong belief in family life and thought that youngsters should be raised by their own parents whenever possible.[25]

Pregnant women were among those who appealed to the bureau. Mary Rogers was expecting when her employer threatened to turn her out of the house where she lived. However, she was able to avoid this "until sufficiently recovered from childbirth to work and earn a support." Women who were not pregnant but had been left indigent as a result of pregnancy also asserted their rights. When Malinda Wheeler's husband, Ned, left her impoverished without cause, he was ordered to pay her ten dollars a month support. Some women became so adamant about protecting themselves and what little they had that former husbands found themselves pleading with the bureau to intervene with their former wives so they could retrieve their "personal effects."[26]

After the Civil War there were black women throughout Texas who became indigent and sought assistance from the Freedmen's Bureau. Although this problem was not widespread, it was still too large for the bureau to handle. Between December of 1865 and July of 1866, the bureau issued only 165 rations to black women in the entire Lone Star State. During June, July, and August of 1868, shortly before the bureau concluded its operations, only six women and ten girls received rations from the agency. A ration, which was supposed to care for an entire family, consisted of ten ounces of pork or bacon, sixteen ounces of flour or cornmeal, ten pounds of peas, eight pounds of sugar, two quarts of vinegar, eight eleven-ounce candles, and two pounds of soap, salt, and pepper. In addition, women and children received a supplement of ten ounces of coffee. This ration was inadequate for the needs of a family, but it did help somewhat.[27]

Houston black women numbered among those who found themselves destitute and sought assistance from authorities. Often they turned to the bureau for information and guidance. An unnamed freedwoman approached the Houston bureau for help in taking care of Rachel Hester, who was ill. An agent referred her to a judge with the recommendation that Hester be sent to the poorhouse, since she had no visible means of support. Tina Washington was another person without means who could not support herself; a bureau agent routed her to the county chief justice. Lucinda Graves sought bureau aid because she was unable to provide for her four children due to poor health. Joe Moore appealed to the bureau for help in a sad situation. He related that the child of Nellie Keene had just died and that she did not have the money to bury it. Keene, through Moore, sought whatever aid the bureau might see fit to extend.[28] However, such abject need was rare. Blacks across the state, and in Houston, generally took care of their own. Although the bureau was certainly parsimonious in distributing rations, it did offer some needed aid to black women and children.

Women and Work

Harris County freedwomen in Houston labored at a variety of tasks when slavery ceased. Some worked for wages and shares as agricultural laborers on the plantations surrounding the city. Enterprising black women also found employment in other areas, particularly domestic service to whites. Both types of work closely resembled the labor they had performed as slaves. But now the relationship between blacks and whites had dramatically changed, and black working women in Harris County took their freedom to work with them. Their change in attitude and behavior did not please white employers, who loudly and often criticized their lack of servile deference. Black women also complained about whites, especially when white women charged them with dishonesty. They also hailed other blacks before the bureau for non-payment of wages and unfair treatment. Through these cases it is possible to catch a glimpse of how black women in Houston fought to establish their economic rights.

As employees black women consistently were treated unfairly. Throughout the Reconstruction era, women who labored in the fields, or who labored at all, were paid less than men, black or white. For agricultural labor, first-class workers (always men) received ten dollars in specie per month while second and third-class workers, including women, were paid proportionally less. Women who worked on farms, for example, received only one-half to two-thirds the pay of men when cash was still used as payment for plantation work. This gender division in the wage system did not change significantly during the postwar years. When women contracted, even if married, their agreement with employers was considered binding. Authorities did not permit husbands to interfere, although spouses were allowed to make any arrangement concerning working with their wives to which the employer might consent.[29]

Black women from the surrounding plantation area used the Houston bureau headquarters to bring complaints about threatened or actual physical abuse associated with their employment. They also desired settlement for services rendered and complained bitterly to the bureau when they were denied their wages. One aggressive woman named Margaret even brought charges against the vice-consul of Russia for defrauding her out of her wages. The bureau warned him that "as a worthy representative of your august Master," he should not "violate with impunity the laws" of the United States.[30]

Black women did not always direct their demands for fair compensation at whites. Kizzy sued Catherine, another black woman, for wages for labor performed in January, 1866. Although most individuals compromised their differences between themselves, other conflicts were resolved because women used the bureau to gain additional leverage. The Freedmen's Bureau courts gave these black women a legal tool they did not previously possess, and the women used it often.[31]

Women who worked the plantations surrounding Houston registered claims to wages or shares for themselves as well as their children when they felt a settlement was unfair. In 1867 a number of white farmers decided to act together in dismissing black women with whom they had contracted for the year. The bureau saw to it that these women remained employed. However, authorities also held black women to their obligations, since contractual agreements bound employees as well as employers. Thus in 1866 C. B. Sojourner was allowed to retain the services of a freedwoman (the "wife of Leroy") until she performed enough work to reimburse him for the cost of transporting her to the job site. She had been destitute with a sick child when Sojourner hired her, and he had employed her at her own request.[32] At other times, blacks sued other blacks for debts. Mary Vick, a Houston freedwoman, was sued by freedman George Cooper for payment of seven dollars due him for building a small house. Cooper's complaint was sustained, and he collected.[33] A black woman named Minerva also collected. She had worked for W. G. Nolan for four months at ten dollars a month — good wages for her, since this was the standard rate for men. She testified that Nolan acknowledged his indebtedness and had promised to pay her but had not. Minerva claimed she had received only a pair of shoes, worth about two dollars and fifty cents, and that Nolan now was trying to stall by saying somebody else was responsible for half of the money due. Minerva was described as being very destitute and deserving of the money.[34]

Black women were no less aggressive in protecting their working children's economic rights than in protecting their own. While Polly was unsuccessful in trying to collect wages for her children in 1866, because they were judged too young, Rachelle West had more luck a year later in claiming twenty-five dollars for work her children performed.[35] Black women did not refrain from suing other blacks where payment for their children's work was concerned. Julia Heard hauled Ben Lyons before a bureau court demanding four dollars in salary, which she received, for the whitewashing her son had done for Lyons. Mary Sellers sought the bureau's help in obtaining child-care pay from Newman Jackson, a black man, who had left two of his children in Sellers's house. He had agreed to pay her six dollars a month and owed her for three months. The bureau ordered Jackson, who worked on a nearby plantation, to pay up.[36]

Houston black women, just emerging from slavery, had very little property, but they did vigilantly guard what they had. Land naturally was of primary importance to them. Tenna's claim for one acre of land was validated, although it is not known how she acquired the real estate. America Lord proved her title to a house erected on the property of Mary E. Shea. When John Kennedy purchased the land, he attempted to remove Lord. However, the bureau prevented this action until Kennedy could prove his right to evict Shea.[37]

Black women in the Bayou City had to be wary about their economic status and their ability to support themselves lest they become vagrants or paupers. In 1866 Houston authorities charged indigent freedwomen with vagrancy and compelled them to work on the city's streets. The bureau investigated this and discovered that the police had arrested some black women as well as a white man for disorderly conduct. Unable to pay the fine for the charge, all were sent to work it off on the street. The bureau agent would have complained had city officials made any distinction in the punishment of blacks and whites, but they had not.[38] However, a bureau agent did intervene to request permission from a city judge for a surgeon to visit Harriet Anthony in the city prison. The surgeon said she had aborted due to hard labor on the street, and the agent also asked that she be released from confinement at once.[39]

Economic catastrophe also forced some black women to enter the world's oldest profession. For those who were young and attractive enough, working as a prostitute was an alternative to vagrancy and poverty. Although the number of black prostitutes in Houston following the war is not known, several young women were brought into court for maintaining a "disreputable house" near the T.&A. Depot.[40]

Violence: An Enduring Problem

For both blacks and whites the adjustment to freedom was a gradual and often painful process in which blacks were often the victims of force. Many such incidents involved the brutalization of black women. White planter David Hill assaulted Agnes Alexandra, a black woman who worked for him, despite the presence of two witnesses, both of whom later testified against him. Such treatment was sufficient cause for employment contracts to be annulled and blacks freed to seek work elsewhere. That is what happened when Mony, a household worker, was struck many times and generally poorly treated by the white woman who employed her. Although the actions of the white woman were defended as "simply the outbursts of a violent temper provoked by great obstinacy and ill-behavior of the servant," the bureau canceled the work contract between the two, allowing Mony to search for better employment. Sometimes violence was more calculated — a way to try to cheat black workers out of their yearly earnings by running them off the plantation. Premeditated violence against black workers normally occurred toward the end of the contract year when black workers were due to be paid.[41]

Many former slaveholders abused black women after the war. Selina Parker's suit in early 1866 illustrates how reluctantly some whites relinquished authority and power over their former slaves. Parker was Michael Linney's former slave. Once free, she chose to live with one of Linney's daughters in Liberty, Texas, and in September, 1865, she decided to take her daughter and move to Houston. When Linney learned she had decided to make this move, he appeared at her home, physically abused her, stole what money she had to make any move difficult, and abducted her daughter. After scattering Parker's clothing, he rode off, forcing her little girl to walk in front of his horse. Authorities did not always punish other whites for such behavior, but Linney was found guilty of assault, robbery, and kidnapping. He was fined two hundred dollars in gold and was ordered to pay Parker thirty dollars for damages and restitution. Cases similar to this were not uncommon.[42]

While the black community in Houston apparently did not suffer the savage brutalities occurring in rural areas of the Lone Star State, racial violence did take place in the Bayou City. Milly Graham and Emily Matthews complained that the white women who employed them had treated them badly and had physically driven them from their work site. Investigators found Adeline Williams's white employer so abusive that they fined her fifty dollars. In a similar case, the bureau assessed another white employer ten dollars, notwithstanding that the black woman who brought charges against him was "very abusive and used the foulest language." In another incident, a husband-and-wife team, Adeline and Levi Tanks, charged a white physician for chasing them with an open knife. Throughout Texas, white-against-black violence continued after slavery was abolished.[43]

Black women sought to protect their children from violence, and they brought complaints against those who abused their offspring. Julia Brown charged that a white woman who employed her son had beaten him with a cowhide whip, and the bureau ordered the woman to pay the youngster five dollars. However, the bureau did not always rule in favor of black complainants. For instance, Dinah Wren charged a Dr. Hartridge with unjust treatment of her daughter, Rebecca. Investigation, though, revealed that Rebecca was legally apprenticed to Hartridge, as the law required, and that he had agreed, as was normally the case, to furnish her with an education. Investigators found no evidence of abuse on his part and dismissed the charges against him. Rebecca remained under his care. Her mother could have been using the suit as an attempt, for whatever reason, to nullify the apprenticeship contract with Dr. Hartridge. In any event, Wren and other black women consistently attempted to ensure that their children were treated fairly, and the law as well as the bureau helped them do this during Reconstruction.[44]

Violence was a frequent side effect of marital complications for black women in Houston. Dollina Williams, although apparently never legally married to Andrew Johnson Williams, lived with him about three months in late 1865. She complained that during this time Williams drank heavily and beat her. Investigation sustained her charges, and Williams spent ten days at hard labor in a military prison. Emma Matthews made the same complaint against her spouse, who also served ten hard days. The bureau made certain that both men completed their sentence.[45]

Cases of wife abuse often involved other marital complications. Zenobia Johnson, for example, charged that her husband Wash had not only mistreated her, but had abandoned her to live with another woman. Moreover, Zenobia complained that she had "contracted a disease from him."

Given these circumstances, she had no desire to be reconciled with him, and the bureau allowed her to move and live anywhere she wanted. The bureau's verdict specifically warned Johnson to stay away from Zenobia lest he be severely punished. However, bureau investigations did not always sustain the accusations made by women. Lucy Ann King, for example, claimed that her husband Wesley King abused her, owed her money, and had abandoned her. But the bureau discovered evidence proving that she was not the wife of Wesley and furthermore had an unsavory reputation as a "desperate character, having attempted to poison her master and mistress, also having been put in jail for bad conduct."[46]

Black women also charged black men with other forms of violence against them and their children. They claimed that black men assaulted and battered them and threatened their lives. They also brought charges of rape and attempted rape against black men for attacks on them as well as their daughters. Alice James, for example, alleged that Peter Smith had tried to ravage her daughter. Melissa Hill brought the same charge against Albert Williams in 1867, and the bureau referred the complaint to the Houston city recorder. Hill was unable to prove her accusation to the satisfaction of officials who therefore dismissed the charge against Williams. In other similar complaints, men had to post rather large bonds — up to five hundred dollars — to assure their appearance before the bureau or civil court. Although rape was not a common crime in the postwar Houston black community, it did happen occasionally. There were also instances of women fighting violence with violence. The records reveal cases of women being charged with drawing knives, disorderly conduct, fighting, and using "bad language."[47]

Conclusion

Black women in Houston made strides in consolidating whatever social and economic rights they could establish through a combination of their own efforts, the law, the Freedmen's Bureau courts, and community resources. They focused first upon the reunification of families and kin, especially trying to find children. Encountering white opposition, and occasionally conflicts within their own community, they used the bureau and whatever other support they could muster to bring children into families. This included the few indigent or orphaned black children in the Bayou City. They also did their best to see that black children were adequately supported by pressing claims for child support from men. Although not completely successful, black women tried to limit the social and economic violence done to themselves and to their children in postwar Houston.

The early years of Reconstruction were characterized by turbulence and disorder for urban black women who lived and worked in and around Houston. They struggled to carve out a niche for themselves and to consolidate the gains they had been reluctantly granted by Congress despite a begrudging, if not outwardly hostile, white South. Within their own community, the adjustment to freedom brought forth turmoil and clashes between blacks themselves. To ascertain what rights and protection they had, black women in Houston used the bureau and occasionally civil officials to determine where they stood legally. They were quick to employ the few legal redresses to which they were entitled and attempted to begin defining a dignified existence for themselves. By the end of the Reconstruction era a stable black community had begun to form in Houston. Much of the credit for this properly belongs to women for asserting and testing their newly won legal rights.

Some recent arguments contend that blacks gained little or nothing from emancipation or from national efforts to reconstruct the South. But surely, as Willie Lee Rose has observed, the "difference between slavery and freedom is about the greatest difference in status we can imagine, no matter how kindly a view some historians might want to take of slavery, no matter how limited and curtailed freedom may have turned out to be."[48] By frequently using the Freedmen's Bureau courts in postwar Houston to prevent curtailment of their freedom, black women in the Bayou City established a legacy for the future and forged a base for continued progress.

Notes

1. Suzanne Lebsock, *The Free Women of Petersburg: Status and Culture in a Southern Town, 1784-1860* (New York, 1984), p. 88; W. E. B. Du Bois, *The Souls of Black Folk: Essays and Sketches* (Chicago, 1903), pp. 68-69; *Darkwater: Voices from within the Veil* (New York, 1920), pp. 164-65, 169-70, 178. See also his "Reconstruction and Its Benefits," *American Historical Review* 15 (July, 1910): 781-99, and his *Black Reconstruction in America: An Essay toward a History of the Part Which Black Folk Played in the Attempt to Reconstruct Democracy in America, 1860-1880* (New York, 1935). An overview is in Darlene Clark Hine, "Lifting the Veil, Shattering the Silence: Black Women's History in Slavery and Freedom," in *The State of Afro-American History: Past, Present, and Future,* Darlene Clark Hine, ed. (Baton Rouge, 1986), pp. 223-49.

2. The most important histories of black women are Jacqueline Jones, *Labor of Love, Labor of Sorrow: Black Women, Work, and the Family from Slavery to the Present* (New York, 1985); Deborah Gray White, *Ar'n't I a Woman: Female Slaves in the Plantation South* (New York, 1985); Gerda Lerner, ed., *Black Women in White America: A Documentary History* (New York, 1972). There are several other books on black women, but they are polemical, poorly researched, or written for a popular audience, making them of little value. Although not concentrat-

ing on women, an extremely valuable work for this period is Herbert G. Gutman, *The Black Family in Slavery and Freedom, 1750-1925* (New York, 1976).

3. Barry A. Crouch, "Hidden Sources of Black History: The Texas Freedmen's Bureau Records as a Case Study," *Southwestern Historical Quarterly* 83 (Jan., 1980): 46-58; Crouch, "Freedmen's Bureau Records: Texas, A Case Study," *Afro-American History: Sources for Research,* Robert L. Clarke, ed., (Washington, D.C., 1981), pp. 74-94. A local study is Crouch, "The Freedmen's Bureau and the 30th Sub-District in Texas: Smith County and its Environs during Reconstruction," *Chronicles of Smith County, Texas,* 11 (Spring, 1972): 15-30. See also Ross N. Dudney, Jr., "Texas Reconstruction: The Role of the Bureau of Refugees, Freedmen and Abandoned Lands, 1865-1870, Smith County (Tyler), Texas" (master's thesis, Texas A&I University, 1986). It is a characteristic of the Texas Bureau records that blacks are sometimes only referred to by a first name, as had been the practice during slavery.

4. Michael Perman, *Emancipation and Reconstruction, 1862-1879* (Arlington Heights, Ill., 1987), p. 24. It is also important to see John A. Carpenter, *Sword and Olive Branch: Oliver Otis Howard* (Pittsburgh, 1964); George R. Bentley, *A History of the Freedmen's Bureau* (Philadelphia, 1955), especially pp. 152-68, 249-53; William S. McFeely, *Yankee Stepfather: General O. O. Howard and the Freedmen* (New Haven, Conn., 1968); Herman Belz, *Emancipation and Equal Rights: Politics and Constitutionalism in the Civil War Era* (New York, 1978), and Sara Rapport, "The Freedmen's Bureau as a Legal Agent for Black Men and Women in Georgia: 1865-1868," *Georgia Historical Quarterly* 73 (Spring, 1989): 26-53.

5. Cary D. Wintz, "Blacks," *The Ethnic Groups of Houston,* Fred R. Von der Mehden, ed., (Houston, 1984), pp. 15-20, 22; David G. McComb, *Houston: A History,* rev. ed. (Austin, 1981), pp. 57, 60; Kenneth W. Wheeler, *To Wear a City's Crown: The Beginnings of Urban Growth in Texas, 1836-1865* (Cambridge, Mass., 1968), pp. 150-66. See also Susan Jackson, "Slavery in Houston: The 1850s," *Houston Review* 2 (Summer, 1980): 66-82; Paul D. Lack, "Urban Slavery in the Southwest," *Red River Valley Historical Review* 6 (Spring, 1981): 8-27. For a comparison, see Alwyn Barr, "Occupational and Geographic Mobility in San Antonio, 1870-1900," *Social Science Quarterly* 51 (Sept., 1970): 396-403.

6. Willie Lee Rose, *Slavery and Freedom* (New York, 1982), p. 101.

7. Julia B. Nelson, interview with Louis W. Stevenson, Oct. 30, 1869, Box 42, Records of the Bureau of Refugees, Freedmen, and Abandoned Lands, Texas, Record Group 105, National Archives, Washington, D.C. See also Barry A. Crouch and Larry Madaras, "Reconstructing Black Families: Perspectives from the Texas Freedmen's Bureau Records," *Prologue,* 18 (Summer, 1986): 109-22, reprinted in *Our Family, Our Town: Essays on Family and Local History Sources in the National Archives,* comp. Timothy Walch (Washington, D.C., 1987), pp. 156-67; Robert H. Abzug, "The Black Family during Reconstruction," in *Key Issues in the Afro-American Experience,* 2 vols., Nathan I. Huggins, Martin Kilson, and Daniel M. Fox, eds. (New York, 1971) vol. 2, pp. 26-41. A marvelous survey of blacks regarding their family and social activity is Leon F. Litwack, *Been in the Storm So Long: The Aftermath of Slavery* (New York, 1979). Unless otherwise indicated, all references are to the Texas Bureau records in RG 105.

8. J. C. de Gress (agent, Houston) to James R. Lynch (commander, Houston),

Oct. 24, 1865, vol. 100, p. 7; Charles C. Hardenbrook (agent, Houston) to S. H. Lathrop (commander, Houston), Sept. 18, 1866, vol. 100, p. 263; J. D. O'Connell (agent, Houston) to J. M. Davis, Aug. 30, 1867, vol. 102, pp. 173-74; L. H. Warren (agent, Houston) to Edward Miller (agent, Millican), June 22, 1867, vol. 102, p. 46.

9. Byron Porter (agent, Houston) to C. C. Morse, Jan. 5, 1866, vol. 100, pp. 127-28; George Gladwin (agent, Houston) to Mr. Calhoun, Dec. 30, 1865, vol. 100, p. 108; Gladwin to C. Culsheans (Fort Bend County), Jan. 15, 1866, vol. 100, p. 162; Porter to Mr. Hills, Jan. 15, 1866, vol. 100, p. 166.

10. Gladwin to John H. Murphy, Dec. 29, 1865, vol. 100, p. 104; Gladwin to Henry Sampson, Jan. 2, 1866 (three letters), vol. 100, pp. 118-19; de Gress to "To Whom It May Concern," Dec. 1, 1866, vol. 100, pp. 364-65; Porter to William Austin (Crockett), Jan. 27, 1866, vol. 100, p. 182; Porter to M. Joseph Jerkes (Navasota), Feb. 12, 1866, vol. 100, p. 192. The legal aspects of black rights at the time are explored in Donald G. Nieman, *To Set the Law in Motion: The Freedmen's Bureau and the Legal Rights of Blacks, 1865-1868* (Millwood, N.Y., 1979).

11. Porter to Dr. Whitehead (Danville), Mar. 12, 1866, vol. 100, p. 202; de Gress to William Austin (near Danville), Nov. 6, 1866, vol. 100, p. 315.

12. Chauncey C. Morse to Provost Marshal (Houston), Oct. 1, 1865, vol. 4, p. 10; Order by Porter, Jan. 3, 1866, vol. 100, p. 123; Porter to Hugh Kelly (Clear Creek), Jan. 6, 1866, vol. 100, p. 137.

13. Porter to Dr. Tait (Tyler), July 5, 1866, vol. 100, pp. 238-39; Barbara Alfred v. Jerry Gross, Sept. 5, 1868, vol. 108, pp. 184-85; Gladwin to Louisa (freedwoman), Jan. 11, 1866, vol. 100, pp. 153-54; Doney Hamilton v. Caroline Flash, Aug. 25, 1868, vol. 108, pp. 176-77. The relationship between the army and the Bureau is told in William L. Richter, *The Army in Texas during Reconstruction, 1865-1870* (College Station, Tex., 1987), pp. 32-46. For the alleged involvement of a Bureau agent in a kidnapping, see Porter to C. C. Gillespie (editor, *Houston Telegraph*), Sept. 5, 1866, vol. 100, p. 261, and Richter, *The Army in Texas*, p. 151.

14. Clara Parker v. Louisa Hutt, Aug. 19, 1868, vol. 108, pp. 170-71; de Gress to Cynthia Ann Hickman, Oct. 15, 1866, vol. 100, p. 275; Case of Rosa Johnson, Feb. 12, 1868, vol. 108, pp. 104-105.

15. Porter to Mr. Fulton, Jan. 4, 1866, vol. 100, p. 125, and Jan. 5, 1866, vol. 100, p. 135; de Gress to Fulton, Oct. 29, 1866, vol. 100, p. 297.

16. Pease to "To Whom It May Concern," Feb. 28, 1868, vol. 103, p. 69. The Texas Bureau believed, in principle, that black parental rights were supreme. This seems not to have been the case in North Carolina, where Rebecca Scott has drawn an overly harsh portrait of bureau agents in "The Battle Over the Child: Child Apprenticeship and the Freedmen's Bureau in North Carolina," *Prologue* 10 (Summer, 1978): 10-23.

17. Pease to Sarah White (freedwoman), Feb. 1, 1868, vol. 103, pp. 54-55; Porter to Martha Rodgers (white custodian), Jan. 1, 1866, vol. 100, pp. 111-12.

18. Porter to T. C. Powell (Waverly), Jan. 18, 1866, vol. 100, p. 171; Gladwin to A. F. Oliver (Austin County), Dec. 23, 1865, vol. 110, p. 102; Theodore Brantner Wilson, *The Black Codes of the South* (University, Ala., 1965), p. 110; *General Laws of the State of Texas Passed by the Eleventh Legislature* (Austin, 1866), pp. 61-63; John Pressley Carrier, "A Political History of Texas during the Reconstruc-

tion, 1865-1874" (Ph.D. diss., Vanderbilt University, 1971), p. 75. For civilian action, see "Book of Indentures to Bonds of Apprenticing, 1867-1870, University Archives, James G. Gee Library, East Texas State University, and Carrier, "The Era of Reconstruction, 1865-1875," in Robert W. Glover, ed., *Tyler and Smith County, Texas: An Historical Survey* (Tyler, Texas, 1976), pp. 65-66.

19. Porter to O. A. Runnels, July 18, 1866, vol. 100, pp. 244-45; Porter to Washington Brown (freedman), May 1, 1866, vol. 100, p. 216. For additional examples, see Porter to Sarah W. Gover (Polk County), Jan. 19, 1866, vol. 100, p. 172; Porter to Carrie Toland, Jan. 20, 1866, vol. 100, p. 173; Porter to J. E. Foster, Jan. 27, 1866, vol. 100, p. 181.

20. Pease to J. P. Kirkman (AAAG), Mar. 6, 1867, Operations Reports, P-149, Box 13.

21. Orphan Society v. Octavia Williams, June 10, 1867, vol. 108, pp. 4-5. See also Kathleen C. Berkeley, "'Colored Ladies Also Contributed': Black Women's Activities from Benevolence to Social Welfare, 1866-1896," in Walter J. Fraser, Jr., R. Frank Saunders, Jr., and John L. Wakelyn, eds., *The Web of Southern Social Relations: Women, Family, and Education* (Athens, Ga., 1985), p. 181-203. A general survey of the Texas effort is Ira Christopher Colby, "The Freedmen's Bureau in Texas and Its Impact on the Emerging Social Welfare System and Black-White Social Relations, 1865-1885" (Ph.D. diss., University of Pennsylvania, 1984).

22. Milly Barnes v. Alfred Harroll, June 24, 1867, vol. 108, pp. 16-17; Lucinda Reed v. Charles Reed., Aug. 22, 1868, vol. 108, pp. 174-75; Maria Flowers v. Wash Sessuns, Feb. 3, 1866, vol. 109, pp. 38-39; Porter to William H. Sinclair, July 11, 1866, vol. 100, pp. 241-42; Warren to Maj. De Bathligethy, July 10, 1867, vol. 102, p. 78; Priscilla Bennett v. Peter Bennett, June 25, 1868, vol. 108, pp. 134-35. For background, see Christie Farham, "Sapphire? The Issue of Dominance in the Slave Family, 1830-1865," in Carol Groneman and Mary Beth Norton, eds., *"To Toil the Livelong Day": America's Women at Work, 1780-1980* (Ithaca, N.Y., 1987), pp. 68-83.

23. de Gress to Rhode Ann Licks, Oct. 8, 1866, vol. 100, p. 270; de Gress to Anna Allen, Oct. 22, 1866, vol. 100, 286; Moses Jackson v. Carlinda Jackson, July 6, 1867, vol. 108, pp. 24-25; Charles Smith v. Lizzie Smith, Aug. 24, 1868, vol. 108, pp. 176-77; Smith Welton v. His Wife, May 25, 1866, vol. 109, n.p.; Amy Robinson v. Richard Robinson, May 2, 1866, vol. 109, n.p.; O. E. Pratt to Agent, Houston, Oct. 1, 1866, vol. 46, p. 3; Porter to John (freedman), Jan. 12, 1866, vol. 100, p. 156. In one strange case, a woman complained that her husband had married another woman, but the complaint was dismissed without reason; Millie Lisles v. James Lisles, Aug. 25, 1868, vol. 108, pp. 176-77.

24. Pease to Kirkman (AAAG), Mar. 6, 1867, Operations Reports, P-149, Box 13; McFeely, *Yankee Stepfather,* p. 131. For information on forced marriages among Texas slaves, see Edwin H. Fay to "My Own Darling Wife," Jan. 24, 1863, in Bell Irvin Wiley, ed., *"This Infernal War": The Confederate Letters of Sgt. Edwin H. Fay* (Austin, 1958), pp. 216-17.

25. Emeline Anderson v. George Gentry, Apr. 28, 1868, vol. 108, pp. 114-15; Juliann Stevens v. Durke Woodall, Sept. 15, 1868, vol. 108, pp. 194-95; Rachel

Neal v. Adam Neal, Feb. 9, 1866, vol. 109, pp. 38-39; Porter to Jacob (freedman), Jan. 10, 1866, vol. 100, pp. 146-47.

26. Mary Rogers v. Colonel Anderson, June 12, 1867, vol. 108, pp. 6-7; Pease to Judge Noble, Feb. 1, 1868, vol. 103, p. 55; Malinda Wheelers v. Ned Wheelers, Nov. 9, 1867, vol. 108, pp. 54-55; Warren to Carlinda Jackson, July 5, 1867, vol. 102, p. 70; de Gress to "To All Whom It May Concern," Dec. 11, 1866, vol. 100, p. 384.

27. "Rations Issued to Women by the Bureau since December 1, 1865," vol. 4, pp. 271-72; Porter to C. C. Morse, Jan. 5, 1866, vol. 100, pp. 128-29; Porter to J. E. George (Danville), Aug. 22, 1866, vol. 100, p. 256; Warren to H. R. Bell (judge, Montgomery County), Aug. 2, 1867, vol. 102, p. 128; Joseph B. Kiddoo (assistant commissioner, Texas) to O'Connell, June 18, 1867, vol. 5, p. 82; Warren to O'Connell, Aug. 10, 1867, vol. 102, p. 142.

28. William M. Van Horne (agent, Houston) to Judge John Brashear (chief justice, Houston), Sept. 3, 1867, vol. 102, p. 181; Dec. 2, 1867, vol. 103, p. 20; O'Connell to Dr. Moodie, Aug. 19, 1867, vol. 102, p. 165; Nov. 22, 1867, pp. 210-11; Joseph J. Reynolds (assistant commissioner, Texas) to Oliver Otis Howard (commissioner), Oct. 20, 1868, vol. 5, p. 438.

29. Porter to John M. Sapp (Montgomery), Jan. 31, 1866, vol. 100, p. 184; Porter to Orra M. Carter (Plantersville), Mar. 28, 1866, vol. 100, p. 209; Order by Porter, Jan. 24, 1866, vol. 100, p. 176; Jan. 26, 1866, vol. 100, p. 180. For an analysis of the relationship between black and white workers elsewhere in the South at this time, see Julie Saville, "A Measure of Freedom: From Slave to Wage Laborer in South Carolina, 1860-1868" (Ph.D. diss., Yale University, 1986); Jonathan W. McLeod, "Black and White Workers: Atlanta during Reconstruction" (Ph.D. diss., University of California, Los Angeles, 1987); Richard Paul Fuke, "Planters, Apprenticeship, and Forced Labor: The Black Family under Pressure in Post-Emancipation Maryland," *Agricultural History* 62 (Fall, 1988) pp. 57-74; and Peter J. Rachleff, *Black Labor in Richmond, 1865-1890* (New York, 1989).

30. A. A. Emerson (agent, Houston) to Mr. Wolf (vice-consul of Russia), Oct. 1, 1866, vol. 4, p. 350.

31. Gladwin to Thomas Taylor (Washington County), Jan. 3, 1866, vol. 100, p. 122, plus a series of similar letters immediately following; Gladwin to Catherine, Jan 6, 1866, vol. 100, p. 138; Porter to F. D. Inge (agent, Leona), May 4, 1866, vol. 100, p. 218; Hardenbrook to H. W. Allen (agent, Hempstead), May 30, 1866, vol. 100, pp. 226-27.

32. Porter to C. B. Sojourner, Jan. 15, 1866, vol. 100, pp. 166-67. See also Kizzy King and Miranda King v. Josiah King, Feb. 14, 1866, vol. 109, pp. 40-41; Parcilla Enridge v. Mr. Pugh, Jan. 6, 1868, vol. 108, pp. 88-89; Warren to Dave Roberts, July 5, 1867, vol. 102, pp. 67-68.

33. George Cooper v. Mary Vick, July 5, 1867, vol. 108, pp. 22-23.

34. Pease to Abner Doubleday (agent, Galveston), Feb. 7, 1867, P-8, Box 42; Warren to Brashear (chief justice, Harris County), June 24, 1867, vol. 102, p. 48.

35. Case of Polly, May 2, 1866, vol. 109, pp. 48-49; Van Horne to Mr. Hennessey, Dec. 16, 1867, vol. 103, p. 35; Moses Anthony v. Mr. Alexander, June 20, 1367, vol. 108, pp. 12-13; Warren to Mr. Alexander, June 20, 1867, vol. 102, p.

41; Porter to Mr. Taylor (Grimes County), Jan. 9, 1866, vol. 100, p. 145; O'Connell to Miller (agent, Millican), Aug. 13, 1867, vol. 102, pp. 157-58.

36. Julia Heard v. Ben Lyons, June 13, 1867, vol. 108, pp. 8-9; Van Horne to J. S. Randall (agent, Sterling), Sept. 2, 1867, vol. 102, pp. 178-79.

37. Pease to John Kennedy, Jan. 21, 1868, vol. 103, 50; Tenna v. Mr. Raphael, July 17, 1867, vol. 108, pp. 28-29; O'Connell to E. M. Wheelock (agent, Galveston), Aug. 13, 1867, vol. 102, pp. 156-57; Porter to Dan Linton (Montgomery), Jan. 11, 1866, vol. 100, p. 153; Van Horne to J. J. McKeever, Dec. 24, 1867, vol. 103, pp. 37-38; Joe Davis v. Patience Wynn, June 12, 1867, vol. 108, pp. 6-7. For writings on the rights of white women, see Suzanne Lebsock, "Radical Reconstruction and the Property Rights of Southern Women," *Journal of Southern History* 43 (May, 1977), pp. 195-216.

38. Emerson to de Gress, Oct. 26, 1866, vol. 4, p. 363; de Gress to H. A. Ellis (AAAG), Oct. 26, 1866, vol. 100, p. 296. It is worth noting, however, that no white women were ever put to work on the city's streets.

39. Julia Wilkes v. City of Houston, June 11, 1867, vol. 108, pp. 4-5; de Gress to Judge Hadley, Oct. 24, 1866, vol. 100, p. 289.

40. Warren to Judge Fuller, June 24, 1867, vol. 102, p. 51; Warren to George Lancaster (agent, Hempstead), June 8, 1867, vol. 102, p. 13.

41. Porter to Charles F. Allen (agent, Hempstead), May 22, 1866, vol. 100, p. 223; Mony v. Mary Mortimer, Aug. 24, 1867, vol. 89, pp. 3-4. For white violence on Texas black women, see Barry A. Crouch, "A Spirit of Lawlessness: White Violence; Texas Blacks, 1865-1868," *Journal of Social History,* 18 (Winter, 1984), pp. 217-32.

42. Selina Parker v. Michael Linney, Jan. 22, 26, 1866, vol. 109, pp. 28-29, 34-35.

43. Milly Graham v. Louisa Thompson, May 2, 1866, vol. 109, pp. 48-49; Emily Matthews v. H. F. Matthews, June 7, 1867, vol. 108, pp. 2-3; Hardenbrook to Marple, July 27, 1866, vol. 100, p. 250; U.S. v. Tobin, Dec. 19, 1865, vol. 109, pp. 12-13; Levi and Adeline Tanks v. Dr. Blake, June 18, 1867, vol. 108, pp. 12-13; Warren to Judge Fuller, June 22, 1867, vol. 102, p. 44; Margaret Downs v. Milton McGowan, May 2, 1866, vol. 109, pp. 46-47.

44. Julia Brown v. Jamison, May 4, 1866, vol. 109, pp. 54-55; Dinah Wren v. Dr. Hartridge, June 18, 1867, vol. 108, pp. 10-11.

45. Dollina Williams v. Andrew Johnson Williams, Feb. 12, 1866, vol. 109, pp. 38-39; Emma Matthews v. Frank Matthews, Feb. 15, 1866, vol. 109, pp. 40-41; Porter to Officer in Charge of Military Prison, Feb. 23, 1866, vol. 100, p. 194; Pease to Judge Fuller, June 18, 1867, vol. 102, p. 37; July 27, 1867, vol. 102, pp. 120-21. See also Elizabeth Pleck, *Domestic Tyranny: The Making of Social Policy against Family Violence from Colonial Times to the Present* (New York, 1987).

46. de Gress to "To All Whom It May Concern," Dec. 3, 1866, vol. 100, p. 367; Lucy Ann King v. Wesley King, Jan. 2, 1866, vol. 109, pp. 18-19.

47. Houston Agent to Autry Wright, Aug. 9, 1867, vol. 102, pp. 142-44; Lucinda Reed v. Osburn Smith, Sept. 14, 1867, vol. 108, pp. 192-93; Warren to Mayor DeDigethaby, June 13, 1867, vol. 102, p. 24; Warren to Judge Fuller, June 26, 1867, vol. 102, pp. 57-58; Melissa Hill v. Albert Williams, June 13, 1867, vol. 108, pp.

6–7; U.S. v. M. McGuire, Dec. 30, 1865, vol. 109, pp. 16–17; U.S. v. Holda Cotton, Dec. 28, 1865, vol. 100, p. 104; Dec. 28, 1865, vol. 109, pp. 16–17; Kissya Lee v. November Ashville, Nov. 12, 1867, vol. 108, pp. 58–59; Virginia Haardley v. Louisa Fernandos, Dec. 14, 1867, vol. 108, pp. 72–73. See also Jacquelyn Dowd Hall, "'The Mind That Burns in Each Body': Women, Rape, and Racial Violence," in Ann Snitow, Christine Stansell, and Sharon Thompson, eds., *Powers of Desire: The Politics of Sexuality* (New York, 1983), pp. 328–49.

48. Rose, *Slavery and Freedom,* p. 93; Eric Foner, *Nothing But Freedom: Emancipation and Its Legacy* (Baton Rouge, 1983); Barry A. Crouch, "Black Dreams and White Justice," *Prologue* 6 (Winter, 1974), pp. 255–65. Bess Beatty portrays how black women were viewed in black newspapers during this time in "Black Perspectives of American Women: The View From Black Newspapers, 1865–1900," *Maryland Historian* 9 (Fall, 1978): 39–50.

Richard Allen: The Chequered Career of Houston's First Black State Legislator

Merline Pitre

In the last three decades massive revision in Reconstruction history has drastically altered the traditional stereotyping of black leaders as being ignorant, penniless individuals, ascending straight from the cornfield to the legislative hall.[1] While earlier revisionists have made a genuine effort to eradicate this stereotype, they have also tended to perpetrate yet another stereotype by portraying black leaders as unselfish, single-minded individuals dedicated only to improving the lot of freedpeople.[2] It is hoped that as revisionism becomes more balanced, historians will produce more nuanced accounts that avoid inaccurate generalizations. Indeed, such accounts have already begun to appear.[3] During the Reconstruction and post-Reconstruction eras, southern blacks and whites had to fashion a new modus operandi in their relations with one another to replace the rules and regulations of interracial contact associated with slavery. Richard Allen, Houston's first black state legislator, was a complex man whose career spanned these equally complex periods.

Allen's Early Political Goals and Accomplishments

Richard Allen entered Texas Republican politics from almost total obscurity. Unlike many black political activists in the Lone Star State, he was not free born, relatively affluent, well educated, or widely traveled.

Richard Allen was born a slave in Virginia in 1826. Fragmentary sources do not indicate when he was taken to Texas, but evidence does reveal that upon his arrival he settled in Harris County where he was owned by J. J. Cain. While still a slave, he acquired the skills of carpentry and demonstrated his talents on many outstanding buildings in Houston. The Houston *Union* noted in 1870 that the "finest and most elegant mansion that once graced our city—[that of] Mayor J. R. Morris—was the handiwork of [the] Honorable Richard Allen while he was a slave; not the mere mechanics only, but the design, the draft and all." Combining his carpentry talent with that of an engineer, Allen also became a bridge builder after his emancipation in 1865 and built one of the earliest bridges over Buffalo Bayou in Houston.[4] At about that time, in 1867, he likewise took his first step into politics by becoming an agent for the Texas Freedmen's Bureau.[5] One year later he joined the Republican party and became a controversial registration supervisor in the Fourteenth Senatorial District. These experiences whetted his interest in a political career. Subsequently, in 1869, Allen won election to the Twelfth Legislature as a representative of Harris and Montgomery counties. He was forty-three years old.[6]

As a lawmaker, Allen's political behavior reflected a deep concern for civil rights, education, laborers, veterans, and internal improvements. As with virtually all of his black colleagues in politics, his faith in the power and the necessity of universal education was unequivocal. Accordingly, he urged the passage of the first comprehensive Free School Bill—a bill designed to give all students equal access to education.[7] Likewise, Allen was responsible for successfully introducing an act to incorporate the Gregory Institute of Harris County. The Institute was first established by the Freedmen's Bureau in 1866 to train teachers. After its incorporation in 1871, however, all the schools previously established by the Freedmen's Bureau in Harris County were abolished and their students transferred to the Institute. It was largely due to Gregory's new status that Harris County in 1871 had the largest number of blacks enrolled in public schools in the entire state—760 females and 734 males.[8]

With the same amount of determination that he used in obtaining the incorporation of the Gregory Institute, Allen pushed to exempt the wages of laborers and others from a writ of garnishment.[9] Although he failed at that, he met with more success when he presented a petition for a Confederate veteran concerning the ex-soldier's pension. Out of this effort evolved the Texas Independent Veteran Bill, which became law on August 13, 1871. By its provision, the state granted Texas veterans $250 per year, with an additional like amount for those wounded during their service.[10]

Allen performed great work in the legislature as head of the Roads and Bridges Committee. Under his leadership, the committee improved and extended the transportation system of the state. In order to encourage commerce and communications, he facilitated the construction of a toll bridge across the Sabine River at Lake Fort in the southern part of Wood County between present-day Mineola and Tyler. Numerous other bridges and a number of ferries were authorized during Allen's tenure as head of the important legislative committee.[11]

Biracial Politics in Action: the Allen-Tracy Partnership

In addition to serving his constituents, Allen also served himself. Both during and after his service in the legislature, he spent much of his time in Houston wheeling and dealing with James G. Tracy, a newspaper editor and executive chairman of the Texas Republican party.

Tracy, a newcomer to politics, had come to Texas prior to the Civil War and learned the newspaper trade at the Houston *Telegraph*. He joined the Republican party early in 1868 and established his Houston *Union* as the official organ of the party in the city.[12] A conservative turned radical, Tracy became the driving force behind the Grand Old Party in Houston throughout most of the postwar years. As early as January of 1868 he was appointed recorder of the city of Houston by General Joseph J. Reynolds, who commanded the district of Texas.[13] The city council refused to seat him, but he was reappointed in October.[14] A year later, largely through his ties and connections with the "Radical Establishment" of the city, Tracy was appointed justice of the peace, postmaster of Houston, and voter registrar of Harris County.[15] In order to maintain both himself and the Republican party in power, in 1869 Tracy established and became president of the Republican County Club of Houston, largely composed of newly enfranchised black voters.[16]

By 1870 Tracy had worked his way up through the ranks of the Republican party to become head of the State Executive Committee. He used his newspaper freely to support the policies of Governor Edmund Davis's administration. The newspaper also advocated more internal improvements, larger railroad subsidies, and broader and more liberal Republicanism. Tracy had the ear of the governor on these and other matters. In 1870, for example, the replacement of most of Houston's city officials with men of Governor Davis's political persuasion was largely based on Tracy's recommendations. These appointments enhanced Tracy's net worth as well as his reputation; several months after T. H. Scanlan was appointed mayor of Houston, he and Tracy founded the Bayou City Bank.[17] A year later, Scanlan, using his position as mayor, obtained the charter to establish the City Railway Company. He boldly arrogated himself as president of the company and named Tracy to the board of directors.[18]

As Tracy and Scanlan were partners, so were Allen and Tracy. They functioned as politicians during the period of Reconstruction and tried, along with many others, to restore the nation politically, economically, and physically after a bitter and protracted war. The whole process of Reconstruction was in the hands of fallible human beings—politicians, entrepreneurs, humanitarians, Southerners, Northerners, whites and blacks—driven by all kinds of motives, passions, and prejudices. As they sought their diverse ends, these people fought and compromised; they made alliances as well as enemies; lofty principles became entangled in political chicanery; and greed mixed with far nobler impulses in a campaign to bring a new measure of dignity to women and men just out of slavery. Neither Tracy nor Allen could escape the influence of such a charged and tricky environment.

The key advantage for Allen, or any other black, in developing a relationship with a white person like Tracy lay in the whites' contacts within the ruling class. Using his contacts, Tracy was able to provide funds, jobs, and protection to his allies. Some blacks knew that in a white-controlled society, white representatives would have the best access to power and to all of the things that power commanded. Probably no black person in Houston realized this better than Richard Allen.

Hence Allen — a skilled laborer, politician, and man on the make — established an opportunistic, paternalistic relationship with Tracy from 1868 to 1884. This relationship with Tracy proved to be the key to Allen's success. It benefited Tracy as well. Republicans such as Tracy were pleased to have an able and articulate leader like Allen to influence newly liberated and enfranchised blacks to support the Grand Old Party. By associating with Tracy, of course, Allen was almost assured that he would reap political and economic gains. He was, in fact, a delegate at every Republican State Convention between 1870 and 1896, and he also served as a delegate to nearly all of the Republican National Conventions during the same period. The same holds true for Tracy.[19]

As early as 1869, Tracy and Allen were in control of the Republican party in Houston.[20] Indeed, their relationship was cemented by their activities in the Bayou City after the war. In numerous towns and cities of the South, including Houston, skilled blacks waged an uphill battle to earn a living at carpentry, shoemaking, smithing, building, and related occupations. They faced implacable opposition from most native whites as well as many immigrants, all of whom regarded black workers as unwelcome competitors. Thus, it was natural for individuals like Tracy, who wanted to establish a Republican party in Texas that rested on black voting strength, to foster the interests of his black partner, Allen. Hence, through his association with Tracy, Allen by 1872 obtained a contract to construct sidewalks for the city. Because the chief concern of the Houston City Council was internal improvements that year, it awarded contracts for the construction of 140 blocks of sidewalks to Hitchock and Company to do brick and asphalt paving, and to Richard Allen to do wooden sidewalks. The property owners on the blocks affected were allowed to decide which type of siding they preferred.[21]

This and similar deals forged a strong relationship between Tracy and Allen. Nevertheless, although Allen was a great supporter of Tracy, his reliance on a black constituency to remain in power sometimes required him to act contrary to Tracy's wishes. Thus, for example, Allen allowed his name to be placed in nomination for the Third Congressional District seat held by William Clark in 1871, even though he was not serious about this post; at that time, in fact, Allen was making plans to seek reelection as representative from the Fourteenth State Senatorial District.[22] Even if he had been interested in the congressional post, his association with Tracy would have prevented him from pursuing it, since Clark was Tracy's man. Hence, when the nominating convention for the Third Congressional District seat was held, Allen withdrew his name on the first ballot. He went on to win successful reelection to the State House of Representatives of the Thirteenth Legislature, but he was unseated two months after being sworn into office.[23] Allen appealed his case to the Committee on Elections and Privileges, but to no avail. According to the Majority Report issued by the committee, many blacks who voted for Allen either did not reside in Harris or Montgomery County, or their names did not appear on the registration list.[24] Allen's dismissal ended his legislative, but not his political, career.

When Houston Republicans met in August of 1873 to select delegates to the state convention, they were split over whether or not they should select Tracy as a delegate. Blacks, in particular, opposed him. They had not forgotten that it was James G. Tracy who, as head of the Republican party, in 1871 tried to break up the largely black Loyal Union League of Texas. The Loyal Union League of America had been organized in the North during the Civil War, at which time it did an effective job in rallying support for the conflict against secession. Organizers later branched out into the South, establishing the League in Texas in 1867. As a protective and benevolent society, it welcomed black members, catechized them politically, and relied on their votes to establish and maintain the Republican party in the South. Tracy, however, believed that many whites refused to join the Republican party because they thought they would have little influence in an organization where the Union League was the dominant force—opponents branded the Republican party as a "Nigger Party." Tracy designed a plan to attract more whites into the party in an attempt to regain Republican control of the Texas legislature in 1872. His strategy was to dissolve or break up local chapters of the League and to replace them with Republican County Clubs, as he had effectively done in Houston since 1869. His effort was foiled, however, when it met with stiff opposition both from blacks and from whites, who used the League as a political power base.[25]

The opposition of Houston blacks to Tracy in 1873 was clearly justified, yet before the vote on delegates was taken, Allen was able to persuade a large number of blacks to cast their ballots in favor of Tracy. Of this incident the Houston *Telegraph* noted that "Negroes showed their power, yet they were not free from white control."[26] The next year, in part because of the rumor that Houston blacks would hold their own political caucus and bar all whites, Houston Republican leaders, who were mostly whites, decided to hold a secret meeting, rather than a public one, to select candidates for local offices. At this gathering, only whites — including some who were Democrats — were nominated, all with the blessing of Richard Allen.[27] Some blacks naturally regarded Allen's behavior as rank opportunism, if not outright betrayal of his own race. Notwithstanding, Allen had no full-time job other than that of politician-at-large after the legislative portion of his career ended in 1873. His livelihood depended on how he resolved the differences between his idealistic desire to serve his people and his ambition and willingness to serve himself.

Allen's Later Political Goals and Accomplishments

Nowhere is Allen's ambiguous nature better shown than in his simultaneous opposition to and support of independent candidates and tickets. Even though Allen was bitterly opposed to independent candidates on the state ticket, he sided with local white Republicans in supporting independent Democrats in local elections.[28] Similarly, in 1878, when most blacks turned to the Greenback Party at the urging of former governor Edmund Davis, and because it represented a good opportunity for them to win elections, Allen opposed the move. Instead, he lent his support to the Straight-Out ticket, on which he was nominated as lieutenant governor.[29] Yet while Allen opposed the Greenback party on the state level, he was endorsed by that same party and won a seat for street commissioner of Houston on an independent ticket the same year.[30]

Another example of Allen's contradictory behavior was his effort to capitalize on the feelings of disenchanted blacks in 1879 by encouraging them to join the mass exodus to Kansas. Because of his enthusiasm for this project, in July of 1879 Allen was chosen as a delegate to represent black Texans at the Nashville Convention on the Exodus.[31] When blacks returned to the state, they called for a convention of their own to be held in Houston in order to discuss whether or not they should join the Kansas Fever. Despite the efforts of Henry Adams, organizer of the conference, to exclude politicians from the meeting, Allen not only attended the conference but was elected as its presiding officer.[32]

After a lengthy discussion, the majority of blacks at the meeting decided that they should leave the state of Texas as a way of improving their condition. However, they were undecided about where they ought to go — whether to other places in the United States or to Africa. Richard Allen proposed that they take refuge on a large area of land in northwest Texas that would be reserved exclusively for the settlers, much like Indian reservations, and protected from white occupation.[33] But Allen's proposition was weak. The prevailing policy of the period did little to vouchsafe the rights and property of Native Americans when they conflicted with the ambitions of whites. Given the status of blacks, there was no reason to suppose that a black reservation would remain any more secure than an Indian reserve if whites decided to intrude.

Although Richard Allen has been regarded as one of the most vocal supporters of the Exodus, his support of the movement appears to have been motivated by his political ambitions rather than by any real desire to promote the welfare of impoverished blacks. Despite his rhetoric about his leaving the state along with other blacks, Allen quickly lost interest in the movement when his plan for settlement in northwest Texas failed. His effort to gain black votes through his flimsy support of the Exodus substantiates the criticism of one of his detractors who stated: "Dick Allen is ambitious and feels that he cannot satisfy that ambition [by leaving Texas]. He not only wants the praise of the Negro but also the white."[34] This criticism was further substantiated when in July, 1881, Allen was elected secretary of the American Baptist Missionary Association. At that time, the association said nothing about the Exodus but instead urged black Texans to educate their children and give support to any movement or any party that advocated the extension of educational facilities and that encouraged blacks to show themselves to whites as thrifty and honest citizens.[35] The blessing given to this resolution by Allen must have pleased a number of white conservatives who were afraid that Allen's support of the Exodus would cause them to lose cheap, local labor.

If white conservatives had any reason to doubt Allen's militancy in the past, they could breathe a sigh of relief in and after 1884. In that year, after being elected as an at-large delegate to the National Convention, Allen bolted the regular State Republican Convention and joined forces with dissident Republicans who formed a Straight-Out convention. He was suitably rewarded by this group by being appointed as head of the important Committee on Address, which named speakers for the convention. Moreover, Allen was elected chairman of another bolted convention, called by John Grant in 1896, that opposed Norris W. Cuney and the regular Republicans.[36]

Leaving the controversial 1896 convention at the ripe old age of three score and ten, Allen was old enough to think about retiring. But politics had become the bone of his bone and the flesh of his flesh. While he played no further role in statewide politics after the turn of the century, Allen remained a feisty participant in Houston affairs. As late as 1908 he was still trying to dictate to blacks who they should vote for, who should be the main speaker for the annual Juneteenth celebration, and who should hold office in the Emancipation Park Association.[37] Allen continued to engage in such activity until his death in the Bayou City in 1911.

Richard Allen was articulate, talented, and manipulative — qualities desperately needed as blacks struggled for a place in the political life of Houston, of Texas, and of the nation. But Allen's faults eclipsed even these virtues. Proud and arrogant, he often displayed a tendency to help people especially when he could help himself even more. Allen longed for power, status, and prestige. However, his overweening ambition, coupled with an abrasive personality, led him into trouble wherever he went. He attracted people by his oratorical ability and by his intelligence, but he also antagonized people of both races by his blatant opportunism. His role in the Exodus affair typified his interest in promoting his own welfare more than that of the blacks he claimed to represent.

Allen's inability to transcend his paternalistic relationship with James G. Tracy offers a clue to some of the weaknesses of black leadership during and after Reconstruction. Both men rode to power on the strength of reform politics, which were then supposedly embodied within the Republican party, and each man needed what the other had to offer. Tracy, a white man in a white-dominated society, had power. Allen, a leader among recently liberated blacks, had votes. It was natural for the two to develop a relationship; the experiment in biracial politics demanded cooperation between political activists of both races. But cooperation did not imply equality, and blacks were always the junior partners, often forced to make painful choices between the demands of their white patrons and the needs of their black constituency. While it would be remiss to say that Allen was divorced from the interests of black voters, it can be said that on some issues that concerned blacks he was outspoken, while on others he simply spoke loudly but carried a small stick.

Notes

1. Claude G. Bowers, *The Tragic Era: The Revolution after Lincoln* (Cambridge, Mass., 1929); Charles Ramsdell, *Reconstruction in Texas* (New York, 1910).

2. W. E. B. Du Bois, *Black Reconstruction* (New York, 1935); Alrutheus A. Taylor, *The Negro in South Carolina during Reconstruction* (Washington, D.C., 1924); Horace M. Bond, *Negro Education in Alabama: A Study of Cotton and Steel* (Washington, D.C., 1931).

3. Thomas Holt, *Black over White: Negro Political Leadership in South Carolina during Reconstruction* (Chicago, 1977).

4. J. Mason Brewer, *Negro Legislators of Texas* (Austin, 1935), pp. 49, 53, 125; Paul Casdorph, *The Republican Party in Texas, 1865–1965* (Austin, 1965), p. 39;

Lawrence Rice, *The Negro in Texas* (Baton Rouge, 1971), pp. 38, 49, 57, 65; Houston *Union*, July 6, 1870.

5. In March, 1865, Congress created the Bureau of Refugees, Freedmen and Abandoned Lands to aid emancipated slaves. The life of this agency was extended in 1866, at which time the Freedmen's Bureau provided food, clothing, fuel, medicine, and education to the destitute, both black and white.

6. Dallas *Herald*, Feb. 8, 15, 1868. See also Thomas Stubling, "To Whom It May Concern," Apr. 18, 1867, a letter authorizing Allen to establish a charter of the Union League of America throughout Texas, in the J. P. Newcomb Papers, Barker Texas History Center, University of Texas, Austin; Brewer, p. 125.

7. *Texas House Journal*, 12th Legis., Called Sess., p. 485.

8. Ibid., pp. 428, 865; H. P. N. Gammel, *The Laws of Texas, 1822-1897*, vol. 6 (Austin, 1898), pp. 323-24. See also Ira Bryant, *The Development of Houston Negro Schools* (Houston, 1928), p. 10; Texas Superintendent of Public Instruction, *First Annual Report, 1871* (Austin, 1872), pp. 88-100.

9. *Texas House Journal*, 12th Legis., Called Sess., p. 384.

10. Ibid., Regular Sess., p. 474.

11. Ibid., Adjourned Sess., pp. 58-59, 635-37.

12. Carl H. Moneyhon, *Republicanism in Reconstruction Texas* (Austin, 1980), pp. 109-10.

13. Minutes of the Houston City Council, Feb. 1, 1865, to July 1, 1869, microfilm, Texas and Local History Department, Houston Public Library; U.S. Army, Fifth Military District, Department of Texas, "General Orders 1869-1870," Barker Texas History Center. See also Office of the Adjutant General, "Papers Relating to the Legality of Appointments and Removal of Civil Officials in Texas by General Joseph J. Reynolds, March 1867 to January 1868," microcopy, National Archives, Washington, D.C.

14. Houston *Times*, Oct. 2, 4, 1868.

15. *Daily Houston Telegraph*, Sept. 4, 1869; ibid., Oct. 2, 1869. See also U.S. Army, "General Orders 1869-1870."

16. *Daily Houston Telegraph*, Nov. 17, 18, 20, 1869; Houston *Union*, Nov. 20, 1869.

17. *Daily Houston Telegraph*, Nov. 27, 1870; Houston *Union*, Nov. 26, 1870.

18. *Daily Houston Telegraph*, June 25, 27, 1871; ibid., Nov. 23, 1871.

19. Casdorph, pp. 36, 39, 47, 48, 66, 251; Dallas *Herald*, Feb. 5, 8, 1868.

20. *Daily Houston Telegraph*, July 11, 14, 1869; Galveston *Daily News*, July 3, 4, 1869.

21. *Daily Houston Telegraph*, Feb. 4, 6, 9, 10, 11, 17, 1872; ibid., Mar. 1, 22, 1872; ibid., Apr. 20, 21, 26, 28, 1872.

22. *Flake's Daily Bulletin* (Galveston), Aug. 3, 6, 1871; Galveston *Daily News*, Aug. 3, 1871.

23. Austin *Daily Statesman*, Mar. 19, 1873; *Texas House Journal*, 13th Legis., Reg. Sess., 60; Galveston *Daily News*, Mar. 12, 1873.

24. *Texas House Journal*, 13th Legis., Regular Sess., pp. 68, 249.

25. J. G. Tracy to J. P. Newcomb, June 1, 1871, J. P. Newcomb Papers; *Flake's Daily Bulletin*, June 22, 1871; Galveston *Daily News*, July 9, 1871; Moneyhon, pp. 146-47, 155-56; Houston *Union*, Mar. 5, 1869.

26. *Daily Houston Telegraph,* Aug. 12, 14, 24, 1873.

27. Galveston *Daily News,* Dec. 24, 1874.

28. Galveston *Daily News,* Dec. 24, 1874.

29. Ibid., Aug. 19, 1878; Ernest Winkler, ed., *Platforms of Political Parties in Texas* (Austin, 1916), pp. 190-93. The Greenback Party consisted of many diverse elements (discontented farmers, disgruntled Democrats, and advocates of soft money) and was first established in Texas in 1878. The term Straight-Out refers to Republicans who were opposed to fusing with independents or third parties to win elections.

30. *Daily Houston Telegraph,* Jan. 8, 9, 16, 1878; Galveston *Daily News,* Jan. 8, 9, 1878. It has been mentioned by one source that Allen was collector of customs of the Port of Houston, but an investigation into Group 56 of the Treasury Department Records at the National Archives indicates that Allen was never appointed to the post (Ahola South to author, May 5, 1985).

31. Panola *Watchman,* May 21, 1879.

32. Galveston *Daily News,* July 4, 5, 1879; *Daily Houston Telegraph,* July 4, 5, 11, 1879. See also Leonard Wilson, Jr., "Texas and the Kansas Fever 1879-1888" (master's thesis, University of Houston, 1973); "The Proceedings of a Mississippi Migration Convention in 1879," in the Documents section, *Journal of Negro History* 4 (1919).

33. Galveston *Daily News,* July 5, 1879.

34. Ibid.

35. Ibid., July 11, 14, 1881.

36. Winkler, pp. 359-60; Austin *Evening News,* Mar. 27, 1896.

37. Houston *Post,* June 19, 1908.

Part III

Economic and Social Development in Black Houston during the Era of Segregation

Introduction

Historical Overview

Racial segregation following the period of Reconstruction imposed massive political, economic, and social restrictions on blacks in Houston and throughout Dixie. Politically they had little formal power; Texas was rapidly becoming a one-party state almost totally dominated by Democrats, and by the end of the century the resurgent Democrats of the Lone Star State were openly dedicated to white supremacy. Economically, blacks were marginalized. Slavery left them with an inheritance of poverty, while whites maintained continued control of the economic sector. White Texans were not inclined to share economic power with blacks or to assist them in improving their circumstances. Indeed, the whites' goal, as in the past, was to maintain blacks as a servile, exploitable laboring class. Socially, the etiquette of Jim Crow required blacks to be deferential and submissive to whites on the job and in casual public contacts they had; off the job the races went their separate ways. In broad terms, then, the historic structure of southern race relations that stressed systematic inequality was merely modified and continued. Whites had the power to incorporate the traditions of the past into the practice of the present. Thus did a slave society become a segregated society in Houston and in Dixie. And, it was within this segregated society that blacks structured their community in Houston.

While segregation by the late nineteenth century certainly dominated black life and defined black-white relations, it was not a monolithic force that affected all blacks equally, and blacks were not merely passive victims of it. Like slavery, the nature and impact of segregation on the lives of blacks varied at different times and in different places. Furthermore, as in slavery, blacks responded to segregation creatively, and they structured communities that enabled them to survive and occasionally to prosper within its restricting confines.

In the late 1860s and early 1870s black Houstonians created the institutions that became the basis of the black community. During the seventy years that followed, blacks built this community in a segregated environment. Segregation, which was perhaps overlooked in the euphoria surrounding emancipation, had become well entrenched in the city by the mid-1870s. More than any other single factor, it determined the nature of black Houston.

Segregation developed in Houston in a somewhat haphazard manner, partly by law, partly by custom. Although Houston never enacted a complete code of laws to regulate black behavior comparable to the slave codes of the antebellum period or the black codes of the early postwar period, from time to time state laws and city ordinances contributed to the growing reality of racial segregation. School segregation was legally imposed by the state's constitution in 1876, state laws segregated the railroads in 1891, and a city ordinance separated the races on Houston's streetcars in 1903. In 1907 the city council enacted a law that authorized segregation in hotels, theaters, restaurants, and other public facilities, and in 1922 a new city code of ordinances segregated parks and outlawed biracial cohabitation. Custom, on the other hand, segregated blacks and whites in the city jail and the city hospital. Blacks had no library facilities until they organized their own in the Fourth Ward in 1907. Public swimming pools, restrooms, and drinking fountains were also segregated. Black doctors had no medical facilities in which to practice until the first black hospital opened in 1910. In 1928 at the Democratic National Convention, black spectators were seated in a small area of the gallery that was fenced off by chicken wire. In 1933 city officials rejected architectural plans for a new Southern Pacific Railroad station because blacks and whites would have to use the same ramps to board the trains.

Houston had no ordinance segregating residential areas. Nevertheless, distinctive black residential areas developed. By the end of the nineteenth century the centers of black population were southwest of downtown in the Fourth Ward, especially along San Felipe Street, southeast of downtown in the Third Ward, and in the Fifth Ward, northeast of the business district. Although none of these areas were totally segregated, in the early twentieth century the largely black parts of the city were becoming increasingly black, and by the 1930s white families in these areas were rare.

The influx of blacks that began with emancipation continued in the years that followed. The black population increased from 3,691 in 1870, to 23,929 in 1910, to 86,302 in 1940. Most blacks who came to Houston during this period arrived from rural areas in Texas and Louisiana, and they usually moved to Houston to attend high school or to get a job. When they arrived, they often lived for a time with relatives or friends and relied on these contacts to help them find jobs and adjust to life in the city. Black neighborhoods retained many of the qualities of small-town life well into the twentieth century for a number of reasons. These included Houston's

Table 7
Black Population in Houston, 1850–1980

Year	Total Population	Black Population	Percent Black
1850	2,396	533	22.2
1860	4,845	1,077	22.2
1870	9,382	3,691	39.3
1880	16,513	6,479	39.2
1890	27,557	10,379	37.7
1900	44,633	14,608	32.7
1910	78,800	23,929	30.4
1920	138,276	33,960	24.6
1930	292,352	63,337	21.7
1940	384,514	86,302	22.4
1950	596,163	125,400	21.0
1960	938,219	215,037	22.9
1970	1,232,802	316,551	25.7
1980	1,594,086	440,257	27.6

SOURCE: United States Census Data

rapid growth, family ties that stretched from city to country, Houston's relative small size and low population density, and the fact that blacks were not concentrated in a single concrete ghetto. Many blacks recalled the small-town atmosphere of black neighborhoods as late as the 1930s and early 1940s. The absence of legal residential segregation and the continued presence of a few whites—usually either poor Houstonians or immigrants who had businesses in the neighborhood—also tended to soften some of the harsher aspects of ghetto life.[1]

As the black population of the city grew, new black enclaves developed in the wards and beyond their boundaries. For example, Independence Heights, initially a separate black-governed suburb northwest of the city, was annexed in 1927. Even more interesting was Frenchtown, a Fifth Ward neighborhood of approximately five hundred Louisiana blacks of French descent who imported their Creole culture into the city in the early 1920s. The blacks of Frenchtown were French-speaking Catholics, most of whom worked as skilled or semi-skilled labor for the Southern Pacific Railroad. With their distinctive language, religion, cuisine, and music, they maintained their cultural integrity within the larger black community. Finally, as the black population expanded rapidly in the 1920s and again in the 1940s and 1950s, real estate developers created subdivisions that offered blacks middle-class homes comparable to those being built for whites. These black subdivisions were generally built on the fringes of existing black enclaves to the northeast, east, and southeast of the city, and offered sidewalks, paved streets, and other amenities not usually found in the older black neighborhoods.[2]

Despite the improvements found in suburban housing built in the second quarter of the century, most blacks still occupied poor housing in a neighborhood that received less than its share of city services. While a significant number of blacks owned their own homes—the percentage rose from 20.1 percent in 1910 to 31.4 percent in 1930, before the depression reduced black home ownership back to 21.7 percent in 1940—and while many of these homes were substantial dwellings, the typical black family lived in substandard housing. For example, as late as 1940, 23.3 percent of black-occupied housing units in the city did not have running water, while only 5.3 percent of the nonblack households lacked this convenience. Black dwellings were also more crowded. According to 1940 census data, 30.6 percent of black-occupied housing units contained more than one person per room, while only 19.7 percent of the nonblack homes were this crowded. In addition, black neighborhoods—especially the older neighborhoods—often did not have paved streets, street lights, or sidewalks, and they typically suffered from poor drainage that regularly left large areas flooded and inaccessible after heavy rains.[3]

Efforts to improve the quality of black neighborhoods were only partially successful. Some work was done on a volunteer basis. Black newspapers urged their readers to clean up their yards, and they exposed residents who were particularly negligent in doing so. The desire to receive improved city services led to the formation of the first black community and civic associations. These organizations avoided confrontation while quietly working with some success behind the scenes through personal contacts within the city's power structure. While some improvement occurred in the 1920s, especially in the area of street repair, black neighborhoods continued to suffer on the whole from a lack of basic city services.[4]

The most dramatic change in housing came in the late 1930s and early 1940s when the city established the Houston Housing Authority in order to participate in the development of federally funded, low-income housing projects. Initial black fears that the city would ignore their housing needs proved to be unfounded. In fact, the Housing Authority targeted the first two Houston projects, Cuney Homes in the Third Ward and Kelly Courts in the Fifth Ward, for blacks. By 1945 the city had provided low-income housing for 3,868 black Houstonians. While the black community benefitted from these two projects, they suffered from other actions of the Housing Authority. In 1938 the city announced plans to clear a large section of the Fourth Ward north of Dallas Street to construct San Felipe Courts, a thousand-unit housing project for low-income whites. In spite of protests to both city hall and the federal government that this project would dislocate hundreds of poor blacks from one of the city's first black neighborhoods (including the original Freedmantown) and destroy many of the black community's oldest churches, schools, and other institutions, the government went ahead with the project.[5]

Blacks not only endured inferior housing in Houston, but throughout the period of segregation they also were relegated to the poorest jobs. In 1880, for example, 84 percent of the city's black workers were employed as domestic, unskilled, or semiskilled labor, while only 9.1 percent held skilled jobs, and only 1 percent were professionals. In the decades following the Civil War, relatively few blacks successfully engaged in trades like carpentry or blacksmithing. Also, the vast majority of women and children who worked in Houston in 1880 were black. In general, during the late nineteenth century black Houstonians faced job conditions that were significantly worse than those faced by average whites. Even when blacks did enter the skilled trades, they usually received lower wages and performed work that was physically more demanding than white workers did.[6]

Black employment patterns did not change substantially in following decades. In 1940, 89.6 percent of black workers in the city still worked in the lowest job categories (domestic, service worker, and unskilled and semiskilled laborer), while only 4.7 percent were classified as professionals or managers. In contrast, 10 percent of white workers were professionals in 1940, and only 14.4 percent fell into the three lowest job categories. While relatively few black children worked in 1940, black women were still far more likely to be in the work force than were white women. In that year 53.7 percent of black women held jobs outside the home, while only 29.2 percent of white women did. Though the strength of Houston's economy provided a sufficient number of jobs during most of this period, when economic distress occurred, it affected blacks more severely than whites. In 1940, for example, 11 percent of the black work force was unemployed, compared with only 7.1 percent of the white work force.[7]

A major factor that contributed to the low status of black labor in Houston was the poor relationship between black workers and local unions. Even before the Civil War, unions attempted to prevent the employment of blacks in skilled jobs. After emancipation, this hostile relationship between black and white labor persisted, and early unions were segregated. In the early 1870s local blacks helped organize the Texas branch of the National Labor Union (Colored), and for two years this union operated in the city. The most significant union in the 1880s, the Knights of Labor, theoretically opened its doors to workers of all races. In Houston, however, blacks could participate only in separate assemblies. By 1885 two black assemblies existed in the city. There was very little contact between black and white members of the Knights of Labor; all social functions, picnics, and even Labor Day celebrations were segregated.[8]

In the 1890s trade unions replaced the defunct Knights of Labor as the principal voice for labor in the city. Blacks played only a minor role in the trade union movement. The vast majority of blacks were not skilled workers, and those few skilled workers were generally excluded from membership. The American Federation of Labor finally set up segregated trade unions for blacks after the turn of the century. On the whole, however, the black labor movement in Houston was weak and isolated, receiving little assistance or sympathy from white unions. A major exception to this situation occurred on the city docks. After the Civil War ended, black dock workers had become a major force on the wharves of both Houston and Galveston. This was largely because of the influence of Norris Wright Cuney, a prominent black Republican who served for a time as port collector in Galveston, and his associate, Richard Allen, who served for a time as port collector of Houston. When the Houston ship channel opened in 1914, black and white longshoremen organized separate unions and split the work on a fifty-fifty basis.[9]

Not all Houston blacks were relegated to unskilled or semiskilled jobs. There were black businessmen and professionals in the city, although their numbers were relatively small. To a degree these blacks benefitted from the racial situation in the city, because their businesses served the black communities that emerged out of segregation. Most black professionals were ministers and teachers. A 1915 survey identified only seven black attorneys, eight physicians, five druggists, and two dentists.[10] These professionals, plus the black teachers and ministers, served an exclusively black clientele. Of the nearly four hundred black business establishments identified in the 1915 survey, most were barbershops, grocery and meat markets, restaurants and cafes, and delivery services.[11] All but the latter catered to blacks. The result was that by the turn of the century, blacks in Houston could obtain most items and services within their communities. However, most of these establishments were small, because black businessmen lacked sufficient capital or credit to expand and also because they faced stiff competition from white businesses that operated both in black neighborhoods and downtown. Despite these obstacles, some black entrepreneurs became quite prosperous. J. H. Harmon, for example, opened a thriving dry goods store in the city in 1903. Five years later Rev. N. P. Pullum spoke of his business successes at the convention of the National Negro Business League in Baltimore. Pullum noted how he had used his income as a minister to finance a brickyard, a shoe store, and two drugstores.[12]

In the mid-1920s several community leaders attempted to promote black business in the city. Clifton F. Richardson, publisher of the black weekly newspaper, the Houston *Informer*, took the lead in these efforts. Richardson urged his readers to patronize black-owned establishments; in 1923 he established the first of several black businessmen's associations, each

African Americans unloading a ship in 1922. An agreement that was worked out in the 1880s divided jobs at the port of Houston between black and white longshoremen. *Courtesy Houston Public Library, Houston Metropolitan Research Center*

of which enjoyed a brief flurry of success before fading from the scene. Even the Houston Negro Chamber of Commerce, chartered amid great fanfare in the mid-1930s, had little real impact on the growth of black business and rather quickly evolved into a social organization.[13]

On the whole, black-owned businesses and black business leadership have not had a major impact on Houston, dominated as they have been by service establishments oriented toward the black community. In 1929, for example, 71.8 percent of black businesses were either dining establishments or food markets; and even these types of black businesses faced competition within their neighborhoods.[14] Greeks, Italians, Germans, Jews, and Chinese operated similar establishments there, and a large number of blacks preferred to patronize white businesses, where they believed that they received better products, service, and prices. Only businesses that offered services specifically oriented toward black needs—barber shops, beauty salons, photographers, and funeral homes—encountered little outside competition. Despite these shortcomings, Houston's black businesses compared very favorably with those in other American cities. In 1929, Houston's black population was the thirteenth largest in the nation, but Houston ranked tenth in the number of black-owned businesses and seventh in average sales per black business. Furthermore, in sales per capita of black population, Houston's black-owned businesses eclipsed other major southern cities, including New Orleans and Atlanta. They also surpassed New York City, which had the largest black population in the nation, by a better than a two-to-one margin.[15]

During the period of segregation, black churches and black schools, not black businesses, were the most significant and influential institutions in the black community. Almost every black Houstonian was an active member of a black church during the period before World War II. Divisions between churches usually reflected political and social divisions within the black community. The largest black denominations were Baptists and Methodists, although there were a significant number of Catholics, especially in the Fifth Ward, and a large number of small evangelical congregations and storefront churches. Although Antioch Baptist remained the most prestigious black church, by 1941 St. John Baptist Church, on Dowling Street in the Third Ward, boasted the largest congregation in the city. By the early 1930s over 180 Baptist congregations claimed 80 percent of black Houstonians as their members. Several divisions of the Methodist Church also operated in Houston's black communities. The oldest black church in the city, Trinity Methodist Episcopal, continued to exert significant influence. In addition to Methodist Episcopals, the city also contained active congregations of African Methodist Episcopals and Christian Methodist Episcopals. The first black Catholic church, St. Nicholas, was organized in the Fifth Ward in the 1880s. By 1945 St. Nicholas had approximately 3,000 members, while a second black Catholic church, Our Mother of Mercy, located near Frenchtown, had 800 parishioners. Both Catholic and Protestant churches were social and civic centers as well as houses of worship, and black ministers provided much of the leadership for the community.[16]

During this period the fraternal orders, mutual aid societies, and social and civic clubs that had emerged immediately following emancipation continued to play an important role in the community. The most visible were the fraternal lodges, which demonstrated their vitality by erecting imposing edifices during the 1920s. The most prominent lodge, the Grand United Order of Odd Fellows, established in 1881, occupied the most impressive lodge building. In addition to the social functions they sponsored, these fraternal orders provided members with death and burial benefits—often the only insurance that members possessed. Mutual aid societies provided similar services, but they rarely had the financial assets of the fraternal lodges and consequently had a poor survival rate. However, during the depression many of the fraternal lodges discovered that they had commit-

Black women's clubs were a force for social progress throughout the period of segregation. Pictured here are members of the Alpha Kappa Omega chapter of Alpha Kappa Alpha, circa 1942. Members include Martha Sneed Robinson (who served briefly on the Houston City Council in 1990-91 following the death of her husband, Judson, who was the first black elected to the city council since Reconstruction) and Erma Sweatt, whose brother, Heman Sweatt, played the major role in desegregating the University of Texas. *Courtesy Houston Public Library, Houston Metropolitan Research Center*

ted too many of their resources to their buildings. Several failed because of their inability to meet their financial obligations. Most of the social clubs focused their attention on entertainment and recreational activities, although several also funded scholarships. The civic associations, on the other hand, were interested principally in upgrading black neighborhoods, particularly by obtaining more city services for these areas.[17]

Next to churches, schools were the most important institutions in the black community. From its inception, the Houston Independent School District was segregated, and as early as 1871 a separate facility existed for black children in each ward. Throughout the period of segregation black schools suffered consistently from substandard facilities and inadequate funding. In the 1880s, for example, black male teachers were paid only 58 percent as much as white male teachers, and in 1918 the state provided

$9.06 for the education of each white child but only $6.90 for each black student's education. By the early 1920s most black schools suffered from dilapidated facilities and severe overcrowding. Because of poor drainage, the Gregory Institute sat in a lake each time it rained; in 1923 Colored High School had only five hundred seats for an enrollment of over a thousand students.[18]

Although inequality in educational facilities continued, blacks did benefit from a massive program of school construction in the mid-1920s, as well as from a determination on the part of the Houston Independent School District administration to upgrade both white and black education. In 1921 there were sixteen black elementary schools and one black high school in the city; by 1940 the number had increased to twenty-four elementary schools, three junior high schools, and three high schools. In addition to the construction of new schools, many older black schools, including Gregory Institute, received new buildings.

Even more significantly, in 1927 the school board established Houston Colored Junior College, a black version of the concurrently established Houston Junior College. The establishment of the black junior college ended a long struggle on the part of the black community to bring higher education to black Houstonians. This struggle began with Jack Yates's unsuccessful efforts to locate Bishop College in Houston, and in the early 1920s it resulted in the decision of Wiley College of Marshall, Texas, to offer extension classes in a local black high school. Houston Colored Junior College was founded primarily to certify and upgrade the quality of black school teachers; it began serving this mission by offering night classes in a black high school. Like black institutions of the Houston Independent School District, it suffered from discriminatory funding formulas and discrimination in faculty salaries (as well as the fact that lower qualifications were required of its faculty). Despite these handicaps, it grew steadily, becoming a four-year college in 1935, acquiring its own campus in the Third Ward, and then in 1947 becoming a state university, Texas Southern University.[19]

Despite the advances made in the 1920s and 1930s, black education remained inferior to that available to whites. Reflecting this, illiteracy among blacks was significantly higher than among whites throughout this period. While white illiteracy stood at less than 0.5 percent in 1930, black illiteracy remained at over 7 percent. On the other hand, the advances in black public education of the 1920s had an effect. Black illiteracy in the city declined from 10.8 percent in 1920 to 7.1 percent in 1930. In 1930 the rate of black illiteracy in Houston was lower than the average rate of black illiteracy for urban areas with a population of greater than 25,000. Furthermore, by 1930 the percentage of Houston's black youth attending school was greater than

Public school teachers were a core part of the black, professional middle-class in Houston. Mollie Brown taught for years at Douglass Elementary School in Houston's Third Ward, where this photograph was taken circa 1906–11. *Courtesy Houston Public Library, Houston Metropolitan Research Center*

that of either Atlanta or New Orleans, although it was not quite as high as that of New York or Detroit.[20]

Segregation of schools and other institutions led to the development of a self-contained black community in Houston. Most blacks responded to segregation by turning inward, relying on their own families and communities, creating their own institutions, and avoiding, as much as possible, contact with the outside white world. Blacks in Houston had their own schools, newspapers, parks, baseball teams, and amusement facilities. There were black restaurants, saloons, theaters, and movie houses. Blacks celebrated their own holiday, Juneteenth, and around the turn of the century they established their own fall festival, De-Ro-Loc ("colored" in reverse), a black version of the historic No-Tsu-Oh carnival ("Houston" spelled backward). In one sense segregation thus stimulated the black community. Many black businesses existed primarily to serve the black population; segregated schools provided employment for black teachers and administrators. The price of segregation, however, was very high. Blacks frequently lived in inferior housing and worked at low-paying jobs; black schools were poorly funded, and black illiteracy was many times higher than white illiteracy; black neighborhoods did not receive their share of city services; and, most telling, the death rate for blacks in Houston in 1930 was over twice as high as it was for whites.[21]

The price of segregation must be measured in more than just economic terms. For most blacks segregation was a humiliating experience. Custom dictated that blacks address whites with respect and enter white homes and businesses only through the back door. In some stores blacks were served only in a separate section of the shop and only after all white patrons had been served. In most dress shops black women were not allowed to try on clothing—if they were interested in purchasing a hat, a white woman had to model it for them. If white movie theaters admitted blacks at all, it was through a side door, and there was either a separate showing for them or else they were seated in a special section of the balcony. Blacks were also subjected to verbal and occasionally physical abuse, especially if whites judged their demeanor to be inappropriate. Newspapers often referred to blacks in insulting terms, and whites usually addressed blacks as "boy," "uncle," or "Sal."[22] Perhaps the most destructive aspect of segregation was the feeling, voiced by a black mother, that her children were cut off from most of the world and would never have the experiences and opportunities for growth that were available to white children.[23] Nevertheless, by the early twentieth century segregation was so well entrenched that most blacks chose not to confront it. Indeed, some even seemed to endorse it. In 1915 the editors of the *Red Book of Houston,* a black publication describing the leaders and institutions of the black community, advised their readers, "A worthy man in his race, whatever it is, loses that worthiness when he

Two of the most popular annual social events for black Houstonians in the early twentieth century were Juneteenth Day, which celebrated the day in June, 1865, when emancipation was proclaimed by federal forces in the vicinity, and De-Ro-Loc ("colored" spelled backwards), a fall festival. Martha Yates Jones and Pinkie Yates are in a buggy decorated for the 1908 Juneteenth parade. In the background is the Yates family home in the Fourth Ward. *Courtesy Houston Public Library, Houston Metropolitan Research Center*

attempts to obliterate social and racial barriers imposed by a benevolent Jehovah. He must stay in his own to prove the worthiness of his life."[24]

In This Section . . .

Segregation resulted in the continued development after the Civil War of a color-coded community in the Bayou City. For blacks, segregation combined with a growing black population to create a distinct black Houston that, if not separate from white Houston, was nevertheless terra incognita to most whites. Unfortunately, our knowledge of black Houston during the enormously important formative period from the end of Reconstruction to 1900 has also remained mostly uncharted territory. Filling this gap in Houston's history must be a high priority for scholars. Throughout the South, the late nineteenth century was the time when black religious colleges were founded, when blacks began to attend public schools, and when in southern urban areas the black "city-within-a-city" formed around black newspapers, black sororal and fraternal societies, black branches of the YMCA and public libraries, and similar organizations and institutions. Within black Houston a fledgling black middle class formed to meet the needs of the black population. The core of this middle class was composed of those in such professions as education and the ministry, for which segregation provided a guaranteed, captive black clientele unwanted by whites. Around the black core middle class were others, principally in business, who had to compete with whites for the allegiance of black customers. Collectively this black elite advocated a gospel of racial unity—a goal likewise endorsed and promoted by leaders as diverse as Booker T. Washington, W. E. B. Du Bois, and Marcus Garvey. Black entrepreneurs in Houston particularly encouraged black consumer solidarity as a necessary building block of collective racial economic progress.

One of the ablest and most energetic of this group was Clifton F. Richardson. Himself an immigrant to the Bayou City, Richardson was a founder and editor of two of the most widely read black newspapers in Houston, both of which had to compete with the white press for black readers. He helped establish the Houston *Informer* in 1919, and some ten years later he founded and edited the Houston *Defender* until his sudden, premature death in 1939. Richardson's profile of black Houston in the 1920s is one of the four following essays that examine black Houston between the turn of the century and the end of World War II. Lorenzo Greene's portrait of black society in the Bayou City during the opening months of the Great Depression is all the more valuable because he viewed what he saw with the discerning eye of an educated, well-traveled visitor to the city. Frances Dressman's essay has the virtue of examining in detail the birth, life, and death of one particular black business in Houston, the jitney or taxi trade, while James SoRelle provides a more panoramic view of black economic and ideological developments through the end of World War II. These essays about twentieth-century black Houston confirm that while slavery had ended over a half century earlier, white-sponsored racial discrimination nevertheless survived and was commonplace in the Bayou City in all aspects of community life. Indeed, Houston's long historical experience with slavery shaped the era of segregation that followed.

Notes

1. This picture of the migration into the city and the nature of life in the black communities was confirmed by numerous oral history interviews. For examples,

see Sylvia Harrison, interview with Shelly Jarmon, Houston, Tex., Apr. 3, 1981 (audio tape in possession of Cary D. Wintz); Robert J. Terry, interview with Cary D. Wintz, Houston, Tex., May 30, 1981 (audio tape in possession of Wintz). Senfronia Thompson recalled that her grandmother ran a boarding house for blacks who migrated into the city seeking jobs. See Senfronia Thompson, interview with Shelly Jarmon, Houston, Tex., Dec. 15, 1981 (tape recording in possession of Cary D. Wintz).

2. Patricia Smith Prather, "Town Pride," *Houston Chronicle,* Jan. 17, 1987; Jack E. Dodson, "Minority Group Housing in Two Texas Cities," in *Studies in Housing and Minority Groups,* ed. Nathan Glazer and Davis McEntire (Berkeley, 1960), pp. 103-105.

3. U.S. Department of Commerce, Bureau of the Census, *Sixteenth Census of the United States: 1940,* vol. 2, *Housing* (Washington, D.C., 1943), pp. 282, 284, 287, 290; SoRelle, pp. 228-30.

4. Houston *Informer,* July 28, 1923; SoRelle, pp. 227-32; William M. Patterson, interview with Cary D. Wintz, Houston, Tex., Apr. 20, 1981 (tape recording in possession of Wintz).

5. SoRelle, pp. 241-48; Houston *Informer,* Dec. 10, 1938, Oct. 7, 1939, Mar. 30, 1940, Apr. 20, 1940, Apr. 27, 1940, July 13, 1940.

6. Robert E. Ziegler, "The Workingman in Houston, Texas, 1865-1915" (Ph.D. diss., Texas Tech University, 1972), pp. 34-36, 41, 51; *Department of the Interior, Census Office Statistics of the Population of the United States at the Tenth Census* (Washington, D.C., 1883).

7. U.S. Department of Commerce, Bureau of the Census, *Sixteenth Census of the United States: 1940, Population and Housing: Statistics for Census Tracts, Houston, Texas* (Washington, D.C., 1942), p. 21; and *Sixteenth Census of the United States: 1940, Population,* vol. 3, *The Labor Force: Occupation, Industry, Employment, and Income,* pt. 5, *Pennsylvania-Wyoming* (Washington, D.C., 1943), pp. 595-96.

8. Ziegler, pp. 83, 85-86.

9. Ibid., pp. 97, 158-63.

10. *The Red Book of Houston: A Compendium of Social, Professional, Religious, Educational and Industrial Interests of Houston's Colored Population* (Houston, [1915]), pp. 164-71.

11. Ibid.

12. "Life Members of National Negro Business League" [1908], Afro-American Files, Institute of Texas Cultures, San Antonio, Texas.

13. SoRelle, pp. 257-62; Howard Beeth, "Houston and History, Past and Present: A Look at Black Houston in the 1920s," *Southern Studies* 25 (Summer, 1986) 2:172-86.

14. U.S. Department of Commerce, Bureau of the Census, *Negroes in the United States: 1920-1932* (Washington, D.C., 1935), pp. 525-26, 578.

15. Ibid., p. 578. Blacks interviewed frequently admitted they shopped in white stores for the reasons cited in the text. See, for example, Tommie Allen Smith, interview with Shelly Jarmon, Houston, Tex., Sept. 26, 1981 (tape recording in possession of Cary D. Wintz).

16. SoRelle, pp. 310-16.
17. Ibid., pp. 321-30.
18. Ibid., pp. 79-82.
19. Sharon Johnson, "The Development of the Houston College for Negroes," pp. 9-12, unpublished paper in possession of Cary D. Wintz. Originally Texas Southern University was named Texas State University for Negroes; it became Texas Southern University in 1951. See Ira B. Bryant, *Texas Southern University: Its Antecedents, Political Origins, and Future* (Houston, 1975).
20. *Negroes in the United States,* pp. 224, 252.
21. The death rate for diseases clearly linked to poverty and a poor environment, such as pneumonia and tuberculosis, even more clearly illustrate the price of segregation. The death rate from pneumonia for blacks was 1.65 per 1,000 and only 0.48 per 1,000 for whites, while the death rate from tuberculosis for blacks was 1.51 per 1,000 and for whites 0.44 per 1,000. *Negroes in the United States,* pp. 452, 454-55.
22. SoRelle, pp. 69, 98.
23. Hortense Dugar Smith, interview with Cary D. Wintz, Houston, Tex., Sept. 11, 1981 (tape recording in possession of Wintz).
24. *Red Book,* p. 3.

The Emergence of Black Business in Houston, Texas: A Study of Race and Ideology, 1919-45

James M. SoRelle

Introduction

   In his controversial study of the black middle class in the United States, E. Franklin Frazier criticized black professionals and entrepreneurs for formulating an elaborate social myth that exaggerated the benefits of black business endeavors. "This social myth," he wrote, "has been one of the main elements in the world of 'make-believe' which the black bourgeoisie has created to compensate for its feeling of inferiority in a white world dominated by business enterprise." Moreover, Frazier contended that the ideological framework employed by black business leaders to justify the establishment of a separate black economy represented little more than a smokescreen for greed — a desire to accumulate wealth and status at the expense of a captive economic audience.[1]
  Certainly Frazier offered his readers many valuable insights into the motivations and actions of the black middle class in American society. There can be little doubt that members of the African-American elite who attempted to spawn a viable black economy occupied a very tenuous position in relation to the economic mainstream in the United States. Such were the consequences of black powerlessness. At the same time, however, Frazier dismissed too easily the extent to which African-American leaders were committed to various aspects of black racial ideology to generate a pragmatic response to the real world of Jim Crow. Although some members of the black elite undoubtedly invoked philosophical arguments as a mask for avarice, many black community leaders embraced the concepts of self-help, race pride, and racial solidarity to combat the considerable economic manifestations of racism.[2] The evolution of black business in Houston, Texas, demonstrates just how closely important elements of African-American thought were linked to black economic development.

Houston's Black Economy

Like their counterparts throughout the South, and indeed throughout the entire nation, black Houstonians in the years between the two world wars confronted limitations imposed upon them by segregation in housing and social activity. Furthermore, they found themselves excluded from the mainstream of political and economic life in a city that the local white chamber of commerce depicted as "Heavenly Houston." Many African Americans responded to these conditions by seeking opportunities within their own neighborhoods. The existence of a steadily growing black population presented Bayou City blacks with the alternative of developing their own social and political organizations as well as fostering their own commercial enterprises.[3]

Although black leaders proclaimed that the emergence of a separate black economy would strengthen the entire African-American community in Houston, the chief beneficiaries of such a program were clearly black professionals and businesspersons—a group that Blaine Brownell has described as "the commercial-civic elite"—who depended upon black customers for their livelihood.[4] Hence, this professional and business elite profited from local mores that created a need for separate goods and services in the black community. Just as the existence of Jim Crow schools and separate religious institutions provided numerous teaching positions and pulpits for the city's black educators and clerics, so too did other black professionals and entrepreneurs depend upon the existence of a separate society to make a living. Among professional occupations, for example, black physicians, dentists, pharmacists, and lawyers provided services for an almost entirely black clientele. For these professionals to have anticipated serving white clients would have been to engage in self-delusion or to have themselves labelled incurable optimists. The limitations of race also led other black entrepreneurs to rely heavily if not completely upon the African-American community. For example, Hobart Taylor, Sr., owner of the HT Taxi Company, rarely expected to handle white fares, just as surely as Yellow Cabs refused to carry black passengers in Houston. Black undertakers like Thornton Fairchild, Elvidge Jackson, and John M. Frierson thrived in the Bayou City because, while they occasionally buried whites, they handled all black corpses due to the requirements of Jim Crow.[5]

Black-owned businesses, then, generally were oriented to the African-American market, and most of these enterprises were service trade establishments, such as barbershops, restaurants, grocery stores, and blacksmith shops. Food service establishments dominated the field of black-owned businesses, since African Americans could not patronize most white cafés and restaurants. Of 259 black retail businesses enumerated by the census bureau in 1929, restaurants, cafeterias, lunchrooms, or refreshment stands accounted for 43.6 percent. The next largest group of enterprises included various types of food distributors, such as grocery stores and fruit, vegetable, or meat markets (73 establishments, or 28.2 percent of the total). The third largest group of black businesses (22 establishments, or 8.5 percent of the total) consisted of automotive services, such as filling stations and garages. In addition to these businesses, numerous barber and beauty shops, such as the Orgen ("Negro" spelled backward) Barber Shop, the White Swan Barber Shop, and especially Madame N. A. Franklin's beauty establishments, catered solely to black patrons.[6]

Houston's black-owned businesses compared quite favorably with black enterprises in other cities throughout the country. The Houston Chamber of Commerce boasted in 1919 that "Colored people [in Houston] are engaged in all avenues of business and some have made a very creditable showing."[7] Statistics for 1929 indicate that the Bayou City's black population, the thirteenth largest in the nation, ranked tenth in number of black-owned establishments, seventh in average net sales per store, and third in net sales per capita of the black population.[8] In fact, during the years between the world wars, black business enterprises abounded in Houston, and local blacks praised them as manifestations of an emerging racial consciousness. Why, they asked, should whites benefit at the expense of black professionals and entrepreneurs who could provide many, if not most, of the same goods and services to black customers?

These attitudes were expressed frequently in the pages of the Houston *Informer,* the major black weekly in the city. In a discussion of the numerous instances of mistreatment of black women by white merchants, for example, editor Clifton F. Richardson asked his readers, "Have we no race pride? no self-respect? . . . Are we content to forever serve in the 'Sambo,' 'Uncle Ned,' 'Aunt Dinah' and 'Sally Ann' role both from a political, commercial and civic viewpoint?" Black Houstonians, Richardson argued, must unite in a cooperative effort to build and support their own business interests. The *Informer* editor suggested that black entrepreneurs emulate the Jews, who "by pooling their moneys and combining their interests . . . dominate the financial and commercial world."[9] Richardson's point was clear, albeit exaggerated and laced with stereotypical assumptions.

On another occasion, Richardson surveyed the problem of black economic dependency and wrote: "There was a time when we were justified in giving our business to others, but that was before the advent of reputable and responsible race enterprises. . . . We can never be a substantial and successful race as long as we build up concerns of other races to the detriment and exclusion of our own. . . . From a business point of view we must think more in terms of racial solidarity, co-operation, teamwork, and group action."[10] In the same vein, he implored, "Let us not slacken our speed, but let us pull full steam ahead to the distant port of economic independence, racial solidarity and inter-racial amity."[11]

Opponents of this philosophy charged that encouragement of separate black business operations represented an undesirable, self-imposed segregation, but Carter Wesley, Richardson's successor as editor of the *Informer*, pointed to the argument of W. E. B. Du Bois in behalf of the idea of separate black cooperatives and concluded that "segregation or no segregation, we must in the last analysis make our own way. . . . So, why not take the little institutions that we have, and the few opportunities for self-improvement and development that are ours, and make the most of them . . . ?"[12] Black leaders in the Bayou City repeatedly called for cooperative efforts to expand business operations independent of white control. "We must go into business," wrote Dr. Theodore E. Bryant. "We must sell as well as buy. . . . We must support our own enterprises."[13] When, in 1923, the Houston *Informer* asked a group of prominent black citizens, "What is the most crying need among Houston's Colored Citizenry?" several responded that blacks must pool their efforts and resources to launch and support black businesses.[14]

The prevalence of this attitude toward expanding black business operations in Houston led Simeon B. Williams, a local educator who wrote a humor column for the *Informer* entitled "Cimbee's Ramblings," to believe that he had detected "w'ite coller feaver" in the Bayou City's black community. This ailment, Williams observed through the character of Cimbee, a semi-literate raconteur and man-about-town, prompted young blacks to enter the business world where they "kin set down in er swivvul cheer an' throe dere foots up on de des' an' tawk laud erbout de financhul wurl." Although Cimbee appeared to be critical of this movement, within a few years he, too, had been won over. "We's got ter bil us up er passel uv biznesses," he told his fictional friend, Gus, "'fo we kin ever call ourse'ves er race wurthy ter live long side uv uther races, dat's de thing we ain got."[15]

A leading advocate of black business expansion in Houston was C. F. Richardson. Through his editorial columns in the *Informer*, Richardson spearheaded the promotion of racial solidarity for the purpose of forming large black businesses and corporations. While continuously boasting of the business opportunities available to Bayou City blacks, he criticized his readers for lacking the foresight to understand the importance of establishing and supporting their own businesses to cater to black patrons. Moreover, he chastised black entrepreneurs for what he viewed as their lack of cooperative spirit.[16] Even in the wake of the nation's economic collapse, Richardson maintained his campaign to foster black enterprise in the city. "This is the day of big business," he wrote in 1929 with unchained optimism, "and Negroes must form combinations and establish corporations to engage in business on a large scale, if the businesses conducted by our people are to survive and thrive."[17] The arrival of the Great Depression in the 1930s, however, turned the attention of black Houstonians to the immediate problems connected with economic adversity, and whatever potential existed for the realization of Richardson's dream of large-scale business development within the black community dissipated in the midst of economic chaos and hardship.

Building Black Economic Consciousness

In addition to their efforts to promote black-owned businesses by encouraging self-help and racial solidarity, black community leaders argued that the development of a black economy also required expressions of racial consciousness and pride on the part of black consumers. But racial consciousness, let alone pride, remained a distant prize so long as black Houstonians continued to trade with white merchants who did not serve the best economic interests of African Americans. "The time has arrived," proclaimed one *Informer* column, "for the colored people to have some racial self-respect and stop spending their money with merchants who are base ingrates and mercantile hogs."[18] Particularly galling to the promoters of black business were fair-skinned blacks who "passed" for white in order to shop in stores that otherwise refused service to African Americans. Although critical of the racist policy of those stores, the *Informer* denounced passing as a clear sign of a lack of racial self-respect.[19] That not all black Houstonians agreed with the *Informer*'s complaint was evident in the statement of Rosalee Mitchel, a mulatto boardinghouse manager, who justified her passing, claiming, "I don't try to slight my color but I don't see why I ought to deny myself things."[20]

The prevalence of foreign-born proprietors, especially Chinese, Greeks, and Italians, who operated stores in predominantly black neighborhoods, provided another irritant to members of Houston's black commercial-civic elite. Cimbee expressed this concern when he complained: "It gives me de 'Nigger Blues' ever time I goes thru de parts uv our town an' sees de culler uv de fokes whut is sellin' our peepul awl dey eats an' wares, an' awl de wood an' cole dey burns."[21] These distasteful arrangements became especially unbearable when foreign-born storeowners or clerks mistreated black customers, although black residents at times seemed to ignore such abuses. For example, when a foreign-born café owner who catered solely to blacks shot one of his customers during an altercation, no significant protest followed, and within an hour of the shooting the café was once again filled as though nothing had happened. At other times, however, black leaders and local residents voiced their disapproval of abusive treatment. One such incident occurred when a Chinese clerk at Wing Chong's grocery on West Dallas in the Fourth Ward, adjacent to downtown, kicked two young black girls. Some two thousand black residents responded to this relatively minor assault by organizing a picket line around the store. The protest continued until Wing Chong issued a formal apology, fired the clerk responsible, and hired a black in his place. In addition, Chong paid each girl's family $150 as restitution.[22]

As far as some black Houstonians were concerned, the best way to prevent shootings and incidents such as the Wing Chong affair from recurring was for local blacks to open their own establishments and for African-American shoppers to patronize only those businesses owned and operated by blacks. Such recommendations reflected the desire to put into practice the concepts of self-help, race pride, and racial consciousness and solidarity. These concepts were often manifested in admonitions to "Buy Black." One *Informer* editorial concluded: "If we would spend as much time trying to build up and fortify our own race as we have been doing from time immemorial in strengthening and solidifying other racial groups, we would not always be the recipients of such acts of ingratitude, discourtesy and insult!"[23] The *Informer* also articulated this "Buy Black" philosophy on numerous occasions in advertisements boosting race enterprises. In 1919, for example, the paper urged its readers to purchase their groceries from R. L. Andrews, one of the black community's leading businessmen, in order to "help fortify your own business concern and strengthen the race commercially." Two years later, the *Informer* announced the opening of Fitch's Photography Studio as the "latest race enterprise" in Houston and added, "It is our duty to support all deserving enterprises owned and operated by our people."[24]

Emphasis upon the concepts of race pride, racial solidarity, and self-help in Houston culminated in the 1920s and 1930s in attempts by local black leaders to create and maintain a business association as a forum for the discussion of the commercial needs of the city's African-American population. These efforts demonstrate how civic boosterism, which was an inextricable part of the "business progressivism" of the South, also abetted the movement to expand black business interests in Houston.[25] The earliest of these organizations was the Houston Colored Commercial Club, which emerged in 1923 under the guiding hand of C. F. Richardson, who served as executive secretary. The members secured office space in the United Brothers of Friendship building and within a year boasted a membership of 260, including many of the city's leading black professionals and entrepreneurs. The club soon affiliated with the National Negro Business League and initiated programs to inspire black Houstonians to support black-owned businesses within the community. In addition, the Colored Commercial Club encouraged black storeowners to take pride in their businesses by making them physically attractive and urged proprietors to advertise special sales to promote "Negro Trade Week" as a device for building black consumer consciousness.[26] Some observers may have viewed "Negro Trade Week" as an example of racial chauvinism, but club members preferred to regard this observance as a valuable effort to instill the concept of self-help in the minds of black residents and consumers. On behalf of the Houston Colored Commercial Club, the *Informer* argued that "it is not the intention of the organization to endeavor to commercialize prejudice nor appeal to class and race distinctions; but to educate and train our people to the utter importance and necessity of trading with and patronizing those of their own race who are qualified and situated to render the service they desire."[27]

The early activities of the Houston Colored Commercial Club stimulated great expectations among many African Americans interested in the development of independent black business in Houston. Cimbee hoped that the club would "cunvert sum uv de ole moss backs ter at leas' lurn whare sum uv de cullud bizness places uv our sitty is located."[28] Naturally Richardson's newspaper remained a staunch supporter, but its pages also cautioned the commercial club not to rest on the laurels of its initial progress. The *Informer* praised these early efforts but warned that failure to follow through on programs or to maintain community interest in the club's operations would have the same effect as having "fed pearls to swine."[29] Apparently such exhortations went unheeded, and despite its encouraging beginning, by 1926 the Colored Commercial Club had fallen into "a state of suspended animation."[30] Appeals from C. F. Richardson to revive the organization failed to strike a responsive chord among black community leaders, a fact that angered and disappointed the activist editor. "Really, it is a sad reflection upon the boasted intelligence, business acumen and racial pride of the Houston Negroes," he editorialized, "that we do not have a business league, commercial club or chamber of commerce, or that we seem to be unable to keep one functioning like our racial brothers are doing in other Southern cities."[31]

Richardson, however, did not abandon his efforts to organize a viable business league, and in the summer of 1927 he joined forces with Homer E. McCoy, a local businessman, and Hobart Taylor, the wealthy owner of the HT Taxi Company, to launch a membership drive to create a local branch of the National Negro Business League. This project apparently was stillborn and was soon followed by the short-lived Business Men's Luncheon Club, organized in January, 1929, by James B. Grigsby, director of the American Mutual Benefit Association, a local insurance company.[32]

Not until the organization of the Houston Negro Chamber of Commerce in the mid-1930s did black Houstonians succeed in establishing a black business association of any note. But even then some community

Organized in the mid-1930s, the Houston Negro Chamber of Commerce worked to promote black businesses and a "buy black" consumer consciousness among local African Americans. Shown here is its headquarters, at 224 West Dallas, close to Houston's downtown. Posed in front are some members, including C. W. Hicks, a waiter (front row, second from right); Sam Payne, a postman (front row, third from right); and L. H. Spivey, a print-shop owner and president of the Chamber (front row, fourth from right). *Courtesy Houston Public Library, Houston Metropolitan Research Center*

leaders questioned the organization's usefulness. The chamber's major objectives were cooperation with the white chamber of commerce, boosting black commercial enterprises, and stimulating "a buying and selling consciousness among our group," but in practice the chamber's actual work fell far below expectations. Carter Wesley expressed concern that the chamber used 80 percent of the funds collected from its members to cover office expenses and the salaries of officials, and his unrelenting criticism of leading officers in the organization forced the resignation of Dr. William M. Drake as president in 1939. A local printer, L. H. Spivey, succeeded Drake, and the chamber members passed resolutions promising to continue the struggle to develop and support the best business interests of the black community, including patronage of black-owned stores and enterprises. Nevertheless, problems continued. Factionalism erupted when a dissatisfied group of members, including Dr. Drake and supported by Wesley, sought to unseat executive secretary O. K. Manning and to expose certain financial improprieties. As a result of these disputes, within two years the Negro Chamber of Commerce lost most of its momentum.[33] Financed largely by whites in the early 1940s and active mainly in sponsoring dances, bathing revues, and boxing exhibitions, the organization had ceased to make a contribution to the city's black business interests. "Yes, the faces of the people who run the Chamber are black," Carter Wesley reported, "but the voice is likely to be found to be that of the white Chamber and white businesses which provide the funds."[34] In 1945 an Urban League survey reported that the Negro Chamber of Commerce had "little or no relationship with the organized channels of business in the city."[35]

Conclusion

Although the existence of a large black population provided a potentially lucrative market for black professionals and entrepreneurs in Houston, several factors inherent in the black community of the time limited the success of many of these endeavors. In the first place, the capital required to initiate large-scale business operations presented a major obstacle, especially since white banks were reluctant to extend loans for black ventures. Even in a city like Houston, with a large number of well-to-do black inhabitants, African-American entrepreneurs faced difficulties in convincing potential investors of the desirability of the proposed projects or of the possibility for success. C. F. Richardson noted that many blacks who were financially able to invest in worthy projects hesitated to do so. He therefore suggested that reducing the cost of shares of stock to a reasonably low figure would create a cooperative movement within the entire black community that could put several black businesses on their feet. Still, the masses of African Americans were unwilling or incapable of making such investments.[36]

In addition to withholding their support from new business endeavors, many black Houstonians displayed an indifference toward black businesses already in existence. In some cases, black customers complained that African-American proprietors failed to provide the same variety and quality of goods as white storeowners. Other African Americans criticized black entrepreneurs for providing poor service and engaging in lax business methods. Some charged that blacks providing services available only in the black community because of the requirements of segregation took advantage of this situation to gouge patrons. Certain trades that attracted particular condemnation included black barbershops and black-owned cleaning establishments that charged their customers much more than their white counterparts. Black-owned taxi companies represented another chief offender because their fares were twice as high as those of the white-owned cab companies that would not service the black community.[37] Richard R. Grovey, a local black civic leader in the 1930s, found the basic problem easy to identify. "[Black Houstonians] expect the Negro to have better services than the white man before they will even agree to give him a trial," Grovey told an interviewer. "It really keeps the Negro who is trying to do something in a strain."[38]

This attitude on the part of many local African Americans also handicapped black professionals who depended upon black clients for their livelihoods. Some black residents simply had no faith in the abilities of these professionals. For example, some black Houstonians questioned the skills of black physicians whose practices were composed almost entirely of black patients. Freddie Collins, a black maid, reported that she always called black doctors "unless the case is very serious, then I have a white doctor." Said Collins, "I don't think they [black physicians] know as much as a white doctor and you can't depend on them. I just ain't got no faith in a colored doctor." A similar response came from another black domestic, Manilla Lovelady, who claimed, "I believe that white doctors treat you better than Negro doctors anyway." On the other hand, Carter Wesley criticized black doctors in the city who complained that African-American patients preferred white physicians, when those same doctors sent their patients to white pharmacists because they claimed that black pharmacies did not have adequate medicines in stock or did not give fresh prescriptions.[39]

The foregoing serves to clarify the dilemma confronting black professionals and entrepreneurs in the Bayou City. Existing in what Gunnar Myrdal termed the backwater of discrimination, the members of Houston's black commercial-civic elite were forced by the demands of legal and customary segregation to depend upon a separate African-American market for their subsistence.[40] To many members of the black elite, Jim Crow had delivered a rather cruel set of opportunities. On the one hand, it presented to black professionals and entrepreneurs a large black market for their services. On the other hand, basic prejudices within the black community led African-American customers to fill the cash registers of white merchants more frequently than those of black proprietors and professionals. Black community leaders might articulate the concepts of self-help, race pride, and racial solidarity as strategies for either accommodation or protest, but too many black Houstonians remained unwilling or financially powerless to support a philosophy of "race first."

Notes

1. *Black Bourgeoisie: The Rise of a New Middle Class* (Glencoe, Ill., 1957), pp. 24-26. While the foregoing by no means provides a complete summary of Frazier's conclusions, it does represent a statement of the major assertions that drew so much praise and condemnation from reviewers. For a thoughtful critique of *Black Bourgeoisie,* see August Meier, "Some Observations on the Negro Middle Class," *Crisis* 64 (Oct., 1957), pp. 461-69, 517.

2. The most complete discussion of the concepts of self-help, race pride, and racial solidarity among African Americans is found in August Meier, *Negro Thought in America, 1880-1915: Racial Ideologies in the Age of Booker T. Washington* (Ann Arbor, 1963). Meier presents evidence of the continued influence of these ideologies into the "New Negro" era of the post-World War I period. Moreover, he demonstrates that these racial concepts were employed both by accommodationist and protest leaders among African Americans.

3. Houston's total population in 1910 of 78,800 persons included 23,929 blacks (30.4 percent); by 1920, the black population had increased to 38,960 (24.6 percent). In 1930, 63,337 (21.7 percent) of the city's 292,352 inhabitants were black, and by 1940 there were 86,302 blacks (22.4 percent) living in a city whose population stood at 384,514. United States Department of Commerce, Bureau of the Census, *Negro Population: 1790-1915* (Washington, D.C., 1918), p. 74; ibid., *Negroes in the United States, 1920-1932* (Washington, D.C., 1935), pp. 54-55; ibid., *Fourteenth Census of the United States Taken in the Year 1920,* vol. 3, *Population: Composition and Characteristics of the Population, by States* (Washington, D.C., 1923), p. 47; ibid., *Sixteenth Census of the United States: 1940,* vol. 4, pt. 6, *Population: Characteristics of the Population* (Washington, D.C., 1943), p. 1044.

4. Blaine A. Brownell, *The Urban Ethos in the South, 1920-1930* (Baton Rouge, 1975).

5. Comments on the monopoly enjoyed by black cab companies and morticians can be found in Ira B. Bryant, interview with H. J. Walker, Houston, Tex., Aug. 7, 1939, in Charles S. Johnson, "Source Material for *Patterns of Negro Segregation:* Houston, Texas" (research memoranda for use in the preparation of Dr. Gunnar Myrdal's *An American Dilemma,* New York, 1940), p. 15; B. T. Brooks, interview with Walker, Houston, Tex., Aug. 10, 1939, ibid., pp. 11, 13; and Rosalee Mitchel, interview with Joseph Taylor, Houston, Tex., Aug. ?, 1939, ibid., p. 7. Mitchel even suggested that too many black funeral homes operated in the city. "There are over twenty Negro undertakers here," she said, "enough to bury Cox's [Coxey's] Army."

6. Bureau of the Census, *Negroes in the United States,* pp. 518-19, 523; Melvin James Banks, "The Pursuit of Equality: The Movement for First Class Citizenship among Negroes in Texas, 1920-1950" (D.S.S. diss., Syracuse University, 1962), p. 23; Bruce Alan Glasrud, "Black Texans, 1900-1930: A History" (Ph.D. diss., Texas Tech University, 1969), p. 129. For more about Madame Franklin's beauty establishments in the Bayou City, see the voluminous Madame N. A. Franklin Beauty School Collection, Houston Metropolitan Research Center, Houston Public Library.

7. Houston *Informer,* June 14, 1919. The chamber at that time and for many years following did not admit black members.
8. Bureau of the Census, *Negroes in the United States,* pp. 518-19.
9. Houston *Informer,* May 28, 1921.
10. Ibid., July 5, 1919.
11. Ibid., June 16, 1923.
12. Ibid., May 12, 1934.
13. Ibid., June 14, 1919.
14. Ibid., Mar. 3, 1923.
15. Ibid., Oct. 17, 1925, Feb. 11, 1928.
16. Ibid., Mar. 31, June 16, 1923, Aug. 29, 1925.
17. Ibid., Nov. 2, 1929.
18. Ibid., Nov. 27, 1920.
19. Ibid., Sept. 22, 1928.
20. Mitchel interview in Johnson, "Source Material for *Patterns of Negro Segregation,*" p. 5.
21. Houston *Informer,* Jan. 6, 1923.
22. Ibid., Feb. 2, 1924, Sept. 1, 4, 29, 1937. For additional complaints among blacks concerning foreign-born proprietors in black neighborhoods, see ibid., May 30, 1925, Oct. 31, 1931; Bryant interview in Johnson, "Source Material for *Patterns of Negro Segregation,*" p. 13; Brooks interview, ibid., p. 8.
23. Houston *Informer,* Jan. 4, 1930.
24. Ibid., June 28, 1919, Feb. 26, 1921.
25. For a discussion of boosterism as an essential element of southern progressivism, see George Brown Tindall, "Business Progressivism: Southern Politics in the Twenties," *South Atlantic Quarterly,* 62 (Winter, 1963): 92-106. For the adoption of this booster spirit by blacks in the urban South, see Brownell, *The Urban Ethos in the South,* pp. 56-58.
26. Houston *Informer,* Feb. 17, Mar. 24, Apr. 7, 28, July 14, Sept. 29, 1923.
27. Ibid., Oct. 13, 1923.
28. Ibid., Mar. 3, 1923.
29. Ibid., Oct. 20, 1923.
30. Ibid., Oct. 23, 1926.
31. Ibid., Apr. 9, 1927.
32. While the full history of these two business associations is unknown, the Business Men's Luncheon Club probably fell victim to the onset of the Great Depression. See ibid., July 16, 1927, Jan. 26, 1929, as well as Jesse O. Thomas, *A Study of the Social Welfare Status of the Negroes in Houston, Texas* (Houston, 1929), p. 72.
33. Houston *Informer,* Oct. 26, 1935, Nov. 11, 18, 25, Dec. 9, 1939, June 8, 1940. In the spring of 1940, a group of young black professionals and businessmen organized the Houston Negro Junior Chamber of Commerce for "men of good standing" between the ages of twenty-five and thirty-five, but little is known of the activities of these black Jaycees. See ibid., Mar. 16, 1940.
34. Ibid., Sept. 19, 1942.
35. National Urban League, *A Review of the Economic and Cultural Problems*

of Houston, Texas, as They Relate to Conditions in the Negro Population (n.p., 1945), p. 61.

36. Houston *Informer,* Mar. 5, 1921, Aug. 29, 1925.

37. Ibid., Feb. 16, 1924, Mar. 8, 1930, Aug. 12, 1933, Sept. 11, Oct. 2, 16, 1943, Jan. 15, Mar. 11, Nov. 4, 1944. See also Ellie Walls Montgomery, "Possibilities of Improving Negro Business through Better Business Methods" (Study Number 1, Department of Sociology, Houston College for Negroes, 1935), p. 3; Willis Johnson, interview with Joseph Taylor, Houston, Tex., Aug. ?, 1939, in Johnson, "Source Material for *Patterns of Negro Segregation,*" p. 8.

38. R. R. Grovey, interview with Joseph Taylor, Houston, Tex., Aug. ?, 1939, in Johnson, "Source Material for *Patterns of Negro Segregation,*" p. 13.

39. Freddie Collins, interview with H. J. Walker, Houston, Tex., Aug. 6, 1939, ibid., p. 5; Manilla Lovelady, interview with Walker, Houston, Tex., Aug. 8, 1939, ibid., p. 7; Houston *Informer,* Nov. 8, 1941. The monetary impact of these prejudicial views was demonstrated in a report on black businesses in Texas. The report claimed that of the $50 million paid each year by black Houstonians for various goods and services, black customers spent less than $1 million in black-owned stores or in the offices of black professionals. Montgomery, "Possibilities of Improving Negro Business," p. 3.

40. Gunnar Myrdal, *An American Dilemma: The Negro Problem and Modern Democracy* (New York, 1944), pp. 29, 304-305.

"Yes, We Have No Jitneys!"
Transportation Issues in Houston's Black Community, 1914-24

Frances Dressman

An impulsive idea that was begun mostly to fill a gap in the mass transportation systems of America's fast-growing cities, the jitney was always on the periphery of the transportation and business world. Jitneys were privately owned cars that carried passengers over a regular route according to a flexible schedule—a way for a fellow with an old Ford to make a few extra dollars by taking people to town faster and cheaper than the cumbersome streetcars could manage. Jitneys lasted for less than ten years in the United States, but many cities, including Houston, took the interlopers to heart and its citizens soon depended on jitneys to get them where they wanted to go.

By 1923-24, when the Houston City Council gradually abolished the jitney, there were nine lines operating in the city with nearly two hundred drivers—and this was much reduced from the nearly three hundred jitneys in the city in 1918.[1] One of these nine, the San Felipe Line, catered to black Houstonians who could not ride in the white jitneys. This line's jitneys, owned and operated by blacks, were a part of the black community: a business, if somewhat on the edge of respectability and only marginally profitable, that provided a needed service. But Houston's black-owned jitneys were prevented from operating for a year before the white-owned jitneys were forced to shut down, as the black community became the biggest losers in a power struggle involving white business interests and local government.

Jitneys Sweep the Country . . .

Jitneys began on the west coast in late 1914; by the beginning of 1915 they had already spread east to cities like Omaha, Kansas City, San Antonio, and Houston, and the jitney phenomenon had caught the attention of the national press. There were an estimated twenty-five hundred jitneys west of the Mississippi, and, according to a Kansas City citizen, their growth was spurred by the "'public be damned' attitude of streetcar corporations." Indeed, jitneys were born out of the inefficiency of trolley lines; they were popular because they offered, for the same price as a trolley ride, a flexible routing that could deliver people closer to their destinations; and they were deemed "cheap, comfortable and quick."[2] It was only logical that "as the automobile became a sturdier, more powerful product, its possibilities as a money-making passenger carrier were increased."[3]

It was not long before streetcar companies complained about unfair competition because jitneys were not subject to regulation, did not pay taxes like the traction companies, and had no "rolling stock" to maintain. Jitney competition took an estimated $3 million worth of business away from the trolley lines annually.[4] There were questions, too, about the safety of the vehicles and the advisability of adding them to the already congested urban streets. By mid-1915 regulation of jitneys, mostly in the form of hack licenses, had thinned their ranks.[5] Yet while the jitney drivers admitted that it was hard to eke out a living charging so little fare and carrying so few passengers, and although civic and business people wondered how they could maintain their cars and still make a profit, the number of jitneymen continued to grow. Even with regulations, over one hundred cities in the United States and Canada had jitneys, and "in Houston, Texas, 350 cars are reported running under stringent traffic-regulations."[6] For a time at least, jitneys made themselves part of the mass transit system of America's cities.

. . . And Challenge Houston Streetcars

Electric streetcars began operating in Houston in 1891, and in 1900 when the Houston Electric Company took control of the streetcars, there were already thirty-five miles of track.[7] But after 1900, Houston's burgeoning central business district and rapidly growing population put a strain on a mass transit system dependent on the laying of expensive track and overhead wiring. A magazine published by the Galveston and Houston railway companies reported in 1912 that there had been great difficulty in maintaining route schedules due to traffic, narrow streets, few bridges, and many railroad crossings. Add to these difficulties the automobile — on sale in Houston beginning about 1902 — and the city was primed and ready for the jitney when it arrived.[8]

Jitneys became a firmly established part of Houston's transportation system very quickly, as evidenced by the city council's ordinance in June of 1915 revising the city code to add an article on jitney rules and regulations. The ordinance defined jitneys not as licensed hacks but as

> . . . regular transportation . . . that travel up and down the streets soliciting patronage and for a certain fee demanded by those in charge. . . . persons are carried to and from destinations and over routes designated and fixed by said owners, managers and drivers of such vehicles.

Further, the ordinance stated that since public safety was "affected and endangered by unlicensed and unrestricted methods of such use," jitneys must be licensed, have definite routes and schedules, and obey all traffic laws.[9]

Race and Transportation

The black community in particular welcomed the advent of the jitneys. Not only was the new mode of transportation cheap and convenient, but it also offered the means to protest the inequities of segregation on the streetcars. Texas had a long-standing tradition of racial separation in mass transit, beginning with the railroads. Civil rights legislation in the last quarter of the nineteenth century slowly advanced the notion of equal accommodations for equal fare, but separate cars were fixed by both law and custom. In 1903 the City of Houston, supplementing state law, passed an ordinance providing for the separation of black and white passengers on cars in the street-railway company. The revised city code of 1904 designated "separate but equal" compartments, with each divided and lettered, and provided that any person sitting in a car not designated for his or her race was to be charged with a misdemeanor. The law required the use of a moveable screen to separate the races, whites in front, blacks behind.[10] From 1903 to 1905 Houston's black citizens, like those in several other southern cities, responded to discriminatory streetcar ordinances with a boycott.

The boycotts were possible because blacks still dominated the traditional jobs of hackman and drayman in many southern cities. In Houston, "a negro visitor reported that the protestors had developed an informal transit system of passenger vans, wagons and carriages," charging a five-cent fare.[11] Some whimsical black hackmen set aside "whites only" spaces in their cabs, or joshed that they were sorry they could not pick up white passengers, since they did not have screens. However, the boycott neither ended streetcar segregation nor prevented the increase in segregation laws of the following decade, which included the 1913 establishment of separate waiting rooms for the races at Union Station.[12]

The streetcar situation was always volatile in Houston. There were many incidents, and a series of confrontations between black soldiers stationed at Houston's Camp Logan and discourteous streetcar conductors played a significant part in polarizing racial tension, leading to the violent race riot of 1917.[13] In 1919, one of the first issues of the Houston *Informer*, soon to become black Houston's foremost minority paper, featured a front-page story about a black passenger's being assaulted on a streetcar by the conductor and a white passenger. Another editorial in July of that year condemned the nation's common carriers for charging blacks and whites the same fare but giving blacks poorer service. Blacks' "place" on the streetcars was a constant reminder of their oppressed status and thus a constant source of friction between the races.[14]

Jitneys as a Black Business

The black jitneys became a well-established part of the city's transportation system and of black life in Houston. The social and political situation at the time encouraged such black transportation enterprises:

> Because of deteriorating conditions [within the black political situation], there had been a shift in emphasis from agitation and politics to economic advancement, self-help, and racial solidarity, often coupled with a philosophy of accommodation. The development of transportation companies, therefore, functioned in three ways: as a means of protesting against discrimination, as a fulfillment of the dream of creating substantial Negro business by an appeal to racial solidarity, and — hopefully — as a practical solution to the transportation problems faced by the masses of boycotting Negroes.[15]

Jitneys were typical of Houston's black businesses in many respects. They oriented to the black market because of the laws, but they also provided a needed service to that community. They were generally small in size and capital investment, as were most black Houston enterprises. Jitneys were also a facet of the historical pattern of blacks' being employed as public drivers, such as hack drivers and draymen. Jitney drivers were an obvious extension of an ongoing, almost totally black-dominated trade that later evolved into several black-owned taxi firms (such as Hobart Taylor's HT Taxi Service in the late 1920s).[16] The black jitneys were a highly visible and important part of the city's community as a whole, since much of their operation involved getting black patrons to and from domestic and yard work in white neighborhoods. In a 1919 editorial in the Houston *Informer*, editor Clifton Richardson called for the San Felipe Jitney drivers to clean up their appearance, noting that they operated "mostly in white residential areas where protest is imminent." He felt that an "unbecoming appearance" reflected poorly on their race and showed a lack of respect for their black patrons.[17]

Exactly who Houston's black jitneymen were is hard to establish, although the *Informer* and the city and telephone directories are of some use in determining how they functioned. Advertisements for car services appeared regularly in the *Informer*, although it is not certain these were all jitney owners. In several issues in 1921, the paper congratulated a new transfer company, the Red Star Line, operated by Richard Fortson and Johnny Reese and formed from the consolidation of two separate lines. In the 1921 Houston *City Directory*, Fortson is listed as owner of the San Felipe Auto Repair, while Reese is listed as a driver in 1921 and as "service car" in the 1922 directory.[18] A sampling of telephone directory listings for 1918-20 shows over fifty auto livery or jitney companies. It appears that the jitney or car business was a second income for many blacks, including G. B. M. Turner, who was a school principal and whose wife was president of the San Felipe Jitney Association.[19]

One well-known jitney operator was George S. Goodson, who owned several cars. First listed in the 1903-1904 *City Directory* as a porter, Goodson subsequently is listed in the directories and in *Informer* ads as a hack driver (1910), proprietor of a hack line stand at 603 Travis (1912-13), manager of the West End Transfer Company (1919), manager of the Cut Rate Auto Line for "rent cars" at 1515 Prairie (1920), proprietor of the Union Station Auto Transfer Company and operator of an auto repair service and soft drink stand (1922), and owner of a filling station at 610 Heiner (1927). Goodson moved into auto repair and service after the abolition of the jitneys.[20] In addition, during the early 1920s, Goodson's photograph appeared as manager of the Frierson and Company casket company in another *Informer* advertisement, which also included the information, "first class cars for hire by the hour or trip," and three telephone numbers.[21]

While the black jitneymen were small entrepreneurs whose livelihoods often depended on the condition of an old "flivver," they were, nevertheless, part of the black business community and vital to the black community's transportation needs. They were also acknowledged and regulated by the white-dominated city government, but in the coming jitney-streetcar controversy neither their importance to the blacks nor their acceptance by the whites would matter.

The End of the San Felipe Line

Almost as soon as jitneys appeared in the Bayou City, the Houston Electric Company complained of lost profits. By 1919 Luke Bradley, vice president of the company, told the Kiwanis Club that the company was losing $400,000 a year to the jitneys and could no longer "afford nor maintain the line."[22] In September, 1922, the Houston Electric Company made a formal request to the Houston City Council that jitneys be abolished on streetcar lines and within two blocks of these streets. The company said it was unable to continue operation at the same fare, intimating it was not making enough revenue to pay the interest and dividend charges that it needed for its credit standing. Apparently the council had already reduced the number of jitneys by 100 but there were still over 180 cars left.[23] On September 12, "in view of the complications that have arisen one after another, in the matter of the jitney question since 1914," Houston City Commissioner T. L. Waugh suggested "that the proposition be submitted to the vote of the citizens" in a public referendum. But the Houston Electric Company did not want voters to determine its constitutional rights; the company stopped improvements and requested a fare hike from seven to nine cents.[24]

Fares had increased four years earlier, and Mayor Oscar Holcombe vowed to fight this new increase.[25] Houston Electric Company Manager W. E. Wood declared that the company's return was not enough to pay interest on the money borrowed to make the improvements, "let alone pay a return on our investment." The reported dividend to investors had been eight percent.[26] But tempers cooled temporarily as the Houston City Council agreed not to take over the franchise and the company agreed to wait to file for an injunction as well as to provide a complete report, including an accountant's check on operations. A few days later, the council announced that the question of whether or not jitneys should be abolished in Houston would come to a vote at the general election on November 7. Within a week of this decision, however, the council once again changed its mind, and by October 15 the mayor and council had declared the question of outlawing the jitneys dead.[27]

With the jitney question settled for the time being, the city council introduced a motion to accept the streetcar company's proposition that the company resume improvement work immediately if the council would agree to reduce the nearly 190 jitneys operating in Houston to 150 by January 1, 1923. On October 16, under the headline "Streetcar-Jitney Fight Ended," the *Houston Post* reported that Mayor Holcombe and streetcar company officials had worked out a deal. Forty jitneys were to go; the council and mayor declined to say which ones, but it was believed that the reduction would come gradually.[28]

Houston blacks soon found out that the city's plan to solve the jitney dilemma meant the elimination of their line. On November 1, as part of a city council compromise with the streetcar company, eleven of the twenty-three jitneys on the San Felipe Line were ordered to discontinue service by November 15. Then, on November 10, the papers reported that the "Last San Felipe Bus Runs December 15." Under the compromise, the remaining twelve black jitneys and seventeen other jitneys from various white lines would be abolished by December 15, 1922. Even though the black jitneymen, under the leadership of Richard Fortson, got an injunction to prevent the city from revoking their licenses until January 1, 1923 (when they expired), by January 3 the black San Felipe jitneymen were gone. They had been served notice that their licenses would not be renewed, and "officials of the traction company drove around the line to see that the job had been done," making sure that bootleg black jitneymen were arrested and fined.[29] In the spring of 1923, jitney operators were still trying to reestablish the line, circulating a petition to get the issue of its closure put to a popular vote. However, they were unable to get the necessary 3,000 to 3,500 signatures — ten percent of the votes cast in the last city election — even after weeks of trying. Houston's black population was 33,843 in 1920; in his *Informer* editorials, Richardson claimed that there was no lack of qualified black voters, only a lack of interest. Even a good number of the black jitneymen themselves had not qualified to vote because they had not paid the required poll taxes.[30]

Voting for Jitneys

To Richardson, the black vote was the key to the whole situation. When the San Felipe Line was first shut down, sacrificed by the city council to placate the Houston Electric Company, Richardson speculated in an editorial that it was because black jitneymen were poorly organized and unable to resist, and that the series of legal restrictions and qualifications that effectively limited black voting power made black opinion negligible: "If the colored citizens of Houston participated in the mayoralty elections, no such summary action would have been taken."[31] Black citizens might be upset, Richardson reported, but it did not matter because the race was just a football of city officials. White lines were not decimated because "whites could resent the discrimination and confiscatory legislation on election days." His advice: "Pay your poll tax and get ready for the elections of 1923."[32] The chance to vote on the jitney-streetcar issue occurred in the spring.

The reduction in jitneys was not enough for the streetcar company. The city council tried to reroute the jitneys to avoid direct competition with streetcars, but the council members could not agree on routes and in desperation decided to put the issue to a popular vote on June 9, 1923. Simeon B. Williams, writing in May 1923 as "Cimbee," the *Informer*'s own "social observer," ruminated on whether blacks should vote "fer dem w'ite jitney men's what had er chanst ter he'p our black jitney boys an' turnt de cole shoulders ter 'em," or the streetcar company, which was the main reason there were no black jitneys. If he voted with the streetcar company, Cimbee asserted it would not be because he thought they were not making money or because their drivers gave polite service.[33] Richardson felt assured there was little concern among blacks with this election. His paper took no stand on the election, except to remind readers that the white jitneymen had asked for black support, but had not given any to the blacks when the latter had asked them to help keep their line alive. Richardson changed his stand on election day, urging that the jitneys be abolished. He decided that the streetcar company was a "real asset to the community" and "helped the city grow." Taking a position as a civic booster, Richardson forgave the streetcar company for past indiscretions against blacks, saying it was not a question of big corporation versus small business but "equity and dependable transportation facilities."[34]

In the June election, however, the streetcar company lost by 1,100 votes, and the white jitneys remained in business. The Houston Electric Company sought an injunction to restrain the city from continuing to enforce the seven-cent fare, while the mayor traveled around the country to find a transportation consultant—finally hiring one from New York—to investigate the situation. The expert declared the streetcar system efficient, but reported that as long as there were jitneys, the streetcars would continue their fight. Meanwhile, prominent Houston businessman A. S. Moody headed a citizens' committee to work out a solution.[35]

About half of the black votes cast favored the jitneys in the June election, perhaps partly because some white jitneymen held out the hope that if the white jitneys won the June election, the permits of the black jitneymen might be renewed. But black hopes were dashed when, to combat a planned lawsuit to force the city to issue permits for the San Felipe Line, the Houston City Council "in an informal preliminary meeting Thursday morning [June 28, 1923] agreed to meet Thursday afternoon and abolish the line altogether."[36] In their haste, however, the council passed the resolution without the proper signature of the mayor on a letter requesting the council's action on the matter. So the council reconvened the following Saturday, Mayor pro tem Allie Anderson signed the document, and the council voted two to one to pass the resolution abolishing the San Felipe Line. It was a simple matter to eradicate the whole line, which was established by city ordinance. The one "no" vote came from Street and Bridge Commissioner W. R. Britton, who said "he did not think the city should discriminate, especially since the voters have shown they want the jitneys."[37] But the city would brook no opposition from any black jitneymen. With little fanfare, a whole economic enterprise within black Houston and a vital method of mass transit for the black community was gone.

A Change of Allegiance

Meanwhile, the white jitneys were also in jeopardy, despite the public vote in their favor. A. S. Moody's citizen's committee worked out a plan whereby the Houston Electric Company would resume its improvements and withdraw its suit for a fare increase, in return for the city's abolishing all jitneys. This bargain was approved by both bodies, and the council agreed to a second vote on jitneys on January 19, 1924. Moody said the "transportation problem is an economic one and should be settled in a businesslike manner without allowing a lot of extraneous matter to confuse the issue."[38]

Six weeks away from the January referendum, Richardson launched into high gear with weekly editorials telling his readers to vote for the traction company and against the white-owned jitneys. If the jitneys were retained, he foresaw increased streetcar fares, lack of adequate transportation, and loss of potential growth for the city. A *Houston Post* editorial concurred, saying that when all the transportation needs of a city had been put on the jitneys, they had failed to provide adequately.[39]

But Richardson's real point was that one white power structure had put the black jitneys out of business and another should not also be allowed to keep the black community from the only means of transportation left to them: the streetcars. He noted that jitneys did not employ blacks, gave no money to black causes, and were above the law, as "no other public carriers in Texas are permitted by law to operate without making provisions for the accommodation of both races." A full-page advertisement loudly proclaimed: "Help Houston Grow! Vote to Abolish the Jitneys." This ad and others placed by the Colored Citizens Club and the Houston Electric Company were carried in Richardson's newspaper up to election day. Richardson painted the traction company as a benificient patron of the black community for its jobs and philanthropy, while pointedly noting that the white jitneys had never done any of this.[40]

In the week following the election, Richardson reported that the jitneys had lost soundly by a general margin of two to one, and by a vote of over three to one in the black community. "[The] part the colored voters played in the election is not only an encouraging sign, but also a redeeming one," he wrote. Most of the blacks who voted had cast their ballots in favor of streetcars this time, whereas the previous year more than half of them had supported the jitneys. Even the former San Felipe jitneymen who had hoped to have their line reinstated after the earlier vote were supporters of the ordinance to abolish jitneys altogether. This election was a good sign that black indifference to civic matters was on the wane, Richardson felt, adding that the traction company now had to try to assure better service for *all* its patrons and extend lines to the new black neighborhoods.[41]

The demise of the jitney was probably inevitable as urban areas grew, technology improved, and big business ruled the marketplace. But although all jitneys were abolished, the attention given by civil authorities and citizens to the effects of the white jitneys' demise was much greater than that given to the ending of the black jitneys. The closure of the San Felipe Line highlights two important, ongoing issues in the black community: segregation in mass transit systems and the effort to establish black businesses.

The black-owned jitneys served a need not adequately filled by the established transportation system, and thus were of significance to the whole black community. They were small, service-oriented businesses with little capital and certainly no political leverage. These facts, and the lack of support from the black community, perhaps caused by years of having no effective political voice, left the black jitneys vulnerable. Like the jitneys, black business at this time remained fragile and on the fringe — barely avoiding being undone by government, by white business, and especially by economic adversity. Houston sacrificed the black jitney business for the sake of progress and civic improvement, and no significant voice was raised in protest. With the end of the San Felipe Line, a thriving business enterprise had been wiped out, without any thought given to its economic or social impact.

As in the case of the jitney-streetcar controversy, public transportation with its separate-but-equal segregation was a focal point for racial inequality throughout the United States. The black community found adequate transportation difficult to achieve, whether on the streetcars with their signs, screens, and incidents, on the jitney lines so easily abolished, or on newer forms of mass transit. The transportation controversy did not end in Houston with the jitneys; the same news story that announced their demise promised the addition of buses to the streetcar lines. But the buses initially excluded black passengers, despite the efforts of local black leaders to obtain separate compartments or separate buses. When members of the white elite in River Oaks protested that their black servants could not get to work and petitioned city council to establish a separate bus line for them, some blacks were then allowed to ride the buses. However, it was not until 1932 that the Houston City Council amended the ordinances to allow blacks segregated bus transportation.[42] The black jitney line was easily abolished, but the larger issue of mass transportation for Houston's blacks would remain an issue for many years to come.

Notes

1. Writer's Program, Works Progress Administration, *Houston: A History and Guide* (Houston, 1942), p. 115.
2. "The Jitneys," *Literary Digest* (Feb. 13, 1915), pp. 302–303; "The Jitney,"

New Republic (Feb. 13, 1915), pp. 43-44; "The Jitney," *World's Work* (Apr., 1915), pp. 618-19; Stanley I. Fischler, *Moving Millions: An Inside Look at Mass Transit* (New York, 1979), p. 39.

3. Fischler, p. 39.

4. "The Jitney," *World's Work* (Apr., 1915), pp. 618-19; "The Jitney 'Bus' and Its Future," *American Review of Reviews* (Nov., 1915), pp. 624-25; Fischler, p. 167.

5. "The Jitney 'Bus' and Its Future," pp. 624-25; *Literary Digest* (July 3, 1915), pp. 3-4.

6. "The Jitney 'Bus' and Its Future," pp. 624-25; *Literary Digest* (July 3, 1915), pp. 3-4; "The Jitney Unprofitable," *Literary Digest* (June 19, 1915), pp. 1509-10.

7. Fischler, p. 75.

8. Peter Papademetriou, *Transportation and Urban Development in Houston, 1830-1980* (Houston, 1982), p. 28.

9. City of Houston, Jitney Ordinances, June 16, 1915.

10. August Meier and Elliott Rudwick, *Along the Color Line: Explorations in the Black Experience* (Urbana, Ill., 1976), pp. 267-68; *Charter of the City of Houston* (Houston, 1903); *Charter and Revised Code of Ordinances of the City of Houston* (Houston, 1904); James M. SoRelle, "The Darker Side of 'Heaven': The Black Community in Houston, Texas, 1917-1945" (Ph.D. diss., Kent State University, 1980), p. 93. See also SoRelle, "'An De Po Cullud Man Is In De Wuss Fix Uv Awl': Black Occupational Status in Houston, Texas, 1920-1940," *Houston Review* 1 (Spring, 1979) 1:15-26.

11. Meier and Rudwick, pp. 273-74.

12. Ibid.; David McComb, *Houston: A History* (Austin, 1981), p. 109.

13. Robert V. Haynes, *A Night of Violence: The Houston Riot of 1917* (Baton Rouge, 1976), pp. 64-68.

14. Houston *Informer*, June 7, July 12, 1919.

15. Meier and Rudwick, p. 274.

16. SoRelle, "The Darker Side of 'Heaven,'" 259, 268; Meier and Rudwick, p. 273. A brief mention in the Houston *Informer*, Jan. 1, 1921, shows that jitneymen were an organized group that contributed to the community. The paper reported that the San Felipe Jitney Association had donated $15.00 to the municipal Christmas tree for colored children and had donated gingham material for the girls of the Dorcas Home.

17. Houston *Informer*, July 5, 1919.

18. Ibid., Feb. 19, 1921; ibid., Mar. 12, 1921; *Houston City Directories*, 1920-22; *Houston Classified Telephone Directory*, Fall, 1921.

19. *Houston Classified Telephone Directory; Houston City Directories;* Houston *Informer*, Jan. 8, 1921.

20. George Nelson, telephone interview with author, Mar. 17, 1986; *Houston City Directories*, 1903-27.

21. Houston *Informer*, Mar. 6, 1920.

22. McComb, p. 74.

23. *Houston Post*, Sept. 6, 1922.

24. Houston City Council Minutes, Book U, Sept. 12, 1922.

25. *Houston Post*, Sept. 22, 1922.

26. Ibid., Sept. 23, 1922; McComb, p. 107.

27. *Houston Post,* Sept. 30, 1922; ibid., Oct. 3, 15, 1922; *Houston Chronicle,* Oct. 1, 1922.

28. *Houston Post,* Oct. 15-17, 1922; Houston City Council Minutes, Book U, Oct. 16, 1922; *Houston Chronicle,* Oct. 17, 1922.

29. *Houston Post,* Nov. 2, 10, 1922; *Houston Chronicle,* Nov. 26, 1922; ibid., Jan. 3, 1923; Houston *Informer,* Nov. 11, 1922; ibid., Jan. 6, 1923; ibid., Jan. 5, 1924. Apparently the San Felipe jitneymen had run bootleg operations after their licenses were not renewed, as the *Houston Chronicle* reported on June 28, 1923.

30. Houston *Informer,* Apr. 7, 14, 1923. Comparative population figures can be found in Jesse O. Thomas, *A Study of the Social Welfare Status of the Negroes in Houston, Texas* (Houston, 1929), p. 8.

31. Houston *Informer,* Nov. 11, 1922.

32. Ibid., Jan. 6, 1923.

33. Ibid., May 26, 1923; *Houston Chronicle,* Jan. 20, 1924.

34. Houston *Informer,* June 2, 9, 1923; SoRelle, "The Darker Side of 'Heaven,'" pp. 351-52.

35. *Houston Post,* June 9, 10, 1923; *Houston Chronicle,* June 21, 1923; Jan. 20, 1924.

36. Houston *Informer,* Dec. 22, 1923; *Houston Chronicle,* June 28, 1923; City of Houston Jitney Ordinances, June 30, 1923.

37. *Houston Post,* July 1, 1923.

38. *Houston Chronicle,* Jan. 20, 1924.

39. Houston *Informer,* Dec. 8, 1923; *Houston Post,* Dec. 3, 1923.

40. Houston *Informer,* Dec. 22, 29, 1923.

41. Ibid., Jan. 26, 1924; *Houston Chronicle,* Jan. 20, 1924.

42. SoRelle, "The Darker Side of 'Heaven,'" pp. 95-96.

Houston's Colored Citizens: Activities and Conditions among the Negro Population in the 1920s

Clifton F. Richardson, Sr.

Editor's Introduction

Clifton F. Richardson was born in Marshall, Texas, and graduated from Bishop College, a popular all-black school located in his hometown, with a degree in journalism. Shortly thereafter, like many other Texans of both races born in small towns and rural areas around the state, Richardson sought his future in urban America and moved to Houston. After gaining some working experience in the newspaper business, he founded the weekly Houston Informer *in 1919 and served as its managing editor. Subsequently he shared the ownership of the newspaper with partners, among whom was another recent migrant to Houston, Carter Wesley. After a bitter falling-out with his partners, Richardson lost control of the paper. However, almost immediately, in 1930, he established a rival weekly newspaper, the* Houston Defender, *which he owned and managed until his sudden, unexpected, and premature death in 1939.*

    Richardson was one of black Houston's leading and most outspoken activists. He served as president of the Houston chapter of the National Association for the Advancement of Colored People and was a founder and member of the board of directors of the city's Negro Chamber of Commerce. He also served on the executive committee of the National Negro Business League and was affiliated with many other local, regional, and national organizations. Although only a small fraction of his correspondence survives, his editorials in both the Informer *and the* Defender, *as well as the other portions of those newspapers, remain invaluable primary sources for events and developments concerning black Houston during the 1920s and 1930s. The following article originally appeared in August, 1928, in* Civics for Houston, *a progressive white magazine that was briefly published in the Bayou City.*

With the largest colored population of any city in Texas — variously estimated from 55,000 to 60,000 — "Heavenly Houston" can rightfully boast of as intelligent, thrifty, substantial, upstanding, law-abiding, and patriotic a group of colored citizens as can be found in any other city in America, without regard to geographical lines or location. This is as it should be, for the progress, peace, growth, and well-being of this community are indissolubly linked and intertwined with the black race; since it is an accepted fact that no community or social order can rise, permanently, above its lowest member.

A recent survey of colored business enterprises in twenty southern cities, made under the auspices of the National Negro Business League of which Dr. R. R. Moton of Tuskegee Institute is president, reveals that Houston tops the list with business concerns owned and operated by members of the colored race.

Professionally, colored Houston has twenty-two physicians, fourteen dentists, seven registered pharmacists, and four lawyers. These professionals are graduates and post-graduates from some of the leading colleges and universities of the country, including Harvard, Yale, Columbia, Pomona, Illinois, Chicago, Northwestern, Howard, Meharry, Pennsylvania, Fisk, Bishop, Wiley, Prairie View, and other institutions of learning.

According to available statistics, more colored citizens own or are acquiring homes in Houston than in any other purely southern city. It is further estimated that Houston's colored population has approximately $7,000,000 deposited with local banks and financial houses.

The religious or church life of colored Houstonians has been given the most prominent place on the racial program, resulting in about 116 churches of various denominations. Frankly and candidly, the writer holds to the opinion that "colored Houston" is top-heavy with churches. The leading churches of the city are: Antioch Baptist, Rev. E. L. Harrison, pastor; St. John Baptist (Dowling), Rev. S. A. Pleasant, pastor; Bethel Baptist, Rev. J. R. Burdette, pastor; Trinity Methodist Episcopal, Rev. J. H. Lovell, pastor; Wesley Memorial African Methodist Episcopal, Rev. J. B. Butler, pastor; Bebee Tabernacle Colored Methodist Episcopal, Rev. L. G. Porter, pastor; Mt. Corinth Baptist, Rev. A. Hubbard, pastor; Brown's Chapel African Methodist, Rev. L. J. Sanders, pastor; Boynton Chapel Methodist Episcopal, Rev. T. M. Jackson, pastor; St. Nicholas Catholic, Father Carl Schappert (white), pastor; Gregg Street Presbyterian, Rev. J. H. M. Boyce, pastor, and other smaller churches of many and sundry denominations.

The residential sections inhabited by colored citizens, which, during the last two or three years, have received considerable civic consideration and physical improvement, are still lacking (many of them) in the permanent type of improvements so essential to the moral, physical, civic, and aesthetic welfare of the community. Rent houses are built in such close proximity to each other that one can stand in one house and hear the inmate in the adjacent house change his mind. This is both literally and figuratively true!

If the city of Houston has an ordinance on its statute books regulating and prohibiting this method of building houses for tenants, the law is neither invoked nor enforced when it comes to rent houses for colored citizens. Surface privies are still ubiquitous in many sections occupied by colored residents, while drainage is extremely bad in most of these colored sections, with cesspools and ponds of stagnant water that seldom dry up between rains.

Street lights are few and far between, and the resultant darkness obtaining in these colored neighborhoods becomes a potential and actual incubator of crime and criminals; for the Holy Writ is true when it proclaims the doctrine that evildoers prefer darkness to light. These districts have very little fire and police protection, and it is becoming increasingly difficult for colored Houstonians to get much fire insurance upon their homes and household effects.

Furthermore, the jamming of houses so close to each other, as is done by some avaricious landlords, renders and maintains such districts as fire menaces and hazards to the entire city; for most conflagrations that wreak havoc to cities usually have their beginnings in such ghettos and quarters.

In the face of such unhealthy and unsavory living conditions, the death rate among colored Houstonians is alarmingly high, and the city government and public-spirited citizens should immediately address themselves to the holden task of rectifying and remedying these conditions as a matter of self-preservation, if from no other motive.

Emancipation Park, located at Dowling, Tuam, and Elgin, Third Ward, which the colored citizens of the community bought years ago and turned over to the city during the Campbell administration, is the only colored park in the city. Though under municipal management and control, the city has done very little towards beautifying and improving this park.

Through the generous gift of Hon. J. S. Cullinan, white local philanthropist, the colored citizens of this community have in the Houston Negro Hospital the most modern and novel eleemosynary institution of its kind in the country. Mr. Cullinan donated a building costing $80,000, and the city council provided land valued at $25,000. The hospital is run by a colored board of directors, assisted by a white advisory board. Mrs. M. H. Bright, formerly superintendent of nurses, is now superintendent of the hospital, and the colored board members are J. W. Hubert, president; H. P. Carter, vice-president; C. H. McGruder, secretary; W. E. Miller, treasurer; Rev. E. L. Harrison; Rev. J. S. Scott; and C. F. Richardson. A. J. Johnson is financial agent, and Dr. H. E. Lee, local colored surgeon, is chief of the hospital staff.

This hospital, located at Ennis and Elgin, Third Ward, is the first unit of a proposed health center for Houstonians of color, and the following inscription on the bronze tablet at the institution very clearly and succinctly sets forth the spirit and object of the donor: "This building, erected A.D. 1926 in memory of Lieutenant John Halm Cullinan, 344th F.A., 90th Division, A.E.F., one of the millions of young Americans who served in the World War to preserve and perpetuate human liberty, without regard to race, creed or color, is dedicated to the American Negro, to inspire good citizenship and for the relief of suffering, sickness and disease amongst them."

Houston has a colored branch of the Young Women's Christian Association, located on the ground floor of the Odd Fellows' Temple, Prairie Avenue and Louisiana Street. This organization maintains a cafeteria, assembly room, social hall, and employment bureau at its downtown quarters, and it operates a residence at 406 Saulnier Street. Under the leadership of Miss Doris B. Wooten, former executive secretary, this organization has done and is still doing a wonderful piece of religious, social, and community work.

The Colored Young Men's Christian Association occupies a three-story brick building at Prairie Avenue and Smith Street, where constructive work is being done for the colored men and boys of the community. Gilbert T. Stocks, Morehouse college graduate, is executive secretary. Both of these organizations have outgrown their present limited quarters and are in dire need of buildings in keeping with Houston's prestige and standing.

There are three colored weekly newspapers published in Houston: *Texas Freeman,* C. N. Love, editor; *Houston Sentinel,* J. M. Burr, editor; and the Houston *Informer,* which is edited by the writer. The *Informer* is printed in its entirety in the printing plant owned and operated by the Webster-Richardson Publishing Co., publishers and printers, 409-411 Smith Street. This plant is said to be the most modern and best equipped owned and operated by the race in Texas. In addition to the newspapers, there are eight job printing offices run here by colored printers.

The following colored lodges have more than $1,000,000 invested in buildings, alone, in Houston: Grand United Order of Odd Fellows, Louisiana and Prairie; United Brothers of Friendship and Sisters of the Mysterious Ten, Milam and Prairie; Knights and Daughters of Tabor, Prairie near Milam; Ancient Order of Pilgrims, West Dallas and Bagby; Ancient Free and Accepted Masons, Schwartz and Providence. Subordinate lodges of these and other colored fraternal organizations have several halls here.

The Lincoln Theatre, 711 Prairie Avenue, of which O. P. DeWalt is proprietor and owner, is rated as the finest exclusive colored playhouse in the South.

Colored Houstonians are known far and wide for their musical ability

Teacher Pinkie Yates with her class at Colored High School in Houston's Fourth Ward, circa 1910. *Courtesy Houston Public Library, Houston Metropolitan Research Center*

and talents, and they boast of the premier musical organization of the South — the Coleridge-Taylor Choral Club, composed of nineteen trained singers and musicians, with Mrs. P. O. Smith, popular music teacher, as directress. In Miss Ernestine Jessie Covington, local musical prodigy and thrice winner of the Juilliard Musical Foundation annual award of $1,000 for advanced musical study under the music masters in New York City, Houston has an artist who has already taken front rank among the leading pianists of the country. Miss Covington, the only child of Dr. and Mrs. B. J. Covington, 2219 Dowling Street, is also an honor graduate from Oberlin Musical Conservatory, Oberlin, Ohio.

Civic improvement associations are being fostered in some of the populous colored residential sections, and though rather sporadic in their activities, they are doing much to inspire the race along the lines of civic beautification, health, hygiene, and sanitation.

Houston has three colored senior high schools (something that no other city in America possesses), one [colored] junior high school, and the only municipally owned and operated colored junior college in the entire world. There are also seventeen elementary or grade schools (public) here for colored scholastics, with the largest colored teaching personnel of any city in the entire South—if, in fact, any other southern city approaches Houston in this respect.

At the recent commencements of the Washington and Jack Yates senior high schools, the graduating classes numbered 116 and 106 respectively, or a total of 222—the largest number of colored high school graduates ever turned out by any city in the United States at one commencement.

Houston offers the colored group the greatest opportunity of any southern city for industrial employment and commercial and professional activity. There are about ninety colored postoffice carriers here, one postoffice clerk, two postoffice terminal clerks, thirty railway postal clerks with headquarters in this city, among whom are fifteen clerks-in-charge; to say nothing of mail weighers, mail truck drivers and other postal employees.

There are four plain clothes officers of color on the local police force, two patrolmen; one public school physician; three nurses with the Social Service Bureau; three nurses at Jefferson Davis County-City Hospital; three nurses connected with the public schools; one family case worker with the Social Service Bureau; three workers at Bethlehem Negro Day Nursery.

Additional parks should be provided in the Fourth and Fifth Wards for colored citizens, and the colored residents of the Heights should have a park. There is no swimming pool provided for our colored population, although playground activities are being conducted at two or three of the ward public schools.

Housing and living conditions among the colored residents of Houston should be surveyed and studied in the immediate future, and the findings made a basis for a well-defined program for the amelioration of these shameful, shocking, and startling conditions under which thousands of colored Houstonians are forced to live and eke out a bare existence.

Additional colored patrolmen should be added to the local police force to patrol colored districts on all beats, and thus minimize the danger of clashes between minions of the law and colored citizens.

With its extremely large colored population and their various and varied activities and achievements, it is next to impossible to give a free and full account in such an article as this, but the writer has endeavored to give the readers of this magazine a graphic cross-section of Houston's colored citizenry, who constitute an important and integral part of our heterogeneous and polyglot population.

Sidelights on Houston Negroes as Seen by an Associate of Dr. Carter G. Woodson in 1930

Lorenzo J. Greene

Editor's Introduction

At 2:30 on the afternoon of September 4, 1930, Lorenzo J. Greene arrived in Houston, driving an old Model T Ford and accompanied by two students. Greene and his companions had been on the road since June. Their mission was to raise money for the struggling Association for the Study of Negro Life and History by peddling books on black history throughout the country. They also hoped to raise the historical consciousness of blacks and to persuade local schools to add books on black history to their curriculum. The success of their undertaking was limited—Carter G. Woodson apparently gave the expedition only his "skeptical blessings" and belittled its importance and seriousness. Nevertheless, Greene and his partners persisted. While the financial impact of their efforts is unknown, as is their impact on school curriculum, Greene did leave a written account of his journeys, which provides interesting insights into black life in the early years of the depression. This alone made his trip worthwhile.

Lorenzo Johnston Greene was born in Ansonia, Connecticut, in 1899. He received his bachelor's degree from Howard University in 1924, and he received both his M.A. in 1926 and Ph.D. in 1942 from Columbia University. In addition to his life-long affiliation with the Association for the Study of Negro Life and History, he served black history as an educator (primarily at Lincoln University in Jefferson City, Missouri) and as a scholar (for years he edited the Midwest Journal *and in 1942 wrote* The Negro in Colonial New England, 1620–1776*). From 1928 to 1933 he served as Carter G. Woodson's research associate at the Association for the Study of Negro Life and History. He was em-*

ployed in this capacity when he undertook the trip that brought him to Houston in the late summer of 1930.

Houston in 1930 had just ended one of the most exciting and successful decades in its history. The opening of its deep water port in 1914 and the city's emergence as the industrial and corporate center for the booming Texas oil industry added to the general prosperity of the 1920s to create a growth spurt in Houston that saw its population soar from 138,276 in 1920 to 292,392 ten years later. While blacks certainly were not the primary beneficiaries of the city's economic success, they did share in it. Black population grew by more than 85 percent during the decade. Black education benefited both from a major program of school construction and renovation and from the establishment of the Houston Colored Junior College in 1927; black business, fraternal institutions, and churches engaged in a construction program that created the black-owned buildings that so impressed Greene. While the depression moderated Houston's boom, and while the city's blacks suffered disproportionately during the hard times, the Houston that Greene described in 1930 seemed relatively unscarred by the depression except, of course, for the growing problem of unemployment.

The Houston that Greene saw was almost totally invisible to most whites of that period. Indeed, there is no evidence from his journal entries that he ever encountered a white Houstonian or that white Houstonians were even aware of his presence in the city. This is not surprising. Black Houston in 1930 was a city unto itself. White Houstonians certainly knew that blacks lived in the city—they knew the districts where they lived and, perhaps, the schools that their children attended. Most even knew a few blacks, at least superficially, as domestics, gardeners, waiters, or as janitors or unskilled workers at the office or the plant. But few, if any, white Houstonians in 1930 had any real knowledge of black life in the city.

Greene's essay exposes a segment of black Houston to us. In the two weeks that he stayed in the Houston area, Greene met with most of the significant personages in black Houston, including businessmen, labor leaders, ministers, and educators. His impressions of the city and its inhabitants are always interesting and often insightful. As an articulate and observant outsider, he provides a perspective on black Houston that is, unfortunately, rare, while his youthful energy, impatience, and sometimes naiveté add color and humanity to his comments. Although

Greene does not provide a definitive look into all aspects of black life in Houston—his contacts and experiences are almost entirely with the middle-class—he does furnish us with a tantalizing but brief glimpse into the black experience in Houston.

Greene presented the following extract from his diary, with brief introductory comments, as a paper at the 1986 annual meeting of the Association for the Study of Afro-American Life and History held in Houston. The editors are indebted to Thomasina Greene, Dr. Greene's widow, for permission to publish it. A longtime friend of the Greenes and an active member of the association, Arvarh E. Strickland, is preparing a complete version of Dr. Greene's diary for publication.

In June 1930 I left the Association for the Study of Negro Life and History in Washington, D.C. with four students, in a used Model T Ford loaded with books on Negro History. We departed with the skeptical blessings of Dr. Carter G. Woodson, founder and Director of the Association.

Our purpose was to help maintain the solvency and ongoing of the Association, to prevent it, if possible, from becoming a victim of the Great Depression. To do so, we were 1) to induce state boards of education to adopt books for schools, 2) to enlighten people about the history and culture of the Negro, 3) to sell the books of the Association thereby helping to keep the Association financially afloat.

Starting out with $12.00, our odyssey lasted ten months, during which we covered most of the South, Middle West, Pennsylvania, and Delaware.

Thursday, September 4, saw us enroute to Houston, Texas. Part of the Diary was lost but a few observations follow:

Thursday, September 4, 1930

Left Austin at 6:30 after giving Oliver Lagrone instructions to work Austin and San Antonio. John Poe and Wilkey accompanied me to Houston.

Reached Prairie View about 112 miles from Austin about 10:30. This is the seat of Prairie View State College for Negroes. There is nothing here but the school. Largest Negro Land Grant College—1450 acres. Some fine buildings, but they are thrown up helter skelter....

Met Dean Austin, Head of the School of Liberal Arts, a Mr. Reeves, whom I had met at Alabama State Normal who teaches education here, and Mr. Southern, a "frat" brother.

Mr. Reeves introduced us to Mrs. Banks, wife of the President, T. R. Banks. The latter is in Galveston, attending an Institute. The Banks have a very pleasant home, rather large. Mrs. Banks told me there is already a considerable interest here in Negro History. Used to have a Negro History program during the entire month of February. Now it lasts only 17 days. Became boresome. The library, she said, has many of our books, but was sure her husband would take mine. School opens next week, September 11. She wants me to return to address the faculty and students. Promised her I would.

Next I saw my "frat" brother, Mr. Southern. He took us to a much welcome dinner in the cafeteria. Good meal. Southern showed me around the campus. Pointed out the new mechanical arts building and the hospital. There are two resident physicians, two nurses, a surgeon and a pharmacist, all paid by the state. The administration building, sorry to relate, is an old stone structure. The boys' dormitory is fair; so are the toilet accommodations.

Reached Houston at 2:30. Saw Dr. Peacock, Dr. Joe Gathings, and Dr. Davis. First two were college-mates of mine at Howard University. Dr. Davis is the brother of Marylou Davis of Shreveport, Louisiana, whom I had met earlier. Had lots of fun, after they had recovered from the shock of seeing us. Dr. Gathings is doing well. Practicing here two years. One of the best surgeons here. Dr. Davis secured us a room on Dowling Street. We didn't like it. Couldn't change, for we were "broke." I have had to "carry" Poe. Poor fellow! His money "ran out" in Waco.

Went to a party. Could not enjoy myself because of lack of money. Moreover, had not had suit pressed. Felt very self-conscious. Met a Mr. L—— who teaches at Prairie View. Told me salaries are very low there. Range from $80 to $120 a month and teachers must board themselves and pay room rent. Earn less than teachers in city schools here. Maximum is $1600. That is the minimum for whites. There are three senior high schools here, Mrs. Scott, a teacher, told me, and one Junior High School. Poe became enamored of lovely Miss Johnny Mae Newton, a Fisk graduate. I could not blame him. Her complexion was a treat to the eyes.

Retired, after writing in diary, about 12:30.

O, yes! Received two letters from Dr. Woodson. Told me he had received requisitions for *The Rural Negro*. Was sending them to New Orleans.

Was also sending the blanks that I ordered from Waco. Then wanted to know what is being done with them. Angered me when he asked whether we are distributing them among children to play with. Said we must be having a fine time with the ladies, judging from the letters coming to the office.

I shall write Dr. Woodson and give him an equal amount of sarcasm in return. This trip is netting me nothing financially. It is being done by me solely because of my deep interest in and devotion to the Association. He cannot see that, however, or else every little thing bulks so large that it occludes his vision. It is such petty things which will impel me ultimately to sever connection with Woodson and tell him to go to hell.

Friday, September 5, 1930
Rose at 6:30. Wrote in Diary until 7:30. I had 73 cents. Ashamed to meet the landlady because we could not pay her. For breakfast we sat in the car and ate a few grapes and graham crackers. Bought a gallon of gas. Reduced the exchequer to 15 cents.

Called on John Harmon. He keeps a store on West Dallas Street. He told me it was a department store. Did not seem like my idea of a department store (Macy's or Gimbels) as everything was on one floor. Yet it is an effort in a field entered into by very few Negroes. Harmon is married. Eloped. Wife is very charming and hospitable. Harmon cashed a five dollar check for me. Took me to his bank.

Told me employment situation here is very bad. 2,000 Negroes out of work. General depression the cause. Says Houston has become second largest city in the South and the largest in Texas. Ship canal has taken priority in shipping away from Galveston. Latter was dependent upon cotton for huge volume of trade. The ship canal makes Houston a great port. Ocean-going ships can now come into the interior and load this staple which formerly had to go through Houston to Galveston by rail. Most of Galveston's trade now is that which comes from the far western or southern part of Texas. It has been totally eclipsed as a port by Houston. And to think that before the ship canal was constructed, the volume of Galveston's trade was second only to that of New York.

Harmon took us to dinner at the "Nu Way" Cafe, following his wife's failure to prepare lunch for us at the store. Like most women, she desired to show up to best advantage and have us take dinner with her Sunday. The proprietor of the "Nu Way" Cafe, Smith, has succeeded in driving out of business two Greeks who thrived upon Negro trade. The result is he serves a great quantity and variety of food. No quality. I did not enjoy my dinner, for neither the place nor the food attracted me. It is patronized chiefly by laborers.

Passed by Pilgrim's Life Insurance Company's building on West Dallas Street. An imposing office building. The most beautiful, owned by Negroes, I have yet seen. It has a unique style of architecture. I must add, too, that the Odd Fellows also have a fine building on Milam Street.

Had been trying to get to Galveston all morning. But, being without money, was detained. Gave Poe money to pay our room rent. We are going to leave our present lodgings. Don't like either the tenants, landlady, or the location of the house.

Returned to Harmon's store after filling car with gas and oil. Was ready to leave for Galveston. Mrs. Harmon, telephoning, told me she had a prospect for me. Tried to put it off until tomorrow that I might go to Galveston. Could not. Therefore I went to see Mr. G. V. Henry, a railway mail clerk. Has a fine house on Shepherd Street. Told me of economic plight of Negroes here, which is terrible. One third out of work. Even street work is done by whites. Once in a while, Negroes can be seen driving garbage wagons but that is infrequent. Says trash gangs are nearly all white and Mexican. Recalled coming into a town where a railroad bridge was under construction. All laborers were white. Informed me Mexicans have so hurt Negroes in San Antonio, that wages are terribly low and Negroes have little or no work. Only labor which Negroes have real hold on in Houston is loading and unloading ships. Such work is heavy and in the sun. Whites and Mexicans dislike it. Negroes are well paid, however. Sometimes can make $12 a day. Work is irregular, however. Depends upon ships entering or leaving the harbor. Told me Mexicans' haven is railroad work. Too hot for Negroes. Strange because the Negroes had been enduring the heat until the depression. I considered it a case of cheaper labor by the Mexicans whose standards of living are lower than the Negroes just as theirs is lower than the whites (generally).

Mr. Henry bought the books. Told me he is usually a hard man to sell. Told me to see Mr. White, another railway clerk. He duplicated the order after I had persuaded him to buy the books for his son. Asked me, upon Mr. Henry's suggestion, to speak at the meeting of postal employees tonight about 9:30 at the Odd Fellows Hall. Felt I might be able to sell something. I promised to be there.

Called upon Mrs. Johns, secretary of the Y.W.C.A. A fine woman. "Y" is in Odd Fellows Temple. Very attractively furnished. Mrs. Johns knows many people with whom I am acquainted, including the Rev. Vernon Johns, Gladys McDonald, Miriam Atkins, Ned Pope and others. The latter is now engaged in social work; has been here several times, in fact. Comes here two or three times a year. Mrs. Johns says the "Y" expects to build within the next few years. Needs building badly to care for social problems here. Mrs. Johns is interested in starting a Negro History Club. Wants me to speak here at Houston upon my return from New Orleans. She and Carter Wesley, lawyer, newspaperman, etc., whom I met last night, will sponsor it in connection with Reverend Pleasant. I am to see them tomorrow morning. Mrs. Johns took a set of books for the Y.W.C.A.

After dinner wrote Woodson. Referring to his sarcasm in respect to the use made by us of the subscription blanks, I said, "I am at a loss to understand your very excellent sarcasm in this respect. If you expect that for every subscription blank which *leaves* the office, a corresponding order will *enter* the office, then I see that you know nothing about practical selling in the field. Since you are ignorant of this fact, let me enlighten you. Some people, when interviewed by the agent, do not find themselves in a position to buy at that time. Some do not intend to buy. However, they will often ask that we leave blanks which they will forward to the office with the initial deposit before the sale ends. And *we leave them.* If this may be called distributing blanks or souvenirs for juveniles, then we plead guilty. And it shall continue until *you* order otherwise, since we are interested in arousing the interest of these people in our work, even if we are not able to sell them. You ought to know that a subscription blank in the hands of an interested person, can mean an order when a book on Negro History or some kindred topic is needed."

Referring to his ironic statement concerning our advertising the office through the fair sex, I wrote: "Yes, the ladies are advertising the office. And we *are* having a lovely time. My love letters kindly hold until my return that I might choose the lady who offers most, fiscally." I felt better after writing him this letter. Some day Woodson may learn how to deal with his subordinates but I fear death will cut short its consummation.

Returned home. Nice house, but on a terrible street. Dress after waiting ¾ of an hour to get into the bathroom. Rushed out. Spoke to railway mail clerks. About 12 present. Sold three sets of books. Mr. Walls, the president, promised to take a set later today. Pleased with the day's work.

From the meeting went to a dance. Saw no one who interested me until Miss Johnny Mae Newton introduced me to Miss Ella Robey. Both girls are beautiful. Miss Newton's complexion is a thing of beauty to behold. Shall call Miss Robey tomorrow. Is a school teacher here. A Bishop graduate. Returned home at 12:45. Retired about 1:20. Houston, I believe, will be a good town for business.

Saturday, September 6, 1930

After breakfast, called on Mr. Carter Wesley, who had promised to arrange for a meeting for me here next Sunday. It is so difficult to find one's way about Houston that I actually passed his office several times without knowing it. Wesley is a man of diversified interests. A graduate of Northwestern University, he is a lawyer, real estate man, publisher, and insurance man, among others. And he is a *young* man only about 35, I should judge. He introduced me to Mr. Webster, Mr. Atkins, and the entire office force associated with him. Made a fine publicity man for me by telling them all about my work with Dr. Woodson.

Tried next to sell them the books. Mr. Webster squirmed out of it by pleading "lack of time," he had to go to the bank, prepare the payroll, and so forth. Then failed — perhaps deliberately — to be available at 2 P.M. at which time he had promised to see me. Mr. Wesley, after expenditure of much persuasion by me, finally succumbed when I appealed to his ego. Told him that his name listed [among the purchasers] would induce others to do likewise. He took a set, to be sent him C.O.D. ($9.98) in November.

Mrs. Workman, formerly a school teacher in New Orleans, now head of one of the departments in the insurance company, also took a set to be sent C.O.D. October 5.

From Mrs. Workman, I went to the Pilgrim Temple to see Professor Ryan. Found him in the most beautiful, colored-owned building that I have ever seen. A fine, golden-colored brick building, triangular in shape, standing at the apex of West Dallas and Bagby Streets. Is four stories in height with a roof garden. Its interior amazed me, for here was a real attempt at beautification, such as few other Negro-owned buildings can boast. The very lifts of the steps were decorated; the walls were inlaid with white marble and granite. The elevators, too, were the roomiest and most elaborate that I had seen in any "race" building. There were stores, of course, on the first floor, one a white-owned pharmacy.

I told Mr. Ryan, who is also Secretary of the Pilgrims Life Insurance Company, how much I admired the structure and how I ranked it first among those I had seen, owned by Negroes. Thanked me and told me that there must be resident in my comment some truth, for several people, who are qualified to know, had told him the same thing. Ryan is stoop-shouldered, rather thickly set, with a large head, sitting upon broad shoulders. His complexion is brown. He seemed to be an inveterate smoker, puffing on a long cigar during our entire conversation, while his straw sailor hat sat on the back of his head.

Told him of my mission. Recounted the gist of the books to him. He bought them readily.

Went back to Odd Fellows Building. This is also a fine structure on Louisiana Avenue. Clean too. Could do nothing there. Went then to Bastrop Street, after securing directions from Miss Henry. Found Mr. Walls. Had been expecting me. Is a mail man, President of the Postal Employees here. Said post office was rotten when he entered it years ago. The old-time Negroes had made it difficult for a young, intelligent, colored carrier to get a job. Were "hat in hand" Negroes. Took all manner of abuse and would remove caps when delivering mail into office buildings. Tried also to keep young Negroes out. White superintendent would not hire intelligent colored men. Preferred more ignorant ones who were more pliable. Walls got on, however, organized the Postal Employees Alliance, fought to break the power of the old Negroes, and brought in men who were eager for promotions through efficiency, rather then holding their jobs through their obsequiousness. Refused to take off his cap, when entering office buildings. Considered it part of his uniform, like a soldier. Whites tried to prevent his delivering mail in business district. Failed.

Alliance, through his persistency, caused a shake-up in the office here two years ago. Succeeded in bringing the post office inspector from Washington, D.C., to Houston. The result of his (latter's) investigation was the dismissal or demotion to carriers of all the supervisors and even of the superintendent himself. The inspector congratulated Walls.

Told me that Negroes could have had a post office supervisor position but none was qualified. W. E. Scott was the only one so fitted but, unfortunately, he was addicted to drink. There was a fine opportunity for a Negro to gain such a position, for of all those fired, according to Mr. Walls, not one had the qualifications for the position.

There are in Houston now, Mr. Walls informed me, more than 100 Negro mail carriers. This is more than half of the total force which stands at about 200. In contrast to this imposing showing, there are only 8 Negro carriers in San Antonio, the second largest city in the State; none in Dallas or Fort Worth and none in Waco.

This is not because of prejudice, according to Mr. Walls, but largely because of the inclination of the Negro to follow the path of least resistance. Afraid of a little resentment by whites. Complained they could not get application blanks. If such were so, they could have been secured with ease from New Orleans or Washington. The chief reason is, Negroes do not take the examinations. If many took the exam and passed among the first three, they would stand an excellent chance of getting on. Where only a few take it, of course, such a consummation is minimized. An example of mass examination taking was described by Mr. Walls when he told me that, as soon as examinations are announced, the Alliance gets the examination blanks and distributes them among the Negroes. At the last examinations held, 1400 Houston Negroes took them. Of these, 600 passed and nine were put on as carriers.

Walls has already manifested his worth to the service by a suggestion which, when adopted, saved the post office the services of more than 200 substitutes for three hours in getting out the extra heavy Friday mail. Where they had hitherto worked five hours on Monday delivery, he had them come in two hours on Sunday and arrange the mail. The postmen, saved this trouble, had nothing to do but deliver the mail. The Superintendent congratulated him upon his practical suggestion. Walls also told me he asked the superintendent for Negro supervisors. Latter told him it would be hazardous for him to do so, since there were none before he came. Promised to give Negroes monopoly on carrying the mail.

Walls threatened to hold him to his promise. Says another vicious practice among the whites, in order to keep Negroes from promotion, is to give them freedom to break the rules, wink at it, then hold these infractions as a club over their heads when seeking higher positions.

The Alliance tries to correct this by persuading the carriers to observe the rules. Walls even attacked the superintendent about it. He is a very interesting speaker and impressed me as a hard and conscientious worker.

I easily sold him a set of books. Said he would not be without them, since he had children.

From Walls, I called upon Rev. Pleasant. Said to be the most active Negro minister here. Told me a meeting could be held at his church next Sunday at 3 o'clock. Bought a set of books to be sent September 15, $9.98 C.O.D.

I then hastened to the Y.W.C.A. to see Mrs. Johns but she had gone, having waited for me until four o'clock. Carter Wesley had left too. Failing to get in touch with them by telephone, I called upon Professor Fox, head of the Junior College here. Thinks Howard University is the finest black school in the country; I agreed. Fox was graduated from Howard in 1904, a classmate of Dean Dwight Holmes. Fox says Houston has three colored high schools. It is the only city in the South in this respect. Teachers must all have degrees to teach in the elementary schools. Fox kept me talking an hour. Bought nothing.

The streets of Houston are terrible. This applies of course to the Negro section. They are mostly unpaved and many of them are as narrow as alleys. They are death to automobile tires with crushed rocks just dumped into holes and even on the surface. The section around George Street is horrible. Drinking water in many cases is out-of-doors; so are the toilets. The same can be found in some streets all over town. The homes, of course, vary from fine brick or frame structures to hovels. All in all, however, the Negroes are more progressive here than anywhere else in Texas.

I want to go to New Orleans today but Poe has sold nothing, which detains me. I believe he is doing more socializing than anything else. Can't "carry" him much longer, for I too must live.

Negroes, due to the lack of employment, are steadily converging upon the cities looking for work. Today I met a young fellow from Sante Fe, New Mexico. Had been doing well working on a ranch shearing sheep for 70 cents a pound of wool. His sister induced him to come to Houston. Jobless for weeks, he finally found work as a hod carrier. Hard work. Such laborers get 40 cents an hour. Much of this went for car fare, which is 10 cents here.

To add to the glutted market, whole families of Mexicans in Ford touring wagons, or what not, have crossed the border and flocked to the cities, displacing Negro workers by their willingness to work for wages varying from one quarter to one half that paid Negroes.

Monday, September 15, 1930
After breakfast, I called upon Dr. B. J. Covington, father of Jesse Covington, the well-known pianist. He had given me his card yesterday, and

invited me to call upon him. The doctor is an elderly, dark man of medium build, who resembles my Uncle Tom (Coleman). I told him so. He marvelled, but remarked it might be possible, for his father was sold South from Virginia and he had no recollection of any relatives.

All too frequently that did happen in slavery, for antebellum Virginia, says Bancroft, was one of the leading slave breeding states for the lower South. Dr. Covington congratulated me upon my speech of yesterday, saying he thought it was extremely informing. His favorable comments gave me the cue to ask him about the books. He replied that he would have to consult his wife and daughter. The latter is the well-known pianist, Jesse Covington.

During our conversation, I remarked that Houston Negroes had the greatest potential for development of any group of Negroes I had yet seen in the South. He agreed but stated that there were many things which nullified, to some extent, their advantages. Racist attitudes especially toward Negro women here, he added, are such that, if he can help it, he does not ride with Mrs. Covington on the street cars, because his wife, like any Negro woman, is prone to be insulted by any person with a white skin. Worse, it is impossible for him or any Negro to be a man in the presence of his woman. For any Negro to resent such an insult whether he be husband, father, brother, or sweetheart, would be tantamount to suicide. Just last week, he went on, a wealthy, Negro woman, driving a fine car, was ordered by a policeman to take her car off Main Street, and leave it on Milam Street (in the Negro district) where the "niggers" belonged. She was infringing upon no law, therefore took the officer's number and reported the incident to the chief of police. That officer did nothing. A citizen committee of Negro men also waited upon the Chief to the same end. All the satisfaction they received, however, was that he would investigate the matter. Later it developed that he did not know *who* was on duty there at that time. It is such things as this, according to Dr. Covington, which make the Negro's situation in the South so insecure, that it is equivalent to sitting on a volcano. One never knows when an eruption will occur. If he could have secured reciprocity from the State of Illinois, the doctor added, he would have left the South long ago. But an examination is now required of all older physicians and he feared he could not pass it. I left Dr. Covington, but his words made me realize, as never before, the racial dilemma faced daily by Southern Negro men who love their women yet who feared to protect them against the insulting advances of the most ignorant white man.

Later I called upon Dr. Forde, a West Indian physician. He regretted he could not subscribe, but introduced me to his friend, Dr. Roett, also from the West Indies. The latter is tiny; I daresay he weighs no more than 100 pounds. Roett expressed much interest in the books, especially *African Myths*, which he wanted for his son. I would not stop at that, however; it was the set I desired to sell him. He suggested I come back tomorrow morning after he had consulted with his wife. I always fear such a maneuver. The wife in such cases usually kills the sale. Further, I believe if the man is writing the check, he ought to be able to decide for himself, and make his wife a present of the books. However, I shall see to the doctor tomorrow.

Off then to the Y.W.C.A., where I met three very charming ladies, a Miss Jefferson, Miss Hill, and a Miss, (whose name escapes me). Mrs. Johns, the Director, apologized for the small audience last night. I reassured her, however, that she should not feel badly about yesterday, since she had put forth every effort to make the meeting a success. She replied that the teachers showed absolutely no interest in it. I knew that; so does Woodson, which is one reason for our book-selling campaign. Although she had called many teachers personally, inviting them to the meeting, generally they retorted that they knew everything about "niggerology." No one could tell them more. God help them! (Most of them are Prairie View graduates, which means that their Negro education is relatively meager.)

Later I made an attempt to see Mr. DeWalt, the movie theater owner. He was too busy, but promised to see me at two o'clock tomorrow afternoon. Taking leave of DeWalt, I tried to find Henry Lee Moon and Poe, whom I was to meet at Harmon's Department Store at that hour. Unfortunately, I got there ten minutes too late.

I then stopped at Bill Jones' filling station. Jones is an interesting old man who spoke at the Democratic Club meeting Sunday. He styles himself a "race" man, patronizing Negro business exclusively. Said he once paid a white doctor $12 just to taste the medicine a Negro physician was prescribing for his wife. Since she showed little signs of improvement, friends advised him to engage a white doctor, claiming the Negro physician was "killing" her. To appease them, he engaged a white doctor, informing him of the Negro physician and the medicine he had prescribed for his wife. Asked whether the Negro doctor had prescribed the proper treatment. White doctor tasted the medicine. Told Jones he would have prescribed the same. It cost Jones $12 to have the medicine tasted but it confirmed his faith in the Negro physician.

Told me also of the arrest of his son on a flimsy murder charge in Michigan. Jones' friends advised him to get a white lawyer. Others admonished him to let his son hang. Jones did neither. Secured colored lawyers — Harold Bledsoe of Detroit, a classmate of mine, and another. His son was acquitted and once more his confidence in his race was vindicated. So staunch a race supporter is he, that Jones says he lost twenty-five cents on a case of soda water, in order to patronize a Negro establishment. That was during the time he kept a store.

Interesting man. Could have talked to him indefinitely. Jones promised to come to hear me speak tomorrow night and to take a set of books. Introduced me to his daughter who came by just as I was leaving.

From Mr. Jones, I called upon Professor W. L. D. Johnson, Principal of Blackshear School. He was registering students for Junior High School. Could not see me until tomorrow morning at 7:30. Promised to take a set then.

Dr. Martin, the druggist who promised to take a set last Saturday and pay cash, pleaded an unexpected financial obligation. I grinned but persuaded him to take a set $9.98 C.O.D. on October first. He may take them and then he may not.

En route to dinner, I met Miss Jefferson and Miss Boozer, Y.W.C.A. workers. Chatted with them for 15 minutes. Miss Boozer is charming.

After dinner I had an engagement with Miss Gladys Davis, to whom Mrs. Harmon had introduced me. Poe had to get a haircut before going to see Miss Newton. The upshot of the matter was that Henry Lee Moon had to drive me to Miss Davis' home, then return for Poe to take him out to Miss Newton's. Moon was supposed to return for me. After spending a few hours with Miss Davis, who proved a delightful companion, I returned home by trolley and foot. When I reached there, Poe and Moon had already arrived. They expected I would be "peeved" but I came in laughing. They had gone for me, but were told I had departed about ten minutes earlier.

Tuesday, September 16, 1930

This proved to be a pretty full day. My first task after breakfast was to call upon Mr. Covington. Although he told me his wife wanted but one book, he ended by taking a set. From there I went to Dr. Forde's office. In the interim, I had sent Moon and Poe away in the car with instructions to meet me at John Harmon's Department store on West Dallas Avenue, at 2:30. I jotted down a couple of topics at Dr. Forde's office, while Miss Landy, his office girl, smiled and talked with me.

I then called upon Dr. Roett, the brilliant West Indian physician, who is smaller than I. He asked me to return at 6 P.M. On my way downstairs, I met Carter Wesley and James Nabrit, who had sponsored the meeting for me on Sunday. They took me to dinner at the Y.W.C.A. Nabrit, who had been Dean of the College at Pine Bluff (Arkansas A.M.&N. College), told me that Howard University, among Negro institutions, paid the biggest salaries. I replied Tennessee State did. Nabrit remarked he had been offered $3,000 to teach Political Science at Howard. I doubted it. My friend Ralph Bunche, a Harvard M.A., took the position in 1929 for only $1,800 a year. (Mr. Nabrit later became President of Howard University.) Salaries at Howard, I contended, are, and have been, low, comparatively speaking, on account of the relatively small appropriation for such, from federal funds. We argued to no conclusion.

After leaving Nabrit, Mr. DeWalt, the colored theatre owner, who sat at a table behind us, called me. I told him I had been trying to get an audience with him for almost two weeks. He invited me then and there to his office. He claims to have the best Negro-owned theatre in the South. He escorted me through the building; it is large, well-decorated, and contains the latest sound-recording equipment.

I spent two hours talking with Mr. DeWalt, although both of us pleaded "busy." He emphasized the precarious economic position of the Houston Negro, his difficulty in finding jobs, and commented upon the utter levity with which the Negro viewed his position. He was laughing, said DeWalt, while Rome burned, dancing while his very economic foundation was crumbling beneath him. DeWalt considered the Negro teacher almost hopeless, unconcerned with Negro History and its benefits for the Negro children. Most of the teachers, he added, assume a "know-it-all" attitude, while the children, who come to them seeking inspiration, instead are crushed by the vicious propaganda circulated about Negroes in the textbooks they use.

He spoke of the failure of the Standard Life Insurance Company, adding that he was a director of that ill-fated business. It also had a Bank and Trust Company as well as the Insurance Company. At the first board meeting, DeWalt said he warned against the evil of interlocking directorates, at the head of which were bishops, including Bishop Hurst (now deceased). Seeing that the same directors were at the head of the Banking and Trust Company, the parent company, and the Insurance Company, he tried in vain to have it changed. However, he successfully protested against directors coming from Atlanta to meetings at the company's expense and succeeded in having the three directors reduced to one. The Company also distributed dividends of 20% before it was able to do so. When the 1929 crash came, DeWalt said it was the result of poor business management. Here Moon told me later that Robert R. Moton, successor to Booker T. Washington at Tuskegee, tried in vain to save the Company. In desperation he sought the aid of Julius Rosenwald, philanthropist, of the Rosenwald Fund. But when he learned that $250,000 was necessary to save the Company, Rosenwald withdrew his support.

Mr. DeWalt subscribed, although he had two of the books. I substituted two others for them. He asked me to be sure to call upon him when I again came to Texas. A fine man, with good business acumen, yet has never attended a business school. He is a graduate of Prairie View College.

I phoned John Harmon and asked him to tell Henry Lee Moon and John Poe to meet me for dinner at 3:30. Later I called upon Mr. McGruder,

Grand Secretary for the S.M.T. or something (a fraternal organization). He took a set and referred me to the President, Mr. Robinson. During a long talk, he told me that he knew Maude Cuney-Hare, the author of "Antar of Araby," one of the poems included in the set of books. Robinson was also a good friend of her father, Mr. Cuney, who he added, excelled as a politician and an orator in Galveston, Texas. Robinson later regretted his inability to subscribe, pleading lack of funds. Later I called upon Mr. Davis of the same order; a very humorous, kind, and interesting man. I sold him so easily, that he said I made him part with his money quicker than any person he had ever known.

Leaving him, I went thenceforth to Dr. Roett's office. While waiting for him, the mother of his office girl, who goes to Fisk, came in. I tried to sell her, but she gave me the old answer: "Will see you later."

When Dr. Roett was available, he told me he could take but one book, *African Myths*. That was letting him off too easily, therefore, I stayed with him until I persuaded him to write a check for $4.00, initial payment on a full set. He has a boy and I played upon that knowledge.

It was now 6:30. I rushed home to eat dinner which I did in ten minutes. Poe and Moon had already eaten. I had one hour to jot down notes, dress, and get to the hall where I was to speak. On my way home, as will happen when one is in a hurry, we suffered a flat tire, which delayed us fifteen minutes. Arriving home, I made a few notes, changed my shirt, and hurried to the hall.

When we reached the hall, I found the crowd disappointing. Still I spoke more than an hour on "Present Unemployment Among Negroes: Causes and Remedies." I was applauded; the people told me I was wonderful. I felt as if I had done fairly well.

C. W. Rice, the head of the Colored Laborers' Association, who sponsored the affair, also spoke. He is an eloquent speaker, very emotional. I think he would make a good preacher, is heavy-set, dark and of medium height. He wanted to take me from church to church here with the speech I delivered. I told him I had no speech, just notes. Rice invited me to speak at the Teacher's Convention in San Antonio, in November. He is trying hard to save jobs for Negroes here, but he has a difficult task on his hands. Dr. Shadoner, a pompous man, sporting a goatee, then spoke and read letters from a Houston banker, a Galveston merchant, and a Texas and Pacific railroad official, purporting to give the people confidence in Rice. Rice is very long-winded, talks so much he ruins a man's speech. He gave me $6.00, pleading that the crowd was small. I shall speak no more, however, without setting a price in advance. Moon had to leave to keep an engagement. Poe and I went home. Moon was still out at 11:30 when I retired.

Wednesday, September 17, 1930

Immediately after breakfast, I called upon Dr. Shadoner, to secure his order for a set of books. This wealthy doctor does not have as well-equipped an office as Drs. Covington, Forde, and the others. He pleaded "broke" after congratulating me upon my speech, but I persuaded him to let me send him a set of books ($9.98 C.O.D.) by October 1st. There is always more than one way of getting these fellows.

I went over to Carter Wesley's office in the International Longshoremen's Association building. He is a progressive young man, scarcely 32 years old. As I aforestated, he is interested in insurance, newspapers, and financial companies. I wanted him to cash some checks, but he was not in. I did see Mrs. Workman, however. She had a letter already addressed to me with a money order enclosed. She gave me the $4.00 instead. It was welcomed. Mrs. Webster, the assistant editor of the newspaper, also subscribed. She had promised to take a set Saturday before last, but did so only after much coaxing and even then, it was $9.98 C.O.D. She may or may not accept the books when received, and whether I shall receive my $4.00 commission is problematical.

From there we stopped by Mr. DeWalt, the movie owner, who told me that after my speech last night, business and professional men should pay all of my expenses. He invited us to attend his theater *gratis* and also invited me to stop with him whenever I visited Houston.

We left Houston about 3:00 P.M., after pulling a deal with a filling station man, whereby I secured a fairly good tire to replace one that had been badly worn. The proprietor asked $1.50 difference, but I "beat" him down to $1.25. Think I got the better of the bargain. Hope I did, at least.

Now to take stock of Houston: a big, sprawling city — largest in Texas, second largest in the South. The total population is about 300,000, of whom approximately 70,000 are Negroes. The latter form the most enterprising and most appreciative group of colored people in the South. Some idea may be gleaned by the subjoined jottings:

Negro Business: There are about eight colored gasoline filling stations here, one finance company, several chain drug stores, independent drug stores, several insurance companies, beauty shops, two hat shops, one dry goods store, ten or more groceries, one soda water manufacturer, several ice and fruit dealers, and a theatre. The busiest Negro lunch room in the South is here. It is called the "New Day."

Schools: Houston has the best Negro school system in the South. It comprises about twenty schools, including three senior high schools and one junior college. They are all large, airy, brick or stucco buildings. This is especially true of the Phyllis Wheatley High School, which for sheer artistic beauty, surpasses any colored school that I have yet seen, even Dun-

The 400 block of Milam in downtown Houston was a center of black businesses, including a clothing and dry goods stores, a photographer, a physician, and a dentist. Pictured circa 1910 are men who worked there and who were also members of a choral group at Trinity Methodist Episcopal Church on Travis Street, the oldest black church in the city. In the center, holding a cigar, is Stafford Harrison, who later volunteered for duty in WWI and was killed. *Courtesy Houston Public Library, Houston Metropolitan Research Center*

bar High School in Little Rock. There are more than 400 Negro teachers. Nearly all have degrees. Indeed, no person can now teach here, not even in the grades, without a degree. This fine system is due to the efforts of Mr. Oberholtzer, a native of Pennsylvania, who is Superindendent of Eduation for the city, and who formerly held that position for the State of North Carolina.

Library facilities: Houston has the largest colored public library in the South. What it needs is a younger and more energetic librarian.

Amusements: Most of the recreational facilities include dance halls, miniature golf courses, pool rooms, etc. The best Negro theatre in the South is here, owned by Mr. DeWalt. All, of course, are segregated.

Politics: Negroes can vote here, but many will not pay the poll tax to avail themselves of the privilege. This is a common fault. A movement is on foot here under the auspices of the Negro Democratic Club to correct this failure. If Negroes *would* vote, it would go far toward correcting some of the many inequalities which they endure.

Labor: Most of the Negroes are engaged in common labor, such as stevedores, laborers in factories, filling stations, garages, stores, porters, janitors, etc. Most of the women are domestics. Some men and women work in laundries. But Negroes are hard pressed economically. Whites are driving garbage wagons, cleaning streets, serving as waiters in hotels and restaurants, acting as doormen, working on road construction, and on railroads; in short, doing all sorts of work that Negroes formerly did. C. W. Rice, the labor man, has Negro Houston fairly well aroused over this situation; but in general, although thousands of Negroes are out of work, they laugh, dance and drink corn whiskey, he tells me, while their economic foundation is crumbling about them. To add to their economic woes, large numbers of Mexicans are coming in and taking over their work. About 10,000 to 15,000 Negroes according to Rice are unemployed.

Race Relations: Very good here for a Southern city.

We arrived in Galveston about 4:40 P.M., crossing from the mainland to the island upon which Galveston is built. What a beautiful sight across the water as we sped over the bay! The city is beautiful. Wide streets with stately palm trees in the center lead into the city. It is very well laid out, the streets being either numbered or lettered.

Jobs are scarce here for Negroes. Work at the wharves has been reduced, due to the competition of Houston as a port and the lower dock rates at the municipal piers there. Then, too, Mexicans, Italians, poor whites, and others, are taking this work more and more from Negroes since the Depression. Port Arthur, Beaumont, Corpus Christi, and Orange all are cutting down Galveston's once vast commerce, due to their development as ports, and reducing jobs for Galveston's Negro laborers correspondingly. Most of the latter are dependent upon loading or unloading ships, chiefly with cotton. There are huge warehouses and cotton presses here. Negroes, I am told by a Negro janitor, have been driven out of the hotels. Whites have taken their places. I had a chance to verify this statement during a drive along the beach. Not a Negro was seen in the hotels as waiters or bellboys.

I endeavored to sell Dr. Mosely a set of books. He passed the decision on to his wife, whom I easily sold. I failed to see the doctor afterwards for he was called out on a confinement case.

After dinner I called upon Professor G. W. Gibson, the principal of the High School. He lives in a white neighborhood on the main residential street of the city. He is an elderly man about 75. And what a wealth of experience and knowledge he has! He had heard Wendell Phillips, the great abolitionist orator, speak at Wilberforce University in 1877, where he had enrolled as a student in 1876. Bishop Lee taught him. Later Lee became president of Wilberforce. He knew Maude Cuney-Hare well. She is the author of "Antar of Araby" which appears in *Negro Plays and Pageants*. He taught her. Mr. Cuney, her father, was a personal friend of Professor Gibson's. Cuney was the "biggest" Negro in Texas. Few, said Gibson, excelled him in handling white men. He was also one of the greatest forces in organizing Negro schools, and was the founder of the Cotton Screwmen's Association of Galveston, which made it possible for whites and blacks to work together harmoniously on the wharves. When he died, said Mr. Gibson, more white men followed his funeral cortege than ever has occurred here for any person, black or white. He died about 1897. Cuney lived on Avenue J, a few doors from Professor Gibson. The latter invited me to speak to his students tomorrow morning at 8:30. I promised to do so. I left, very much impressed with Professor Gibson.

After securing a room at the Orlando Hotel (God help us) where we paid just 50 cents a night, Moon and I went down to get a view of the gulf at night. We drove along the boulevard which borders the gulf. The city is protected by a sloping sea wall about 12 feet high. All along the beach are imposing and picturesque hotels, most of Spanish design. The colored people also have a dance hall and a few homes fronting the boulevard. But, just as the pavement usually ends where the Negro section begins, just so were the beautiful lights on the boulevard discontinued in front of the Negroes' property. In the white hotels, all the help we saw was white.

After driving along the beach and watching the swishing waves of the gulf from a distance, Moon and I walked down a pair of steps, until we sat just above the huge rocks against which the relentless waves rolled and broke unceasingly. The water was beautiful. It was bewitching. There was no moon and the white-capped billows, starting afar out on the black water, appeared like great lights shining in the distance. Then suddenly they took shape and began their surge landward. As they rolled nearer, they seemed to stretch out lengthwise at a furious pace, until they reminded me of legions of enormous snow-white horses galloping madly down the gulf, only to swerve and pour their foaming, undulating forces against the shore. But terrific as were their onslaughts, the immovable rocks met their countless charges, received their tremendous impact unshaken, and hurled their watery ranks backward, broken now and reduced to a fine spray. There was something in the relentless courage and tenacity of the water that seemed to grip and hold me. I remarked to Moon, that, though these same waves now retreated again and again, like beaten gladiators, they would return with greater force for the next onslaught and continue to crash against these rocks until, ages hence, they would ultimately triumph, by reducing these seemingly irreducible crags to fine and shimmering sand.

Both of us left with a deeper appreciation of the spiritual, and with a more assured conviction that after all, despite His various appellations, there existed a greater One than man somewhere, regardless of His nature, who rules wisely over the destinies of us mortals.

Thursday, September 18, 1930
At 8:15 I was in the office of Principal J. W. Gibson at the Central High School, where I was to speak to the student body upon some phase of Negro History. The school is a large white stone building and makes an imposing appearance from the outside.

While waiting for the assembly period, Professor Gibson told me some very interesting things about himself, which were reinforced by certain plaques, certificates, and commissions hanging on the walls of his office.

In the first place, he served as Consul for Liberia here for 20 years, having been appointed by President William McKinley on August 12, 1901. His commission from Liberia also hangs on the wall and bears the signature of President J. W. Gibson. He also served as a four-minute speaker during World War I and has a certificate of honor from the Federal Government, and a letter of congratulations, signed by President Woodrow Wilson, bearing date of November 29, 1918. This letter commends him for his valuable services during the War. Mr. Gibson also has the dubious honor of having been the only man to "whip" Jack Johnson, former Negro heavyweight champion of the world. Jack was formerly a pupil of his, went as high as the fourth grade, but would go no further. Mr. Gibson said he had to whip him for fighting, the very field in which he was to rise to world renown. Gibson told me that many times he regretted doing such, for he might have thereby crushed Johnson's pugilistic talents.

It was now time for me to speak. I addressed about 600. They gave rapt attention, although for a moment, they were amused by my embarrassment caused by a maladjustment of a portion of my wearing apparel. Perhaps I did well, for one of the teachers congratulated me afterwards, told me that I must have been a Lincoln (Pennsylvania) man. They are noted for an oratorial ability which I sorely lack. Mr. Gibson told me that I could have held the students there all day. I felt encouraged because I knew it is difficult to keep the attention of high school students when one is speaking to them. I remember how boresome it was from my own high school days. Professor Gibson tried to persuade me to stay in town to speak at his church Sunday, but I told him it was impossible. He then subscribed to a set of books for the school library.

His next act was to show me through the school. First we went to the Library. It is called the Rosenberg Library, in honor of Harry Rosenberg, a Swede, who came to Galveston in the 1850's, became a slave owner, amassed a large fortune, and bequeathed $500,000 for a library for whites.

Negroes and white friends fought to gain funds from the bequest for a Negro library. They were successful enough to secure a school library, which is also open to the public. Mr. Gibson is in charge. Naturally, it is small and inadequate for the demands made upon it. The school's chemistry and physics laboratories are well equipped. The laboratories in particular were in excellent condition. I accompanied Mr. Gibson through the carpentry shop, the sewing department, domestic arts department and other mechanical areas. All made a fine impression upon me. I took leave of Mr. Gibson with regrets, for he is full of historical information.

We went therefrom to the post office where I sent a report to Dr. Woodson, including the largest single number of orders yet — 19; Poe sent 15. The number ought to be heartening to Woodson.

Part IV

Segregation, Violence, and Civil Rights:
    Race Relations in Twentieth-Century Houston

Introduction

Historical Overview

Not all Houston blacks quietly accepted the denial of their civil rights. Many protested various aspects of segregation, sometimes subtly, sometimes more aggressively. Even as segregation was being established in the city in the late nineteenth century, some black citizens resisted limits on their rights. Beginning in the 1920s there was an almost constant struggle, first against the inequality that accompanied segregation, then against segregation itself. Houston was not the site of the dramatic confrontations that characterized the civil rights movement in the 1950s and 1960s, and black Houstonians did not hold leadership positions in the national civil rights movement. However, events in Houston, especially the legal struggle for black suffrage, not only illuminate local developments but also demonstrate the degree to which the antecedents of the movement for civil rights can be found in locations besides Montgomery, Birmingham, and Atlanta. They also illustrate the manner in which national events affected events in local communities.

The Struggle against Segregation in Houston

Houston blacks were in the forefront of the legal struggle to overturn restrictions on black suffrage. In the years following Reconstruction, even though they ceased to hold public office, some local blacks continued to play an active, though diminished, role in the Republican Party. For example, between 1876 and 1912, three black Houstonians—Richard Allen, John M. Adkins, and M. H. Broyles—served as delegates to the National Republican Convention. Allen also served on the Rules Committee of the 1876 and 1884 conventions. However, by 1908 the conservative, "lily-white" faction had gained control of the Republican Party in Texas and had eliminated blacks from influential positions in the state Republican organization.[1]

Blacks also found their influence at the ballot box diminished in the early twentieth century. Unlike other southern states, Texas never completely prohibited blacks from voting. However, the implementation of the white primary for local and state elections severely limited the political impact of blacks. Although they could and often did vote in general elections, their exclusion from the primary in a one-party state effectively negated their political power. In the 1920s when the white primary was fully in place, blacks devoted much of their energy and resources to the struggle against this impediment to their political rights. In January of 1921 the City Democratic Executive Committee of Houston approved a resolution expressly prohibiting blacks from voting in the next primary election. C. F. Richardson, editor of the Houston *Informer,* condemned the decision as a direct violation of constitutional rights, while C. N. Love, editor of the *Texas Freeman,* joined with a group of local black leaders to file suit against the chairman of the Harris County Democratic Party.[2] This suit was the first step in a legal battle that would last almost a quarter of a century and involve Houston's black newspapers, much of its legal talent, and many of its civic leaders. Many black Houstonians blamed their early setbacks in this struggle on the failure of the national office of the NAACP to cooperate with local black leaders in pushing the legal struggle to the level of the Supreme Court.[3] In 1940, however, after raising sufficient funds from local branches of the NAACP and obtaining the full cooperation of the national office (including the services of attorney Thurgood Marshall), Houston blacks launched their final assault on the white primary. On November 15, Marshall filed suit in federal court on behalf of Dr. Lonnie Smith, a local dentist and NAACP member, against the election judges in the Fifth Ward precinct where Dr. Smith had attempted without success to cast his vote in the Democratic primary election. On April 3, 1944, the Supreme Court ruled in the case of *Smith* v. *Allwright* that any effort to exclude blacks from voting in a primary election was a violation of the Fifteenth Amendment of the United States Constitution. That summer, for the first time in many years, black Houstonians went to the polls and voted in the Democratic primary without experiencing any major problems.[4]

The victory in *Smith* v. *Allwright* did not lead immediately to black political power. Although several blacks were elected precinct judges in neighborhoods with a predominantly black population, for the next twenty years blacks would win election to major offices only rarely. Between 1948 and 1965 blacks competed in eighteen races but won in only three. The first black in the twentieth century to win to a major position was Hattie Mae White, elected to the school board in a citywide race in 1958. For the most part, however, blacks did not take advantage of the newly re-

Helen Glover Perry conducting a voter registration drive at a well-known nightspot, Club Matinee, circa 1961. Perry was active in voter registration drives beginning in the late 1940s. Such drives were organized by the Fifth Ward Civic Club on the city's northeast side and registers received five cents for every person they registered. *Courtesy Houston Public Library, Houston Metropolitan Research Center*

gained right to vote—at least not immediately. Instead, for many years after *Smith* v. *Allwright* the majority of blacks in the city remained politically apathetic. Initially only a handful of middle- and upper-class blacks paid the poll tax and registered to vote. Although black voter registration increased at a slow but steady pace during the 1950s, it would not be until the mid-1960s that black voting strength was sufficiently marshaled and organized to elect black candidates or to influence the election of whites on a regular basis.[5]

Two developments increased black political power in post–World War II Houston. First, the NAACP conducted a series of voter registration drives in an effort to increase black voting in the city. The most successful of these drives, following the 1966 Voting Rights Act and the division of the state into single member legislative districts, achieved measurable results. The following year Barbara Jordan won election to the Texas Senate and Curtis Graves gained a seat in the state House of Representatives. By the mid-1970s five black Houstonians represented their city in the state legislature, one held a seat in Congress, and a large number held elected or appointed positions in local government. In 1971 Judson Robinson, Jr., became the first black in almost a hundred years to be elected to the Houston City Council.[6]

The second development that increased black political influence in the city was the organization of several black political pressure groups. The first of these, the Harris County Council of Organizations (HCCO), was formed in 1949 to conduct voter registration drives and voter education programs. It achieved its greatest success through a candidate endorsement program. As black voting strength grew, more candidates, both black and white, sought the endorsement of the HCCO and similar black political action groups. By the mid-1970s the endorsement of these organizations became almost essential to win the black vote—a factor that more and more frequently determined the outcome of citywide elections.[7]

During the 1920s and 1930s Houston blacks also attempted to mitigate some of the effects of educational segregation. Community leaders did not challenge segregation per se, but they demanded that separate facilities be equal. They focused their efforts on ending the discrepancies in teacher salaries. While black teachers and administrators were usually reluctant to complain about their pay publicly, as early as 1919 the black press and several prominent blacks protested against the wage scale. As a matter of policy, black teachers were paid only about 60 percent as much as white teachers, even though they taught the same curricula and performed the same duties.[8] After obtaining improved facilities during the massive school building and renovation program of the mid-1920s, in the early 1930s the Houston *Informer,* the local chapter of the NAACP, and the Houston Negro Chamber of Commerce tried unsuccessfully to correct inequities in teacher pay. No real progress was made in resolving this issue until the early 1940s, when a group of elementary school teachers finally joined in the demand for salary equalization. In 1943, threatened with a lawsuit that they did not think they could win, the school board gave in to the demands of the black teachers and raised their salaries to the level of their white counterparts.[9]

Most blacks avoided direct confrontation during this period of segregation, but this was not always possible. One continuing problem was the relationship between the black community and the police. Blacks in the city complained that they faced regular harassment and verbal abuse from policemen, sometimes to the point of police brutality. Black newspapers, especially C. F. Richardson's Houston *Informer,* frequently publicized these incidents and blamed them on the caliber of men hired for the city's police force. In 1938 the *Informer* charged that the Houston police force consisted mainly of "ex-convicts, discarded police officers from other towns, roughnecks, and a few earnest men, green and untrained in the duties of a police."[10] Black leaders attempted to address these problems by pushing for the prosecution of officers guilty of brutality and by adding black officers to the force to patrol black neighborhoods.

Police brutality was related to the worst example of racial violence in the city's history—the 1917 riots. Trouble began when northern black soldiers stationed at Camp Logan, just west of downtown Houston where Memorial Park is today, encountered Houston's version of segregation. Tension between black soldiers and local whites increased for several weeks before violence erupted. The riot was triggered by rumors that a Houston policeman had killed a popular black soldier in the Fourth Ward. Although the rumors were false, earlier encounters between the soldiers and the local police made them believable. On the evening of August 25, 1917, approximately a hundred armed black soldiers marched down Washington Avenue and then down San Felipe, toward downtown Houston, determined to obtain vengeance against the police and against white Houstonians in general. Before the army restored order, sixteen whites and four blacks lay dead, and eleven more whites were seriously wounded. In the series of courts-martial that followed, nineteen black soldiers were executed, sixty-three received life sentences, twenty-eight received lesser prison terms, and seven were acquitted. Although no black Houstonians were involved in the riot, they were affected by it. Shortly after the riot, Houston police conducted a house-to-house search of black neighborhoods and temporarily confiscated all firearms owned by blacks.[11]

The Houston riot occurred during the period of heightened racial tensions in America that accompanied World War I and persisted into the 1920s. Even though most white Houstonians blamed the 1917 riots on outsiders brought to the city by the army, not on local blacks, the riot nevertheless contributed to the deteriorating racial climate that continued into the early 1920s and witnessed the revival of the Ku Klux Klan in the city. In March, 1921, a Klan mob brutalized a black dentist, and four years later another Klan mob tarred and feathered a local black doctor.[12] The Klan also threatened outspoken black leaders who criticized their actions, including Houston *Informer* editor C. F. Richardson. In June, 1928, several years after Klan influence in the city had diminished, Houston recorded its only documented lynching. The victim, Robert Powell, had killed a white policeman in a Fourth Ward shoot-out. A white mob took Powell from Jefferson Davis Hospital, where he was recovering from wounds, and hanged him from a bridge that crossed a gully on Post Oak Road, west of the city. This act shocked and outraged both black and white Houstonians. The city appropriated funds for an investigation, while the governor and

Houston's "night of violence" on August 23, 1917, which involved the all-black Third Battalion of the Twenty-fourth United States Infantry stationed in the city at Camp Logan, in some respects previewed the racial clashes of the infamous "Red Summer" of 1919. In Houston, however, African Americans initiated the armed clash, and more whites than blacks lost their lives. *Courtesy Houston Public Library, Houston Metropolitan Research Center*

several citizens groups offered rewards for the apprehension of the guilty parties. Although the county eventually indicted seven men for the crime, only two came to trial, and they were acquitted.[13]

In spite of events such as these, Houston was relatively free of racial violence during the period of segregation. Even the outspoken Houston *Informer*, which never soft-pedaled racial violence or police brutality, observed in 1930 that blacks were fortunate to live in a city like Houston where "the mob spirit" was not rampant.[14]

Black Houston in the Late Twentieth Century

The two most significant events that have occurred in the black community during the second half of the twentieth century are the breakdown of legal segregation and the rapid growth of the black population in Houston. Desegregation in Houston began in 1950 when five blacks filed suit to gain access to municipal golf courses. Three years later the public library integrated its facilities, and in 1954 segregation ended on the city buses.[15] School desegregation took longer. Following the 1954 Supreme Court school desegregation ruling, several blacks tried, without success, to register at all-white schools. In December, 1956, the NAACP backed a lawsuit filed on behalf of Beneva Williams and Dolores Brooks to end school segregation. Endless delaying tactics utilized by the conservative majority of the school board finally prompted federal district judge Ben C. Conally to order the desegregation of all first grades in September of 1960, following which desegregation would proceed at the rate of one grade per year. However, the school board placed such severe restrictions on transfer eligibility that only twelve black students met the requirements to attend white schools during the first year.[16] This and similar tactics caused the federal courts to intervene again, and in 1966 all schools were ordered to desegregate. While no schools are totally segregated, most black students still attend predominantly black schools. Nevertheless, in 1980 the Houston Independent School District was found to have complied substantially with the desegregation order. Most black parents surveyed informally in 1981 expressed more concern about the quality of the education that their children receive than with the continuing pockets of segregation.

The desegregation of restaurants, lunch counters, and other public facilities began in the spring of 1960, when students at Texas Southern University staged the first Houston sit-in demonstration at the lunch counter of Weingarten's grocery store in the Third Ward. Within a few days the sit-in movement spread to downtown lunch counters and to the city hall cafeteria. Officials at Foley's department store, eager to avoid the negative publicity the civil rights demonstrations were bringing to other southern cities, convinced other Houston store managers to cooperate with black organizations so that downtown dining facilities could be desegregated as quietly as possible. Consequently some racial barriers began to disappear as city leaders adjusted to the new realities. By 1963 city and county parks, beaches, and swimming pools were integrated. The only violence during this period occurred during two confrontations on the Texas Southern University campus between students and the police in 1965 and 1967, and during a shoot-out in the Third Ward between police and a black militant group known as People's Party II in the summer of 1970. However, most changes came fairly peacefully, and by the early 1970s most of the old barriers of segregation no longer existed. While all traces of discrimination certainly have not disappeared, those that remain are more subtle and more likely to be based on economics rather than solely on race.

Equally dramatic as the breakdown of segregation was the rapid growth in the city's black population. Between 1940 and 1980 the number of blacks in the city grew from 86,302 to 440,257 — a dramatic increase of more than 400 percent. The need to absorb this growth has had a tremendous impact on the black community. The most visible change has been the expansion of black neighborhoods. While the traditional enclaves of the Third, Fourth, and Fifth wards absorbed some of the newcomers, as did the black neighborhoods that were developed in the 1920s and 1930s, most of the new growth occurred outside of these neighborhoods. New black subdivisions opened northeast, east, and southeast of the city. Meanwhile the demand of black professionals and the black middle class for quality housing brought blacks into the previously all-white Riverside area south of the Third Ward in the 1950s and 1960s. In the 1970s, residential segregation began to break down as some blacks moved into racially mixed neighborhoods and apartment complexes, especially in the west and southwest sections of the city. Housing desegregation was facilitated by a fair housing ordinance that outlawed discrimination in the sale or rental of housing. In spite of these changes, in 1970 almost 10 percent of the city's census tracts were more than 90 percent black, and in the mid-1970s three-fourths of the black population still lived in areas that were at least 70 percent black. In 1980 the proportion of census tracts that were at least 90 percent black had risen to over 13 percent, although the percentage of blacks living in census tracts that were greater than 70 percent black had declined slightly to about seven out of ten.[17]

Some blacks expressed concern that residential desegregation would weaken the traditional black neighborhoods by draining away middle- and upper-class blacks.[18] In other words, those who could afford to move from the old, segregated neighborhoods would do so, leaving behind only the poorest. There has been a tendency for this to happen, especially among younger blacks, and especially in the Fourth and Fifth wards. But this process had begun earlier, before desegregation, as many younger, more affluent blacks abandoned the old neighborhoods for newer all-black subdivisions. A more serious problem was the negative impact that desegregation had on many black businesses as more and more blacks patronized white-owned businesses outside their immediate neighborhoods. As a result of the dispersion of black population into new areas of the city, and with the breakdown of the more overt manifestations of racial discrimination and segregation, the self-contained black communities — with their small-town atmosphere that was common in the early twentieth century — ceased to exist.

A major effect of these changing residential patterns was the transformation of the traditional geographical alignment of black Houston. Until the mid-1930s, the Fourth Ward was the economic center of black Houston. West Dallas (formerly San Felipe) and nearby streets were the home of more than 95 percent of the city's black-owned businesses. By the early 1950s the Fifth Ward had gained the largest share of the city's black population, and Lyons Avenue and Jensen Drive had replaced West Dallas as the main streets of black enterprise. The Fifth Ward's dominance did not last long, however. The city's rapid population growth led to the development of new, more attractive black neighborhoods, especially in the southern part of the city. At the same time, black businesses lost an increasing number of customers to white-owned competitors downtown, and particularly to the new suburban shopping malls.

The Third Ward, on the other hand, prospered during this period. By the mid-1960s, although the three inner-city wards no longer contained the majority of Houston's black population, the Third Ward had supplanted the Fifth Ward as the area with the greatest concentration of black business in the city. Even though only about 7 percent of the city's blacks lived in the Third Ward in 1970, almost 10 percent of the black-owned businesses were located there, and more significantly, the Third Ward was the home of Riverside National Bank, Houston's only black-owned bank, as well as Standard Savings Association, the state's only black-owned savings and loan association, and the Houston Citizens Chamber of Commerce, the principal black business organization in the city.[19]

During the last thirty years, the Third Ward has also become the cultural center of black Houston. To a large degree, the Third Ward's cultural preeminence was based on the emergence of Texas Southern University as a major educational institution. The original mission of the university was to provide black Texans with "educational opportunities equal to and comparable with those offered by other [state supported] institutions."[20] As higher education in Texas became desegregated, TSU's focus shifted to the problems and issues of the urban environment that confronted inner-city residents. With an enrollment today of over ten thousand students,

Artist John Biggers helped found the Texas Southern University art department in the late 1940s. He is pictured here in 1983 in front of the mural that he painted at Christia Adair Park south of Houston. *Photo by Cary D. Wintz*

Texas Southern is the second largest historically black university in the United States. Although it no longer serves an exclusively black clientele, the school has remained a predominantly black institution and a center of black education. In addition, with its FM radio station, library, art gallery, and active programs of music, art, and theater, it is a center for black culture in Houston. Furthermore, the presence of Texas Southern in the heart of the Third Ward has stimulated cultural development in the surrounding area. Today the Third Ward is the home of the city's two leading black newspapers, its black-owned radio stations, and black theater, art galleries, and book stores. Texas Southern faculty members helped make the nearby Riverside community the most desired place of residence for Houston's black elite.

While the Third Ward has emerged as the center of black business and culture in Houston, the overall impact of changing residential patterns on the older neighborhoods has been negative. Even though the black popu-

Table 8
Comparison of Black Neighborhoods, 1970 and 1980

Neighborhoods	Total Black Population	Percent of Population that Is Black	Percent of Blacks Who Are High-School Graduates	Median Income of Black Families	Percent of Black Families below the Poverty Level	Percent of Black Homes that are Owner-Occupied
			1970			
Third Ward	46,777	91.1	39.0	$5,637	27.4	20.2
Fourth Ward	6,347	69.4	15.0	$3,385	50.7	3.5
Fifth Ward	33,656	69.6	24.8	$4,895	36.1	23.5
Sunnyside; Scottcrest	27,204	97.2	37.4	$7,409	17.7	73.4
Southpark; MacGregor	48,687	66.1	44.6	$7,603	18.0	68.4
Pleasantville	10,619	88.6	32.9	$8,086	16.6	72.3
Total Wards	86,780	79.8	31.7	$5,172	32.5	20.3
Total New Neighborhoods	86,510	76.1	40.7	$7,601	17.7	70.5
TOTAL: Entire Population of City	316,551	25.7	51.8	$9,876	10.7	48.4
			1980			
Third Ward	34,652	92.7	48.1	$11,566	29.6	23.2
Fourth Ward	4,361	63.4	29.2	$6,350	48.6	5.0
Fifth Ward	23,957	73.9	37.1	$9,126	36.9	27.2
Sunnyside; Scottcrest	25,033	95.9	49.7	$16,542	19.5	70.4
Southpark; MacGregor	71,391	94.2	59.0	$16,190	17.6	59.3
Pleasantville	7,536	86.7	45.1	$19,838	11.2	76.8
Total Wards	62,970	82.1	42.6	$10,307	33.7	23.5
Total New Neighborhoods	103,960	94.3	55.4	$16,549	17.6	63.4
TOTAL: Entire Population of City	440,257	27.6	68.3	$21,817	10.1	48.0

SOURCE: U.S. Department of Commerce, Bureau of the Census, *1970 Census of Population and Housing, Census Tracts, Houston, Tex., Standard Metropolitan Statistical Area* (Washington: Government Printing Office, 1972), P133–P150, H67–H150; and *1980 Census of Population and Housing, Census Tracts, Houston, Tex., Standard Metropolitan Statistical Area* (Washington: Government Printing Office, 1983), P543–P602, H93–H105.

lation grew by more than 120,000 during the 1970s, the number of black residents in the wards declined slightly. In addition, the more affluent elements in the black community have tended to move out of the wards since the 1960s. As a result, as Table 3 indicates, by 1970 residents of the older black areas were generally more poorly educated, had lower incomes, were more likely to fall below the poverty level, and were less likely to own their own homes than were the residents of the newer black neighborhoods (those that were established in the 1920s or later). These trends accelerated between 1970 and 1980, and they showed no sign of abating during the 1980s. Furthermore, if the relatively prosperous and well-educated residents near

Texas Southern University are eliminated from the Third Ward figures, the differences between the older and newer black areas are even more pronounced.

The major problems that confronted blacks during the post–World War II era continue to be poor employment and economic status, a high crime rate, and substandard health care. New problems include substance abuse, increased juvenile delinquency, and the weakening of the black family. Indicative of this latter problem is the high rate of teenage pregnancy and illegitimacy in the black community. In 1985, for example, 53.3 percent of the black births in the city were illegitimate, a rate that far surpassed that of either the city's white or Mexican-American populations.[21]

Although blacks in Houston do not enjoy the same economic position as whites, their status has improved significantly since the 1940s as blacks have shared in the city's growth and prosperity. For example, black unemployment in Houston through the 1970s was about half the national average, even though it was still higher than that of white Houstonians. Black income continued to lag behind that of whites, although the gap narrowed. The median income of black families was 54 percent that of white families in 1950, 65 percent in 1970, and 70 percent in 1980. Similar improvements have occurred in the employment status of blacks. In 1960, 8 percent of the city's blacks were classified as professionals, semiprofessionals, proprietors, or managers, while 79.3 percent of black workers were employed as domestics, service workers, or unskilled laborers. By 1980 the percentage of black professional and managers had risen to 13.1 percent, and the number of domestics, unskilled, semi-skilled, and service workers had dropped to 45.9 percent. As Table 4 indicates, black employment status has steadily improved since 1940. Most notably, the percentage of black professionals and managers has risen more than 300 percent since 1920, while the percentage of unskilled and semi-skilled labor has decreased. Even more significant is the increase in black technical, clerical, and sales workers and the decline in the percentage of black service workers. Reflecting these advances, between 1940 and 1970 the proportion of black owner-occupied homes rose from 21.7 percent to 44.7 percent. Even with rapidly escalating home prices and interest rates, as well as the addition of more than 120,000 blacks to the city's population, the number of black homeowners had dropped only slightly to 43.4 percent by 1980.[22]

In spite of these gains, blacks still occupy the lowest rungs on the economic ladder, and unemployment is a major problem among inner-city black youth. Furthermore, the severe recession that hit Houston in the early 1980s and sent the unemployment rate into double figures struck blacks and other minorities especially hard. While we will have to wait for the 1990 census to document whether or not the economic gains of the preceding two decades were lost, obvious symbols of the impact of the reces-

Table 9
Black Occupations, 1920-80

Occupation	1920	1940	1960	1980
Professionals & Managers	3.0%	4.7%	8.0%	13.1%
Technical, Clerical, Sales	1.7%	2.1%	6.1%	28.8%
Craft & Skilled Workers	8.3%	3.6%	6.0%	11.5%
Service Workers	42.9%	54.7%	42.5%	20.5%
Unskilled & Semi-Skilled Labor	43.3%	34.9%	36.8%	25.4%

SOURCE: United States Department of Commerce, Bureau of the Census, *Fourteenth Census of the United States, Taken in the Year 1920*, vol. 4, *Occupations, 1920* (Washington: Government Printing Office, 1923), pp. 1114-16; *Sixteenth Census of the United States: 1940, Population*, vol. 3, *The Labor Force: Occupation, Industry, Employment, and Income*, pt. 5, *Pennsylvania-Wyoming* (Washington: Government Printing Office, 1943), pp. 595-96; *U.S. Census of Population and Housing: 1960, Census Tracts, Houston, Tex., Standard Metropolitan Statistical Area* (Washington: Government Printing Office, 1961), p. 75; *1980 Census of Population and Housing, Census Tracts, Houston, Tex., Standard Metropolitan Statistical Area* (Washington: Government Printing Office, 1983), pp. 569, 571.

sion on the black community include the restructuring under white ownership of Riverside National Bank (now Unity Bank) and the bankruptcy of black entrepreneur Percy Creuzot, owner of the popular fried chicken restaurant chain, Frenchy's.

Most of the problems that the black community faces in the area of crime and health care are related to its economic status. Economic pressures and a relatively high level of unemployment have contributed to the high crime rates in the black community. Crime affects black Houstonians in two ways. First, blacks are more likely to be arrested, especially for serious offenses, than are whites. Although blacks constituted only 25.7 percent of the city's population in 1970, they accounted for 39.6 percent of the total number of arrests and 52.4 percent of those arrested for violent crimes (murder, rape, robbery, and assault). Second, since most crime is intraracial in nature, blacks run a higher risk than whites of being victims of crime. For example, in 1985 black Houstonians were more than three times as likely to be victims of homicide than were their white counterparts.[23]

Although the problem of inadequate law enforcement is a citywide issue, it particularly affects the black community. Most black Houstonians believe that their communities are insufficiently protected by the police. Many also feel they are more likely than whites to be victimized by excessive use of police force. Relations between the Houston Police Department and the black community deteriorated during the 1970s due largely to the perception (especially among black youth) of racial discrimination in the police department and of widespread police brutality directed toward the black community. One of the unfortunate results of this perception was the reluctance of qualified blacks to join the police department. The appointment of a black chief of police in 1982 seems to have led to a more positive relationship between the black community and the police. Chief Lee Brown had been fairly successful in removing the police department from the center of controversy prior to his 1989 resignation to head the New York City Police Department. Since his departure, however, heated conflict between Houston police and the black community over the use of excessive force has once again arisen.

The level of health care available to black Houstonians is even more clearly related to economic status. Today all health care facilities are integrated. The black health-care system that developed during the period of segregation has all but disappeared. Of the four black hospitals still operating in the city in 1970, only two — Riverside General Hospital in the Third Ward, and St. Elizabeth's Hospital in the Fifth Ward — were still open in 1982. By 1988, Catholic authorities decided to close St. Elizabeth's, and Omni International Hospital, a black-owned facility that opened in northeast Houston in the early 1980s, had declared bankruptcy. Only Riverside General seemed to have any future.

With the desegregation of health facilities, income level became the principal determinant of the quality of health care available to blacks. Middle- and upper-income blacks generally patronize the same hospitals as others of their economic class, while low-income blacks rely on public health care facilities. In response to the rapid growth of the black community, the Harris County Hospital District expanded its services in low-income black neighborhoods. In spite of this, blacks continue to suffer from a higher rate of infant mortality and a higher general death rate than whites. In 1985 the clearest indication of the health care problem confronting the black community was the high rate of infant mortality. Black infant mortality that year was over 50 percent higher than it was for whites, and the percentage of black newborns suffering from low birth weight was over 100 percent higher than for white infants. These problems persist in the black community despite the fact that pregnant black women were slightly more likely than white women to receive prenatal care.[24] Part of the health care problem confronting the black community is related to the proportionately low number of black doctors and dentists practicing in the city. In the early 1980s, there were only some seventy black dentists and black doctors in the whole county out of a black population of nearly half a million.

Blacks have assumed a more visible and active political role in the city during the last forty years. More blacks held public office, and black voters currently have a greater impact on local elections than at any time in the city's history. Also, black political organization has become more sophisticated in recent years. In addition to pressure groups, such as the Harris County Council of Organizations and Blacks Organized for Leadership Development, other blacks worked behind the scenes to influence the appointment of blacks to administrative posts in the city government and the school district. In spite of this, most blacks feel that they still do not have an adequate voice in local governments, although nearly all agree that the situation has improved dramatically during the last twenty-five years. Perhaps the greatest source of frustration has been the failure of blacks to achieve the highest administrative posts — mayor of the city and superintendent of the Houston Independent School District. The first of these positions seems particularly illusive because of political divisions within the black community, the ability of white candidates like Mayor Whitmire to marshal strong minority support, and changing demographics that seem to be working against black candidates.

Leadership in the black community has always tended to come from professionals, especially ministers, lawyers, teachers, physicians, and journalists. Black businessmen, on the other hand, generally have not sought positions of leadership. A survey of black leadership in Houston in the mid-1970s identified twenty-five community leaders, thirteen of whom held elected offices. Of the total only three were businessmen, while fifteen were professionals. Nothing has occurred in the last ten years that would substantially change the results of that survey.[25]

What is the sum total of the black experience in Houston? What has it meant to be black in Houston? Unlike other ethnic minorities who have made Houston home, blacks have not become assimilated — indeed, the visible physical differences between blacks and whites seem to make complete assimilation impossible. To most nonblacks, skin color is the most distinguishing characteristic of blacks. Blacks, however, do not see themselves in this way. For most blacks (at least the ones surveyed for this study), the most important factors defining their ethnic identity are having been relegated to a second-class status as well as having been the victims of prejudice and discrimination. In other words, blacks do not feel that they are intrinsically different from other groups in society, but they feel that they have been treated differently. They also believe that they have had to struggle to overcome barriers that most nonblack Houstonians do not face. Ironically, most blacks also believe that this struggle has had positive effects. Some feel that it has strengthened blacks; others feel that it has given them a unique approach to life that makes them more compassionate and enables them to make the most of difficult situations; still others believe that it has reinforced their ties to family and friends. Black Houstonians stress, however, that at the core they are not different. They are Houstonians, like their nonblack neighbors, but they are Houstonians whose history has included special hardships, and confronting these hardships has created a special relationship among Houston blacks and between blacks and their community.

In This Section . . .

Blacks mounted no collective resistance to slavery in Houston, although rumors of slave plots were a staple of local white society. Following the Civil War and into the twentieth century, the strictures of segregation were made somewhat more tolerable to blacks because of the constant growth and relative economic prosperity of the Bayou City. Consequently, the single most violent episode between the races in Houston primarily involved not native blacks but the soldiers of the Third Battalion, Twenty-Fourth United States Infantry, who were on temporary assignment in the city. Houston's "night of violence" on August 23, 1917, foreshadowed the famous "red summer" of 1919, when many other American cities had somewhat similar interracial clashes. Despite the relative affluence of Houston, however, historian Robert V. Haynes argues that blacks in the Bayou City nevertheless took the lead in undermining the basis of racial segregation in Texas by legally attacking one important aspect of it—the white primary. This effectively disenfranchised blacks in Texas, which was a one-party state. Thus Houston experienced what are arguably two of the most visible aspects of race relations in the United States during the first half of the century—overt, collective interracial conflict, and attempts by blacks to use the law to protect themselves and to achieve their goal of social and political equality. James SoRelle's essay places interracial violence and legal maneuvering in a wider context in his treatment of race relations in Houston between the two world wars.

Following World War II the struggle for civil rights in the nation entered a new phase that was characterized by public marches, demonstrations, sit-ins, and other direct-action tactics that eventually demolished legal segregation in America. F. Kenneth Jensen details the early sit-in movement in Houston, which led to the end of de jure, sanctioned racial segregation in the Bayou City. In an accompanying essay, Cecile E. Harrison and Alice K. Laine discuss how Houston blacks began to address the important issue of economic development and economic power. However, just as the period of slavery was succeeded by one of segregation, so the era of segregation has been followed by an ongoing practice of racial and economic discrimination. Robert D. Bullard ably documents these practices with his analysis of housing in the Bayou City. And, in the final selection of this volume, historian Robert Fisher examines Houston's politics of power, which promote continued elite control, and recommends specific ways that elite power can be curbed and perhaps displaced by effective, democratic community mobilization. In any event, surely the future battles for human rights in Houston and throughout Dixie will center on the intersection of ethnic and economic discrimination, the third component of a historical slavery-segregation-discrimination triptych — a triptych that measures both the progress as well as the shortfalls in combatting racial prejudice in Houston, Dixie, and the United States.

Notes

1. James Martin SoRelle, "The Darker Side of 'Heaven': The Black Community in Houston, Texas, 1917-1945" (Ph.D. diss., Kent State University, 1980), p. 43.
2. Houston *Informer*, Feb. 19, 1921; SoRelle, pp. 173-74.
3. Darlene Clark Hine, "Blacks and the Destruction of the Democratic White Primary, 1935-1944," *Journal of Negro History* 62 (Jan., 1977): 49.
4. Ibid., p. 51. See also Darlene Clark Hine, "The Illusive Ballot: The Black Struggle against the Texas Democratic White Primary, 1932-1945," *Southwestern Historical Quarterly* 81 (Apr., 1978), pp. 371-92.
5. Alice K. Laine, "An In-Depth Study of the Black Political Leadership in Houston, Texas" (Ph.D. diss., University of Texas, 1978), pp. 42-43; Chandler Davidson, *Biracial Politics: Conflict and Coalition in the Metropolitan South* (Baton Rouge, 1972), pp. 84-87.
6. Laine, pp. 43-44.
7. Laine, pp. 38-42; Davidson, pp. 41-44.
8. Houston *Informer*, June 7, 1919; SoRelle, pp. 88-89.
9. SoRelle, pp. 91-92.
10. Houston *Informer*, July 16, 1938; SoRelle, p. 72.
11. Emile Oliver, interview with Cary D. Wintz, Houston, Tex., Sept. 16, 1981 (tape recording in possession of Wintz). For the best description and analysis of the 1917 riots, see Robert V. Haynes, *A Night of Violence: The Houston Riot of 1917* (Baton Rouge, 1976). For a further discussion of this event, see also C. Calvin Smith, "On the Edge: The Houston Riot of 1917 Revisited" (Paper presented at the second African American History in Texas Conference, Dallas, Texas, Feb., 1991), published in *The Griot* 10 (1991): 3-12. Although the Houston Police Department had appointed its first black patrolman in 1870, the number of blacks on the force was always small, and their authority was severely limited. See W. Marvin Dulaney, "The Texas Negro Peace Officers' Association: The Origins of Black Police Unionism," *Houston Review* 12 (1990) 2:59-78.
12. SoRelle, pp. 73-74.
13. Ibid., pp. 76-77.
14. Houston *Informer*, May 10, 1930.
15. David G. McComb, *Houston: A History* (Austin, 1981), p. 166.
16. Ibid., pp. 169-71.
17. U.S. Department of Commerce, Bureau of the Census, *1970 Census of Population and Housing, Census Tracts, Houston, Tex. Standard Metropolitan Statistical Area* (Washington, D.C., 1972), P177-P216; U.S. Department of Commerce,

Bureau of the Census, *1980 Census of Population and Housing, Census Tracts, Houston, Tex. Standard Metropolitan Statistical Area* (Washington, D.C., 1983), P104-P129.

18. This concern was expressed by a number of black Houstonians interviewed in 1981. See, for example, Senfronia Thompson, interview with Shelly Jarmon, Houston, Tex., Dec. 15, 1981 (tape recording in possession of Cary D. Wintz).

19. Robert D. Bullard, "Houston's Third Ward: A Center for Black Business," unpublished paper, 1981, in possession of Cary D. Wintz.

20. Quoted in "Texas Southern University General Catalog/Bulletin, 1983-85," p. 1.

21. City of Houston Health and Human Services Department, *The Health of Houston: Births, Deaths and Other Selected Measures of Public Health, 1981-1985,* pt. 1, *Citywide Measures,* n.d. [1986], p. 1.14.

22. *1970 Census,* P133-P150, H67-H71; *1980 Census,* P543-P602, H93-H105.

23. Naomi W. Ledé and Hortense W. Dixon, "Urban Minority Groups in Houston: Problems, Progress, and Prospects," an unpublished report by the Texas Southern University Urban Resources Center, May 1973, pp. 209-14; *Health of Houston,* p. 3.6.

24. *Health of Houston,* p. 1.18-1.19, 2.6.

25. Laine, pp. 93-94.

Race Relations in "Heavenly Houston," 1919-45

James M. SoRelle

Introduction

In spite of the obvious seriousness of the Houston race riot of August 23, 1917, most sources—both black and white—in the years between the two world wars characterized race relations in the Bayou City in a positive light.[1] The local chamber of commerce sought to include African Americans in its booster motto—"Heavenly Houston"—and carefully enumerated the many benefits and opportunities available to Bayou City blacks. The city's fledgling black weekly newspaper, the *Informer,* expressed its gratitude to the chamber and noted that this attitude on the part of local white business leaders "presages a better day between the races." And yet, given the continued patterns of racial discrimination, reinforced by a pervasive system of Jim Crow, the Bayou City presented an environment for most black Houstonians that was a good deal less than heavenly. This fact notwithstanding, black commentators continued to note the lack of serious racial friction in the city. Jesse O. Thomas, southern field representative for the National Urban League, concluded in 1929, "The relationship existing between the races in Houston is much more cordial than is found in many places of the South," and despite the prevalence of Jim Crow laws and customs, "there is a freedom from the tension and the intensity that characterizes the behavior of the two groups in a larger measure than is true in the average Southern community." A decade and a half later, this environment had changed little in the eyes of Urban League analysts, who noted in a 1945 survey, "Compared to other southern cities, race relations in Houston are good. . . . Periodically, minor rifts occur and only occasionally have major conflicts disturbed the current of race relations." These generally peaceful relations, however, were not a product of brotherly love. The Urban League studies admitted that black Houstonians occupied a subordinate status in the community, and yet "there were no manifestations of bitterness or acute intolerance observed." This seemed to be a result of white Houstonians' adamant adherence to local racial mores and the fact that Houston blacks tended to accept the city's racial status quo "with little outward evidence of resentment."[2]

Houston's amicable race relations depended in part upon the infrequent contacts between the races. Given the pattern of residential segregation in the city, intermingling of black and white Houstonians was limited primarily to work relationships or to incidental meetings on the city's downtown streets. Most black Houstonians realized that they could avoid racial conflicts by remaining in their designated "place."[3] Several local blacks described this attitude during interviews conducted in 1939 for the famous Carnegie-Myrdal study. B. T. Brooks, an employee of Hughes Tool Company and part owner of a local funeral parlor, noted, "As long as a Negro attends to his own business, he gets along all right." An unemployed laborer, Willis Johnson, reported, "I never get myself in the place where I have any trouble with [whites]." Ira B. Bryant, principal of Booker T. Washington High School, expressed the mutual disregard between the races in Houston when he responded that white Houstonians "just don't pay any attention to you [in public places] and I don't pay any to them." These comments substantiate the earlier conclusion of the Urban League's Jesse Thomas that "each group seemed to have decided to 'play in its own back yard.'"[4]

While black Houstonians frequently avoided direct confrontations with their white counterparts, the pervasiveness of discrimination in the city prevented African Americans from forgetting that whites viewed them as an inferior caste. In their daily activities, black Houstonians confronted traditional patterns of race relations that required them to exhibit a submissive attitude toward whites. For example, southern mores required blacks to address whites with the utmost respect and to enter white homes and many places of business only through the rear door. Moreover, custom demanded that black men remove their hats in the presence of all whites. In addition, the public abuse heaped upon black citizens became a common complaint among the city's black leaders. White store clerks rarely referred to black patrons as "Mr.," "Mrs.," or "Miss," but addressed them instead as "boy," "uncle," or "Sal." Correspondence from whites to blacks often carried the odious suffix "Colored" or "Nig." as a badge of inferiority and discourtesy. Local white newspapers championed this practice by consistently applying insulting labels to blacks. They referred to black women as "negresses" and to blacks in general as "darkies" and "coons."[5] When the *Houston Post* editorialized that every black soldier who fought in France should have been rewarded with a watermelon, the black Houston *Informer* indignantly responded, "We fought for freedom and liberty —not watermelons. . . . The black man and watermelons are not so indissolubly linked together. . . . The race is tired of ridicule and jest at its expense in the white press."[6] The complaints of the black press, however, did little to prevent a continuation of such public abuse. It persisted, accompanied by other practices common to white supremacist rule throughout the South—violence against blacks by the Ku Klux Klan as well as the police, and rigidly enforced segregation in schools, on public transportation, and in other public facilities.

Police and Klan Violence

Although insults were humiliating and potentially damaging psychologically, black Houstonians could endure them more easily than physical black-white confrontations that occasionally resulted in deadly violence. Among the most objectionable of these episodes, because they involved whites sworn to keep the peace, were the numerous conflicts between white policemen and black citizens. Police brutality, which had produced the incident that sparked the 1917 riot, continued to pose a problem for African Americans in the Bayou City in the period between the world wars. The *Informer,* which kept a vigilant watch for police attacks on black citizens, placed much of the blame for them on the low character of the persons hired by local law enforcement agencies. "A fair appraisal of the personnel of the Houston Police Department," the paper declared, "will reveal that it consists of ex-convicts, discarded police officers from other towns, roughnecks, and a few earnest men, green and untrained in the functions and duties of a police."[7]

Certainly some of the clashes were provoked by blacks who resisted arrest, but white patrolmen generally displayed little patience and even less courtesy when dealing with African Americans. On one occasion a policeman accosted a black woman, Mrs. R. V. Brown, as she was selling copies of the *Informer* on Main Street in the central business district of the city. The patrolman ordered Brown to leave the area, telling her to "stay on Milam and Prairie [Streets] with those other 'niggers.'" When Brown did not obey with as much alacrity as the officer desired, he arrested and escorted her to the police station, where she was charged with disturbing the peace. During the ordeal at the station, another white patrolman approached Brown and threatened to "kick her black ———." Learning of the unwarranted harassment meted out to his employee, Clifton F. Richardson, editor of the *Informer,* filed a complaint with the chief of police, and the charges against the woman were subsequently dropped.[8]

At other times physical abuse accompanied or replaced verbal threats. In 1940, for example, white patrolmen arrested a local black photographer, A. C. Teal, for alleged drunk driving. The officers beat Teal and then tried to claim that his injuries had resulted from a drunken fall. The Teal incident was only one of a long history of such beatings, and the *Informer* expressed its concern. "The feeling is growing among Negroes that their position is becoming more insecure, because policemen are beating them at will, and the authorities are refusing to do anything about it, and blandly accepting shallow excuses and explanations even when the arrested person shows obviously that he has been brutalized." Such activities, said the black weekly, would win little respect or cooperation from black Houstonians for the city's law enforcement officials.[9]

Racist policemen were not the only white Houstonians who terrorized blacks. During the first half of the 1920s, a revived Ku Klux Klan made sporadic forays against black residents whom Klan members claimed were challenging white supremacy and espousing social equality of the races.[10] In March, 1921, a Klan mob castrated Dr. J. L. Cockrell, a local black dentist, because of his alleged associations with white women. Another black doctor, R. H. Ward, was abducted, tarred, and feathered in 1925 by three white assailants who claimed to be acting upon orders from the local Klan chief in Houston. Following a report that white nurses at St. Joseph's Infirmary were attending patients in the segregated ward, an appalled citizen wrote to *Colonel Mayfield's Weekly,* the local Klan newspaper, "Not only do white girls have to wait on these Negroes but they are compelled to bathe them and rub their black carcasses. Ye gods!"[11]

C. F. Richardson of the *Informer* became a target for Klan threats on several occasions because of his constant attacks on KKK activities in the Bayou City. Richardson received numerous threats against his life, and the *Informer* office was vandalized by Ku Kluxers as a warning to the editor to halt his searing denunciations of their organization. As a result of these threats, Richardson began carrying a pistol to ward off would-be Klan assailants. Following one unfavorable editorial on the Klan, he found a sign nailed to the front door of his home. Written in red letters with a drawing of a dagger, the notice warned: "Nigger, leave town. Don't let the sun go down on you." Richardson called a group of his cohorts, including O. P. DeWalt, Julius White, and O. L. Hubbard, and the men stood armed watch outside the editor's home, but no Klan vigilantes appeared.[12]

By 1925 the Ku Klux Klan's influence in Texas and Houston had diminished, but assaults against black citizens continued. One of the most brutal incidents of mob violence — and for city fathers, one of the most embarrassing — occurred just prior to the opening session of the Democratic National Convention held in the Bayou City in June of 1928. On June 20 a white mob abducted Robert Powell from a bed at Jefferson Davis Hospital. He was recuperating from a gunshot wound inflicted in a fracas with local police that had left a white detective dead. Powell had been arrested, charged with murder, and placed under armed guard at the hospital. A mob, however, overpowered the guard, carried the wounded prisoner to a waiting car, and sped away. The next morning Powell's lifeless body was discovered hanging at the end of a rope tied to nearby Post Oak Bridge.

White and black Houstonians alike expressed shock over the first lynching in the city's memory. A special meeting of the city council passed an emergency ordinance authorizing Mayor Oscar Holcombe to appoint an investigating committee to act independently of the police inquiry into the matter. In addition, the council appropriated ten thousand dollars to cover expenses for the investigation and prosecution of the guilty parties. Texas governor Dan Moody offered $250 for each lyncher captured, and several local white organizations offered additional rewards. Judge Langston King directed the Harris County grand jury to set aside its other business in order to investigate Powell's lynching immediately, and within a week the jury handed down indictments against six local whites.[13]

Black Houstonians responded to the Powell lynching with both outrage and caution. The *Informer* noted that the incident seriously threatened the future of peaceful race relations in the city and characterized the members of the lynching party as "Houston's Hellish Huns." The local branch of the National Association for the Advancement of Colored People offered a thousand dollars for the arrest of the guilty parties, and it urged state and national anti-lynching legislation to discourage future incidents of mob violence. By contrast, the *Texas Freeman,* a black weekly edited by Charles Norvell Love, was particularly discreet. "The less all Negro critics and fault-finders here and there say about high official authority in Houston and Harris County in handling those white lynchers . . . the better it will be for our group." As trial preparations began, another black weekly, the Houston *Sentinel,* expressed the belief that justice would prevail.[14]

Unfortunately, the *Sentinel*'s confidence in the local courts was misplaced. As the trial progressed, black Houstonians realized that the proceedings were little more than a ruse to save the city's good name from suffering national opprobrium. Simeon B. Williams, creator of an *Informer* column entitled "Cimbee's Ramblings," was certain that the lynchers would go unpunished. As the trial dragged into October, Cimbee wrote in his usual exaggerated street argot to his fictitious pal, Lee, "I mought be rong . . . but ef dem law erbidin w'ite sitersuns gits victed fer dat krime, den yu kin hav my nue fall hat fer er footbawl." A week later Cimbee confessed: "Yu no, Lee, frum awl de everdince dat I has red in dat tryal uv dem ledged linchers, I dun cum ter de klushun dat dat cullud feller Robert Powell aint bin linched a tawl." Williams proved to be prophetic. Two of the accused lynchers were tried and acquitted, and in September of 1931, the district attorney's office dismissed the cases against the remaining defendants. The *Informer,* bitter at this latest example of whitewash justice, commented sarcastically, "We would ask the . . . question of why they [the accused lynchers] weren't turned loose long ago, after having been first decorated by the community with medals for bravery?"[15]

The lynching of Robert Powell, however, did not alter permanently the image of "Heavenly Houston" held by many Bayou City blacks, who continued to boast that they lived in a more pleasant racial environment than many other black southerners. Even the militant *Informer* conceded that Houston fell short of a racial Gehenna. For example, when a white girl charged a black bellhop with raping her in a local hotel, then later retracted her story, the *Informer* claimed: "It was fortunate for this colored youth that he was residing in a community such as Houston, where the mob spirit is not rife and rampant."[16] But even if black Houstonians largely escaped racial violence, as a group they suffered constantly and unrelentingly from the same second-class citizenship as blacks throughout the South. The policies of racial separation or exclusion in the city's schools, transportation system, and public accommodation facilities daily brought into focus the subordinate status of Houston's black population.

Schools and Education

Despite the boast of the Houston Chamber of Commerce that the Bayou City provided "one of the best educational systems in the South for colored children," black education suffered from an unwillingness on the part of the Houston Independent School District to satisfy the statutory obligation of "impartial provisions" in the city's Jim Crow schools.[17] As a result, Houston's black schools were characterized by inadequate physical plants, insufficient classroom space, and limited supplies of equipment and instructional tools.[18] In short, during the period between the world wars, black schools in the Bayou City were as unequal as they were separate. One local black leader contradicted the roseate portrait painted by the white chamber of commerce by asserting unequivocally: "The school situation here is one of the worst that you ever want to see."[19]

During the 1920s several elements within the black community, including the black press, began to voice disgust at the glaring inequalities plaguing African-American education in Houston. Much of this criticism focused on the sad condition of many of the city's black schools. In 1920, for example, the Houston *Informer* published a series of photographs of Gregory Elementary School to demonstrate the unhealthy conditions of that institution. In addition to an obvious absence of sidewalks around the campus, these pictures revealed huge ponds of standing water surrounding the building—the product of heavy rains and poor drainage. "Gregory's campus is almost entirely submerged," the *Informer* reported, and one local wag claimed that students had begun to grow webs between their toes to enable them to navigate on "Lake Gregory." Two Fourth Ward residents suggested that the aqueous environment around the campus provided a suitable site for fishing and duck hunting. In addition to the obvious inconvenience this situation produced for students and teachers at Gregory, the standing water represented a health hazard as a breeding ground for diseases. The *Informer* demanded city action, but school officials apparently remained indifferent to this problem. Three years later the *Informer* described Gregory as a school "situated in the center of a young lake, which undermines the health of both the teachers and pupils, with the result that more teachers have died out of Gregory School than any other school in the system."[20]

Gregory School, unfortunately, was not the only problem. Many of the city's black elementary schools were old frame structures badly in need of repair or replacement. One of these, said the *Informer,* "is likely to fall when a good gust of wind strikes it a center blow." The newspaper described several other black facilities as "totally inadequate and unfit for school purposes" and "a menace to public health." These problems were not limited to the lower grades. The city's sole black high school, known only as Colored High until it was renamed in 1927 in honor of Booker T. Washington, was incapable of meeting the educational needs of the city's black population. In 1923 Colored High provided only five hundred seats for an estimated enrollment of a thousand students. Some classes assembled in a poorly lit, damp basement. "Right here in Houston," an *Informer* editorial complained, "the rat-trap called a colored high school building would reflect discredit upon Podunk Creek or some other jerk-water settlement; while the ward school buildings are fire traps, health menaces and abominations both in the sight of man and God!"[21]

Another common complaint of African-American leaders who sought to improve the city's black schools involved the discriminatory application of school funds at both the state and local levels. In 1918, for instance, the state of Texas appropriated $9.06 for the education of each white student but only $6.90 for each black pupil.[22] Although these appropriations determined to some degree the unequal conditions in Houston's school system, the local board of education compounded the allocation discrepancies by consistently disregarding the educational needs of the black community. School officials frequently discriminated in applying funds from school bond levies for the benefit of African-American education. Occasionally the school board attempted to circumvent black complaints by designating money for a new school building for black students, but such tactics seldom satisfied black critics. A 1923 bond issue, for example, included a proposal for a new black junior high in the city's Fifth Ward, but it said nothing about improving the deplorable conditions at the black schools that already existed. As a result, a Colored Citizens' Committee met with school board members and outlined an extensive program of recommended improvements to meet the needs of the black community. These included requests for a new building for Colored High, a second black high school located to the east in the Fifth Ward, and new brick buildings to replace the frame structures at nine black elementary schools. The committee asked the board of education to designate $500,000 of the proposed $3 million bond to carry out these recommendations and received assurances that between $500,000 and $600,000 would be spent on black schools if the bond passed. Unfortunately the issue failed at the polls, and black Houstonians were forced to wait for the upgrading of their schools. C. F. Richardson expressed bitter disappointment at the defeat and charged that the bond had been a victim of racism. The issue's opponents, he claimed, had sealed the fate of the bond by accusing school board officials of trying to buy black votes by offering the carrot of better school facilities.[23]

The defeat of Houston's 1923 school bond, however, did not deter the board of education from continuing its program to improve the city's school system. Between 1924 and 1930 the city passed a series of multimillion-dollar bond issues, with some of the money earmarked for black education. Still, Houston's black schools never received funds commensurate to the size of the black population in the Bayou City. In 1924, for example, the *Informer* noted that black Houstonians received only 7 percent of all local school appropriations for buildings and equipment, although they constituted approximately 25 percent of the city's inhabitants. The following year, when the Houston Independent School District announced its intention to spend $70,000 for a new black high school in the Third Ward, C. F. Richardson criticized school officials for setting aside so little of the $3 million approved by a recent bond election and suggested that black citizens should consider any amount under $500,000 as unfair and insulting. He added that if school officials wished to be impartial in their allocation, they would designate $750,000 (or 25 percent of the bond) for black schools.[24] When some white officials argued that the amount set aside for the new high school reflected the ratio of taxes paid by blacks in the school district, Richardson countered by saying that "schools are not maintained and supported because of the ratio of taxes paid by any group or race of people, but in view of the fact that such institutions are imperative for the good of the entire social family."[25] Perhaps in response to Richardson's charges that the minuscule appropriations for black education represented little more than "a sop or sugar-tit," the superintendent, E. E. Oberholtzer, announced that the board of education would apply $500,000 of a newly proposed $4 million dollar school bond to building and improving the city's black schools. The *Informer* suggested that a committee of black leaders obtain concrete promises of improvements from Oberholtzer and members of the school board before delivering black support at the polls, but when the board of education published its contemplated improvements, including funds to repair or enlarge facilities at seventeen black plants, the paper gladly endorsed the bond issue.[26]

Although Houston's black schools clearly benefited from the school district's expansion program of the mid-1920s, inequalities continued into the 1930s. When school construction slowed during the depression, black education suffered far more than white education from the inactivity. The *Informer* complained in late 1935 that, while the local school board planned at least five new white schools, it had made no provisions for any black schools in spite of the need for black junior highs in both the Third and Fifth Wards. Richard Grovey, commenting on the lack of money infused into the black community's schools during one particular year (probably 1936), stated that "out of four million dollars that was spent in a building program only about one hundred thousand dollars went to the Negro schools. You can figure out for yourself if that is discrimination."[27]

Complaints concerning discriminatory funding for African-American schools, however legitimate, should not overshadow the fact that black education in the Bayou City did improve over the years. The building program of the 1920s provided new black schools, and many of the older structures were remodeled or replaced by brick buildings. In 1921 black students in Houston attended classes at sixteen elementary schools and one secondary school; by 1940 Houston's black schools included twenty-four elementary, three junior high, and three senior high schools. In addition, blacks attended classes at two Catholic schools, St. Nicholas and Our Mother of Mercy. Moreover, night school classes at the city's black senior highs and at Harper Junior High School provided local African Americans with an adult education program. Noting the availability of the night schools, the *Informer* insisted in 1929 that "it is no excuse for any man or woman, boy or girl, even though forced to work daily for a living, to be ignorant and illiterate in this community." Finally, black Houstonians also benefited from the establishment of Houston Colored Junior College; at the time of its founding in 1927, it was the only publicly supported junior college for blacks in the United States. Administered by the Houston Independent School District but supported by tuition levies, this school became a four-year college (Houston College for Negroes) in 1934; in 1947 it became a state university ultimately named Texas Southern University. Originally planned to provide local blacks with a teacher education curriculum, Houston College for Negroes became a source of pride for the city's black community.[28] By 1939 one local black educator could admit that "Houston is just now getting to the place where it believes in Negro education."[29]

Public Transportation

The Bayou City's dual school system represented only one of the cornerstones supporting Houston's segregated society. Public transportation represented another source of the imposed second-class citizenship of black Houstonians. City fathers argued that the Jim Crow laws pertaining to public transportation served to forestall conflicts on streetcars and buses caused by the more intimate contact of the races, but many local blacks objected to the abusive treatment they received from white conductors and drivers as well as to the manner in which public transportation failed to serve their community adequately.[30]

Prior to the introduction of motor buses in Houston in 1924, electric streetcars provided the chief means of public transportation in the Bayou City. The white conductors determined seating for passengers by placing a movable screen in the car to designate the racial line of demarcation, with black riders required to take seats behind the screen. Bayou City blacks generally observed the Jim Crow car laws, but conflicts did erupt between white conductors and black passengers, especially when the streetcars were filled and seating was at a premium. On several occasions fights broke out as conductors sought rigid enforcement of the law even when seats were available in the white section.[31] Cimbee referred to the slapping of one black woman passenger by a white conductor as "cave man tactics"; in 1927 he wrote of the local streetcar situation. "It looks lack de kumpinny is got de ijea dat dey is got ter hyar de bullinges set er bad mens dat dey kin fine in awl de kuntry on dese lines [in black neighborhoods]."[32]

Between 1914 and 1923, black Houstonians could avoid confrontations with whites by taking advantage of the jitney service that operated a line in the Fourth Ward exclusively for blacks. The jitney lines hurt the profits of the streetcar company, but its service to black neighborhoods was never satisfactory. In 1922 the Houston City Council reduced the number of cars on white jitney routes but completely abolished the San Felipe jitney line. Blacks objected to this, since the San Felipe line had been operated almost entirely by and for African Americans.[33] "This is class discrimination of the deepest dye and is both discriminatory and confiscatory," the *Informer* exclaimed. "Maybe the colored race in 'heavenly (?) Houston' will come to its senses by 2000 A.D., but in the meantime we shall be kicked about at will by those in official authority and all our protestations and petitions will hardly amount to a row of pins."[34] Black jitney operators attempted unsuccessfully to secure enough signatures to petition the city council for a referendum on the San Felipe jitney line. Noting the apparent unwillingness of black citizens to rally over the issue, the *Informer* chastised its readers for their "utter lack of interest in civic matters, even though they directly and vitally affect our group."[35]

The introduction of bus transportation in Houston initially continued the exclusionary policy of the jitneys with respect to black passengers. Local black leaders offered several arguments in their efforts to obtain bus accommodations in the form of separate compartments or separate buses. In the first place, they pointed out that the policy of excluding blacks from the buses violated "separate but equal" transportation statutes. They also noted that the Houston Electric Company's buses operated on paved roads for which black Houstonians had helped pay through their taxes. And, finally, black leaders resented the fact that the buses ran through several predominantly black neighborhoods but refused to stop for black passengers.[36]

Ironically, the first crack in the bus company's policy came as a result of protests from wealthy whites living in the exclusive River Oaks neighborhood. They petitioned the city council to allow the bus company to establish a special line to enable their house servants and maids to get to work on time. The *Informer* argued that if the bus company agreed to allow black domestics on the River Oaks lines, then all buses should carry blacks.[37] Failing this, wrote C. F. Richardson, "we presume that the only hope for our people to ride in these buses will be for all of us to get a job working for some white family in that section of the city, and then we shall all be eligible to ride in these 'pretty little buses'!"[38]

Although the action by the concerned employers of River Oaks opened the bus doors to some blacks, local officials encouraged African Americans to ride streetcars instead. Not until 1932 did the Houston City Council recognize a need to adopt an amendment to the city's Jim Crow ordinances providing for segregation on city buses — and even then some bus drivers, all of whom were white, refused to take on black passengers. According to Charles S. Johnson, however, black Houstonians did enjoy a certain amount of freedom in seating arrangements despite the presence of the ubiquitous Jim Crow screen. In black neighborhoods, Johnson reported, African-American passengers were assumed to have the bus all to themselves, except for the front two seats immediately behind the driver. Black passengers often took seats directly behind these "reserved" seats, and if more whites boarded than the white section could accommodate, the black passengers would move back without a word from the driver. Such responses, however, neither precluded confrontations between black and white passengers nor radically improved the temperament of white bus drivers on those occasions when they did step in to enforce city ordinances. As was the case with the city's streetcars, racial clashes occurred on the buses as a result of the Jim Crow restrictions. The *Informer* suggested that many of these flare-ups could have been avoided if the drivers and passengers did not carry guns and knives with them. Despite these warnings, however, the city bus lines continued to be a source of interracial tension in the Bayou City.[39]

Public Places

As in the case of public transportation, black Houstonians suffered the indignities of second-class citizenship in white-owned stores and places of public accommodation. Several secondhand stores, often those owned by Jewish or Italian immigrants, treated blacks as they did any other customers. But most white-owned establishments either publicized their refusal of service to black patrons or provided special arrangements for African Americans. In some stores, for instance, clerks waited on black customers in a special section, often out of the sight of white customers. Black shoppers also frequently had to wait until the salesperson had assisted all the white customers in the store, although some white owners employed black clerks specifically to attend to black customers. Several clothing and millinery stores refused to allow blacks to try on clothes before purchasing them. In addition to being victimized by poor service, black Houstonians who ventured into certain white-owned establishments often were subjected to abuse, including being physically ejected from the stores.[40]

Houston's white-owned hotels and restaurants typically refused service to blacks, although they employed them as bellhops, maids, and kitchen workers. According to Charles Johnson, interracial contacts in eating establishments were "a very sore spot in this town" although whites occasionally mingled with blacks in black-owned cafes and saloons.[41] Local blacks seldom protested these exclusionary customs, but on at least one occasion the interest of the "wartime emergency" of World War II resulted in a brief episode of integrated dining. In 1942 several white army officers approached the manager of Kelly's Cafe, across the street from the plush Rice Hotel, and asked if he could serve twenty-five soldiers. The manager replied that of course he would be delighted to feed the troops—but was stunned when the officers returned leading a black battalion. After some hesitation and a consultation with the proprietor, the manager allowed the soldiers to sit down and eat. The *Informer* wrote a gleeful account of the incident:

> The soldiers ate. They used knives and forks and spoons and deported themselves as any other gentlemen. Not even one poured his coffee into his saucer to sip it up. . . . Everything finished, they arose at the command, placed their chairs back at the table just as they would do if they were under instructions from Emily Post or had been reading her book on etiquette. . . . There were no casualties . . . and the cafe is still open. This country is at war with a common enemy and strange but necessary things happen in times like these."[42]

Despite the temporary desegregation of Kelly's Cafe, however, black Houstonians doubtless remained aware that most white proprietors frowned upon their patronage.

Movie theaters catering to whites generally excluded black Houstonians also, but some owners occasionally set aside Jim Crow sections for blacks or designated certain days that African Americans might attend the entertainments. In the 1920s only the Palace and Majestic theaters provided balcony seats for black patrons, but even these policies were subject to change. In 1926, for instance, the Majestic management prohibited blacks from all weekend performances, a policy the theater rescinded in 1928. In the next decade, Loew's State Theatre and the Metropolitan Theatre scheduled special midnight showings of movies with all-black casts for a black clientele, but the management nevertheless required the moviegoers to enter through the side entrance or fire escape rather than the front door. Public performances held at the City Auditorium, Music Hall, or Sam Houston Coliseum sometimes excluded blacks but more often provided a special Jim Crow section for these events. On some occasions the performances played to specifically prescribed audiences, with whites and blacks attending on different evenings. This was often the case when such famous black entertainers as Duke Ellington, Cab Calloway, or Fats Waller played in Houston.[43]

Black Houstonians could also expect separate and unequal facilities in various city services—that is, when they were not excluded from such benefits altogether. Jim Crow pervaded the city's hospitals where black patients were relegated to segregated wards, and only Jeff Davis Hospital provided more than a handful of beds for black patients. The city provided scarcely any recreational facilities for its black residents. No public swimming pools catered to blacks, and park as well as playground acreage was almost nonexistent. Houston's black leaders criticized the city fathers' lack of attention to Emancipation Park, a ten-acre plot purchased by a group of ex-slaves following the end of the Civil War and later donated to the city. Located on the outskirts of the Third Ward, the park's upkeep was the responsibility of the city, which did pitifully little. Moreover, the segregation of city parks was prescribed by law in a 1922 ordinance stating, "All other parks in the city now or hereafter existing and not set aside exclusively for the use of colored people shall be used exclusively by white people." In addition, black leaders complained, though with few results, about the lack of additional recreational facilities for African Americans, such as tennis courts and golf courses.[44]

The Colored Carnegie Library represented a source of pride for black Houstonians, but it too fell victim to the inequality associated with Jim Crow. Established in 1913 with the aid of a grant from Andrew Carnegie, following a request for assistance from Booker T. Washington and former Houstonian Emmett J. Scott, this branch was placed under the direction of the Houston Public Library in 1921. Like the city's black schools, this segregated facility suffered the usual problems of inadequate financing. In 1926 and 1927, for example, the Colored Carnegie Library received only

4 and 5 percent, respectively, of the total library expenditures.[45] In criticizing the insufficient apportionment made to this branch, the *Informer* editorialized, "This branch is poorly equipped, and it would be a joke (a very sad one) to compare its opportunities for intellectual and cultural development with the municipal library which Negroes are taxed to support, but from which they are excluded."[46]

Among the city's social welfare agencies, black Houstonians benefited from Community Chest funds, but the agencies that provided services for blacks did so on a segregated basis. Often these separate "agencies" consisted of a single black caseworker who handled the needs and requests of all black applicants. But even the bona fide social service organizations ministering to the city's black population operated on meager budgets. The Dorcas Home, for example, a county center for delinquent females, received no funds from the Community Chest. This situation led black leaders to complain that the home was not receiving a fair chance for success, since financially it was able to provide only the barest necessities. Other organizations, such as the Young Women's Christian Association, the American Red Cross, the Houston Social Service Bureau, and Traveler's Aid, provided assistance to needy blacks in the years between the world wars, but the aid never met the demands within the community. Even with the onset of the Great Depression, New Deal relief programs conducted their activities within the prescripts of separate but equal, thereby continuing a traditional pattern of social welfare assistance in Houston.[47]

Conclusion

Despite frequent claims by members of both races that race relations in the Bayou City were cordial and comparatively free from racial clashes, in actuality relationships between whites and blacks were determined by a set of attitudes and an institutional framework that guaranteed a second-class status for African Americans. Usually segregation, either by custom or statute, was the rule, and only very rarely did equality accompany separation. Indeed, if Houston symbolized heaven, as the chamber of commerce and other boosters suggested, then black Houstonians, conditioned by a lifetime of Bayou City experiences, could anticipate that when the day arrived that they entered the Pearly Gates, they would do so through the portal marked "For Colored Only."

Notes

1. The most accurate, comprehensive study of the Houston riot is Robert V. Haynes, *A Night of Violence: The Houston Riot of 1917* (Baton Rouge, 1976).

For an earlier description of this incident, see Edgar A. Schuler, "The Houston Riot, 1917," *Journal of Negro History* 29 (July, 1944): 300-38.

2. Houston *Informer*, June 14, 1919; Jesse O. Thomas, *A Study of the Social Welfare Status of the Negroes in Houston, Texas* (Houston, 1929), p. 102; National Urban League, *A Review of the Economic and Cultural Problems of Houston, Texas, as They Relate to Conditions in the Negro Population* (n.p., 1945), p. 168.

3. The black sociologist Charles S. Johnson provides the clearest analysis of the patterns of avoidance and acceptance of the racial status quo by southern blacks. According to Johnson, the responses of blacks to segregation often depended upon the individual's social class, age, sex, education, occupation, and degree of intimacy with whites.

Hostility and aggression against southern Jim Crow laws by southern blacks were largely covert and regulated by the demands of physical safety. The behavior of upper-middle-class and upper-class blacks represented a combination of acceptance and avoidance as well as a rationalization for self-respect, although basically these people were resentful and even hostile. Overt expressions of hostility, Johnson determined, were limited mainly to "bad niggers" of the underclass or to more aggressive upper-class blacks. See Charles S. Johnson, *Patterns of Negro Segregation* (New York, 1943), pp. 231, 244, 263, 295, 302.

4. B. T. Brooks, interview with H. J. Walker, Houston, Tex., Aug. 10, 1939, in Charles S. Johnson, "Source Material for *Patterns of Negro Segregation*: Houston, Texas" (Research memoranda for use in the preparation of Dr. Gunnar Myrdal's *An American Dilemma,* New York, 1940), p. 1; Willis Johnson, interview with Joseph Taylor, Houston, Tex., Aug. 7, 1939, ibid., p. 1; Ira B. Bryant, interview with Walker, Houston, Tex., Aug. 7, 1939, ibid., p. 1; Thomas, *Social Welfare Status of the Negroes in Houston,* p. 102.

5. Brooks interview in Johnson, "Source Material for *Patterns of Negro Segregation*," pp. 2-3; Houston *Informer,* June 14, 1919, Jan. 2, 1926, Oct. 29, 1927.

6. Houston *Informer,* June 28, 1919.

7. Ibid., July 16, 1938. For a much less critical but still useful portrayal of the Houston Police Department, see Louis J. Marchiafava, *The Houston Police Department, 1878-1948* (Houston, 1977).

8. Ibid., June 22, 1929.

9. Ibid., Mar. 9, 1940.

10. Klan activities in Houston are discussed in two works by Charles C. Alexander, *Crusade for Conformity: The Ku Klux Klan in Texas, 1920-1930* (Houston, 1962), and *The Ku Klux Klan in the Southwest* (Lexington, Ky., 1965).

11. Kenneth T. Jackson, *The Ku Klux Klan in the City, 1920-1930* (New York, 1967), p. 83; Houston *Informer,* Aug. 15, 1925; *Colonel Mayfield's Weekly,* May 13, 1922 (quotation).

12. Houston *Informer,* Sept. 8, 1923; George T. Nelson, interview with Bruce Fisher and Louis Marchiafava, Aug. 6, 1974, Houston, Tex., and Clifton F. Richardson, Jr., interview with Veronica Perry and Louis Marchiafava, June 9, 1975, Houston, Tex., now deposited in the Houston Metropolitan Research Center, Houston Public Library.

13. Houston *Informer,* June 23, 30, 1928.

14. Ibid. See also *Texas Freeman,* June 30, 1928, Box C-369, and the Houston

Sentinel, July 12, 1928, Box C-347, National Association for the Advancement of Colored People Archives, Library of Congress, Washington, D.C.

15. Houston *Informer,* Oct. 6, 13, 1928, Sept. 19, 1931.
16. Ibid., May 10, 1930.
17. Ibid., June 14, 1919.
18. *Vernon's Sayle's Annotated Civil Statutes of the State of Texas,* 2 vols. (Kansas City, Miss., 1914), 2, p. 2040; Bruce Alden Glasrud, "Black Texans, 1900-1930: A History" (Ph.D. diss., Texas Tech University, 1969), p. 217; Bryant interview in Johnson, "Source Materials for *Patterns of Negro Segregation,*" p. 6.
19. Richard Randolph Grovey, interview with Joseph Taylor, Houston, Tex., Aug. [?], 1939, in Johnson, "Source Material for *Patterns of Negro Segregation,*" p. 3.
20. Houston *Informer,* Feb. 7, 1920, April 21, 1923.
21. Ibid., Apr. 21, 1923, Jan. 26, 1924.
22. Monroe N. Work, ed., *Negro Year Book, 1918-1919* (Tuskegee, Ala., 1919), 274.
23. Houston *Informer,* Apr. 21, May 5, 12, 1923.
24. Ibid., Mar. 15, 1924, July 4, 1925.
25. Ibid., Sept. 12, 1925.
26. Ibid., Sept. 19, Oct. 10, 31, 1925.
27. Ibid., Nov. 2, 9, 1935, June 27, 1936; Grovey interview in Johnson, "Source Material for *Patterns of Negro Segregation,*" p. 4. For a brief discussion of educational discrimination in the South between the world wars, see George B. Tindall, *The Emergence of the New South* (Baton Rouge, 1967), pp. 500-501.
28. Ira B. Bryant, Jr., *The Development of the Houston Negro Schools* (n.p., n.d.), pp. 50-53; Houston *Informer,* Apr. 13, 1929, Sept. 14, 1940. The most thorough history of black higher education in Houston is Ira B. Bryant, *Texas Southern University: Its Antecedents, Political Origin, and Future* (Houston, 1975).
29. Bryant interview in Johnson, "Source Material for *Patterns of Negro Segregation,*" p. 9. Another product of Jim Crow education in this period — lower salaries for black teachers in the Bayou City's schools — is treated in James M. SoRelle, "The Darker Side of 'Heaven': The Black Community in Houston, Texas, 1917-1945" (Ph.D. diss., Kent State University, 1980), pp. 87-92.
30. In spite of the criticism of the city's urban transportation for blacks, C. F. Richardson admitted that Houston blacks received better streetcar service than did their counterparts in other Texas cities. See Houston *Informer,* Jan. 5, 1924.
31. *Charter and Revised Code of Ordinances of the City of Houston* (Houston, 1904), pp. 394-95; Houston *Informer,* June 7, 1919, Oct. 6, Nov. 24, 1923.
32. Houston *Informer,* Nov. 24, 1923, May 21, 1927.
33. Ibid., Nov. 11, 1922, Dec. 15, 1923; David G. McComb, *Houston: The Bayou City* (Austin, 1965), p. 108. The most thorough discussion of the black jitney line is Frances Dressman, "'Yes, We Have No Jitneys!' Transportation Issues in Houston's Black Community, 1914-24," this volume.
34. Houston *Informer,* Jan. 6, 1923.
35. Ibid., Apr. 7, 1923.
36. Ibid., May 23, June 20, July 25, 1925.
37. Ibid., Nov. 28, 1925.

38. Ibid., Dec. 12, 1925.

39. Charles S. Johnson, "Patterns of Segregation and Discrimination: Houston, Texas," in Johnson, "Source Material for *Patterns of Negro Segregation,*" pp. 12-13; Houston *Informer,* Apr. 2, 9, Aug. 14, 1932, May 21, 1938, May 8, July 31, 1943, Apr. 8, May 25, 1944.

40. Johnson, "Patterns of Segregation and Discrimination," pp. 13-20; Houston *Informer,* June 14, 1919, Feb. 26, 1921, Aug. 25, 1937.

41. Johnson, "Patterns of Segregation and Discrimination," p. 4; Brooks interview in Johnson, "Source Material for *Patterns of Negro Segregation,*" p. 4; Bryant interview in ibid., p. 6; Manilla Lovelady, interview with H. J. Walker, Houston, Tex., Aug. 8, 1939, in ibid., p. 3; Houston *Informer,* May 26, 1923.

42. Houston *Informer,* Oct. 17, 1942.

43. Bryant interview in Johnson, "Source Material for *Patterns of Negro Segregation,*" p. 15; Brooks interview in ibid., p. 7; Booker Taylor, interview with H. J. Walker, Houston, Tex., Aug. 9, 1939, in ibid., p. 7; Johnson, "Patterns of Segregation and Discrimination," pp. 6, 15; Houston *Informer,* Mar. 24, 1923, Jan. 9, 1926, Jan. 14, 1928, Jan. 25, 1930, Oct. 15, 1932, Jan. 22, Feb. 12, 1944.

44. Johnson, Patterns of Segregation and Discrimination," p. 7; J. S. Hautier, comp., *The Revised Code of Ordinances of the City of Houston of 1922* (Houston, 1922), pp. 324-25. For complaints concerning the lack of city funds utilized for black recreational purposes, see the Houston *Informer,* June 8, 1929, July 11, 1931, July 13, Aug. 31, 1935. Criticism of the city's indifference toward Emancipation Park was reported throughout the period under discussion. See ibid., Aug. 4, Dec. 29, 1923, Apr. 30, 1932, May 5, 1934. The history of Emancipation Park is discussed in ibid., Dec. 1, 1923, and in Willie Parker Chestnutt, "Recreation and the History of Its Development among Negroes in Houston" (Bachelor of Science essay, Houston College for Negroes, 1936). A second park was donated for black Houstonians in 1939 by Annette Finnegan, but as late as 1942 the twenty-acre plot had not yet been turned over for the use of city blacks; see Houston *Informer,* Oct. 14, 1939, Sept. 26, 1942.

45. Houston Public Library, *Twenty-second Annual Report,* 1926; Houston Public Library, *Report of Houston Public Library for the Year 1927 (Twenty-third Annual Report),* 1927; Houston *Informer,* July 18, 1931. For the development of the black library in Houston, see Fayrene Neuman Mays, "A History of Public Library Service to Negroes in Houston, Texas, 1907-1962" (master's thesis, Atlanta University, 1964), and Orin Walker Hatch, "The Development of the Houston Lyceum and the Houston Public Library" (master's thesis, University of Houston, 1963), pp. 83-88.

46. Houston *Informer,* July 11, 1931.

47. Ibid., Mar. 12, 1921, Feb. 7, 1931; Thomas, *Social Welfare Status of the Negroes in Houston,* pp. 77-89; National Urban League, *Review of the Economic and Cultural Problems of Houston,* pp. 147-58, 177-96. For a discussion of social service agencies and their work among black Houstonians, see the Will C. Hogg Papers, University of Texas Archives, Austin, Texas, Boxes HC 5/47, 6/80; Houston Foundation, *Social Welfare Work in Houston* (Houston, 1916); Houston Survey Committee, *The Meaning of the Houston Survey* (Houston, 1937); and Alice Bruce Currlin, *Community Welfare, Houston, Texas* (Houston, 1946).

Black Houstonians and the White Democratic Primary 1920-45

Robert V. Haynes

In a democratic society, where government rests on the premise that the voice of the people is omnipotent, a broad franchise is essential to the effective operations of government. Black Americans, who found themselves systematically excluded from voting in most states by virtue of their previous condition of servitude or by their visibility and racial heritage, came to regard this right as the essence of democracy and as a prerequisite for survival in a nation dominated by the white man. In the mid-nineteenth century, after a bloody civil war, the United States seemingly adopted the principle of universal male suffrage with ratification of the fourteenth and fifteenth amendments to the Constitution. The latter prohibited the states from denying voting privileges to any citizen "on account of race, color, or previous condition of servitude." One of the principal purposes of these two amendments was to endow blacks, especially those in southern states, permanently with the right to vote in federal and state elections and, incidentally, to perpetuate the dominance of the Republican Party in national politics.

For a brief period of time this policy worked, but northerners eventually became disenchanted with the necessity of continued federal interference in local elections in the South and with the well-publicized but somewhat exaggerated evidence of corruption in those same states. Consequently, in 1877, Republicans agreed to abandon the practice of dispatching federal troops into southern states at election time — in order to protect black voters from white intimidation and to accept the pledges of white Democrats to guarantee universal male suffrage — in exchange for the Democrats' assistance in maintaining Republican control of the White House. As a result of this compromise in 1877, southern Democrats in Congress acquiesced in the election of Rutherford B. Hayes as president of the United States in return for regaining political control of their home states.

Black southerners continued to exercise their constitutional right to vote as long as they made no concerted effort to overturn the implications of this compromise. In fact, most blacks found it advantageous to align themselves with those conservative whites who maintained control of state houses from 1877 to the 1890s, even though southern legislatures began, as early as the 1880s, to restrict black access to places of public accommodation through a series of segregation laws and to reduce the number of black voters through a complex system of registration and voting procedures. In some southern states, violence, intimidation, and fraud further limited black participation in local elections.

Meanwhile, the United States Supreme Court, in a series of important decisions, began to undermine the legal basis of black rights to equality before the law, as guaranteed by the Fourteenth Amendment, and to the right of suffrage, as protected by the Fifteenth Amendment. In *United States v. Reese* (1876) the Supreme Court paved the way for the eventual disfranchisement of blacks when the chief justice asserted that the "Fifteenth Amendment does not confer the right of suffrage upon anyone." Instead, the Court ruled, "it prevents the States, or the United States, from giving preference . . . to one citizen of the United States over another, on account of race, color, or previous condition of servitude." In the civil rights cases of 1883, the Court reinforced this narrow interpretation of the Reconstruction amendments and the subsequent congressional acts designed to protect black rights, including the right to vote, and successfully restricted the power of the states to that of preventing state officials from depriving blacks of their constitutional rights.[1] In the process, however, it left the federal government without the authority to restrain private citizens from doing the same. Frederick Douglass spoke for the vast majority of blacks when he proclaimed that these decisions "had inflicted a heavy calamity" upon black Americans and had "left them naked and defenseless against the action of a malignant, vulgar, and pitiless prejudice." "What does it matter, to a black," he asked, "if a state may not insult and outrage him, if a citizen of a State may?"[2]

The fatal blow to black rights came in 1896 when the Supreme Court in *Plessy* v. *Ferguson* ruled that segregation of blacks by southern states was not in violation of the equal rights guarantees of the Fourteenth Amendment as long as blacks were provided accommodations equal to those of whites. The cogent and prophetic words of Justice John Marshall Harlan that this ruling would, in time, "prove to be quite as pernicious as the decision made . . . in the *Dred Scott* case," went unheeded. The consequences of these decisions were to throw black Americans upon the mercy of prejudiced whites and to pave the way for the complete segregation and disfranchisement of blacks in southern states. The predictable results were not slow in occurring, and by the end of the nineteenth century, black participation in southern politics was almost a thing of the past.[3]

Although Texans eventually reacted to these developments in a typically southern manner, they did not immediately imitate Mississippi by enacting a literacy test or Louisiana by adopting the infamous "grandfather clause," which was later declared unconstitutional. Instead, in the Terrell election laws of 1903 and 1905, Texas established an elaborate direct primary system that permitted county election judges to exclude blacks, and in 1912 the legislature added a poll tax requirement, which discouraged the poor, mostly black, from voting. Nevertheless, black Texans continued to vote, although in increasingly diminishing numbers, in some state and local elections, especially those in the larger cities, until the early 1920s.

The demand for full exclusion of blacks from the ballot box largely grew out of the tense post–World War I atmosphere in the state and nation. During the second decade of the twentieth century, racial tensions in Texas increased noticeably, and serious racial violence erupted in several cities. The bloodiest of these racial outbursts occurred in Houston in 1917 when approximately one hundred black soldiers, resentful of the manner in which the police enforced segregation, marched on the city and killed sixteen whites and seriously injured at least a dozen others. One outgrowth of the Houston riot was the rapid rise of the Ku Klux Klan in and around Houston, and by the early 1920s this avowedly racist organization had attracted to its standard a majority of the city's policemen and most of its public officials. The Klan grew so strong that no aspiring politician dared denounce it publicly. Even though most white Houstonians were never active members of the Klan, they nonetheless sympathized with the organization's aims and philosophy.[4]

While the fears of white Texans that blacks posed a serious threat to their domination of state or municipal governments were unfounded, a controversy broke out in Bexar County that nonetheless fed their paranoia. For years white candidates had solicited black votes in Bexar County, but in the 1922 elections the incumbent district attorney, D. A. McAskill, accused his opponent of inflaming the black community against him because he had prosecuted a black man suspected of raping a white woman, and he vociferously asserted that "any white man who would ask black folks for their votes was not a Democrat." Following his reelection, McAskill launched a campaign to bar blacks from voting in all Democratic primaries, which culminated in passage of a 1923 white primary statute that explicitly instructed election judges to disregard the ballot of any black voter.[5]

Even before the state legislature responded favorably to McAskill efforts, white Houstonians took steps to slam the door on black voters in the Bayou City. On January 27, 1921, the Harris County Democratic Executive Committee passed a resolution excluding blacks from the upcoming primary election to be held on February 9. The reaction of black leaders in Houston was swift and decisive. Charles Norvell Love, a tall, thin, albino editor of the *Texas Freeman,* persuaded W. L. Davis, editor of the *Western Star,* to join him in filing an injunction against G. W. Griffith, chairman of the

Harris County Democratic Executive Committee, to prevent the committee from executing the resolution. Unwilling to acquiesce in the adverse ruling of the District Court of Harris County, they made an unsuccessful appeal to the Court of Civil Appeals for the First District of Texas on advice of their attorney, R. D. Evans, a young, inexperienced black lawyer of Waco, Texas.[6]

Love and Davis had never expected the state courts to respond favorably, and they were prepared to seek a hearing from the United States Supreme Court. Since the resolution of the executive committee applied only to an election that had already occurred, the Supreme Court upheld the decision of the state court that the cause of action had ceased to exist, making the question moot. In its ruling, however, the Supreme Court gave encouragement to the plaintiffs when it observed that, had the cause been presented prior to this election, it would have raised "a grave question of Constitutional law." This statement reinforced Love's strong belief that blacks must "place the problem of the Negro squarely upon the conscience of the nation" and that "our ultimate hope lies in the Federal Court." "It was the Supreme Court," he declared, "that opened the way for the South to develop the dual system and the Supreme Court alone can reverse the trend."[7]

Another important result of their effort was that it attracted the attention of the National Association for the Advancement of Colored People, the only organization with resources enough to challenge the white primary system. The association had been tangentially involved in the recent legal action that invalidated Oklahoma's grandfather clause, and the NAACP was seeking another test case. Therefore, the blatantly discriminatory action of the Texas Legislature in 1923 in specifically barring blacks from participation in any Democratic primary election was a godsend.

The first challenge to Texas' new white primary statute came in El Paso on July 26, 1924, when a black physician named Lawrence A. Nixon presented his poll tax receipt to election judges C. C. Herndon and Charles Porras and requested a ballot. They refused Dr. Nixon's request but agreed to sign a statement declaring that the denial was based solely on the fact that he was black. The NAACP immediately entered the fray and agreed to compensate Nixon's attorney for filing a five-thousand-dollar damage suit against Herndon and Porras. The federal district court dismissed the complaint on the grounds that the primary was only a means of choosing candidates, not of electing officeholders. Therefore, the refusal of a ballot to Nixon was not a violation of his rights under the Fifteenth Amendment. The attorneys for the NAACP successfully carried the case to the Supreme Court of the United States on a writ of error. Although the Supreme Court in 1927 ruled in favor of Nixon and granted him damages, the victory was incomplete, since the justices based their decision on the

Fourteenth Amendment, which provided much weaker grounds for federal intervention than the Fifteenth Amendment. The Texas legislature had made a legal error in using the state to deny blacks the vote rather than leaving the decision to the Democratic Party. As one black attorney quipped, the court "reached the right result for the wrong amendment."[8]

The Texas Legislature, however, was quick to remedy the situation, repealing the unconstitutional discriminatory portion of the 1923 statute and replacing it with one giving political parties, through their executive committees, the right to determine "who shall be qualified to vote or otherwise participate" in party activities. The state executive committee of the Democratic Party hastily adopted a resolution declaring that only "white Democrats . . . and none other" could vote in the primary elections of 1928.[9]

Despite the fact that injunctions had been unsuccessful in the past, two Houston blacks, J. B. Grigsby and O. P. DeWalt, sought on July 20, 1928, to restrain "the county Democratic executive committee from enforcing the state law." On July 23, two days before the primary election, federal district judge Joseph C. Hutcheson, Jr., denied the injunction, declaring that "political parties may prescribe their own membership qualifications and the Democratic Party could therefore bar Negroes from its primaries."[10]

Disappointed by this setback, black Houstonians appealed to the national office of the NAACP for assistance, but their plea arrived too late for serious consideration, since the top officials had already pledged to support the efforts of El Paso blacks who had arranged for Dr. Nixon to present his poll tax receipt to precinct judge James Condon. The confrontation of July 28, 1928, was a repeat of the 1924 incident, with Nixon subsequently filing suit against Condon for five thousand dollars in damages. DeWalt and Grisby expressed intense displeasure over the NAACP's decision not to take up their case. Officials of the organization had considerable difficulty in persuading them to drop their case in the interest of racial unity and to work with other groups in Texas, such as "fraternal orders, clubs and churches, in contributing toward the expense of the Nixon case."[11]

Once again the district court ruled against the plaintiff, allowing Nixon and the NAACP attorneys to appeal the case first to the Fifth Circuit Court of Appeals and eventually, in early 1932, to the United States Supreme Court. In a five-to-four decision, the Supreme Court in the second Nixon case declared unconstitutional the statutory provision lodging the power to exclude blacks from party ranks in the hands of the state executive committee. In the opinion of Justice Benjamin Cardozo, only the state Democratic Party convention, not the state legislature, could give the executive committee power to bar blacks from its primaries. Again, however, the court based its decision on the Fourteenth Amendment and ignored the contention of Nixon's lawyers that "a vote at a primary election is a vote within the intent of the Fifteenth Amendment and that detailed regulation by the state transformed the Democratic Party into an instrumentality of the state."[12]

Although the NAACP hailed the second Nixon decision as another glorious victory in its battle for universal suffrage, a number of black Houstonians were less elated. Still smarting from the NAACP's earlier refusal to support their local efforts, three energetic and race-conscious young black attorneys — Carter Wesley, J. Alston Atkins, and James Nabrit — and a fearless black gambler named Julius White no longer favored working alongside an ineffective and dilatory national organization; instead they decided to take matters into their own hands.

Of the three attorneys, only Wesley was a native Houstonian. Born in 1892, Wesley was a graduate of Fisk University and Northwestern University Law School. After a brief sojourn practicing law in Muskogee, Oklahoma, where he teamed up with his old friend Atkins, also a graduate of Fisk University but with a law degree from Yale University, Wesley and his partner moved to Houston in 1927.

Shortly after their arrival in Houston, Wesley and Atkins joined with C. F. Richardson, Sr., editor of the influential *Informer,* and two black businessmen, George H. Webster and S. B. Williams, to raise twenty-five thousand dollars with which to establish a real estate firm named the Safety Loan and Brokerage Company, Inc. When the bottom dropped out of the real estate market in wake of the stock market crash of 1929, these men concentrated their energies on the newspaper and publishing business. Hard times and personality conflicts took their toll on these men as they vied for control of the Webster-Richardson Publishing Company. In early 1931 Wesley maneuvered Richardson off the board of directors and persuaded C. N. Love to merge his newspaper, the *Texas Freeman,* with the *Informer,* but Richardson kept the competition going by founding the Houston *Defender.* By 1937 Wesley had transformed his publishing interests into a statewide chain of black newspapers, which included the Dallas *Express* and the San Antonio *Express,* and had founded the National Newspaper Publishers' Association.

Wesley and Atkins, two "hard-headed, almost cold-blooded" businessmen, did not limit their activities to business enterprises. In 1930 they persuaded James M. Nabrit, a bright young attorney from Atlanta who had recently received his law degree from Northwestern University, to join them in forming a law firm of Nabrit, Atkins, and Wesley. The partnership lasted only briefly, however, as Atkins left Houston in 1936 to accept the position of acting president of Winston-Salem Teachers College in North Carolina, and Nabrit moved to Washington, D.C., where he later became president of Howard University.[13]

Nevertheless, the three champions of black rights were together long enough to organize an important grass-roots movement in Houston for overturning the white primary in Texas without assistance from the NAACP. In addition to Julius White, who had contacts with the black underworld, they also attracted the cooperation of Richard Randolph Grovey, leader of the militant Third Ward Civic Club. Born in Brazoria County near Sweeney in 1889, Grovey graduated from Waco Colored High School in 1910 and from Tillotson College in Austin in 1914. Upon graduation he briefly served as principal of a rural school, leaving after the white superintendent instructed him to employ a woman of questionable virtue. In 1917 he moved to Houston and opened a barbershop on Dowling Street where, as a community organizer, he became a controversial figure by spearheading several improvements in the Third Ward. Bold and fearless, the outspoken Grovey expressed his guiding principles to anyone who would listen. "I've lived as long as I want without a right to be a citizen," he asserted. "I intend to fight to my dying day — in order that the Negro's right to be a man shall not be curtailed."[14]

As fervent believers in political activism, Wesley and Richardson used the pages of their newspapers to urge blacks to pay their poll taxes in anticipation of the day when they could vote and to buoy up their spirits to continue to fight for political rights in the courts. In order to keep black hopes alive, Wesley and his friends financed several attempts in Houston to prevent Democratic officials from barring black poll tax holders from the voting booth. In the summer of 1930 they assisted Julius White in filing for an injunction on behalf of black Houstonians after he was denied the right to vote. In November the *Informer* announced that it had "employed the law firm of Nabrit, Atkins and Wesley to fight the battle of Negroes of Houston in their effort to obtain the ballot" in the upcoming city elections. Nabrit, on behalf of C. N. Love, brought suit for an injunction against the city's Democratic executive committee. Since the city charter explicitly provided for the right of all qualified poll tax holders to vote in primary elections, Nabrit argued that the courts should invalidate the results whenever anyone was denied the privilege of voting. Judge Hutcheson, who was unmoved by Nabrit's eloquence or by the force of his argument, denied the injunction.[15]

In an effort to broaden the base of their support, black Houstonians called for a statewide meeting to map strategy for blocking the Democratic Party's plans to exclude them from the summer primary elections of 1932. Although the statewide meeting turned out to be a dismal failure, the effort forged unity among Houston blacks. They organized the Harris County Negro Democratic Club, which included Julius White as president, Nabrit as chairman of the board of directors, and Grovey as third vice-president. In explaining the club's strategy, Grovey stated, "We plan to use reason, the public press and the Courts to let the world see Texas Democracy as it really is."[16]

During 1932 the club rallied behind the NAACP's effort to overthrow the white primary in the case of *Nixon v. Condon* and began preparations for black Texans to vote in the July primaries. Believing that they possessed important evidence that would strengthen the NAACP's cause in *Nixon v. Condon*, Wesley, Atkins, and other members of the club filed an amicus curiae brief in the case shortly before the final hearings were to take place and put pressure on the association to permit Atkins, because of his superior knowledge about Texas, to take part in the final arguments before the Supreme Court. Officials of the NAACP were surprised and dismayed by Atkins's unusual request. As one of them said, "I cannot understand what this muddy-minded person is thinking of." Although not anxious to anger the Houstonians a second time, the association officials decided against asking the Court's permission for Atkins to appear before it, but they welcomed any additional information the Texans might furnish the organization.[17]

Though Wesley and Nabrit did not state it at the time, they attributed the NAACP's mishandling of the case to the fact that the association had relied exclusively upon white attorneys to present its cases before the Supreme Court. No individual could "prepare or present Negro cases as well as a trained Negro," Wesley asserted.[18]

Even though members of the Harris County Negro Democratic Club were hardly overjoyed by the Supreme Court's decision in *Nixon v. Condon*, they nevertheless sought to take advantage of it as much as possible. White Texans, however, were just as determined to maintain white supremacy, and the Supreme Court in its decision had shown them the way. If the political party itself and not the state legislature had decided upon who could vote in primary elections, then no infringement of rights guaranteed by the Fourteenth Amendment would have occurred. Led by Judge W. O. Huggins, editor of the *Houston Chronicle,* a number of white Democrats prepared a new resolution to be submitted to the state Democratic convention at its next meeting in Houston. On May 24, 1932, the convention adopted the Huggins plan, which restricted participation in the primary to qualified white citizens.

Undaunted by this development, Wesley and other black leaders urged their supporters to go to the polls despite the latest resolution of the Democratic Party and their unsuccessful attempt of June 27, 1932, to secure on behalf of Julius White a writ of mandamus to force election officials to execute the law and permit blacks to vote. "What do our people expect?" asked a frustrated editor of the *Informer.* "Do they want the judge to tell them to go to the polls and vote?"[19]

In response to these pleas, approximately five hundred blacks in Harris County voted in the Democratic primary on July 23 before 3 P.M., when election judges, on orders from the county headquarters, began to turn them away. Elsewhere in the state, blacks voted without challenge in Bexar and Grayson counties but were prevented from doing so in the cities of Fort Worth, Texarkana, Corsicana, Tyler, and Dallas. Blacks throughout Texas immediately mounted a legal campaign to guarantee their right to vote in the run-off election. In Houston the law firm of Atkins, Wesley, and Nabrit filed in the federal district court two injunctions, one on behalf of White and the other in the name of Dr. William M. Drake, to restrain the "state and county Democratic executive committee from barring Negroes from voting in the primary of August 27." Similar suits were filed in San Antonio, Fort Worth, and Tyler. The state Democratic executive committee at its meeting in Fort Worth on August 8 pledged to fight back. "If the suits were successful," chairman Huggins feared, "they would result in permitting Negroes to vote in every county in the state." In Houston and elsewhere, unsympathetic judges either dismissed the suits or postponed them on technicalities so that few, if any, blacks voted on August 27.[20]

Despite the widespread litigation of black Texans, 1932 ended with as much confusion as it began concerning the legal rights of black voters. Measured in practical terms, the year had witnessed no significant increase in the number of blacks going to the polls. In 1934 the leading candidate for governor, James V. Allred of Bowie, Texas, announced that "in view of the resolution passed by the State Convention of the Democratic Party on May 24, 1932 . . . negroes are not entitled to participate in the primary elections. . . ."[21] After Allred's opinion received widespread support from county chairmen, two blacks from Jefferson County, W. H. Bell and E. L. Jones, filed a petition for a writ of mandamus against every public official they could think of in Texas in order to prevent the court from throwing out their petition for failure to name the right parties. The Texas Supreme Court, as expected, denied the petition eight days before the July primary on the grounds that the Democratic Party was "a voluntary political association" that could determine its own members. The court's decision in *Bell* v. *Hill* was an important factor in Allred's victory in the gubernatorial election of 1934 and a bitter defeat for black Texans. Although disappointed blacks in Houston cooperated with other black Texans in flooding the Justice Department with affidavits recounting voting irregularities at the polls, they could hardly believe this exercise worth the trouble. In the opinion of federal law officials in Texas, however, election judges had acted in good faith and within the law as interpreted in *Bell* v. *Hill* in keeping blacks from voting. The combination of these developments left Houston blacks in a hopeless and defenseless situation.

In spite of these bitter disappointments, blacks in Houston were determined to continue the fight. Convinced that they possessed the necessary funds, leadership, and legal expertise to win where the NAACP had failed, they ignored the admonition of the national leaders that the Supreme Court was dominated by men of conservative leanings. Wesley, Atkins, Nabrit, and Grovey, believing as they did that the NAACP had mismanaged the earlier cases before the Supreme Court, were in no mood to heed this advice. Furthermore, they felt it essential to place all legal preparations in the hands of black attorneys, and the only way to guarantee this happening was to handle the matter themselves. In addition, they were strongly of the opinion that unless blacks possessed the power of the ballot box, they were destined forever to remain mired in "poverty and self-hate." With the right to vote, they would be in a position to correct the injustices that kept them impoverished and to elevate themselves through programs of self-help and through pressure on local governments to alleviate community problems, such as unpaved streets, inadequate schools and hospitals, infrequent garbage pickup, and lack of recreational facilities. In their view, the movement to secure the ballot was more than a middle-class black drive for political rights; it was a broad-based social movement.[22]

In one important particular, the case filed by Atkins and Wesley in the name of Richard Randolph Grovey differed from the previous one against the Texas white primary. Grovey asked for only ten dollars in damages against Albert Townshend, an election judge, and filed the case in a justice-of-peace court in Houston. By this maneuver the two black attorneys took advantage of a Texas law that prohibited all appeals to higher state courts when the damages did not exceed twenty dollars. Consequently, they were able to appeal the case directly to the United States Supreme Court, where, as expected, the decision went against them. In early 1935 the Supreme Court agreed to review the methods used in Texas to exclude blacks from participating in the state's Democratic primaries.

In their argument before the Supreme Court, Wesley and Atkins insisted that the state of Texas (not the Democratic Party) was responsible for disfranchising blacks, since state law required a primary in which party officials were authorized to issue a ballot to all qualified voters except blacks. Consequently, since the legislature determined procedure for the Democratic primary, the state of Texas was clearly in violation of both the fourteenth and fifteenth amendments.

On April 1, 1935, a day many blacks found appropriate in light of the Court's decision, the Supreme Court ruled that the Democratic Party was a private voluntary association of citizens and not a creation of the state of Texas. As such, the party had a right to limit its own membership. The Court was, as Justice Owen Roberts stated, "unable to characterize the managers of the primary election as state officials in such a sense that any action taken by them in obedience to the mandate of the state convention respecting eligibility to participate in the organization's deliberation is state action."[23]

Grovey v. *Townshend* was a serious but not a fatal setback for black Americans. The *Informer* set the tone for black reaction when it compared, in banner headlines, this case with the infamous *Dred Scott* decision of 1857. One black resident of Washington, D.C., believed that *Grovey* v. *Townshend* was infinitely worse, "since the Dred Scott case dealt with only a small handful of fugitive slaves," but this case "affects directly every colored person in the State of Texas and might eventually affect every adult man and woman in every state in the Union." Even the noted black sociologist E. Franklin Frazier saw the decision as an indication "that the path to political power through the white primary offered no promise to disenfranchised blacks."[24]

Angry blacks across the country, especially those in Texas who had opposed the efforts of Wesley and Atkins from the beginning, took out their frustration on the two black lawyers, accusing them of incompetence and stupidity. For instance, R. D. Evans satirically concluded that "their fido pack went bear hunting and treed a skunk." Several NAACP officials feared that everything they had spent years building up had been suddenly destroyed by the legal blundering of Wesley and Atkins. As Walter White, executive secretary of the organization, noted in his autobiography, "Years of hard work and heavy expense appeared to have gone for naught."[25]

The adverse ruling had one edifying effect: Wesley and his Houston friends realized that they must make peace with the NAACP. In turn, the association's officials began to pay closer attention to the grievances of black Houstonians. Consequently, relationships between the two groups were reestablished on a firmer basis than before. For instance, White, sensitive to the charges of Wesley that the NAACP relied too heavily upon white lawyers, successfully pushed the appointment of Charles Houston, vice-dean of Howard University Law School, as special counsel of the NAACP. This appointment pleased Atkins, who interpreted it as a significant "victory for Negro Lawyers." He optimistically wrote Houston that "under the leadership of able Negro counsel like yourself, . . . it is my belief that Negro Texas can be led to go forward with the NAACP."[26]

Delighted by this change of attitude among black Houstonians, officials of the NAACP moved quickly to launch a new membership drive in Texas. They persuaded the forceful editor of the Oklahoma *Black Dispatch,* Roscoe Dunjee, to join with William Pickens, an NAACP field worker, in conducting a tour of key cities in Texas for the purposes of increasing membership and of raising funds for the organization. Carter Wesley threw his full support behind this effort and gave their visits special coverage in his chain of Texas newspapers. One immediate result of this campaign was the establishment, on October 16, 1936, of the Texas State Conference of

Branches of the NAACP, which, at its first meeting in Dallas, named R. D. Evans president.

While black Houstonians applauded the work of Charles Houston in strengthening the role of black lawyers in the association, they did not lessen efforts to secure voting rights in the city and state. On October 21, 1938, an injunction was filed on behalf of C. F. Richardson, Sr., Will Gree, Dr. William M. Drake, and Julius White against the executive committee of the Democratic Party of Houston, asking the court to restrain the committee from prohibiting black participation in the upcoming November primary. On this occasion the black petitioners retained the legal services of the white law firm of W. A. Combs and Otto Mullinax to plead their case before Judge Kennerly's court. This action reflected the fact that even black Houstonians had grown unhappy with the way Wesley and Atkins handled the Grovey case. The following day, on October 25, a meeting of interested black citizens took place in the YMCA cafeteria, where they approved the suit, donated over sixty dollars to the cause, and named a committee to solicit additional funds across the state.

In order to disprove the plaintiff's contention that the state convention's ban against blacks' voting in primaries did not apply in city elections, white Democratic officials in Houston hastily called a "convention" that unanimously passed a lilywhite resolution. In fact, this resolution was identical to the one adopted by the state convention of 1932 except that the words "Houston" and "Harris County" were substituted for "Texas."

In addition to insisting that the city charter contained no provision for party conventions, Combs and Mullinax argued that, since the National Democratic Party had permitted blacks to participate in party affairs, even seating them as delegates in the 1936 national convention, party officials in Houston had no right to bar them from local primaries. These arguments failed to impress Judge Kennerly, who ruled that there was no difference between this case and the one instigated by Drake in 1933 against the executive committee of the Democratic Party for the city of Houston. In addition, he contended that the Texas Supreme Court in *Bell* v. *Hill* and the United States Supreme Court in *Grovey* v. *Townshend* had fully settled all questions concerning the white primary in Texas.

In commenting on this latest setback in the bitter fight for black rights, the *Informer*, in an editorial entitled "The Primary and Hitlerism," enunciated the similarities between America's subjugation of its black population and Hitler's repression of Jews in Germany. In fact, this argument would become standard fare in the rhetoric of black Americans throughout the late 1930s and the early 1940s.[27]

Although Richardson pleaded with the NAACP to appeal the case to the Supreme Court, the association refused out of fear that it would result in another Grovey disaster and promote further dissension within the Houston branch. Locally, Richardson came under attack for violating a traditional rule of the NAACP against endorsing political candidates; as president of the Houston branch, he threw his support behind John Nance Garner in the summer of 1939. Carter Wesley joined high-ranking officials in the national office in repudiating Richardson's actions after earlier defending him against the charge of being weak and ineffective.

Following accusations that Richardson had mishandled association funds, Walter White sent Daisy Lampkin, an NAACP field worker, to investigate affairs in the Houston office. She uncovered evidence of graft and corruption as well as personal animosity, reporting incidents of "threats of murder" by one member against another. Nevertheless, she also found a number of honest and hardworking members, and she approved of their plan to call a new election, with the understanding that unless "honorable men were elected" she would recommend discontinuing the Houston chapter.[28]

Fortunately for the Houston branch, a change in leadership took place because of Richardson's death in 1939, the departure of Atkins and James Nabrit from the city, and the retirement of veteran warriors, such as C. N. Love. Their places were quickly taken by such individuals as Mrs. Lulu White, wife of Julius White; Rev. Albert A. Lucas, pastor of Good Hope Baptist Church, one of the largest black churches in Houston; Dr. Lonnie Smith, a successful dentist; Sidney Hasgett, a hod carrier; and C. F. Richardson, Jr., who took over the *Defender* following his father's death. Together with Carter Wesley, R. R. Grovey, and Dr. Drake, they worked to restore black solidarity, to pump new life into the movement for black civil rights, and to renew cooperation with the national office of the NAACP. In November, 1939, they selected as president of the Houston branch Albert A. Lucas, a young dynamic minister with unusual organizational skills and fund-raising talents. By the end of the year the Houston office reported a total of 1,484 new members, attracted by a well-coordinated membership drive.

Rallying black Houstonians behind the NAACP with his infectious enthusiasm, Lucas began preparing for another all-out assault on the white primary. Following a citywide meeting of black Houstonians in March of 1940, Lucas, in the name of the Houston branch, issued a call for blacks throughout the state to attend the annual conference of NAACP branches in Corpus Christi and dispatched a special invitation to the national office, which sent Thurgood Marshall, one of the organization's brightest young black attorneys.

At the Corpus Christi meeting, Lucas was named president of the conference, and together with Marshall and other prominent black Texans, they laid plans for another suit. They decided to place general direction in the hands of the National Legal Committee of the NAACP, although attorney W. J. Durham of Sherman, Texas, was retained as Texas resident council, with Houstonians Wesley and Henry S. Davis, Jr., as his assistants. In selecting a suitable plaintiff, Lucas suggested two members from his own congregation—Dr. Lonnie E. Smith and Sidney Hasgett—after Wesley adamantly objected to Clifton F. Richardson, Jr., editor of the Houston *Defender,* on the grounds that he would never give "publicity to a competitor." Embittered by this decision, Richardson accused Wesley of treachery. By this time, Wesley ran the *Informer,* after he and others had forced Richardson off the paper. In his personal column in the *Informer,* "The Ram's Horn," Wesley labeled Richardson's accusation as unfounded and irresponsible and scolded his competitor for belittling Hasgett's occupation.[29]

Although both Smith and Hasgett were refused ballots in the primary election of July 27, 1940, the local legal committee waited to file suit until Hasgett, accompanied by Grovey, Wesley, and Julius Smith, was also denied a ballot in the run-off election of August 24. The election judge involved in the second incident demanded to know who was behind the request. "You haven't been coming up here for the past nine or ten years," he said. "Now speak out, who sent you here?" Wesley replied that the black citizens of Houston had sent them, and Grovey explained that they sought the same privileges as Mexican Americans, who were allowed to vote in primaries. After telephoning the local Democratic headquarters for advice, the election judges turned Smith and Hasgett away.[30]

On January 14, 1941, Davis, accompanied by Lucas, filed suit in the United States district court in the name of Hasgett against election judges Theodore Werner and John H. Blackburn, asking for five thousand dollars in damages. After denying a motion by the defendants' attorney to dismiss the case, Judge Kennerly set the hearings for April 25. Marshall and Durham argued that the denial of a ballot to Hasgett, in an election authorized by state action, constituted a violation of the Fifteenth Amendment. Both the primary and general elections were "an integral part of the election machinery of the state of Texas since the Democratic Party," they contended, was in actuality the only organized political party in Texas. As proof of this assertion, they pointed out that "since 1859, the nominees of the Democratic Party had been elected in a major election with two exceptions." On May 5 Judge Kennerly ruled that Werner and Blackburn had a right to exclude Hasgett from the Democratic primary.[31]

Although the Fifth Circuit Court of Appeals granted Hasgett's request for an appeal, Marshall and the NAACP decided to drop the case before the hearing took place in New Orleans. The reason for this unexpected development was Marshall's belief that the Supreme Court's decision in *United States* v. *Classic* had important implications for overturning the white primary. Although this case involved fraudulent election officials in

Louisiana and had nothing to do with the right of black voters, it concerned primary elections, and therefore Marshall believed it was relevant to the NAACP's effort to invalidate the Texas white primary.

In the *Classic* case, the Supreme Court in a five-to-three decision held that Congress possessed "the authority to regulate primary elections when . . . they are a step in the exercise by the people of their choice of representative in Congress." In other words, the court ruled that the right of qualified voters to cast their ballots in a primary and to have them counted was a right "secured by the Constitution." Thurgood Marshall and Durham not only found the decision "striking and far-reaching," but they also instantly recognized its importance to the NAACP's case before the courts. As Durham said, this decision put the Supreme Court "on our side of the question and we must press forward with new hope and determination."[32]

In light of these considerations, the NAACP attorneys decided to drop *Hasgett* v. *Werner* and to file a new suit "based upon the theory of the case of *United States* v. *Classic*. . . ." White and Marshall then traveled to Texas to break the news to black Texans, who were understandably disappointed by the decision to drop the Hasgett case. For example, Julius White warned Marshall that he "had better win the next case or not return to Texas." Wesley, on the other hand, believed that Marshall was right and defended him vigorously in the pages of the *Informer*. "The tables are turned," he predicted, "and whereas the Democratic Party has had all of the protection . . . now the Negroes are on top of the world."[33]

Since Dr. Lonnie Smith had been refused a ballot in the primary of July 27, where nominations for federal offices were determined, Marshall, on November 13, 1941, filed a new suit in his name against S. E. Allwright and James E. Luizza, election judges of Harris County, seeking a declaratory judgment and five thousand dollars in damages.

In his arguments before the district court, Marshall pointed out that the Democratic Party did not possess the usual characteristics of a closed organization, such as a constitution, a set of bylaws, or a list of active members. He also stressed the similarity between this case and *United States* v. *Classic,* where the Supreme Court had ruled that the primary election in Louisiana was an integral part of the election machinery of that state and, therefore, subject to federal control. Neither District Judge Kennerly nor the judges on the circuit court were convinced by Marshall's logic. They ruled that primaries were party affairs, not elections in the constitutional sense.

Marshall and the other black attorneys filed a petition for a writ of certiorari in the United States Supreme Court. When Marshall delivered his statement to the court on November 12, 1943, an optimistic and excited Carter Wesley was one of the spectators. To his surprise, the justices "sat

Legal victories, such as *Smith v. Allwright,* opened the door for black participation in local politics in the mid-1940s. Shown here are African Americans participating in the 1948 Democratic Harris County Rump Convention. *Courtesy Houston Public Library, Houston Metropolitan Research Center*

on the edge of their seats" during the presentation but afterwards "asked no questions." The Supreme Court delayed rendering a decision until the attorney general of Texas had an opportunity to file a last-minute brief, which rehashed the old argument that the Democratic Party was a voluntary organization of members "banded together for the purpose of selecting individuals" to be candidates in the general election.[34]

In a landmark eight-to-one decision, the Supreme Court in January, 1944, declared the white primary unconstitutional. Justice Stanley Reed, a Kentucky Democrat, in delivering the majority opinion, acknowledged that primaries were an integral part of the election process and therefore neither the state nor the Democratic Party could legally deny blacks the right to vote in them.[35] At last the long and frustrating struggle for the right of blacks to vote in primary elections in the South was over. While the abolition of the white primary did not result either in any dramatic increase in the number of black voters in Texas and in Houston or in any noticeable shift of political power for the white establishment, this victory was a significant boost to black morale and an important stimulus for an upswing of interest in the NAACP, which experienced a tremendous growth in membership in 1945 and 1946. Carter Wesley proudly asserted that membership in the Houston branch had "reached more than 4,000 netting over $5,000."[36]

J. Alston Atkins, a former Houstonian, fittingly summarized the struggle when he proclaimed that it revealed "the patience, and endurance, and character of the Negro race at its best."[37] Black Houstonians can properly take pride in the accomplishments of their forbearers who successfully secured for them the political weapon that they so effectively use today.

Notes

1. *United States* v. *Reese,* 92 U.S. pp. 214-56 (1876); John Hope Franklin, *Reconstruction: After the Civil War* (Chicago, 1961), pp. 208-209; Milton R. Konvitz, *The Constitution and Civil Rights* (New York, 1947), pp. 8-28.

2. Quoted in LaWanda Cox and John H. Cox, *Reconstruction, the Negro and the New South* (New York, 1973), pp. 144-51.

3. *Plessy* v. *Ferguson,* 163 U.S. 537, 165 Sup. Ct. 559 (1896); Darlene Clark Hine, *Black Victory: The Rise and Fall of the Black Primary in Texas* (Millwood, N.Y., 1979), 17; Paul Lewinson, *Race, Class, and Party: A History of Negro Suffrage and White Politics in the South* (New York, 1963), pp. 111-12; Lawrence D. Rice, *The Negro in Texas, 1874-1900* (Baton Rouge, 1971).

4. Robert V. Haynes, *A Night of Violence: The Houston Riot of 1917* (Baton Rouge, 1976); Charles C. Alexander, *The Crusade for Conformity: The Klu Klux Klan in Texas, 1920-1930* (Houston, 1962).

5. San Antonio *Express,* May 11, 1923, July 25, 1923; Harold M. Taver to D. A. McAskill, 1922, Eugene V. Baker Library, Texas State Historical Library at University of Texas in Austin; *General and Special Laws of the State of Texas, Thirty-Ninth Legislature, Second Called Session* (Austin, 1923), pp. 74-75.

6. C. N. Love to W. L. Davis, Mar. 18, 1922, quoted in Melvin Jones Banks, "The Pursuit of Equality: The Movement for First Class Citizenship among Negroes in Texas, 1920-1950" (Ph.D. diss., Syracuse University, 1962), p. 144; *Love* v. *Griffith,* 236 S. W. 239 (Tex. Civ. App. 1922); Authur B. Spingarn to W. E. B. DuBois, Oct. 31, 1924, A. B. Spingarn Papers, Box 3, Library of Congress Washington, D. C.; Hine, *Black Victory,* pp. 59-60.

7. Love v. Griffith, 266 U. S. 32, 45 Sup. Ct. 12 (1924); C. N. Love to W. L. Davis, Mar. 18, 1922, quoted in Banks, "Pursuit of Equality," p. 144.

8. *Nixon* v. *Herndon,* 273 U. S. 538 (1927); Houston *Chronicle,* Mar. 8, 1927; Loren Miller, *The Petitioners: The Story of the Supreme Court of the United States and the Negro* (New York, 1966), p. 233; Hine, *Black Victory,* pp. 76-85.

9. *General and Special Laws of the State of Texas, Fortieth Legislature, First Called Session* (Austin, 1927), p. 193; R. W. Hainsworth, "The Negro and the Texas

Primaries," *Journal of Negro History,* 38 (Oct., 1933), p. 428; Houston *Informer,* Mar. 12, 1927; Houston *Post-Dispatch,* June 3, 1927.

10. *J. B. Grisby et al. v. Guy Harris,* 17 Fed (2nd) 942, (S.D. Texas, 1928); Walter Lindsey, "Black Houstonians Challenge the White Democratic Primary, 1921-1944" (master's thesis, University of Houston, 1969), pp. 12-13; A. W. Jackson, *A Sure Foundation and a Sketch of Negro Life in Texas* (Houston, 1940), p. 385.

11. O. P. DeWalt to Robert Bagnall, Sept. 8, 1928, NAACP Papers, Box D-64: Marshall to William T. Andrews, Oct. 29, 1928, ibid., Box C-69, Library of Congress.

12. *Nixon v. Condon,* 286 U.S. 73 (1932); Miller, *Petitioners,* pp. 223-24; Hine, *Black Victory,* pp. 119-26; Henry J. Abraham, *Freedom and the Court: Civil Rights and Liberties in the United States* (New York, 1972).

13. Hine, *Black Victory,* p. 129; Lindsey, "Black Houstonians," p. 25.

14. Hine, *Black Victory,* pp. 126, 129-30; Lindsey, "Black Houstonians," pp. 26-27; Houston *Informer,* Feb. 16, 1935; Banks, "Pursuit of Equality," p. 214; Jackson, *A Sure Foundation,* pp. 681-83.

15. Houston *Informer,* May 5, May 10, 1930, Nov. 22, 1930, Dec. 13, 1930, Jan. 17, Jan. 31, 1931. A copy of the brief in this case is in Nixon papers, Lyndon Baines Johnson Library, University of Texas at Austin, Box 2. See also Carter Wesley to Knollenberg, Jan. 14, 1931, NAACP Papers, Box D-63.

16. Houston *Informer,* Jan. 9, 1931; *Houston Post,* July 1, 1934; Hainsworth, "Negro and Texas Primaries," p. 433.

17. Carter Wesley to Herbert Seligman, May 10, 1932; James Marshall to Spingarn, Feb. 12, 1932; White to Spingarn, Jan. 22, 1932; Nathan Margold to Charles Houston, Mar. 1, 1932, NAACP Papers, Box D-63; White to E. O. Smith, Nov. 2, 1932, ibid., Box D-62.

18. Houston *Informer,* July 16, 1932; Hine, *Black Victory,* pp. 144-45.

19. *White v. County Democratic Committee,* 60 Fed (2nd) 973 (S.D. Texas, 1932); Houston *Informer,* July 22, 1932.

20. Wesley to Knollenberg, May 30, 1931, NAACP Papers, Box D-63; *White v. Harris County Democratic Executive Committee,* 60 Fed (2nd) 973 (S.D. Tex., 1932); Houston *Informer,* July 30, 1932; Hainsworth, "Negro and Texas Primaries," p. 447.

21. James V. Allred to D. B. Wood, June 9, 1930, NAACP Papers, Box D-63.

22. R. D. Evans to White, Apr. 28, 1935, NAACP Papers, Box D-92; Houston *Informer,* Sept. 29, 1934, Jan. 16, 1935, Mar. 2, Mar. 30, 1935.

23. Thurgood Marshall, "Rise and Collapse of White Democratic Primary," *Journal of Negro Education,* 26 (Summer, 1957): 252; *Grovey v. Townshend,* 295 U.S. 45 (1935).

24. Houston *Informer,* Apr. 6, 1935; William J. Thompkins to Marvin Hunter McIntyre, Apr. 23, 1935, quoted in Hine, *Black Victory,* p. 172; E. Franklin Frazier, "The Negro in the American Social Order," *Journal of Negro Education,* 4 (July, 1935): 302.

25. Evans to White, Apr. 28, 1935, NAACP Papers, Box D-91; Walter White, *A Man Called White: The Autobiography of Walter White* (Bloomington, Ind., 1970), p. 88.

26. White, *A Man Called White,* pp. 143-45; Atkins to Charles Houston, Sept. 29, 1935, and Nov. 11, 1935, NAACP Papers, Box D-92.

27. Houston *Informer,* Nov. 5, 1938.

28. Daisy Lampkin to White, Oct. 30, 1939, Nov. 6, 1939; White to Lampkin, Nov. 15, 1939, NAACP Papers, Box G-204; Gillette, "Rise of NAACP in Texas," *Southwestern Historical Quarterly* 81 (Apr., 1978): 396.

29. Houston *Informer,* Aug. 10, Sept. 28, 1940; Lindsey, "Black Houstonians," pp. 55-56.

30. Houston *Informer,* Aug. 31, 1940.

31. "The Ballot: Texas Primary Case," NAACP, annual report, 1941, p. 15; memorandum from Legal Department to members of the National Legal Committee, re: Texas Primary Case, *Hasgett* v. *Werner,* NAACP Papers, box 22; Houston *Informer,* Feb. 8 and Apr. 29, 1941; *Sidney Hasgett* v. *Theodore Werner and John H. Blackburn,* Civil Docket No. 449, U. S. District Court for Southern District of Tex., Houston. Jan. 14, 1941. Smith files, Federal Records Center, Fort Worth, Tex.

32. Hine, *Black Victory,* pp. 202-206; Marshall, "White Democratic Primary," pp. 249-54; Houston *Informer,* Nov. 14 and 22, 1941; *United States* v. *Classic,* 313 U.S. 299 (1941).

33. Hine, *Black Victory,* pp. 206-207; Houston *Informer,* Nov. 22, 1941; Gillette, "NAACP in Texas," p. 408.

34. Houston *Informer,* Nov. 20 and 27, 1943, and Dec. 4, 1943.

35. *Smith* v. *Allwright,* 321 U. S. 657, 64 Sup. Ct. 757 (1944); Lindsey, "Black Houstonians," pp. 105-106.

36. Houston *Informer,* Apr. 8, 1944, and Dec. 23 and 30, 1944; Banks, "Pursuit of Equality," p. 332; Lindsey, "Black Houstonians," pp. 111-15.

37. J. Alston Atkins, *The Texas Negro and His Political Rights: A History of the Fight of Negroes to Enter the Democratic Primaries of Texas* (Houston, 1932), p. 6.

The Houston Sit-In Movement of 1960-61

F. Kenneth Jensen

Sit-ins erupted spontaneously in hundreds of southern cities in the spring and summer of 1960. Manifesting the aspirations and hopes of black youth at the dawn of a new decade, these demonstrations employed old tactics, developed earlier by labor unions and subsequently used by small, relatively unnoticed pacifist and civil rights groups.[1] But in 1960 these old techniques of protest won unusual popularity among a rising generation of blacks. They bolstered the established civil rights movement and helped make the 1960s the dramatic time it was. The sit-ins were the opening gambit in a decade that would be characterized by an escalating strategy of direct action to eliminate the most overt expression of racial discrimination—segregation.

Racial segregation became firmly entrenched in Houston in the early twentieth century. During those years, blacks suffered increasing social discrimination and political disabilities. The Texas legislature established a racially motivated poll tax in 1902. The Terrell election laws permitted the exclusion of blacks from primaries. Although the state legislature did not uniformly bar blacks from voting in primaries until 1923, Houston had introduced all-white primaries by 1918.[2]

Before World War II most Texas blacks resided on the farms of East Texas. During and after the war many of them, responding to new job opportunities, moved to Texas cities, such as Houston. In cities they found strength in numbers and felt less vulnerable to white intimidation and terrorism than they had in rural areas. The urbanization of blacks thus stimulated their collective resistance to traditional patterns of exclusion imposed on them by the white majority.[3]

Houston felt some of the earliest stirrings of urban black protest in Texas. During this time two important lawsuits originated in Harris County that challenged the racial status quo.[4] These cases were important parts of the long, expensive struggle by the National Association for the Advancement of Colored People (NAACP) to subvert the legal basis of segregation. Both cases resulted in victories for blacks. In 1944 in *Smith v. Allwright,* the

United States Supreme Court outlawed the all-white primary. In 1950 in *Sweatt* v. *Painter,* the court effectively opened the graduate and professional schools of the University of Texas to blacks. These decisions hastened beneficial changes for Texas blacks. In Houston, Rev. L. H. Simpson became the first black in the twentieth century to run for public office when he attempted election to an at-large position on the city council in 1946. Simpson pastored the largest black Baptist church in the Bayou City and was a leading figure in the Houston chapter of the NAACP. Although he lost the election, Simpson's call to move the city "Toward Democracy" did not fall on deaf ears. Two years later the Democratic Party integrated its Harris County convention.[5]

Inspired by these successes, Houston blacks filed many civil rights suits against the city and Harris County in the early 1950s. These mainly aimed at opening public facilities to blacks and at expanding job opportunities. During the tenure of Mayor Roy Hofheinz, Sr., the city desegregated the municipal golf course after blacks brought suit and after the mayor said that the only alternative to integrating the links would be to construct, at public expense, a new golf course for the city's black citizens. Shortly thereafter the facilities of the Houston Public Library were quietly opened to blacks. Also during the Hofheinz era, racial designations over restroom doors were eliminated in City Hall while integrated waiting rooms, drinking fountains, and restrooms served all at the new city airport.[6]

By the mid-fifties blacks in Houston had made measured progress, but even greater strides were being made elsewhere. In 1954 the high court delivered its momentous decision in the *Brown* case, opening the door to public school integration and completely reversing the separate-but-equal doctrine enunciated in *Plessy* v. *Ferguson* in 1896. The following year Martin Luther King, Jr., and others in Montgomery, Alabama, founded a community organization and action group to protest continued segregated seating on public buses. By adapting methods of nonviolent protest pioneered in India by Mahatma Gandhi, King and his colleagues advanced their cause in Alabama—as well as in the minds and hearts of millions elsewhere.[7]

Although the support for change grew steadily, successes in the modern civil rights movement were not won cheaply. Each skirmish in the struggle normally required hours of hard work, constant pressure on public officials, and often costly lawsuits. White resistance to change also mounted. Those who favored continued segregation exposed civil rights supporters to indignities, harassment, and occasionally death, the threat of which was always present. Segregationists also organized well-financed "massive resistance" campaigns, especially to forestall public school integration. Gov. Orval Faubus of Arkansas provoked a national crisis by blocking the entry of nine black children to Little Rock High School in 1957. In Congress, white Southerners and their sympathizers repeatedly blocked passage of effective civil rights legislation.[8]

Resistance to change was evident in Houston, too, particularly regarding school integration. Despite the extraordinary election in 1958 of a black woman to the board of the Houston Independent School District (HISD), that body remained overwhelmingly white and wedded to the status quo and to traditional racial arrangements. It thwarted every effort to integrate local schools as long as it possibly could. In 1960, when it finally had to administer the desegregation of the first grade, it enforced only minimal compliance. Neither HISD managers nor the mayor were inclined to lead the city further along the difficult road "toward democracy" and into a new era of race relations. Mayor Lewis Cutrer, although elected with black support, tied himself firmly to the business community and paid little attention to the concerns of blacks or other minorities.[9]

The momentary lull in the national civil rights struggle was dramatically ended in February of 1960 when black students in Greensboro, North Carolina, sat down at a segregated, all-white lunch counter; they requested service and continued to sit and wait after they had been refused. This sit-down/sit-in tactic immediately caught on. Throughout the South similar demonstrations soon took place. Students in many cities realized that all they had to do to defy—and perhaps to rend fatally—the patterns of deference upon which segregation depended was to sit down and sit tight. Their primary targets were the lunch counters of southern chain stores that welcomed black clientele but refused to serve them in their sit-down eating facilities.[10]

In Houston, students at predominantly black Texas Southern University paid close attention to the dramatic actions of black students in other parts of the South. They were angered when U.S. senator Lyndon Baines Johnson of Texas remarked that black students in the Lone Star State were too complacent to engage in public protests. This remark, in combination with the momentum created by student activists across the South, inspired T.S.U. students to begin sit-in demonstrations in the Bayou City.[11]

After a series of meetings and intense discussion, T.S.U. students in early 1960 decided to target a Weingarten's supermarket near the campus. Its proximity to the campus made it an inviting target; it was only a few blocks away, within easy walking distance. The store itself was surrounded by the black community, which provided most of its patronage. Moreover, many black Houstonians believed that the Weingarten family, one of the city's wealthiest and most prominent Jewish families, profited enormously from their black clientele. "It was a rather familiar statement on the part of many individuals," Dr. J. B. Jones recalled, "that Joe Weingarten is getting rich off of us." Jones, who was dean of students at T.S.U. at the time and trying to maintain effective contact with student militants, remembers that "the students felt that Weingarten's was the recipient of considerable monies from the black community, and that they should perhaps have been as responsive if not more responsive than other businesses to the sensitivities of the black community."[12]

The Weingarten family's liberal reputation also recommended one of their stores as a target to the students. Otis King, then in his second year at T.S.U.'s Thurgood S. Marshall School of Law, recalls that he and his colleagues knew that Joseph Weingarten, the family patriarch, had recently been the recipient of an award from B'nai B'rith for his generous and outstanding humanitarian and community service. In light of this award, King and other students decided that Weingarten would be particularly vulnerable to pressure to abandon racist policies in his stores. Moreover, the Weingarten's store near the campus — one of several owned by the Weingarten family in Houston — had the added attraction of having a sit-down eating facility. All of these factors, as Jack Weingarten ruefully remembers, made the store "a focal point for black activists' interests."[13]

Houston's first sit-in occurred on March 4, 1960, a Friday afternoon, at Weingarten's Store No. 26 on Almeda near Wheeler. Thirteen T.S.U. students marched from the flagpole in front of Hannah Hall on campus to the store. By the time they arrived at the store their numbers had quadrupled. They immediately occupied the thirty lunch counter stools and requested service. "We filled the counter," Holly Hogrobrooks recalls. She and other students were apprehensive about the possibility of violence that had accompanied many other sit-ins across the South in recent weeks. "I think all of us went with the anticipation that there could be some violence," Hogrobrooks remembers, although none occurred. The store manager quickly closed the counter, after which nobody really knew what to do. "Many stood around," Hogrobrooks recalls. "Spectators stood around. Within fifteen minutes the law enforcement officers got here, and they stood around. Everybody stood around!" The students occupied the lunch counter for almost four hours before leaving the store unmolested.[14]

The students resumed their sit-in at Weingarten's the next day and also sent a detachment to integrate Mading's drugstore a few blocks away. A brawl between whites and blacks in Weingarten's parking lot left one black, James Gates, with a knife wound in the back. None of the sit-in students, however, apparently was involved in the incident. The manager of the store was persuaded to close it for the remainder of the day to avoid further trouble. Nevertheless, the actions of the students dominated the attention of the local news media — attention that the Weingarten family deeply regretted. "We weren't anxious to be the spearhead in this movement," Jack Weingarten recalls, adding that his family's greatest desire at that time was "to get out of the spotlight."[15]

The rapid growth of the sit-in movement in Houston did, in fact, soon dilute the pressure on the Weingarten family. The following Monday sit-in activists appeared at the Henke and Pillot supermarket in the 3600 block of Crawford. There twenty-five blacks, almost half of them women, demonstrated. Sit-ins also resumed at Mading's, but Weingarten's lunch counter was kept closed. On Tuesday a fourth store, Walgreen's drugstore at Main Street and Elgin, was struck. Although one white youth was arrested on the scene for brandishing a razor blade, no actual violence ensued. Mading's management followed the Weingarten example and closed its lunch counter. At Henke and Pillot, the entire lunch counter was torn out and replaced with a display of carpets. When students turned their attention on Wednesday to Woolworth's on the 3200 block of Main Street, management quickly closed the lunch counter for "remodeling."[16]

The sit-in blitzkrieg caught Houston unprepared. Support from the black community, however, was evident from the very beginning. Holly Hogrobrooks, who participated in the original Weingarten's sit-in, recalls that black patrons spontaneously abandoned their grocery carts in the checkout lines, closed their purses, and left the store. As the sit-ins spread, support in the black community grew. "It had become kind of a military thing," Hogrobrooks recalls. She likened community supporters to soldiers and supply sergeants who lined up to provide gasoline as well as automobiles and other necessities to the activists.[17]

The sit-ins had an immediate economic impact on the targeted stores. Closing their eating facilities may have allowed them to avoid the political problem of dealing with black activists and the issue of desegregation, but this tactic caused an unavoidable loss of revenue. And the loss of revenue was not confined to the closing of their lunch-counter operations, because the sit-ins quickly triggered a general consumer boycott by black patrons of the targeted stores. The combination of boycotts and sit-ins — that is, the uniting of the black community behind student activists — put great financial pressure on the managers of targeted stores. Otis King, who participated in the sit-ins from the beginning, recalls that he and other student activists were deeply impressed by the community support they received. He doubts that the Weingarten's store ever regained the patronage it lost during the sit-ins. The effectiveness of black economic and political solidarity, King remembers, "taught us a valuable lesson of just how powerful the black community was, and how effective our actions could be by withholding our economic support of businesses that did not treat us fairly."[18]

At the time of these first lunch-counter sit-ins, Houston newspapers reported several minor racial incidents — mainly rock throwing in black neighborhoods.[19] In a more serious case, young whites assaulted a twenty-seven-year-old black man. Felton Turner was stopped at gunpoint at the intersection of Nashua and 22nd Street, kidnapped, and flogged with chains.

His masked assailants asked Turner whether he had participated in any of the lunch-counter sit-ins. Although he denied having done so, they nevertheless decided to torture him further, explaining that they "had a job to do." The *Houston Informer*, a black weekly, printed a grisly picture of Turner exposing his wounds, which included the initials KKK carved on his chest.[20]

In mid-March student activists, in response to the closing of lunch counters, ceased the sit-ins. However, black consumers continued their boycott by refusing to buy groceries at the stores, and the students themselves, although not making headlines, were far from inactive. They organized as the Progressive Youth Association and chose Eldrewey Stearnes, a T.S.U. law student, as president of the organization. They also established supportive contacts with students at Erma Hughes Business College, a local black insitution, as well as from Rice University, an expensive, prestigious university in Houston whose enrollment was limited to white students under the terms of the will of its founder, William Marsh Rice. Students from both of these schools joined the T.S.U. activists in subsequent sit-ins.[21]

City officials had no policy toward the student protesters. Mayor Cutrer issued contradictory statements that seemed to threaten students with arrest while at the same time acknowledging that they had broken no laws. He spoke of forming a committee on race relations, but then he quickly drew back, saying that he would not establish such a committee under pressure from demonstrators.[22]

While public officials wallowed in confusion and indecision, student protesters—strengthened now by organization and with new members from several institutions—carried their campaign out of the black community and struck like lightning in late March at a cluster of downtown targets— Foley's, Grant's, Kress, Walgreen's, and Woolworth's, all large stores. Five white men and a white woman were among the twenty demonstrators at Woolworth's.[23] On March 26, twenty-five young blacks picketed city hall itself for about half an hour, after which they entered the building and requested service at the municipal cafeteria. The demonstrators sat nervously at first and were the objects of considerable attention from a crowd of city employees who gaped at them from the hallway. Then surprisingly they were served. Only one or two of the onlookers ventured into the cafeteria while the blacks ate.[24]

Blacks hailed the integration of the city hall eatery as a significant victory, although the city's major white newspaper minimized the event's importance by reporting that blacks obtained service only because city officials wished to avoid any disturbance during a visit to city hall by the Argentine ambassador to the United States.[25] However, the other major white daily newspaper told quite a different story. In an interview with a

Houston Post reporter, cafeteria operator Frank Russell and his sister-in-law Elenora Russell indicated that they had previously discussed the possibility of a sit-in by blacks and had decided to provide service to any patron who requested it. Ms. Russell added that they planned to continue to serve blacks as long as they were orderly and behaved themselves.[26]

Shortly after the city hall action, Mayor Cutrer agreed to create a biracial committee to study race relations in the Bayou City. He had refused to consider such a committee when black students suggested it, but he quickly acceded to the wishes of the Retail Merchants Association.[27] On April 7 he named thirty-seven businessmen, including eleven blacks, to the newly created Citizens' Relations Committee.[28]

The committee's work did not proceed smoothly, and the committee soon divided into two factions. The minority, led by A. M. Wickliff of the black Harris County Council of Organizations, advocated immediate municipal desegregation. The larger group, which opposed this goal, included representatives of the Retail Merchants Association as well as chamber of commerce president Leon Jaworski, who in 1974 figured prominently in the investigation of the Watergate coverup, which led to Richard Nixon's resignation.[29]

The May 10 meeting of the committee ended in a noisy, unpleasant verbal exchange. Chairman J. P. Hamblen refused to allow any votes to be cast and apparently decided it best that the committee be dissolved. Accordingly, he made no subsequent calls for a meeting and in June formally recommended to the mayor that the committee be disbanded. Hamblen also suggested publicly that desegregation be left entirely up to individual merchants. Felix Tijerina, a Mexican-American restauranteur and committee member, told reporters that employers might retaliate against blacks for causing trouble with the sit-ins by refusing to hire blacks. He argued that black activists could harm the larger black community by antagonizing whites and prompting a backlash. Neither Hamblen's suggestion nor Tijerina's thinly veiled threat not to hire blacks convinced the minority faction of the committee.[30]

Activists halted the sit-ins in April, May, and June, perhaps in anticipation of some favorable action from the committee. They may also have wanted to give more conservative "establishment" blacks an opportunity to make a deal with their white counterparts. The press of schoolwork and final examinations might also have played a role in diminished protest activity.[31] However, in late July the encouraging civil rights proposals drawn up at the Democratic National Convention inspired Eldrewey Stearnes to organize a spate of sit-ins at the same downtown locations hit in late March plus one new location—the cafeteria in the Continental Bus Terminal.[32] Lack of progress by the Citizens' Relations Committee as well as the failure of black moderates to cut a deal with their white colleagues may also have contributed to this new wave of protest. In addition, school was in summer recess, so students had time on their hands.

Protesters encountered a mixed response to their second major wave of sit-ins. Most lunch counters followed the established pattern and simply closed when they appeared. However, on August 2 eight black students from T.S.U. and Hughes Business College entered the Garden Room of Joske's department store downtown and were served by nervous store officials, who refused payment for the food and encouraged the students to eat quickly and leave fast. At nearby Foley's department store, however, two bouncers unceremoniously and firmly evicted protesters. The uneven reception that greeted activists downtown, however, presaged a major victory for the students: on September 1, nine major downtown stores desegregated their eating facilities without publicity or incident.[33]

The Progressive Youth Association followed up the September 1 breakthrough by expanding the scope of its operations to include integrating the staffs of drugstores, filling stations, and banks in black districts.[34] The organization did not, however, abandon the use of sit-ins to desegregate public facilities. In fact it took a final wave of sit-ins in January of 1961 to open up definitively the city hall cafeteria to blacks.[35] That same month P.Y.A. cadre also sat in at the main police station on Reisner Street adjacent to downtown. Up until that time, all black police department employees, including thirty-nine police officers, had to eat by themselves in the cafeteria kitchen.[36]

February witnessed another action as students confronted segregated movie theaters. Sit-ins continued throughout the spring when twenty-three protesters were arrested for unlawful assembly and fined $250 each. Other activists were later arrested during a protest at Union Station, the main railroad facility in the Bayou City. The police arrest campaign of 1961 clearly was an attempt by officials to end the sit-ins. The fines levied on students burdened them seriously, and they had to resort to appeals for money in the black press to help pay them. By the fall of 1961 most activists faced some sort of legal action. Edrewey Stearnes, arrested at Union Station, refused bail and remained in jail.[37] While the 1961 arrests marked the decline of the sit-in movement in Houston, by then student activists largely had achieved their immediate goal. Downtown eating establishments were mostly desegregated, as were some other public facilities, and students had begun to press the attack for fairer employment practices.

Student activists in Houston achieved what they did despite some serious difficulties. Compared to several other large cities in the South, such as Atlanta and Montgomery, the protest movement in Houston was small. There were not more than a hundred regular activists in the Bayou City, and individual sit-ins seldom numbered more than twenty-five or thirty people. Furthermore, although the protesters in Houston obviously enjoyed wide support within the black community, they never developed a capacity to put thousands of people in the streets, as was accomplished in other large southern cities.

While white reaction to sit-ins was marked by organized, sustained terrorism in other parts of the South, the response of white Houstonians was, with few exceptions, muted. Although the white press invited retaliation against activists by printing their names and addresses, only one was a victim of anything as serious as a cross burning.[38] The savage mutilation of Felton Turner, who was not himself an activist, was the sole instance of a major injury relating to the protests.

A more serious difficulty that student activists faced in Houston, as elsewhere in the South, was opposition from sectors of the black community. Resistance to the sit-ins came from some relatively prosperous blacks; they had political and economic ties with white leaders, and their overall position was a consequence of a racially segregated society. They regarded the changes sought by protesters as a threat to their security and status. Presidents of many black colleges, as well as some of the faculty members at those schools, numbered among those who were fearful of the consequences of protest activity and did not support it. In Houston, for example, President S. M. Nabrit of Texas Southern University, a state-supported institution, disavowed the sit-ins and suggested that they were a threat to his job. He counseled moderation to students and reportedly sent the names of some involved in the sit-ins to the governor for possible disciplinary action.[39] Students at the university labeled Dr. John Lash, who chaired T.S.U.'s Department of Humanities, a "rat" and posted notices on blackboards that he had leaked information "to the wrong sources."[40] Although the university hastily established a legal-aid clinic in early 1960, there is no evidence that it helped students who were arrested in the sit-ins.[41]

The white print media was unsympathetic to the protesters. Neither of the major daily newspapers had black reporters, and the majority of the white reporters who covered the protests, as well as the white editors who approved final copy, were defenders of the racial status quo. Coverage of the sit-ins became very sparse after March, 1960, which was the only month when protests made the front page of the white press. The black newspapers in Houston, of course, generally provided much better reporting on the sit-in movement. One exception, however, was the newest black newspaper in the city, the *Forward Times,* which had only begun publication in January of 1960, scarcely a month before the first sit-in. The announced policy of the *Forward Times* was to limit coverage of the negative side of the news and to stress the positive accomplishments of blacks. Apparently the management of the newspaper believed that student protests aimed at ending segregation were not positive accomplishments and therefore often chose to downplay or ignore them.[42]

For these reasons, Houston was much slower than some other Texas cities in yielding to the demands of student protesters. In the Lone Star State, desegregation appears to have taken place first in midsize cities, then in large cities, and finally in smaller towns. By mid-1960 eating facilities in such midsize cities as Austin, Corpus Christi, Galveston, and San Antonio were serving blacks. Houston eateries in the downtown business district were not fully integrated until later in the year, while Dallas was still experiencing restaurant sit-ins in 1961.[43] Nevertheless, within a relatively short time a small number of young, brave black activists in Houston, supported by a few whites, delivered a lethal blow to the long reign of Jim Crow in the Bayou City. They helped change the face, as well as the soul, of the South.

Notes

1. August Meier and Elliott Rudwick, *CORE: A Study in the Civil Rights Movement, 1942-1968* (New York, 1973), chapters 1-2.

2. Chandler Davidson, "Negro Politics and the Rise of the Civil Rights Movement in Houston, Texas" (Ph.D. diss., Princeton University, 1968), p. 41. Davidson's dissertation was subsequently published, but the material referred to in this and in following notes was not included in the published version.

3. Rupert N. Richardson, Ernest Wallace, and Adrian N. Anderson, *Texas: The Lone Star State* (Englewood Cliffs, N.J., 1970), pp. 399-400.

4. Arthur S. Link and William B. Catton, *The American Epoch: A History of the United States since 1900*, vol. 3, *The Era of the Cold War, 1946-1973*, (New York, 1974), pp. 186-87.

5. The details of Rev. Simpson's long, productive career are in the Rev. L. H. Simpson Collection, Houston Metropolitan Research Center, Houston Public Library. For a critical summary of his career, see Davidson, "Negro Politics," pp. 38-39.

6. Ibid., pp. 50-51, and David G. McComb, *Houston: The Bayou City* (Austin, 1969), p. 230. For the desegregation of the Houston Public Library, see the voluminous Houston Public Library Collection, Houston Metropolitan Research Center, Houston Public Library. Prior to its system-wide desegregation in the 1950s, black Houstonians were restricted to using a single neighborhood branch library.

7. Television, of course, made it possible to bring events in Montgomery into the homes of people in the United States and around the world. These events are detailed in Martin Luther King, Jr., *Stride Toward Freedom: The Montgomery Story* (New York, 1958) and Ralph D. Abernathy, "The Natural History of a Social Movement: The Montgomery Improvement Association" (master's thesis, Atlanta University, 1958). See also three works by David J. Garrow—"The Origins of the Montgomery Bus Boycott," *Southern Changes* 7 (Oct.-Dec., 1985): 21-27; *The Montgomery Bus Boycott and the Women Who Started It: The Memoire of Jo*

Ann Gibson Robinson (Knoxville, 1987); and *Bearing the Cross: Martin Luther King, Jr., and the Southern Christian Leadership Conference* (New York, 1986). See also Adam Fairclough, *To Redeem the Soul of America: The Southern Christian Leadership Conference and Martin Luther King, Jr.* (Athens, Ga., 1987); J. Mills Thornton III, "Challenge and Response in the Montgomery Bus Boycott of 1955-1956," *Alabama Review* 3 (July, 1980): 163-235; and Steven M. Millner, "The Montgomery Bus Boycott: A Case Study in the Emergence and Career of a Social Movement" (Ph.D. diss., University of California, Berkeley, 1981).

8. William Bagwell, *School Desegregation in the Carolinas: Two Case Studies* (Columbia, S.C., 1972); Robbins L. Gates, *The Making of Massive Resistance: Virginia's Politics of Public School Desegregation* (Chapel Hill, 1964); Morton Inger, *Politics and Reality in an American City: The New Orleans School Crisis of 1960* (New York, 1969); Benjamin Muse, *Virginia's Massive Resistance* (Bloomington, 1961); Gary Orfield, *The Reconstruction of Southern Education: The Schools and the 1964 Civil Rights Act* (New York, 1969); Jack Walter Peltason, *Fifty-eight Lonely Men: Southern Federal Judges and School Desegregation* (New York, 1961); Robert Collins Smith, *They Closed Their Schools: Prince Edward County, Virginia, 1951-1964* (Chapel Hill, 1965); and Wilson Record and Jane Cassels Record, eds., *Little Rock, USA* (San Francisco, 1960).

9. Davidson, "Negro Politics," p. 60; McComb, *Houston,* pp. 230-33.

10. Claybourne Carson, *In Struggle: SNCC and the Black Awakening of the 1960s* (Cambridge, Mass., 1981); William H. Chafe, *Civilities and Civil Rights: Greensboro, North Carolina, and the Black Struggle for Equality* (New York, 1980); David R. Coburn, *Racial Change and Community Crisis: St. Augustine, Florida, 1877-1980* (New York, 1985); James Farmer, *Lay Bare the Heart: An Autobiography of the Civil Rights Movement* (New York, 1985); David J. Garrow, ed., *Atlanta, Georgia, 1960-1961: Sit-Ins and Student Activism* (New York, 1989); Robert J. Norrell, *Reaping the Whirlwind: The Civil Rights Movement in Tuskegee* (New York, 1985); David Oppenheimer, *The Sit-In Movement of 1960* (New York, 1989); John R. Salter, *Jackson, Mississippi: An American Chronicle of Struggle and Schism* (Hicksville, N.Y., 1977); Howard Zinn, *SNCC: The New Abolitionists* (Boston, 1964).

11. Holly Hogrobrooks, interview with Jon Schwartz, Houston, Tex., Oct. 27, 1985, Oral History Collection, Houston Metropolitan Research Center, Houston Public Library.

12. J. B. Jones, interview with Jon Schwartz, Houston, Tex., Oct. 18, 1985, Oral History Collection, Houston Metropolitan Research Center, Houston Public Library.

13. Otis King, interview with Jon Schwartz, Houston, Tex., Oct. 27, 1985; Jack Weingarten, interview with Jon Schwartz, Houston, Tex., Nov. 8, 1985, Oral History Collection, Houston Metropolitan Research Center, Houston Public Library.

14. Hogrobrooks interview; McComb, *Houston,* pp. 233-34; *Houston Chronicle,* Mar. 5, 1960.

15. *Houston Chronicle,* Mar. 6, 1960; Weingarten interview.

16. *Houston Chronicle,* Mar. 7-10, 1960.

17. Hogrobrooks interview.

18. King interview. After graduating from T.S.U., King went on to graduate from Harvard law school. Returning to Houston, he served as Houston City At-

torney for several years and became a member of the faculty at T.S.U.'s Thurgood Marshall School of Law.

19. *Houston Chronicle,* Mar. 11-12, 1960.
20. Houston *Informer,* Mar. 19, 1960; (Houston) *Forward Times,* Mar. 12, 1960; Zinn, *SNCC,* p. 25.
21. For a general history of Rice University, see Fredericka Meiners, *A History of Rice University: The Institute Years, 1907-1963* (Houston, 1982). The (Houston) *Negro Labor News,* Mar. 26, 1960, notes the link-up between T.S.U. activists and students at Hughes Business College.
22. Houston *Informer,* Mar. 19, 1960; *Houston Chronicle,* Mar. 25, 1960; (Houston) *Negro Labor News,* Mar. 26, 1960.
23. (Houston) *Negro Labor News,* Mar. 26, 1960.
24. *Houston Post,* Mar. 26, 1960.
25. *Houston Chronicle,* Mar. 26, 1960.
26. *Houston Post,* Mar. 26, 1960.
27. *Houston Chronicle,* Mar. 29, 1960; *Houston Post,* Mar. 30, 1960.
28. *Houston Chronicle,* Apr. 7, 1960; *Houston Post,* Apr. 7, 1960.
29. *Houston Chronicle,* May 10, 1960.
30. *Houston Chronicle,* May 13, June 9, 1960. The papers of Felix Tijerina, who served as national president of a major civil rights organization, League of United Latin American Citizens (L.U.L.A.C.), are deposited in the Houston Metropolitan Research Center, Houston Public Library, along with the papers of the Houston chapter of L.U.L.A.C.
31. Holly Hogrobrooks, one of the most vocal activists, suggested that the demonstrators began when they did in part because it was a slack time in the academic calendar—the beginning weeks of the semester when students had little to do. See Hogrobrooks interview.
32. *Houston Chronicle,* July 28, 1960; Houston *Informer,* July 30, 1960.
33. Houston *Informer,* Aug. 6, Sept. 8, 1960.
34. Ibid., Oct. 22, 29, Dec. 10, 1960; (Houston) *Forward Times,* Dec. 10, 1960.
35. McComb, *Houston,* p. 234.
36. *Houston Chronicle,* Jan. 24, 1961; *Houston Post,* Jan. 25, 1961; Houston *Informer,* Jan. 28, 1961.
37. Houston *Informer,* Feb. 11, May 6, June 10, July 1, July 15, July 29, 1961; *Houston Post,* July 28, 1961.
38. *Houston Chronicle,* Aug. 4, 1960.
39. Zinn, *SNCC,* p. 30; *Houston Chronicle,* Mar. 8, 18, 1960; Houston *Informer,* Mar. 19, 1960.
40. Houston *Informer,* ibid.
41. (Houston) *Forward Times,* Mar. 5, 1960.
42. Ibid., Feb. 27, Oct. 1, 1960. Within a few years, however, the newspaper had become one of the most muckraking black newspapers in the city and was known for its exposés.
43. *Time,* Mar. 28, 1960; *Houston Chronicle,* Mar. 16, 1960; Houston *Informer,* Aug. 20, 1960, Jan. 14, 1961.

Operation Breadbasket in Houston, 1966-78

Cecile E. Harrison and Alice K. Laine

Introduction

Operation Breadbasket in Houston was an effort to deal with the economics of institutionalized white racism. It sought to secure for blacks a share of the economic benefits that whites regularly and systematically extracted from the black community in the Bayou City. This essay focuses on the history, philosophy, organization, program, and strategies of Operation Breadbasket in Houston. It places the local Operation Breadbasket in Houston within the context of the larger civil rights movement in the city; it also describes the relationship between the Houston Breadbasket organization and the Southern Christian Leadership Conference, a national organization headed by Dr. Martin Luther King, Jr., that promoted local Breadbasket operations across the country. In addition, this article discusses how the behavior of established, more traditional black leaders in the Bayou City contributed to severe funding problems for Breadbasket in Houston, which eventually led to its demise.

The Struggle for Black Rights in Twentieth-Century Houston

Prior to World War II, the Houston chapter of the National Association for the Advancement of Colored People (NAACP) took the lead in the struggle for civil rights in Houston. During the war Dr. Lonnie E. Smith, a member of the local organization, appealed a voting rights case all the way to the United States Supreme Court. As a result, the "white" primaries, designed specifically to exclude blacks, were outlawed, and the political process was more democratized.[1] Within a few years, blacks began to run for public office in local elections.[2] To consolidate their influence concerning the benefit of the ballot, voter education, and other issues, blacks founded on January 17, 1949, an "organization-of-organizations," named the Harris County Council of Organizations (HCCO). The council disseminated information and coordinated the activities of member organizations toward common goals.³ At the same time, blacks began to act against economic discrimination by launching successful consumer boycotts against a bakery and a brewery. As a result of the boycotts, the two companies began hiring blacks as drivers and as sales personnel.⁴

These successes were followed in the 1950s with another Houston-based, NAACP victory in the Supreme Court, which desegregated public higher education by forcing the University of Texas Law School to admit a black Houstonian, Heman Sweatt.⁵ Blacks also increased their influence over the local public school system by electing a black woman, Mrs. Charles White, to the Houston Independent School District board in 1957.⁶ Her election followed the Supreme Court's famous desegregation decision in 1954 that marked the beginning of a bitter, protracted struggle between diehard conservatives and liberals in the Bayou City for control of the public school system. Blacks played a significant part in this struggle.

In another notable political victory, a black Houstonian, Barbara Jordan, won a seat in the Texas Senate while another black, Curtis Graves, was elected to the state House of Representatives in 1966. In other respects, the 1960s proved as tumultuous in the Bayou City as elsewhere in the nation. Public controversy erupted over police brutality as well as the location of garbage dumps. Led by the Progressive Youth Association, students from the predominately black Texas Southern University engaged in a wave of sit-ins, which effectively desegregated many eating facilities and other retail outlets in the city. The Civil Rights Act of 1964 legally assured these gains in the sections relating to such public accommodations and facilities as hotels, restaurants, swimming pools, and golf courses. The formation of a group called Friends of SNCC (Student Non-Violent Coordinating Committee) provoked increased police harassment of students and climaxed in a police riot on the campus of the university in May of 1967. One policeman was killed during this police attack on the university and its students.⁷ Although authorities loudly charged five students with his murder, it was later revealed that a police bullet had killed the policeman, and two years later all charges against the students were quietly dropped. During this decade of thrust and counterthrust, two young ministers emerged as prominent local civil rights leaders. Rev. William "Bill" Lawson established the Houston chapter of the Southern Christian Leadership Conference, and Rev. Earl Allen, a more vocally strident leader, founded an organization called Hope Development. This organization later published *The Voice of Hope,* a newspaper that was characteristically outspoken in addressing the needs of Houston's black community.⁸

The response of local and federal officials in Houston to the behavior of blacks during the 1960s was somewhat confused and not particularly

Successful voter registration drives made blacks a formidable element in city politics by the 1960s. Louie Welch, shown campaigning in 1966, was the first Houston mayor to base his election strategy on winning the minority vote. *Courtesy Houston Public Library, Houston Metropolitan Research Center*

successful. After two initial federally sponsored poverty programs failed, in 1967 a third—the Harris County Community Action Association—became the dominant federal anti-poverty organization in town.[9] It compiled a decidedly mixed track record. The mayor of Houston, Louie Welch, commanded a city-sponsored effort to clean up certain problem areas in the black community, notably the "Bottoms," a refuge for shady characters and criminal activity, which even the police were reluctant to enter. Mayor Welch also employed a number of blacks as aides in his office while stationing others, mostly well-known black athletes, throughout black neighborhoods. The Houston Police Department ran an experimental community-relations program. It was not successful because it involved too few people and left those who participated in it with the strong feeling that little could be done to change the attitudes of police about race. Many blacks in the Bayou City were convinced that the police department was infested with Ku Klux Klan members.[10]

The Origin, Philosophy, and Strategy of the National Operation Breadbasket

Operation Breadbasket was founded in the mid-1960s as a second-stage organization. As such, it followed and built upon the accomplishments of earlier civil rights organizations that had successfully won some important political battles and achieved certain legal rights for blacks. By using the political connections and legal leverage blacks had already acquired, the leadership of Breadbasket was able to orchestrate direct-action, pressure-group tactics against the white-dominated private sector in an attempt to stop the gross and continued economic abuses of black America.

Rev. Leon Sullivan of Philadelphia initiated what later became the Operation Breadbasket program. In the early 1950s he organized four hundred ministers and their combined congregations in a massive boycott against companies that discriminated against blacks in the City of Brotherly Love.[11] In 1965 Dr. Martin Luther King, Jr., adopted this technique for the organization he headed, the Southern Christian Leadership Conference. SCLC established chapters of Breadbasket in over fifteen cities across the United States and assigned a young and energetic minister, Rev. Jesse Jackson, to coordinate the national Breadbasket program from a headquarters in Chicago.[12]

Operation Breadbasket was organized around a Saturday morning meeting patterned after a religious service. Despite his heavy schedule, Jackson never failed to appear at these meetings, which typically filled completely a six-thousand-seat movie theater. A choir and orchestra provided gospel music to accompany the business of the meeting, and Jackson himself always delivered a powerful sermon. After the formalities, those in attendance could chat and browse among display tables of merchandise produced by black-owned businesses.

The primary goal of Operation Breadbasket was to encourage black capitalism and economic development. Jackson argued that racism was central to the ideology and practice of capitalism, and that capitalism profited from the exploitation of oppressed people both inside the nation and abroad. Jackson believed that it was absolutely imperative for blacks in America to understand this new form of domestic, at-home colonialism in order to begin to liberate themselves from it and to achieve eventual economic freedom. Accordingly, he challenged black entrepreneurs not to leave the ghetto, but instead to organize co-ops and other business enterprises within them. He also encouraged blacks to "buy black" as part of a larger effort to focus the race upon its own problems and progress. At Jackson's direction, boycotting, or the threat of it, was the main weapon that Breadbasket used to obtain economic concessions from white-controlled companies. In Chicago, Breadbasket launched a boycott of A&P

grocery stores that led directly to agreements with over half of the major food distributors in Chicago's black ghettos. A&P agreed to conduct sensitivity sessions for its executives to help them recognize the existence and effects of racial prejudice. The firm also agreed to use black-owned construction firms to build its ghetto stores, to bank in black-owned banks, to advertise in the black media, to provide more jobs for blacks, to distribute black products in its outlets, and to contract with black-owned janitorial and exterminating companies. The deal with A&P became a model for local Breadbasket chapters across the country.[13]

Operation Breadbasket in Houston

Four ministers from Houston attended a meeting in Chicago in 1966 at which Rev. Martin Luther King, Jr., appointed Jackson to head Operation Breadbasket. All of them left the Chicago meeting and returned to Houston eager to begin an Operation Breakbasket there. One of them, Rev. William "Bill" Lawson, already headed the SCLC chapter in Houston. He soon began a series of weekly meetings with about thirty people interested in Operation Breadbasket. Jackson visited the Bayou City to help nurture this group. A planning committee continued to meet; however, the incipient organization did not continue to mature.[14]

In 1969 an incident galvanized some local blacks, including Lawson, into action. In the spring of that year, Burger King built a fast-food outlet in one of Houston's major black areas. Although several black businessmen applied for the franchise, the company awarded it to a white man. Pluria Marshall, a photographer and SCLC activist, quickly organized some students from Texas Southern University and a group of professional athletes to picket the burger stand in protest. Black customers immediately ceased to patronize it. When a rumor circulated that Burger King officials had promised that no black would ever be given a franchise, many blacks in the city began to boycott all Burger King outlets. The picketing and general boycott proved a spectacular success. Within a month the white owner of the disputed burger stand lost thousands of dollars and was forced out of business. Other Burger King outlets suffered losses as well. The company finally granted the disputed franchise to a group of young black businessmen who acquired a second one soon thereafter.[15]

The quick success against Burger King, a major and very visible company, spurred activists to further efforts, including attention to the entertainment industry. Because of its large black population, Houston was a major attraction to black entertainers, many of whom played the city regularly. However, most of them used white booking agencies instead of local black booking agencies. Once again Pluria Marshall swung into action;

he organized volunteers to distribute leaflets calling for a boycott of specific shows. As a result, two local black promoters began to get a share of the booking business.[16]

In early 1970 Marshall joined with others to address another problem in the entertainment industry, this one involving local radio stations. Two local stations programmed "black," directed their attention to black listeners, and used black announcers and deejays, but both were white-owned. When black employees of the stations decided to approach the owners to discuss better wages, benefits, and working conditions, Marshall and his colleagues supported them by picketing the stations and making other protestations on their behalf. Once again the effort was successful, as the white station owners satisfied some of the concerns of their black employees.[17]

While engaged with the radio stations, Marshall and others completed plans for the formal organization of Operation Breadbasket in Houston, and in April of 1970 Marshall was named its executive director. He subsequently was joined by an associate director and a secretary, and they were all housed in a converted family home in the heart of black Houston, at 2413 Dowling Street in the city's Third Ward. Through the generosity of the owner of the building as well as others in the community, the structure was quickly refurbished, carpeted, furnished, and provided with telephone service.[18]

The administrative structure of Breadbasket in Houston consisted of an executive council, which organizationally should have been subordinate to the national SCLC organization. However, the Houston Breadbasket became increasingly independent of SCLC, and after one failed attempt by SCLC to rein it in, the local organization incorporated separately as Operation Breadbasket of Texas. The original idea was that the executive director and the executive board would share governance of the organization. In practice, however, the energetic Marshall played the dominant role, and the executive board went along with his initiatives. This arrangement might have worked better had Marshall been a more charismatic leader who easily attracted members and money, but he was not. Nevertheless, the organization itself attracted members by its activity. During the summer of 1970, Breadbasket began selling individual memberships for one dollar and organizational memberships for five dollars. Ultimately over a thousand such memberships were sold, mostly to blacks and to black organizations. Although Breadbasket in Houston, as nationally, remained primarily a black organization, it welcomed the support of white members.[19]

Confrontational Activities and Strategies

Marshall and other leading members of Breadbasket in the Bayou City believed that the success of the organization depended upon some quick victories. Consequently they won contracts with nearly a dozen businesses to hire or increase the hiring of black employees. These included two soft-drink bottling companies, a department store, a bakery, a brewery, a dairy, a food store chain, and several independent food stores. Breadbasket also supported the United Farm Workers lettuce boycott and involved itself in local politics by supporting the appointment of a black physician to head the city's health department as well as by entering the controversy about busing school children to integrate public schools.[20]

Breadbasket's negotiations with private companies in Houston—the heart of its program—involved its staff as well as volunteers. It often required sneaking around to collect as much information as possible about target companies. Sometimes the organization was able to make contact with black employees working for target companies, in order to obtain inside information about how many blacks were on the payroll, what positions they held, and in general how the company treated its black workers. Breadbasket also tried, by hook or by crook, to obtain the financial records of target companies or at least to ascertain their profit figures and current economic conditions. On many occasions, however, Breadbasket representatives had to confront a target company without much hard economic or employment data. On those occasions, they simply asked the company to provide them with the data and usually gave them a week to do so. The submission of false data always gave Breadbasket representatives an upper hand in subsequent bargaining. After analyzing the data and running spot checks for verification, Breadbasket wrote a list of demands in the form of a contract to be signed by the target company and Breadbasket. Several negotiating sessions were usually required before such an agreement was reached.[21]

In negotiating sessions, the Breadbasket team consisted of three members, each of whom played a specific role. Marshall, as the executive director of the organization and head of the negotiating team, was the straight man, whose role was to hammer out an agreement with the company. A second negotiator, usually the associate director, played the part of the agitator or man of the people. He was never satisfied with a company offer and always pressed for more. He also frequently emphasized the company's exploitative relationship with the black community and stressed the enormous profits the company squeezed out of blacks. The third representative, often Rev. Bill Lawson or another minister, was the peacemaker who prevented the negotiations from breaking down when they threatened to do so.[22]

In Houston, Breadbasket negotiators always insisted on negotiating rules they believed operated to their advantage. For example, Breadbasket representatives never negotiated with underlings and always insisted on dealing with top management personnel; they preferred the target company's

CEO. They broke off one negotiating session when a company president assigned a staff member to represent him. Furthermore, Breadbasket representatives would not participate in negotiations that included company consultants, lawyers, or public relations specialists. The length of the negotiations varied from one week to about seven months.[23]

When a company refused to negotiate or broke off negotiations, Breadbasket immediately announced a "selective buying campaign," which was its euphemism for a boycott. Volunteers distributed informational leaflets throughout the black community announcing the boycott. Breadbasket asked stores to remove the company's product from their shelves and to post a Breadbasket sign advising customers that the product was not available at that store and asking them not to buy it at other stores. The black media publicized these campaigns. In fact, the black media always kept the black community fully informed of the activities and achievements of Breadbasket, since Breadbasket made the black media one of the chief beneficiaries of Breadbasket's successes. Publicity was vital to the continued efforts of Breadbasket, which depended absolutely on the black community for its strength.[24]

White businesses that became targets of Breadbasket boycotts normally suffered serious profit losses. Their experiences convinced other white companies to make certain changes to avoid becoming targets themselves. One such company, for example, advised Breadbasket that henceforth it was placing some of its funds in black financial institutions. In another instance, a white beer distributor who initially resisted Breadbasket lost twelve hundred dollars during a three-week selective buying campaign when a black drive-in grocery store owner stopped ordering beer from him. Usually the boycotts were not prolonged, lasting from only several days to a few weeks.[25]

Breadbasket and the white companies with which it made agreements had diametrically different attitudes toward those agreements. To Breadbasket they were victories, and the organization made every effort for the black media to publicize them throughout the black community. White companies, however, evidently viewed the agreements as defeats. While they loudly touted their voluntary contributions, such as scholarships, to the black community, they attempted to shroud their dealings with Breadbasket in secrecy and obviously did not want the white community to learn of their less-than-voluntary agreements with a predominantly black, so-called radical organization.

As a result of their victories in Houston, Breadbasket leaders discovered what other civil rights workers elsewhere had discovered: control of the agenda by status quo–oriented persons and groups limits the scope of decision-making to "safe" issues, and thus control of the agenda may be the "second face of power." They realized that those who decide what issues will be given consideration have perhaps even more power than those who simply deal with the relatively safe issues that others have selected for them to debate.²⁶ But Breadbasket's use of direct action and confrontation in Houston showed that a small group with a loud public voice and demonstrated community support could be not only disruptive but also very effective in confronting a much stronger and much larger adversary.

Breadbasket in Houston sponsored secondary and tertiary programs that were also important and did much to solidify its reputation in the black community. It provided tenants with information about tenant rights under the law, investigated evictions that appeared to violate the law, and provided evicted people with assistance in moving. Breadbasket also investigated job-discrimination complaints and made periodic surveys of neighborhood commercial outlets to make sure they were not selling overpriced or inferior goods. Breadbasket was responsible for compiling the first directory of black businesses in Houston, and it helped individual black businesses make valuable financial and legal connections. It also made them aware of available managerial and technical assistance programs. Breadbasket volunteers monitored school board activities and responded to school-related complaints. In a major campaign, Breadbasket personnel put pressure on a number of local radio and television stations to be more responsive to the black community by challenging media license renewals with the Federal Communications Commission. This very successful project led to the establishment of the National Black Media Coalition. Breadbasket was also instrumental in founding two other important organizations: the Texas People's Coalition, a statewide umbrella organization of minority groups working for the rights of minorities and the poor, and the Houston chapter of the Texas Welfare Rights Organization, which had similar concerns.²⁷

The Funding Problem and Demise of Breadbasket in Houston

Breadbasket was never adequately funded, and financial problems led to the demise of the organization in Houston. In fact, the organization was never even able completely to pay its own staff. Only the secretary was paid regularly. Salaries budgeted for the executive and associate director never materialized. On paper, for example, the executive director was allocated an annual salary of $12,000, but in fact he received only a token payment from time to time.²⁸

Several factors contributed to the financial weakness of an organization that was strong in other important respects. The subordination of its board of directors to the executive director generally had the effect of marginalizing the board and its members from the organization itself. Board members thus not only did not personally support Breadbasket as much as they otherwise might have, but in addition were not effectively used as fund-raisers. In short, Breadbasket failed to utilize the talents of its own board of directors and was unable to attract as board members those who had ample assets and useful connections. In a belated and unsuccessful attempt to reverse this self-destructive policy, the executive director informed the members of the board that until they were willing to assume more financial responsibility, "Breadbasket will engage in no other projects but the Media Project."[29]

Another factor that limited the financial viability of Breadbasket in Houston was that it never secured the support of successful, influential establishment blacks who viewed the organization and its confrontational strategies as a threat to their own position as gatekeepers between the races in Houston. If successful, Breadbasket would have competed with more established black groups for funding and power, and it perhaps would have replaced some of those blacks who enjoyed the confidence and patronage of white Houston. Hence, instead of supporting Breadbasket, some powerful black leaders in Houston used their considerable influence to oppose and undermine it at every turn, which they did with considerable success.[30]

A final factor that complicated Breadbasket's existence in Houston was its troubled relationship with its parent organization, the Southern Christian Leadership Conference. This relationship was strained from its beginning but became even more so following the murder of Dr. King in 1968. At that time two of King's lieutenants, Rev. Ralph Abernathy and Rev. Jesse Jackson, vied for leadership of SCLC. Dr. King's widow, Coretta Scott King, intervened on behalf of Abernathy, who silenced Jackson by removing him as head of the national Operation Breadbasket organization. Jackson subsequently resigned from SCLC and established Operation PUSH (People United to Save Humanity). SCLC officials had always felt that Breadbasket in Houston was too closely identified with Jesse Jackson. They filed a suit to remove Houston's Operation Breadbasket from their own national Breadbasket organization only to discover that Pluria Marshall had incorporated as "Operation Breadbasket of Texas" without affiliation with SCLC. Thus, while the issue was moot, it underscored the enmity between two organizations that could have cooperated and helped one another but did not.[31]

Breadbasket leaders in Houston mounted various fund-raising campaigns to try to finance their operations. They organized car washes, cake sales, and art shows. They engaged in membership drives. In addition, black civic and social organizations sponsored promotional affairs and made financial contributions. However, none of this came close to providing an adequate operating budget for the organization. Breadbasket in Houston never achieved solvency.[32]

In 1974 Breadbasket consulted experts to try and salvage the organization. One of them suggested that Breadbasket should be "less public and more organizational."[33] However, the organization's primary strength was its public support, which some were loathe to downgrade or risk alienating. After one attempt to bring Breadbasket under the control of the national SCLC organization, and several local efforts to refocus and revitalize the program, Pluria Marshall resigned as executive director later in 1974 to accept a position as head of the National Black Media Coalition.[34] Two successors to Marshall were similarly unable to place the organization on a sound financial footing. In 1975 Marshall returned to Houston in the dual role as director of the Media Coalition and head of Operation Breadbasket. Breadbasket activities then included investigating the local Small Business Administration office for discriminating against black applicants and mounting a boycott against a local Buick dealer for overcharging black customers for auto repairs.[35] Marshall, however, was unable to bring the organization to sound financial ground, and in 1978 Operation Breadbasket in Houston went out of existence.[36]

Assessment of Operation Breadbasket in Houston

Operation Breadbasket must certainly be considered at least a partial success. Placing employees in private-sector firms did bring payroll money into Houston's black community. Deposits in black financial institutions, advertizing revenue for black media, educational scholarships for Texas Southern University, and professional as well as service contracts with black-owned firms strengthened the local black economic infrastructure and improved somewhat the overall financial condition of Houston's black community.

Operationally, Breadbasket demonstrated the effectiveness of a confrontational strategy in getting issues important to the black community on Houston's agenda. Certainly its visible, public success encouraged a more positive self-image among black Houstonians and improved their collective morale. Even its failure financially to support itself pointed to the importance of a secure economic base for successful community action. In the 1970s, Operation Breadbasket made a modest contribution to the long, ongoing struggle by black Houstonians for equality with whites in the Bayou City.

Notes

1. *Smith v. Allwright*, 321 U.S. 649 (1944), in Richard Bardolph, ed., *The Civil Rights Record: Black Americans and the Law, 1849–1970* (New York, 1970), p. 266.

2. Irma LeRoy, interview with authors, Houston, Tex., Jan. 14, 1970. LeRoy was one of those who ran for public office.

3. *Profile of the Houston Negro Community with Special Tribute to Barbara Jordan* (Houston, 1967, booklet), p. 3.

4. Pluria Marshall, interview with authors, Houston, Tex., Dec. 20, 1970.

5. *Sweatt* v. *Painter,* 339 U.S. 629 (1950), in Bardolph, *The Civil Rights Record,* pp. 273–74.

6. *Profile of the Houston Negro Community,* p. 4.

7. *Houston Post,* May 18, 1967, and the *Informer,* May 20, 1967.

8. Gene Locke, interview with authors, Houston, Tex., Dec. 18, 1988. Mr. Locke served as president of the board of directors of Hope Development.

9. *Houston Post,* May 17, 1967, and the *Informer,* May 20, 1967.

10. In interviews with the authors, several community leaders and activists attested to the belief that the Houston Police Department was a Klan stronghold. This conviction was general throughout the black community in Houston.

11. "What Is Operation Breadbasket?" (Houston, 1970, pamphlet).

12. *Playboy* 16 (Nov., 1969) David J. Garrow, ed., *Chicago 1966: Open Housing Marches, Summit Negotiations and Operation Breadbasket* (New York, 1989).

13. Ibid.

14. Rev. Bill Lawson, interview with authors, Houston, Tex., Sept. 19, 1988. He credited Rev. Sherman Douglass, Rev. Robert Felder, and Rev. E. L. Lott for attending the Chicago meeting with him and for helping establish Operation Breadbasket in Houston.

15. *Houston Post,* July 10, 1974, and *Forward Times,* Dec. 28, 1975. During the Burger King boycott, Marshall discovered that the mayor of Houston was pitting two black organizations, the NAACP and New Directions, against one another in a competition for funding an ex-convict rehabilitation program. Marshall castigated the mayor for manipulative interference in this matter. For more about this, see *Forward Times,* July 6, 1974.

16. Pluria Marshall, interview with authors, Houston, Tex., Dec. 20, 1970.

17. Ibid.

18. Ibid.

19. Vera Jackson, interview with authors, Houston, Tex., Aug. 23, 1988. Ms. Jackson served on the Executive Board of Operation Breadbasket of Texas.

20. Pluria Marshall, interview with authors, Houston, Tex., Dec. 20, 1970; *Forward Times,* Dec. 28, 1974.

21. Marshall provided the authors with a copy of an internal critique that Operation Breadbasket wrote on one of its selective buying campaigns that documents the procedures he described in this interview.

22. Ibid.

23. Ibid.

24. Pluria Marshall, interview with authors, Houston, Tex., Aug. 22, 1988.

25. Ibid.

26. Peter Bachrach and M. S. Baratz, "The Two Faces of Power," *American Political Science Review* 56 (Sept., 1962) 3:947–52.

27. Pluria Marshall, interview with authors, Houston, Tex., Aug. 22, 1988; *Forward Times,* July 27, 1974, Dec. 28, 1974, May 31, 1975.

28. Ibid.
29. Minutes, Executive Council, Operation Breadbasket of Texas, July 9, 1974.
30. Pluria Marshall and Vera Jackson, interviews with authors, Houston, Tex., Aug. 22, 23, 1988.
31. Ibid.
32. Vera Jackson, interview with authors, Houston, Tex., Aug. 23, 1988.
33. Minutes, Executive Council, Operation Breadbasket of Texas, July 9, 1974.
34. *Forward Times,* Dec. 28, 1974.
35. *Forward Times,* June 7, 1975, Sept. 3, 1977.
36. Pluria Marshall, interview with authors, Houston, Tex., Aug. 22, 1988.

Housing Problems and Prospects in Contemporary Houston

Robert D. Bullard

Houston has long been considered a boomtown. Between 1970 and 1980, the city's black community was the fastest growing in the South, increasing over 39 percent in that decade. The Houston metropolitan area contained 2.9 million people in 1980; of these, over 521,512, or more than 18 percent, were black. The city of Houston itself included some 1.6 million people, with over 440,257 blacks, who comprised about 28 percent of the Bayou City's population. They had the distinction of being part of the largest black community anywhere in Dixie.[1]

Housing and Black Neighborhoods

The Houston metropolitan area led the nation in housing starts in the 1970s. Over 487,000 new housing units were built in the area between 1970 and 1980 — an impressive 72 percent increase. However, much of the new housing was constructed in the suburbs with only moderate building taking place in inner-city minority areas. Many lower-income and minority neighborhoods were largely ignored during the peak period of Houston's great housing boom. A case in point is the city's Fourth Ward or Freedmantown, the oldest black neighborhood in Houston. Following the Civil War, thousands of newly freed slaves moved into the Fourth Ward to found the Freedmantown community. It became the center of black social, cultural, political, and economic life. By the 1880s, black settlers had acquired ownership of much of the land in Freedmantown. However, the years of the Great Depression and subsequent decades saw a steady decline in owner-occupancy rates in the neighborhood. By 1900 less than 5 percent of the housing was owner occupied. For the most part, the historic Fourth Ward has become an area of elderly, lower-income black renters vulnerable to wholesale displacement as the adjacent downtown business district expands. It has been a community under siege for some time.[2]

In addition to the Fourth Ward, two other wards have special historical meaning to Houston's black residents. The Third and Fifth wards each have a rich history. These two neighborhoods emerged as mostly black communities due to increased housing demands and pressures in the post–World War II era. Blacks in the 1960s began to move out of these wards southward from the Third Ward and northward from the Fifth Ward; the concentration of the city's black community along this migrant corridor can still be found today. Thus, while growing in size, Houston's black population has also become more spatially decentralized over the past three decades. However, blacks largely remain residentially segregated from whites. The 1980 segregation index (or index of dissimilarity) revealed that over 81 percent of the city's blacks still lived in predominately black neighborhoods, down somewhat from 93 percent in 1970.[3]

Houston's black community is located in a broad belt that extends from the south-central and southeast portions of the city into the north-central and northeast sections of Houston. The black population is largely located in the eastern half of the city, with smaller enclaves in northwest and southwest Houston. While blacks have been moving into Houston's suburbs since World War II, their percentage of the suburban population actually declined in the last two decades. The black share of Houston's suburban population dropped from almost 13 percent in 1960 to less than 9 percent in 1980. The eighty thousand blacks in Houston's suburbs represent a far smaller number than might be expected from the size of the central city black population of more than four hundred thousand.[4]

The black suburbanization trend has often been an extension of the segregated housing pattern that has typified the central city. Black Houstonians often become resegregated or "ghettoized" in suburbia. In other cases, older black suburban enclaves, such as Riceville, Bordersville, Carvercrest, and Acres Homes, have been encircled by new residential and commercial construction with few amenities benefitting nearby black residents. For example, the Houston City Council annexed the all-black Riceville community in 1965. However, as late as 1982 this small black enclave in the rapidly growing southwest sector of Houston did not have running water, sewer or gas connections, sidewalks, paved streets, or regular garbage service.

The Bordersville community is another case of an area that was systematically left out of the economic planning picture. Bordersville is an all-black neighborhood that grew out of an old sawmill settlement or "sawmill quarters." Houston annexed this northeast community in the mid-1960s as part of its bustling Intercontinental Airport complex, and this community straddles an area of considerable and growing affluence. However, the problems in this black neighborhood are not unlike those found in Riceville, which lies nearly thirty miles to the south—namely, the lack of running water, sewer lines, paved streets, regular street repairs, and related amenities that other Houstonians take for granted.

Many of the city's inner-city minority neighborhoods continue to lose residents and a substantial portion of their housing stock for low and moderate-income households. Most noticeably, neighborhood decline is manifested through an increasing number of boarded-up and abandoned buildings as well as empty lots that dot many of Houston's inner-city minority areas. Limited income is a major factor preventing many residents in these areas from competing for housing in the open market. Thus, families with limited incomes are caught in a crushing vise between rising housing costs and a dwindling supply of decent and affordable housing in Houston's inner-city areas.

A disproportionately large share of black Houstonians continue to be ill-housed despite the efforts made by government. Inadequate housing is often clustered in inner-city minority areas where a large share of the city's poor also reside. The housing options and opportunities, including the choice between owning and renting, that are available to blacks and other ethnic minorities have been shaped largely by government housing policies, institutional discrimination in the housing market, the housing construction priorities of builders, demographic changes, and uneven development that has taken place throughout the city. The end result of the interplay between these factors is reduced housing choices and limited residential amenities for black and lower-income residents in the Bayou City.[5]

Suburban development flourished in the past four decades due to federal housing policies. Many of the current residential housing patterns and problems can be traced directly to the government's role during the 1950s and 1960s.[6] Moreover, the failure of the government's first attack on the nation's urban housing problem through urban renewal has been well documented. To a great extent, the "rehousing of displaced residents was subordinated to the primary goal of clearance and redevelopment."[7]

Subsidized Housing for the Poor

In an attempt to allow low and moderate income households to compete for decent, uncrowded, and safe housing, the federal government initiated the Section 8 Rental Assistance Program. The subsidy program was created under the Housing and Community Development Act of 1974. The strategy for providing housing under Section 8 met with some difficulty that was not anticipated by its framers. For example, the program ignored the shortage of decent housing that might develop in response to increased demand. Also, it did not take into consideration possible discrimination based on race, sex, number of children, and welfare status. Finally, landlords often objected to the "fair market rent" ceilings that were determined by the U.S. Department of Housing and Urban Development. The rent ceiling issue became especially critical in Houston during the 1970s, when demand for market apartments was high and vacancy rates were low.[8]

The historical patterns of racial and economic segregation were often perpetuated by Houston's Section 8 housing program. Black program participants, for example, generally secured housing in mostly black neighborhoods, while white program participants secured housing in mostly white neighborhoods. A large share of the black Section 8 tenants secured housing in high density "poverty pockets," where housing was often deteriorating, deficient, and abandoned. Overall, Houston's Section 8 housing program has had a minimal effect in reversing residential housing segregation among lower-income households.[9]

The U.S. Housing Act of 1937 and subsequent Texas enabling legislation led to the establishment of the Housing Authority of the City of Houston (HACH). The city's Housing Authority is responsible for construction of housing under the low-rent housing program. A two-pronged approach was used in carrying out the early mission of the local Housing Authority. First, slums and "blighted areas" were to be cleared; second, decent, safe, and sanitary housing was to be provided. The early Housing Authority boards emphasized the slum clearance provision. However, land acquisition for public housing projects was often mired in controversy. In 1940 the *Houston Post* publicized allegations and charges that the city's Housing Authority Board used slum clearance to "capitalize on poverty" and drive a bargain in Houston's blighted neighborhoods, such as the mostly black Third, Fourth, and Fifth wards.

Today Houston's Housing Authority is the largest of the forty public housing authorities in the Houston-Galveston metroplex. The Houston Housing Authority had a total of 9,893 units of subsidized housing in its 1983 inventory. A breakdown of the Housing Authority's subsidized units indicates that it owned and managed 4,077 units of public housing in fifteen developments scattered across the city. The Housing Authority's Section 8 Housing Assistance Payments Program provided rent subsidies for an additional 5,816 units. The local housing authority, in all, served over twenty-five thousand people in 1983.[10]

The need for additional units of low-rent and assisted housing in Houston far exceeds the current supply. At least one-fifth of the city's more than six hundred thousand households are inadequately sheltered and could qualify for some type of housing assistance. For the past five years the Houston Housing Authority has averaged over five thousand people on its waiting list for public housing.

Conventional public housing construction in Houston suffered a major setback in 1950, when a referendum passed limiting the number of public housing units. As a result, few public housing developments were built in the city between 1952 and 1975. The passage of the local public housing referendum is a major contributing factor in determining the current size of the city's public housing stock. The number of public housing units in the Bayou City lags behind those in other cities of comparable size (see table 10). A 1982 *Houston Chronicle* survey revealed that Houston ranked seventh in the number of housing units but was the nation's fourth largest city.

The city's aging and rapidly deteriorating public housing stock represents an additional problem to the local Housing Authority in its effort to provide decent, safe, and sanitary housing for low- and moderate-income families. These problems are exacerbated by dwindling financial resources, weakened political commitment, and growing citizen opposition to public housing. Public housing has become a volatile political issue that has the potential of creating protests from both suburban whites and inner-city blacks. White suburbanites fear their neighborhoods will be targets for low-income public housing developments as a result of the federal government site-selection policies that restrict new subsidized units in "impacted" areas—that is, neighborhoods with an already high concentration of minorities and low-income residents. Suburban residents also fear that lower-income housing projects would adversely affect their property values and the overall quality of life in their community. Black inner-city residents, on the other hand, voice the fear that public housing developments

Table 10
Number of Public Housing Units in the Ten Largest U.S. Cities, 1982

City	No. of Units	Ranking of Units by Size	Ranking of Population by Size*
New York	207,647	1	1
Los Angeles	26,000	3	2
Chicago	47,000	2	3
Houston	9,500	7	4
Philadelphia	23,000	4	5
Detroit	10,500	6	6
San Antonio	14,000	5	7
Dallas	8,000	8	8
Phoenix	1,800	9	9
San Diego	340	10	10

*Unofficial population ranking in 1982.
SOURCE: *Houston Chronicle*, Aug. 8, 1982.

are being programmed for failure through a policy of neglect and through choices of site locations that are away from the people who need assisted housing the most—lower income households.

The historical development of Houston's public housing projects can be traced to the policy of building separate or segregated housing units for whites and blacks. The location of the city's older public housing developments largely reflects the city's racially segregated housing pattern. In contrast, the site-selection policy of the U.S. Department of Housing and Urban Development has contributed in recent years to the construction of assisted housing in "nonconcentrated" areas of the city and in the suburbs.

The location of the Houston Housing Authority's fifteen developments is presented in table 11. It reveals that the city's black neighborhoods continue to have a substantial share of the city's public housing stock. Specifically, eight of the fifteen public housing developments are located in majority black census tracts. Moreover, there is a discernable pattern of the location of developments for families and developments for the elderly. Houston's public housing complexes that are designed for families tend

Table 11
Houston Housing Authority Developments, 1983

Development	Houston Location	Number of Units	Percent Black in Census Tract*
Family			
Allen Parkway Village	Southwest	1,000	63.4
Clayton Homes	Southeast	348	17.3
Cuney Homes	Southeast	564	99.4
Ewing	Southeast	42	47.2
Forest Green	Northeast	100	78.8
Irvington Village	Northwest	318	6.2
Kelly Village	Northeast	333	94.3
Kennedy Place	Northeast	60	94.3
Lincoln Park	Northwest	264	60.6
Long Drive	Southeast	100	1.3
Oxford Place	Northwest	230	4.3
Wilmington House	Southeast	108	99.5
Elderly			
Bellerive	Southwest	210	4.7
Lyerly	Northwest	200	56.5
Telephone Road	Southeast	200	35.4

*Percentages are based on 1980 Census figures.
SOURCE: Housing Authority of the City of Houston, *Annual Report* (1984).

to be located on the eastern half of the city, while those for elderly people are sited in every quadrant of the city except the northeast.

It is becoming increasingly difficult to build public housing in the Bayou City. A case in point involved the 1982 decision by the Houston Housing Authority to approve the construction of two-family complexes in predominantly white neighborhoods. The Housing Authority approved the building of a 105-unit, low-income development for five million dollars in the Westbury area of southwest Houston. The census tract in which the proposed project was to be built had an ethnic composition of 89 percent white, 7 percent Hispanic, and 4 percent black. The selection of the mostly white neighborhood triggered protests, demonstrations, and legal action. The proposed project was ultimately killed by such opposition as well as the developer's consequent difficulty in securing the large loan required to begin construction.

Citizen opposition to proposed development later influenced the housing authority to revise its application to the U.S. Department of Housing and Urban Development from a family complex to one that would house elderly people. Such a complex likely would have generated less controversy than the original proposal for a low-income family development in the Westbury area. Historically, the city-assisted family developments are composed of minority tenants — mostly blacks, Hispanics, and Indochinese — while the low-rent housing for the elderly is occupied primarily by whites.

Another case involved a proposed public housing development slated to be built in northwest Houston. A $3.5 million, eighty-unit public housing complex was approved in 1982 by the Houston Housing Authority for the predominantly white Spring Branch area. The census tract in which the low-income housing development was to have been built was 87 percent white, 9 percent Hispanic, and 4 percent black. Residents of the area, however, were able to convince the developer not to purchase the land for the proposed project. The Housing Authority subsequently dropped the controversial low-income family development planned for this middle-income neighborhood. The Housing Authority met similar public opposition to its proposal to build a family complex near Pasadena in southeast Houston.

The ethnic composition of the city's assisted developments in 1976 and 1984 is presented in tables 12 and 13. For both years, households made up of minority groups were more likely to be housed in family developments. Whites, on the other hand, comprised the vast majority of tenants in assisted complexes designed for the elderly. However, the percentage of blacks and Hispanics in developments designated for the elderly did show a modest increase between 1976 and 1984.

Table 12
Ethnic Composition of Houston Housing Authority Developments, 1976

ETHNIC COMPOSITION OF DEVELOPMENTS*

Housing Development	No. of Units	Percent Black	Percent Hispanic	Percent White	Percent Oriental/ Other	Percent Black in Census Tract†
Family						
Allen Parkway Village	1,000	66.0	3.0	26.0	5.0	84.3
Clayton Homes	348	58.0	32.0	3.0	7.0	18.4
Cuney Homes	564	99.0	1.0	0.0	0.0	99.0
Irvington Village	318	25.0	55.0	20.0	0.0	7.1
Kelley Village	333	100.0	0.0	0.0	0.0	99.1
Elderly						
75 Lyerly	200	7.0	4.0	89.0	0.0	43.3
Bellerive	210	1.0	4.0	95.0	0.0	0.1

*Ethnic composition of developments as of September, 1976, was calculated by the Houston Housing Authority.
†Census tract data are based on the 1970 Census figures.

The future of Houston's Fourth Ward is often linked to the fate of Allen Parkway Village, one of the city's oldest public housing projects. This linkage is reflected by the commonly held belief that "as goes Allen Parkway Village, so goes the Fourth Ward." Allen Parkway Village has been the subject of much speculation as a result of its close proximity to the expanding downtown area. The public housing project experienced a dramatic change in its tenant population beginning in the mid-1970s. Blacks comprised 66 percent of the project's tenants in 1976, while Orientals made up only 5 percent. However, the black population of the complex plummeted to 34 percent in 1984, while the Asian inhabitants — mostly recent refugees — grew to over 58 percent. This dramatic reversal was the result of the Housing Authority's replacement policy, initiated in the mid-1970s, of selecting Orientals over blacks. The period between 1976 and 1980 was crucial in establishing Allen Parkway Village as Houston's main settlement project for arriving Asian refugees. (see table 14)

The political implications of the Housing Authority's policy is fairly obvious: demolishing a public housing project that sheltered primarily Oriental refugees would arouse less opposition and cause less political fallout than demolishing a complex occupied primarily by black residents. The city's black population is a potent political bloc, but Asians have yet to coalesce as a political force. The Housing Authority has tried to avoid

Table 13
Ethnic Composition of Houston Housing Authority Developments, 1984

ETHNIC COMPOSITION OF DEVELOPMENTS*

Housing Development	No. of Units	Percent Black	Percent Hispanic	Percent White	Percent Oriental/ Other	Percent Black in Census Tract†
Family						
Allen Parkway Village	1,000	34.1	2.8	5.0	58.1	63.4
Clayton Homes	348	47.3	32.0	0.4	20.3	17.3
Cuney Homes	564	98.9	0.4	0.1	0.6	99.4
Irvington Village	318	28.9	60.2	9.9	1.0	6.2
Kelly Village	333	96.1	0.9	0.0	3.0	94.3
Lincoln Park	264	99.3	0.7	0.0	0.0	0.6
Oxford Place	230	87.9	6.5	5.1	0.5	4.3
Forest Green	100	100.0	0.0	0.0	0.0	13.7
Ewing	42	87.5	2.5	7.5	2.5	47.2
Kennedy Place	60	89.8	3.4	0.0	6.8	94.3
Wilmington House	108	98.1	0.0	0.0	1.9	99.5
Long Drive	100	74.0	22.0	3.0	1.0	1.3
Elderly						
75 Lyerly	200	16.2	19.7	64.1	0.0	4.7
Bellerive	210	5.7	20.0	72.9	1.4	56.5
Telephone Road	200	18.1	9.0	70.9	2.0	35.4

*Ethnic composition of housing developments as of August 31, 1984, was calculated by the Houston Housing Authority.
†Census tract data are based on the 1980 Census figures.

a confrontation with either group, however, by closing the complex gradually rather than all at once. The method for this is to allow vacated units to remain vacant and to neglect the physical condition of the settlement. Hence, by mid-1984 only 528 of 1,000 apartments were occupied, and physical deterioration was pronounced; most of the apartment units in the forty-year-old complex, including many still occupied, were not decent, safe, or sanitary.

A 1983 study of the project analyzed its future in conjunction with suggested development and housing options for the surrounding Fourth Ward neighborhood.[11] The Housing Authority voted to demolish the project. Its plan called for replacement units, elderly mid-rise housing in the Fourth Ward, and incentives to leverage additional low- and moderate-income housing units into the thirty-seven-acre site.

Table 14
Ethnic Composition of Allen Parkway Village for Selected Years

Year	Percent Black	Percent Hispanic	Percent White	Percent Oriental/Other	Percent Total
1976	66.0	3.0	26.0	5.0	100.0
1980	45.8	2.3	10.9	41.0	100.0
1983	33.1	2.0	6.9	58.0	100.0
1984	34.1	2.8	5.0	58.1	100.0

SOURCE: Houston Housing Authority, Housing Management Division, *Allen Parkway Village Summary Reports* (1984).

Barriers to Free Choice

While many barriers to decent and affordable housing for Houstonians have been overcome, a sizable portion of the city's black population still does not enjoy complete freedom in the housing market. It has been two decades since the Federal Fair Housing Act of 1968 banned racial discrimination in housing. However, both individual and institutionalized discrimination remain as major obstacles for blacks and other minorities. Discriminatory practices complicate the housing search for thousands of black Houstonians. The various forms of discrimination also contribute to the decline of many inner-city neighborhoods and deny a substantial segment of the community a basic form of wealth accumulation and investment through home ownership. The practice of refusing to sell or lease housing to blacks, coding records and applications to indicate the racial preference of landlords, selective marketing and advertising, racial steering, redlining, and threats or acts of intimidation continue to be problems that limit the housing alternatives available to blacks.[12]

Houston's blacks generally must expend more time, effort, and resources than whites when buying a home. Realtors and lending institutions often serve as gatekeepers in distributing housing and residential packages. The number of black home owners would probably be higher in the absence of housing discrimination by realtors and lending institutions. Some 47 percent of blacks in the Houston metropolitan area owned their homes in 1980, compared with 59 percent of area whites.

The federal and local commitments to the enforcement of fair housing laws have been weakened in recent years. Moreover, "financial and manpower support to rigorously pursue fair housing efforts have been inadequate."[13] There is growing sentiment at the federal level that special efforts are no longer needed to assure equal opportunity for lower-income and

In the mid-1980s inner-city black neighborhoods, such as the Fourth Ward, deteriorated as the downtown business district expanded. Houston's Fourth Ward faces an uncertain future. *Photo by Cary D. Wintz*

minority households. Civil rights violations in the area of fair housing continue to go uncorrected, and this signals the low priority given to federal enforcement of the current fair housing laws. However, even if federal authority vigorously enforced such laws, it could not eliminate housing discrimination by itself. All efforts to strengthen national fair housing laws must simultaneously be coordinated with state and local fair housing agencies and must incorporate strong enforcement measures at the grass roots.

Houston's Fair Housing Ordinance, however, suffers from some of the same defects that limit the federal fair housing legislation—namely, weak enforcement provisions. The city's Fair Housing Division was allowed to seek voluntary compliance only through conciliation with the parties involved in the complaint. In addition, the commitment and financial support for the local fair housing agency have diminished over the years. For example, in 1977 the city agency was staffed by nine full-time employees, four of whom were compliance officers. The agency staff shrank to only three people in 1984—an acting director, a compliance officer, and a secretary. The following year the severely crippled Fair Housing Division was merged with the city's Affirmative Action Division.

Despite the severe problems that the local Fair Housing Division has experienced, Houstonians have continued to file housing discrimination complaints with the city agency. A total of 1,617 complaints were received by the agency between 1975 and 1982 (see table 15). Complaint activity fluctuated from year to year. However, the greatest number of complaints was filed in 1976, soon after the agency was created. The newness and novelty of the agency no doubt contributed to the large number of initial complaints.

The number of housing discrimination complaints filed with the city appears to correspond with the local economic climate and staffing pattern of the local fair housing agency. For example, new housing starts, the number of fair housing employees, and complaint activity were highest from the mid-1970s through the end of the decade. Conversely, a decrease in complaint activity occurred during the economic recession of the early 1980s, which was a recession that dramatically affected the enforcement capability of the city agency.

Discrimination complaints that were filed with the city were disposed of in one of four ways. Some were resolved by formal or informal conciliation. Others were referred to the Houston City Attorney or dismissed. The data in table 16 show the distribution of discrimination complaints for 1979–82. More than two-thirds of the complaints filed during this time were dismissed. The dismissals were usually a result of complaint applications not having the proper applicant signatures or lacking sufficient evidence. On other occasions, complaints were dismissed because applicants withdrew them or because the housing units in question were deter-

Table 15
Housing Discrimination Complaint Activity in Houston, 1975–82

Year of Complaint	Number
1975*	73
1976	478
1977	233
1978	316
1979	175
1980	120
1981	117
1982	105
TOTAL	1,617

*Only includes the period July 9, 1975, through December 31, 1975.
SOURCE: City of Houston Fair Housing Division (1983).

Table 16

Disposition of Housing Discrimination Complaints in Houston 1979–82

Disposition	YEAR OF COMPLAINT			
	1979	1980	1981	1982
Formal Conciliation	8 (4.6%)	2 (1.7%)	2 (1.7%)	7 (6.7%)
Informal Conciliation	32 (18.3%)	41 (34.2%)	38 (32.5%)	35 (33.3%)
Referred to the City Attorney	3 (1.7%)	1 (0.8%)	1 (0.8%)	1 (0.9%)
Dismissed	132 (75.4%)	76 (63.3%)	76 (65.0%)	62 (59.1%)
TOTAL	175 (100.0%)	120 (100.0%)	117 (100.0%)	105 (100.0%)

SOURCE: City of Houston Fair Housing Division (1983).

mined to be outside the Houston city limits and thus beyond Houston's jurisdiction.

Informal conciliation—bringing the concerned parties together in an informal setting to try to resolve their dispute—accounted for more than one-fourth of the complaints disposed of during the 1979–82 period. However, a mere six complaints were referred to the city's legal department for litigation. The Houston City Attorney received only the discrimination complaints that the Fair Housing Division evaluated as having ample evidence to prosecute. Nevertheless, only one housing discrimination complaint case has ever reached the court in the entire history of the local fair housing ordinance—and it was subsequently dismissed.

The western half of the city has consistently registered the largest number of housing discrimination complaints over the years. Nearly two-thirds of the complaints filed between 1979 and 1982 originated in this area (see table 17). The level of complaint activity in Houston's northwest and southwest sectors reflected their rapid development. Southwest Houston, for example, accounted for more than half of the new housing construction during the city's boom era of the 1970s.

Housing discrimination complaint activity also differed significantly with the ethnic composition of the neighborhoods where the complaints originated. In general, complaints were more likely to originate from Houston neighborhoods with few minorities. Nearly 57 percent of the city's housing discrimination complaints filed in 1979 and 1980 originated from individuals living in census tracts where minorities comprised less than 25 percent of the tract population (see table 18). This pattern was demonstrated by cases based upon race/color and national origin. More than 84

Table 17
Geographic Location of Housing Discrimination Complaints in Houston 1979-82

Location	1979 (N = 175)	1980 (N = 120)	1981 (N = 117)	1982 (N = 105)
Northeast	21%	17%	14%	16%
Southeast	24%	18%	9%	21%
Northwest	15%	19%	29%	15%
Southwest	40%	46%	48%	48%
TOTAL	100%	100%	100%	100%

SOURCE: City of Houston Fair Housing Division (1983).

percent of the complaints based upon race/color and almost 93 percent of the complaints based on national origin came from individuals who lived in census tracts where whites were the overwhelming majority.

Sex discrimination complaints, however, did not conform to this pattern. Such complaints were concentrated in both minority and non-minority areas. More than 44 percent of the complaints based on sex were located in census tracts where blacks and Hispanics comprised the numerical majority. Conversely, nearly 41 percent of these sex discrimination cases originated from individuals who lived in census tracts where minorities comprised less than 25 percent of the population. This indicates that sex

Table 18
Type of Alleged Housing Discrimination by Percent Minority in Complaint Census Tracts, Houston 1979-80*

	TYPE OF ALLEGED DISCRIMINATION			
Percent Minority in Complaint Census Tract	Race/ Color	National Origin	Sex	Total
Less than 25	118	18	11	147
	(56.4%)	(66.7%)	(40.7%)	(55.9%)
25-49	58	7	4	69
	(27.8%)	(25.9%)	(14.8%)	(26.2%)
50 or over	33	2	12	47
	(15.8%)	(7.4%)	(44.5%)	(17.9%)
TOTAL	209	27	27	263
	(100.0%)	(100.0%)	(100.0%)	(100.0%)

*There were 295 housing discrimination complaints filed with Houston's Fair Housing Division in the years 1979 and 1980. The above analysis, however, is based upon 263 files in which this type of discrimination was recorded. Thirty-two case files did not list this item.
SOURCE: City of Houston Fair Housing Division (1982).

discrimination in the housing industry complicates the housing search for women, and especially minority women, in both minority and white neighborhoods. Black and Hispanic women are often the victims of a triple whammy of race, sex, and life-style (or single-parent) discrimination. Although race and sex discrimination are covered by local ordinance and are illegal, discrimination against families with children and against single-parent families is not. Such discrimination is consequently practiced without fear of sanction from the city.

Present Realities and Future Prospects

While housing options for many Houstonians have improved during the past several decades, housing for low- and moderate-income blacks has reached a crisis stage. Many continue to be ill-housed, and their search for better shelter is severely complicated by spiraling rents and utilities, high interest rates, and rising construction costs. Minority households and families with children must also contend with institutional housing barriers. Discrimination continues to deny a significant portion of the population decent and affordable housing. Discrimination also denies individuals a basic form of investment through home ownership and contributes to the decline of many inner-city neighborhoods. Moreover, economic hard times in the oil patch have pushed many stable low- and moderate-income black neighborhoods to the brink of depression. In fact, many of these areas have become "foreclosed" neighborhoods.

It appears that black and lower-income households can expect less from government in terms of housing subsidies and programs to stimulate housing production and home ownership. Houston will surely witness an intensification in the competition between incumbent, low-income minority residents of near-town, inner-city neighborhoods and more affluent "urban pioneers" from elsewhere, most of them white, who want to gentrify and occupy older neighborhoods. Once again there is the prospect that poorer minority people will be dislocated to make way for "progress" and "improvements."

Federally assisted housing for the poor has been pushed far down the national agenda, and it is also a low priority at the local level. Few cities, including Houston, can afford to have their public housing taken out of the market. However, many of the nation's public housing complexes are in such a state of abject disrepair that they are literally falling down of their own weight. This problem is a national disgrace. The weakened federal commitment to providing decent, safe, and affordable housing for low- and moderate-income people has left many local housing authorities with extreme fiscal problems that are not likely to disappear in the near future.

Additionally, the "politicization" of the selection of public housing sites, especially regarding family complexes, and the public opposition they have caused, only further complicate the job of local housing authorities. The remainder of the century will likely be a crucial period for big-city housing authorities, such as Houston's, which will almost certainly be faced with dwindling resources.

Barriers to free choice have not all been eliminated in the Houston housing market. Because many of the discriminatory policies and practices employed by landlords, realtors, developers, lending institutions, and apartment managers evolved over several generations, eliminating them will not be an easy task. Discrimination in modern, urban America has reached a level of sophistication that makes it easy to practice but difficult to prove. The solution to this stubborn problem in Houston and elsewhere certainly does not lie in dismantling the local fair housing agency or lax enforcement of the laws that are currently on the books. Indeed, emasculated public service agencies and indifferent enforcement of anti-discrimination laws not only cause worsening housing and related public-sector problems, but become part of the problem itself.

Notes

1. U.S. Bureau of the Census, *State and Metropolitan Data Book, 1982* (Washington, D.C., 1982), p. 386.

2. For a detailed discussion of Houston's wards and the city's other mostly black neighborhoods, see Robert D. Bullard, *Invisible Houston: The Black Experience in Boom and Bust* (College Station, Tex., 1987).

3. Karl E. Taeuber, "Racial Residential Segregation, 29 Cities, 1970-1980," Center for Demography and Ecology, Working Paper, University of Wisconsin, Madison, Mar., 1983, p. 3.

4. See Larry Long and Deanne DeAre, "The Suburbanization of Blacks," *American Demographics* 3 (Sept., 1981) 8:20; Robert D. Bullard, "Black Housing in the Golden Buckle of the Sunbelt, *Free Inquiry* 8 (Nov., 1980): 169-72; Robert D. Bullard and Odessa L. Pierce, "Black Housing in a Southern Metropolis: Competition for Housing in a Shrinking Market," *Black Scholar* 11 (Nov./Dec., 1979): 60-67.

5. For a thorough discussion of this topic, see Jamshid A. Momeni, ed., *Race, Ethnicity and Minority Housing in the United States* (Westport, Conn., 1986). See also Robert D. Bullard, "Persistent Barriers in Housing Black Americans," *Journal of Applied Social Sciences* 7 (Fall/Winter, 1983): 19-31.

6. G. L. Houseman, "Access of Minorities to Suburbs," *Urban Social Change Review* 14 (1981): 11-20.

7. W. R. Morris, "The Black Struggle for Fair Housing: 1900-1980," *Urban League Review* 5 (Summer, 1981): 6-7; Robert D. Bullard, "The Black Family: Housing Alternatives in the 80s," *Journal of Black Studies* 14 (Mar., 1984): 341-51.

8. Robert D. Bullard, "Does Section 8 Promote an Ethnic and Economic Mix?" *Journal of Housing* 7 (July, 1978): 364-65.

9. Ibid.

10. Housing Authority of the City of Houston, *Annual Report* (Houston, 1984), p. 3.

11. Robert Aprea, Robert D. Bullard, Jeff Baloutine, and Jacquline Alford, *Allen Parkway Village/Fourth Ward Technical Report* (Houston, 1983).

12. See Robert D. Bullard and Donald L. Tryman, "Competition for Decent Housing: A Focus on Housing Discrimination in a Sunbelt City," *Journal of Ethnic Studies* 7 (Winter, 1980): 51-63; Franklin James, Betty I. Cumming, and Eileen A. Tynan, *Minorities in the Sunbelt* (New Brunswick, N.J., 1984); and Robert D. Bullard, *Invisible Houston: The Black Experience in Boom and Bust* (College Station, Tex., 1987).

13. U.S. Commission on Civil Rights, *The Federal Fair Housing Enforcement Efforts* (Washington, D.C., 1979), p. 230.

Organizing in the Private City: The Case of Houston, Texas

Robert Fisher

The Private City Rediscovered

One of the central developments in Western Europe and the United States in the 1980s was the rise of the privatization strategy. Under pressure from dramatic economic and social changes in the last decade, the very concepts of the welfare state and public intervention were shaken. In the late 1970s and then especially in Reagan's America, "big government" was declared the main problem, as neo-conservatives sought to dismantle as much of the welfare state as possible.[1] Koch's New York City was the most publicized local example. In Western Europe, Thatcher's transformation of the British welfare state and Kohl's efforts at privatization throughout the Federal Republic of Germany are two significant international examples.[2] Nowhere is this more evident in the 1990s than in central and eastern Europe, where years of repression have created a fertile field for demands for personal freedom and democratic rights. In the current conservative context, this tendency is pushing almost all agendas away from liberal and socialist conceptualizations and toward marketplace solutions. As Paul Starr put it, "Some supporters tout privatization as a sovereign cure for virtually all ailments of the body politic. They prescribe it as a tonic for efficiency and economic growth, an appetite suppressant for the federal budget, a vaccine against bureaucratic empire-building, and a booster for individual freedom, including the opportunities of disadvantaged minorities."[3]

In fact, these authors are talking about "reprivatization," the name said to be first applied to the phenomenon in 1969 by Peter Drucker.[4] Cities in the United States have always been private cities, and privatization was, certainly through the 1920s, the dominant strategy for addressing, or ignoring, urban problems. As Sam Bass Warner, Jr., noted in *The Private City:*

> Under the American tradition, the first purpose of the citizen is the private search for wealth; the goal of a city is to be a community of private money makers. . . . The private market's demand for workers, its capaci-

ties for dividing land, building houses, stores and factories, and its needs for public services have determined the shape and quality of America's big cities. What the private market could do well American cities have done well; what the private market did badly, or neglected, our cities have been unable to overcome.... The twentieth-century failure of urban America to create a humane environment is thus the story of an enduring tradition of privatism in a changing world.[5]

So, the American urban past is filled with potential models for modern-day reprivatizers. But up until 1982, Houston, Texas, was the example of choice, primarily because it was current. The "free enterprise" model of Houston was recognized and touted by those seeking reprivatization from London to Vienna. In the United Kingdom, for example, the Institute for Economic Affairs as well as the Adam Smith Institute, both new-right think tanks, proclaimed Houston as a free-market model of urban planning and policy development for Britain to follow—a strategy they hoped would get the planners and public regulations off the backs of developers and other entrepreneurs.[6] The Institute of Economic Affairs argued, based on its limited research of "the Houston experience," that "the dispensability of land-use controls is not merely arguable in theory: it has been demonstrated in practice.... Perhaps it is an indication of closed minds among the land-use planners and their academic supporters in Britain that they have almost universally ignored the evidence from Houston.... this relatively free regime has had many advantages and few disadvantages or none."[7]

At first glance Houston seems to fit the bill. It is as much a privatized city as is possible for a modern metropolis to be. And Houston has truly been, at least until recently, an engine of growth—spatial, demographic, and economic. Not surprisingly, most of the boosters of reprivatization who tout the Houston model tend to overlook the warts, as if Houston's problems were somehow separate from its success. This paper accepts the argument, ably detailed elsewhere, that Houston's mounting problems are integral aspects of the reprivatization strategy.[8] Whether such policies take the form of load shedding, contracting out, or vouchers, they present to the urban public not only serious problems of accountability, but also an inherent unwillingness or inability to address chronic social needs that are not profitable for private sector investment.[9] The goal here, however, is to use Houston as a case study to examine another element of the reprivatization strategy.

Privatization and Community Empowerment

Neo-conservatives assert that privatization not only solves urban problems better than public programs do but also empowers people at the grass roots.

As Stuart Butler, a consultant with the Heritage Foundation, proclaimed, extolling the virtues of "enterprise zones." "The trend has been for ever greater government spending and intervention within inner city neighborhoods. This has stifled local creativity and made it difficult for communities to adapt to the changing economic climate. The enterprise zone would move policy in precisely the opposite direction, allowing local people and organizations to take the lead in tackling their own problems and opportunities—with the minimum of outside interference."[10]

Privatization, therefore, is seen as the true democratic alternative—the best means of letting the people decide what their needs are and how to meet them. But which people decide? Who participates in the privatization context? Starr argues that "the removal of decisions from the public arena diminishes the individual incentive for community participation."[11] "Use of the political process to control 'private' activity," the Fainsteins note, "is vastly more difficult than employing it to affect government itself."[12] Henig sums up the problem nicely, concluding that

> privatization may diffuse responsibility and thereby increase the perceived costs of mobilizing for political goals. For all the intransigence and imperviousness to input they sometimes exhibit, public officials and public bureaucracies nonetheless are enmeshed in a formal and well-defined system for citizen access. . . . Although the poor suffer disadvantages in competing in this system, they do not enter the arena unarmed. Privatization, however, may shift key decisions to an arena in which market power is the dominant currency, and the poor are well aware that this is an arena in which their victories come very hard indeed.[13]

Houston exemplifies perfectly the proposition that in advanced capitalist economies with representative governments there is a direct, rather than inverse, relationship between the public sector and citizen initiatives.[14] The smaller and weaker the public sector, the fewer and less effective the grassroots challenges; the more privatization, the less potential for local democracy. By delegitimizing the public sector, the privatization strategy makes it extremely difficult for citizens to mobilize in support of collective solutions to urban problems. Contrary to the pronouncements of its advocates, privatization blocks, rather than facilitates, community organizing.

The New Social Movements

Central to this thesis is the contention that the service economy of the corporate central city leads to a different kind of politics of mobilization than does the traditional industrial urban economy.[15] With the shift of the classic forms of industrial production from the central cities of advanced capitalist states to peripheral regions and Third World nations, the structural bases for class-oriented mobilizations move out from under organized labor. Social movements related to such issues as race, gender, and the protection of neighborhood enclaves not only find space to emerge but become the primary arenas of defense and insurgency, which are the primary arenas of social action. The resistances that mobilize and make political demands under such conditions thus turn not on class-based identities, but rather on citizen- or constituency-based identities. They occur in people's communities more often than at the factory, the site of production. Harvey argues, for example, that once the parts of the fragmented metropolis become "the basis for political action, then community consciousness replaces class consciousness as the springboard for action and the locus of social conflict."[16] Identity, community, and culture become the contexts through which people come to construct and understand political life. The point is not that class structures disappear within the context of postindustrial capitalism, but that they become inextricably intermingled with other sources of identity, division, and conflict.

Indeed, movements based on constituency and community are often referred to as new social movements because they depart from the labor- and class-based mobilizations that prevailed in the industrialized nations in the years before and immediately following World War II. Good examples are the civil rights, student, antiwar, black power/community control, women's liberation, environmental, gay and lesbian, and neighborhood organization/protection movements. These major social movements of our time have roots in community, for that is where people most immediately know and experience the grievances that precipitate them. But these social movements cannot be defined totally in relation to the spaces of community and neighborhood, for many of them extend to larger visions of an alternative culture.

Touraine concludes that the principal conflict that has emerged in society is between consumers on the one hand and the large production and management apparatuses on the other, and that this generalized conflict breaks apart into many distinct ones. There are resistances to the bureaucratic control of everyday life not only in the realms of production and in relation to the distribution of the social wage but also in the realms of the school, the family, and sexuality. People challenge the ends of technology, the commodification of the community, the destruction of the environment, and the general despoliation of the quality of life.

Touraine warns that the new social movements, if left totally to their own devices, could open the way for a reactionary retreat into a parochial politics of culture, self-help, and identity. "The main risk," he has written, "is no longer to see social movements absorbed by political parties, as in Communist regimes, but a complete separation between social movements and the State. In such a situation, social movements can easily become segmented, transform themselves into defense of minorities or search for identity, while public life becomes dominated by pro- or anti-State movements."[17] For community- and constituency-based struggles to avoid collapse into anti-movements, their dialectical relation to the state must be understood.

Community Mobilization and the State

There is an abundance of recent literature on the role of community mobilization — covering a range of grass-roots activity from citizen initiatives to community organizations and urban social movements — in forcing urban politics and urban policies to be more attentive to the needs of ordinary citizens, especially groups such as poor racial ethnics.[18] The neo-conservative era in the United States, which began in the late 1970s, not only decimated urban areas but forced social scientists to reevaluate the relationship between the state and community organization. The argument in this paper reflects a reaction against neo-conservative destruction of the state, declaring that public sector expansion and responsibility is critical to community organization. This thinking, of course, runs against the grain of much community organization literature. Midgley points out that central to the rationale of community participation "is a reaction against the centralization, bureaucratization, rigidity, and remoteness of the state. The ideology of community participation is sustained by the belief that the power of the state has extended too far, diminishing the freedoms of ordinary people and their rights to control their own affairs."[19] Actually, community participation literature of the 1960s and 1970s was infused with a contradictory understanding and relationship to the state: on the one hand the state was seen as primarily coercive, the arm of the capitalist system simply seeking to control its workers; on the other, it was viewed as a potential source of support for distributional and service program demands.[20] Out of this came a dialectical view of the state. No longer was it simply seen in Marxian terms as the ruling arm of the bourgeoisie; no longer was it seen in terms of liberal democratic or pluralist theory as a state that reflected and was subservient to its citizenry or one that counterbalanced demands of big labor and corporate capital. The dialectical view saw the state as both a mechanism for social control and a site of political contestation where the working class and poor struggle to address issues and advance their position.[21] As the locus of organizing shifted from the factory to the community, as the old social movements gave way to the new, the targets of organizing moved from the private sector (factory owners, capitalists) to the sources of most community concerns, the state.[22]

As the state expanded and as community groups became more distant from work-based organizing, the state increasingly became the focus of community groups.²³ The state became a battleground for the public debate about issues previously considered private affairs under laissez-faire capitalism.²⁴

According to this dialectical view, grass-roots mobilization is critical to the formation of an expanded public sector. "It is the threat of a powerful working class movement," Gough writes, "which galvanizes the ruling class to think more cohesively and strategically and to restructure the state apparatus to this end. Those countries which have experienced strong centralized challenges to the power of the capitalist class are those which have developed a unified state apparatus to counter these challenges."²⁵

But the dialectical relation between the state and community mobilization also cuts the other way. The expanded state not only comes into being in response to challenges, but in the late twentieth century, where private sector targets seem to disappear in the electronic global economy and where the community replaces the factory/workplace as the locus of organizing, an expanded public sector becomes a critical ingredient — as both arena and target — for continued citizen initiatives.²⁶ In the absence of a sizable and responsible public sector, community organizations, devoid of workplace organizing or obvious private sector targets, wither. Seen from this perspective, current reprivatization strategies to dismantle the welfare state and diminish federal power in social affairs are a last-ditch effort to remove government responsibility for the welfare of citizens and society, so that claims on the government — whether for cleaner air or welfare benefits — are seen as illegitimate and anachronistic. And if such claims are illegitimate, then most community organization is fundamentally undermined.

Houston illustrates well the dialectical relation between the state and community mobilization. The city did not adopt a more state-oriented strategy to urban problems because the city never encountered sufficiently massive problems and never saw itself in a crisis situation that might have produced comprehensive alternatives initiated by either elites or grass-roots insurgents.²⁷ In Houston, government has been kept small and limited in power, and power has been concentrated in private, extra-political bodies. Therefore, it has been nearly impossible to mount anything bordering on an effective challenge to the dominant directive of private economic growth, because of the absence of public arenas for discussing such issues and because challenging groups have had no significant public targets.²⁸ Of course, as will be discussed later, there are numerous other factors mediating against community mobilization in Houston. Continuous boomtown growth, the Jim Crow legacy, a peculiar mix of southern and western political culture, the absence of left-wing alternatives, and repression, as well as other factors, combined to offer a massive obstacle to grass-roots citizen initiatives.²⁹

What is most telling, however, is that when many of these barriers began to diminish in the early 1980s, the social contestation that emerged focused on the public sector and sought to expand it as both a base of power and a base to legitimize claims.[30]

Market Solutions

The dominant ideology of privatization in Houston, certainly from 1948 until very recently, says an expanded public sector is not necessary. It only gets in the way of growth and the market. Unbridled, unfettered capitalism is what made Houston's boom years possible, the argument continues, and the commitment to "free enterprise" is what Houston is all about. As Louie Welch, former Houston mayor, noted in 1980 when he was president of the chamber of commerce, "no city is without poor people but the opportunity not to be poor is greater [in Houston] than in most cities. . . . The free market has functioned in Houston like no other place in America. It has a method of purging itself of slums."[31]

Prior to 1948 in Houston the attitude toward the state was much more ambiguous. As a developers' town, even before World War II, Houston had a tradition of opposition to land-use controls. Advocates of an expanded public sector within the elite almost always lost to opponents, whether the issue was zoning or comprehensive planning. But the battles were often close, and the planners sometimes won, as with the development of an incomplete "emerald necklace"—a park and boulevard system—in the 1920s.[32] There was certainly no united opposition to public sector assistance. As late as 1947, for example, Mayor Oscar Holcombe was not only willing to accept federal funds for public housing projects in Houston, but he actively solicited them by testifying before Congress and requesting additional funding for public housing to address the "daily growing . . . problem—our slums and the great number of people forced to live in them."[33] During the depression, Jesse Jones—"Mr. Houston"—served in the Roosevelt administrations, first as head of the Reconstruction Finance Corporation, then as federal loan administrator, and later as secretary of commerce, channeling government programs to Houston with nary a local complaint.[34]

Beginning in the early 1950s, however, Houstonians began stridently to protest not only federal funds for public housing but also federal support for almost anything that did not directly aid economic growth. This included the rejection of federal funding for school lunch funds and urban renewal.[35] Houston became the "free enterprise city" as the cold war and later the civil rights movement infused antagonism into the public sector with new meaning. The pronouncement of a taxpayers' organization, the Property Owners Association of Houston, associated with the chamber of commerce, put the ideology of privatism into its cold war context, where it remained at least up until very recently. In their opposition to public housing, the association declared, "Thanks to private enterprise, America today is the best housed nation in the world. Whereas Russia — where the government owns all the housing — is the most poorly housed. . . . We are not fighting to save the slums. We ARE fighting to save . . . the American form of government. . . . Come to the membership meeting and get the latest facts on the campaign to stop socialism."[36]

When zoning was defeated in a 1948 referendum in Houston, slightly before the cold war took hold there, the primary argument in opposition to zoning was that it was inherently unworkable and corrupt; by 1962, however, it was crushed in a referendum by opponents who charged that zoning was communistic and socialistic.[37] This is not to suggest that anticommunism appeared in Houston only after the Second World War. Black and Hispanic activists in the 1920s and 1930s continually noted charges of communism being attached to their efforts.[38] Nor is this to suggest that Houston was not always a wide-open and reactionary town. In the 1920s the Ku Klux Klan headquarters was right across from city hall, and the relation between the two was often even closer. Historian Charles Alexander notes how the chief of police in the 1920s "conducted his department according to the instructions Exalted Cyclops H. C. McCall of Klan No. 1 gave him."[39] "White folks here didn't give a damn about what the world thought," black activist Moses Leroy recalled. "Every group we would try to organize they would brand Communist and that would inspire whites frightened to put on those hoods and do some nightriding."[40] But the intensity of the ideology of privatism and the virulent opposition to government social programs did not develop into the city's creed until after the cold war created a hospitable national context for them. And it was the hardening of this ideology, with its delegitimizing of public sector intervention, that made community mobilization so difficult.

Community Organizing in a Sunbelt City

Mollenkopf claims Sunbelt cities are distinguished by "the small size of their governments, their private sector orientation, [and] the lack of political conflict." For him, throughout the Sunbelt "the business community has a virtual monopoly in deliberation on solutions to civic problems."[41] Houston, once the "golden buckle of the Sunbelt," is the shining example of the dominant private city devoid of social contestation. A wide range of sources validates this. Feagin argues that in Houston "fewer instances of urban protest movements appear than in other major cities."[42]

Noting the "somewhat passive role of the black Houston community during the turbulent sixties," Bullard concludes that "although many of the social problems that triggered large-scale protests, demonstrations, and urban riots of the sixties were present in Houston, the city's black community remained relatively calm during this period."[43] Murray suggests that "local voter passivity reflects the widespread feeling in this sprawling, amorphous city that ordinary citizens have little or no influence over public affairs."[44] A recent work comparing housing in Houston and Santa Monica suggests that "the social movements of the 1960s never found any expression in the city" and this helps explain why "the neighborhood empowerment movements of the late seventies and eighties which swept across American cities never took hold in Houston."[45] What did occur in Houston was mild and controllable, especially when compared to events occurring at the same time throughout the "contested cities" of the United States and Western Europe.[46]

It is no accident that the civil rights era of the 1960s is a focal point for discussions about the lack of community mobilization in Houston, for this is the time when such grass-roots activity would be most expected. Houston is a southern city at the western edge of the "Black Belt." It now has one of the largest black populations of any southern city, surpassing Atlanta, Birmingham, and Memphis since 1960, and composing some 28 percent of the city's residents. Throughout the twentieth century the percentage of African Americans has always been large, ranging from 21 percent to 32.7 percent.[47] In most modernizing urban centers in the South with large black populations, there was significant civil rights activity in the late 1950s and 1960s. Moreover, Houston might have been expected to be one of the major sites of civil rights efforts because it had a history of black activism. It was, for example, the locus of one of the most important battles by blacks in the 1930s and 1940s: the overthrow of the white primary.[48] And as late as 1948 an integrated rally of over four thousand people (not all supporters) was held in Houston to promote Henry Wallace's Progressive Party campaign.[49] But the cold war ideology and repression that soon followed in Houston and the nation put an end to this era of black activism.[50] There was, of course, a good deal of activity on the part of both blacks and whites in Houston during the civil rights era, including both conventional and direct action strategies. There were lobbying efforts to desegregate pubic facilities, such as city buildings, swimming pools, golf courses, and the airport;[51] electoral strategies to eliminate the poll tax, register voters, and advance black political candidates;[52] many struggles around school integration;[53] sit-ins at lunch counters in the early 1960s;[54] a student movement at the city's three major universities — Texas Southern University, the University of Houston, and Rice University; and an increasingly militant "black power" movement that developed after 1966, resulting in both a riot on the campus of Texas Southern University, the historically black university in the city, and related police repression to halt such activity.[55] In the late 1960s the black community was hot with the newfound sense that their political activism might have an affect on city and national politics. A contemporary study comparing black attitudes in Houston to those of inner-city blacks in other metropolitan centers concluded that Houston's African Americans were more discontented with the slow speed of civil rights reform than their counterparts in Chicago, Atlanta, and Birmingham.[56] Anyone witnessing student rebellions at Texas Southern University in 1965 and 1967 and the assassination of Carl Hampton, a black activist, by the Houston police in 1970 would not have called Houston a "hotbed of apathy" or an uncontested city.[57] To the contrary, the editors of the *Voice of Hope* believed in April, 1970, that Houston was "on the verge of a Black explosion."[58] So, by suggesting that popular mobilization has not been very strong in Houston, and certainly not strong enough to challenge with any success the political economy of privatization, there is no intent to deny or diminish the efforts of scores of people who struggled to bring about social change.

Nevertheless, it is true that there was much less activism in Houston than in most other comparable cities, southern or northern. The "scope of contagion" remained well contained. F. Kenneth Jensen, writing about the history of the sit-in movement in Houston, confirms in another chapter in this volume that

> compared to several of the other large cities in the South, such as Atlanta and Montgomery, the [sit-in] protest movement in Houston was small. There were not more than a hundred regular activists in the Bayou City and individual sit-ins seldom numbered more than twenty-five or thirty people. Furthermore, although the protesters in Houston obviously enjoyed wide support within the black community, they never developed a capacity to put thousands of people in the streets as was accomplished in other large Southern cities.[59]

Reporter Saul Friedman bemoaned in 1963 in an article in the liberal *Texas Observer* that "the Negroes of Houston are among the most politically docile and backward in the South, if not the nation."[60] And one frustrated black activist complained as late as 1970 that "Houston's problem is that the Blacks have been too quiet. Blacks have been so calm that the white man here has confidence he can submit any type of suppression he wants to use upon Blacks without any retaliation."[61]

Citizen insurgency in Houston after the opening of the cold war was never able to create an atmosphere legitimizing conflict, supporting alternative political ideas, and forcing political elites to alter the dominant hegemony of laissez-faire politics. Despite efforts by activists to expand the

In 1967 Texas Southern University students demonstrated to shut down a major thoroughfare that bisected their campus. These demonstrations climaxed in a confrontation with Houston police that represented one of the most violent episodes in the struggle for black rights in Houston. *Courtesy Houston Public Library, Houston Metropolitan Research Center*

role of local government, by demanding that the public sector implement programs to address the horrid conditions of Houston's slums, Houston's elite continued to toe the privatist line and do as little as possible to address neighborhood needs. Mayor Welch advised in 1964 that other cities should emulate Houston's record on race relations. Its peaceful progress, he noted, was the result of "responsible business leadership, white and Negro." And he warned, on the eve of the passage of the Civil Rights Act of 1964, that "you can expect too much from legislation."[62] Certainly the activism of Houstonians in the 1960s reaped many benefits, personal and collective, but it did little to alter the laissez-faire mindset and privatistic urban policy that characterized the city.

What helps explain the ineffectiveness of social contestation in Houston to move the city beyond its privatistic perspective? Fainstein and Fainstein emphasize that urban social movements and grass-roots contestation are critical for developing democratic urban policy. They change "the whole character of elite response to popular demands and opposition.... In this way, institutionalized politics and power within the economy are strongly although indirectly affected by the availability of popular mobilization as a political resource."[63] But such protest may not be enough. Tarrow suggests that the "political opportunity structure" of a given locale not only yields what it is willing and able to in any given historical epoch but also creates barriers to change that protect it.[64] Fainstein and Fainstein suggest that four essentially political factors help determine whether effective popular mobilization will develop in cities: "(1) The ability of political parties and governmental institutions to contain and channel mobilizations; (2) the relative receptivity of local regimes to action group formation and pressure; (3) the unity of urban elites; and (4) the availability of alternative political ideas that can create an oppositional consciousness among a significant sector of the citizenry."[65] Piven and Cloward argue, furthermore, that without a legitimized public sector that is recognized as being responsible for the public welfare and that becomes, albeit unintentionally, an arena for public discussion and conflict, the effectiveness of urban social protest is severely curtailed.[66] All of these help explain the lack of community organizing in Houston.

The conventional wisdom about why Houston was quieter in the 1960s than most other major U.S. cities, for example, is that Houston was a cosmopolitan "New South" city with a business elite smart and able enough to implement a policy of moderation on civil rights questions. This thinking extends from black radicals of the time to members of the white business elite. According to the militant, black *Voice of Hope* in 1970

> Almost in every instance in which acts of violence and brutality against Blacks have been stopped, the business community has been chiefly responsible for this. Not that members of the business community are so liberal or sympathetic to the Black struggle. In truth, they are not. They are, however, extremely concerned about eliminating any and all conditions that are not conducive to making a profit from the goods and services they have to sell. Therefore, they have in the past exercised considerable influence whenever conditions in the community were of such that they jeopardized the orderly flow of business.[67]

The head of public relations for Foley's department store in the 1950s and 1960s coordinated the efforts of most department stores in the city to defuse the sit-in movement in 1963. His plan to peacefully desegregate lunch counters at private facilities in Houston was adopted by most major retail stores, supported by the newspapers, and approved by key members of the black elite, including the editors of the *Informer* and *Forward Times,* because "the stores were the ones that had the sit-ins, the city hall wasn't. . . . We [were] going to save that business."[68] Clearly, as Tarrow and the Fainsteins would emphasize, a stable, relatively unified elite in the city was able to defuse protest in the city and to contain and manage it within the private sector. In other cities, such as Birmingham, Alabama, where elites were more divided, the political opportunity structure was more open, at least for a time, and protests there were more successful in creating an atmosphere of social contestation and drawing the public sector into it.[69]

In the privatized city, there were also serious structural constraints to community mobilization and protest, which transcended issues of political stability. Quietude, after all, was not simply the result of enlightened, moderate business leadership, no matter how unified and effective it might have been at managing conflict. (It is worth noting, for example, that in the late 1960s when black militant demands escalated, making private sector control of racial tensions difficult, the ubiquitous iron fist of police intervention quickly replaced the velvet glove of moderate reform as the strategy of choice by Houston's leaders.) Other explanations for Houston's relative passivity come closer to the mark. These include the consensus atmosphere in Houston sustained by continuous boomtown growth and economic prosperity,[70] a relatively homogeneous ruling group,[71] a political culture that deemphasized political participation and conflict,[72] the threat and practice of repression,[73] and the absence of an active and expanded public sector.[74] Such structural constraints built a massive obstacle to social change efforts from the grass roots.

Privatization was a major factor affecting the extent and effectiveness of community mobilization in Houston during the civil rights era. Admittedly, measures for examining the relationship between privatization and social contestation need further refinement, and more comparative research on the relation of the civil rights movement and other forms of citizen insurgency to the state needs to be done. Nevertheless, in Houston a political opportunity structure diminished by a weak public sector played a significant role.[75] As Kenneth Gray put it, "Neither labor nor Negroes look primarily to the city government to fulfill their goals; in the South, even more than elsewhere, such groups find local or state appeals relatively futile. Houstonians seem to get from local government what the majority expect from it."[76] Davidson, dismayed by the failure of the black struggle to achieve socio-economic justice, concluded in 1972 that "there does not seem to be any clear-cut connection between the political pressure exerted by Negro interest groups, Negro politicians, and the Negro electorate on the one hand, and progress in obtaining benefits on the other."[77] He argued that this would continue "so long as they do not have a say in what are now called 'private' decisions by those who make them."[78] The trick was to make economic issues public ones, and the only way to begin to do this was with an expanded public sector responsive to heretofore unrepresented or underrepresented groups.[79]

Current Context

Without an expanded public sector aggressively reflecting the will of its poor, racial ethnics, and other "out groups" to address socio-economic issues as well as civil rights, the private sector was not likely to address social problems either. Throughout the nation this has been one of the legacies of the new social movements. Davidson was right in noting that "the groundwork for Negro progress has been laid by the efforts of blacks during the past two decades [1950s and 1960s]."[80] But that groundwork underscored the problem of organizing in a privatized context. Button, in a recent study of the impact of the civil rights movement in southern communities, suggests a number of results relevant to the relationship between the public sector and community organization.

First, regarding the public sector, he suggests that the civil rights movement focused on the public sector because it was easier to effect change there than in the private sector; significant gains from the civil rights movement occurred in the public sector while only moderate ones were won in the private realm. Accordingly, the civil rights movement enabled blacks to expand their participation in the public sector. While municipal jobs are limited, Button notes, these positions have been very important to blacks not only because the work was steadier and the pay better than for comparable private sector tasks, but also because there is a direct relationship between the number of blacks in the municipal bureaucracy and improved service gains in the black community.[81]

This relationship between the legacy of the civil rights movement and the public sector is also evident in Houston. As in other cities, the poor and racial ethnics came increasingly to see the public sector as a base of personal advancement and collective mobilization.[82] For example, as late as the mid-1950s there were no black firemen and policemen, up until 1964 there were no blacks in white collar positions in city hall, and by 1970 little improvement had occurred.[83] Mirroring national trends, significant if limited gains had been made in black participation in the public sector by the mid-1980s. As Bullard notes, in 1985 blacks comprised 15 percent of the city's fire department, 11 percent of city's police department, 5 of the city's 25 department heads, and, overall, half of all the city's personnel (though disproportionately in low-paying and low-skilled jobs).[84] A more recent survey noted that African Americans composed 40 percent of the teachers in the Houston Independent School District.[85] The national gains of the 1960s were most visible in opening up areas of the public sector to racial ethnics, and even in Houston, where the city's public sector remains small (in 1980 1 percent of the population, 16,000 employees; in 1990, with cutbacks in the mid-1980s, just under 20,000 employees) blacks turned to it for individual and collective advancement.

Second, regarding mobilization strategies, Button concludes that black electoral activity and specifically electing blacks to political office "was the most important form of all conventional—and unconventional—political activities."[86] While this became the focus of black efforts in the 1970s and 1980s, black officials were limited in not only effecting change in the public sector but even more so in improving conditions in the private, economic realm. What worked best in the civil rights movement, however, was a blending of electoral activity with grass-roots insurgency. "Protest and violence complemented conventional black politics. . . . Thus it is evident that nontraditional strategies were generally necessary for meaningful community change."[87]

Since the late 1960s electoral efforts have also become the major focus of black activism in Houston. While it was not until 1971 that the first black, Judson Robinson, was elected to city council, the years since 1972 have been the heyday of black electoral representation. By 1985, twenty-nine blacks had held elective office in Houston.[88] Currently on a city council of fourteen elected officials, five councillors are black, of whom two are women. (This high degree of representation on the city council was made possible by a 1973 lawsuit that challenged the at-large system of council election and replaced it with a mix of at-large and district seats.) To the extent that black voters remain relatively unified, as when blacks run against whites or, most recently, against Hispanics, or when the black community endorses a specific candidate in a city-wide race that does not include an African American, blacks often hold the balance of power in Houston elections.[89]

Black advances in the public bureaucracy and elected offices have pointed the direction toward expanding the public sector and making it more responsive to constituencies other than the private sector. But the political culture of privatization continued to undercut any ability the public sector had to address problems and promote redistributional policy. With few resources and little legitimacy to effect change, public sector participation, without grass-roots insurgency, served black individual, more than black collective, advancement. As long as the ideology of privatization prevailed, the impact of black gains in public sector participation remained severely limited.

But the privatization consensus has been challenged recently by worldwide economic events, which in 1982 sent oil prices—and therefore the Houston economy—crashing. In response, many segments of the elite began to call for public-private partnerships to address both increasing infrastructure problems—the social costs of boomtown growth that had been ignored by the private sector—and the inability of the private sector to address such costs.[90] MacManus observed as early as 1983 a rising demand for new public programs.[91] The Houston Chamber of Commerce began to rethink its historical antipathy to public sector intervention on issues other than economic growth. Transportation, public education, air and water pollution, law enforcement, flooding and subsidence, and a host of other mounting citywide problems demanded attention as Houston's "quality of life" was increasingly called into question.[92] The results in 1989 of the Eighth Annual Houston Area Survey suggested that the attitudes of Houstonians "are becoming more liberal, more progressive, more concerned about public spending of sorts, more wanting to see government involved in meeting human needs."[93]

But obviously, private sector demands for an increased public sector — even the desires of most Houstonians for greater government involvement — would not likely translate into benefits for the city's poor and racial ethnic communities. As Warren argues, elite demands for public sector responsiveness tend to focus on allocative (quality of life) rather than redistributive policies.[94] Grass-roots insurgency, complementing electoral strategies, is necessary to put the needs and demands of the poor as well as racial ethnics before a public sector given new legitimacy by the economic crisis.

At first the opposite seemed to be occurring. The growth of the public sector in Houston and the success of strategies to demand public sector responsiveness appeared to be undermined initially by the economic crisis. Cutbacks in the mid-1980s reduced city government from a high of near twenty-two thousand employees to its current just under twenty thousand. Moreover, the funds required to address the rising claims of heretofore ignored groups, such as blacks, Hispanics, gays, and women, diminished at the very moment that Houston called on all its citizens to unite, to be "Houston Proud" and to save the city. The crisis, at first, further dampened the prospects for community mobilization in the private city.

But in actuality the economic crisis has called into question the very idea of the private city, and in so doing has opened the door for more, not less, social contestation directed at the public sector. As elites have begun to look to the public sector for assistance and seek an expanded role for it, so citizen initiatives, building on the legacy of the civil rights movement, have increasingly used local government as an arena and target for their activism. Racial ethnics are not in favor of all public sector expansion — only that which benefits them and which they can affect. In 1985 they voted against a light rail public transportation system because it was not designed to service their neighborhoods. They are well aware of the ambiguous role of the local public sector, which historically has been more coercive and neglectful than helpful to the needs of the poor and racial ethnics. Nevertheless, since the civil rights movement and especially in the past few years, city leaders have had to address the mounting claims of groups for an expanded and more responsive public sector.[95] These groups—from blacks and Hispanics to women, gays, and a host of others —understand the importance of pressuring city hall to address their claims and assure either public sector responsibility for problems or public sector solidarity with their objectives.[96] Citizen action organizations, like the Metropolitan Organization (TMO) and ACORN, came to Houston in the 1970s to empower working-class citizens and sought to build multi-ethnic, multi-racial, neighborhood-based organizations. Their efforts shared a similar approach, first made famous by Saul Alinsky: empower residents by encouraging them to demand that city government be responsive to their needs. As Ernesto Cortes, the founder of TMO, put it at a strategy meeting of Alinsky-style organizers, "The reason you were created is to hold public officials accountable. That whole philosophy is being challenged at the local level, the state level, and the national level. . . . There has to be a public sector. It has to be more effective. It won't be unless you hold them accountable.[97]

Cortes's perspective is reflected increasingly in independent and isolated efforts throughout the city. Tenants in Allen Parkway Village public housing, which sits on choice land on Buffalo Bayou and just outside the downtown area, were able to stop developers and the Houston Housing Authority from razing their homes.[98] The focus of their efforts was the city housing authority and city government, and part of their success was due to the support given by Rep. Henry Gonzalez (San Antonio) who sits prominently on the House Committee on Banking, Finance, and Urban Affairs. But as Lenwood Johnson, the key organizer in the Allen Parkway Village struggle, put it: "We direct our efforts at Earl Phillips [then the head of the Houston Housing Authority]. But the problem is not Earl Phillips. The problem is not Mayor Whitmire."[99] The private sector groups seeking to redevelop the area were the problem, but, unlike City Hall and the Housing Authority, they are much less visible targets.

More recently, students at largely Hispanic Austin High School staged a protest against school conditions, focusing their efforts on the Houston Independent School District (HISD) and receiving in turn a good deal of local and national media coverage. The recent murder of Ida Delaney, a black woman, by off-duty Houston policemen resulted in massive protests that forced the city's woman mayor and black police chief to support the creation of a citizen review process that may begin to guard against future police misconduct. Given recent black electoral victories, a more liberal attitude willing to acknowledge mounting problems as well as the need for public sector intervention, and increased activity in racial ethnic communities around a host of issues—including drugs, education, housing and the homeless, crime, and police brutality—the context seems right for increased community mobilization around demands for increased public sector responsiveness. Even the recent decision by the city council to create a zoning and planning commission reflects demands by middle-class homeowners for greater public responsiveness.

These examples can be viewed as isolated incidents, the social kettle boiling over after years of pressure and neglect. It is, of course, naive to wax optimistic at this point about the decline of privatization and the rising tide of public sector responsiveness and community mobilization. The barriers to the latter two, in both Houston and the nation, are still awesome. After more than a decade of federal social cuts, communities of the 1960s that were once impoverished but stable and often vibrant now find themselves ravaged by crime, drugs, and despair.[100] The argument can be made that elites are still tightly in control, evidenced by their success in dealing with and defusing occasional outbursts and challenges from racial ethnics who are experiencing worsening conditions. Only the future will tell how deep the grass-roots discontent runs, or how much a sense of crisis and social contestation will develop in Houston. But at the least such mobilization and reflexive efforts on the part of elites in Houston denote a shift, increasingly away from privatization as the be-all and end-all, and toward an understanding that the public sector needs to assume increasing responsibility for problems and needs the resources to do so. Citizen initiatives seem implicitly to understand that the initial targets of efforts in the global city cannot be those of the private sector. Rather, the political opportunity structure of the public sector, so inhospitable before, changes as a result of acquiring municipal jobs, winning political office, raising issues in the public sector, and demanding public sector accountability through grass-roots insurgency. Despite worsening objective conditions, this improved opportunity structure has the potential to enable citizens to advance a progressive agenda as perhaps never before seen in Houston

Notes

The author would like to acknowledge that this article began with a presentation, "Working with the Powers That Be in a Privatization Context: Houston, Texas," at the International Conference on Ethnic and Foreign Minorities, Nancy, France, June, 1988. That paper will appear, with others selected from the conference, in forthcoming edited collections, separately published, in France and the United Kingdom.

1. See, for example, Frances Fox Piven and Richard Cloward, *The New Class War: Reagan's Attack on the Welfare State and Its Consequences* (New York, 1982).
2. See, for example, the excellent study by Timothy Barnekov, Robin Boyle, and Daniel Rich, *Privatism and Urban Policy in Britain and the United States* (New York, 1989); Adalbert Evers and Hellmut Woolman, "Big City Politics: New Pat-

terns and Orientations on the Local Level of the Welfare State," *Eurosocial Research Papers* (Vienna, 1986), esp. pp. 1-5; Robin Hambleton, "Urban Government under Thatcher and Reagan," *Urban Affairs Quarterly* 24 (Mar., 1989): 359-88; and Jeffrey Henig, Chris Hamnett, and Harvey Feigenbaum, "The Politics of Privatization: A Comparative Perspective," *Governance: An International Journal of Policy and Administration* 1 (Oct., 1988): 442-68.

3. Paul Starr, *The Limits of Privatization* (Washington, D.C., 1987), p. 1. E. S. Savas, former assistant secretary of Housing and Urban Development during the Reagan years, proclaims its virtues in *Privatization: The Key to Better Government* (Chatham, N.J., 1987). He concludes on page 288 that "this book arrives at the position that privatization is the key to both limited and better government: limited in its size, scope, and power relative to society's other institutions; and better in that society's needs are satisfied more efficiently, effectively, and equitably."

4. See Savas, *Privatization*, p. 12.

5. Sam Bass Warner, Jr., *The Private City: Philadelphia in Three Periods of Growth* (Philadelphia, 1968), pp. x-xi.

6. Judith Allen and Andy Thornley, discussion with author, Central London Polytechnic, May, 1988. See Andy Thornley, "Planning in a Cool Climate: The Effects of Thatcherism," *Planner* (July, 1988): 17-19; Andrew Thornly, "Thatcherism and Simplified Regimes," *Planning Practice and Research* (Sept., 1986): 19-22.

7. Barry Bracewell-Milnes, "Market Control Over Land-Use Planning," in *Government and the Land* (London, 1974), p. 90.

8. The nature and extent of problems facing the poor, blacks, and Hispanics — past and present — are serious and long-standing: poverty, racism, residential segregation, neighborhood decay and destruction, inadequate housing, insufficient health care and social services, and meager public services. These are also the legacies of a laissez-faire city. See Joe Feagin, *Free Enterprise City: Houston in Political-Economic Perspective* (New Brunswick, N.J., 1988); Robert Bullard, *Invisible Houston: The Black Experience in Boom and Bust* (College Station, Tex., 1987); Robert Fisher, "Where Seldom Is Heard a Discouraging Word: The Political Economy of Houston," *Amerikastudien* 33 (1988), esp. 82-86.

9. On accountability as it relates to contracting out, see Bev Cigler, "Contracting Out: Reconciling the Accountability and Information Paradoxes" (Paper presented at Urban Affairs Association meeting, Baltimore, Md., Mar., 1989). On the ideological nature of current privatization efforts and the discrepancy between theory and practice, see Jeffrey R. Henig, "Privatization in the United States: Theory and Practice" (Paper presented at the International Studies meeting, Mar., 1989).

10. Stuart M. Butler, "The Enterprise Zone: Capitalism in the Inner City," *Special Report* no. 21 (Grove City, Pa., 1982), p. 4. The first chapter in Randall Fitzgerald, *When Government Goes Private: Successful Alternatives to Public Services* (New York, 1988) is entitled "Giving Power Back to the People."

11. Starr, *Limits of Privatization*, p. 11.

12. Norman Fainstein and Susan Fainstein, "Regime strategies, communal resistance, and economic forces," in Susan Fainstein et al., *Restructuring the City* (New York, 1983), p. 241.

13. Jeffrey R. Henig, "Collective Responses to the Urban Crisis: Ideology and Mobilization," in M. Gottdiener, ed., *Cities in Stress* (Beverley Hills, Calif., 1986), p. 233.

14. I am not arguing here for Houston's distinctiveness, but it does seem to be an exaggerated example of the private city. See Robert Fisher, "The Urban Sunbelt in Comparative Perspective: Houston in Context," in Robert B. Fairbanks and Kathleen Underwood, eds., *Essays on Sunbelt Cities and Recent Urban America* (College Station, Tex., 1990).

15. This analysis appeared in an earlier form in Bob Fisher and Joe Kling, "Popular Mobilization in the 1990s: Prospects for the New Social Movements," *New Politics* 3 (Winter, 1991): 71-84.

16. David Harvey, *Studies in the History and Theory of Capitalist Urbanization* 1 (Baltimore, 1985), pp. 120-21.

17. Alain Touraine, "An Introduction to the Study of Social Movements," *Social Research* 52 (Winter, 1985): 780.

18. See, for example, Harry Boyte, *The Backyard Revolution* (Philadelphia, 1981); Robert Fisher, *Let the People Decide: Neighborhood Organizing in America* (Boston, 1984); Gary Delgado, *Organizing the Movement: The Roots and Growth of ACORN* (Philadelphia, 1986); Stuart Lowe, *Urban Social Movements: The City after Castells* (London, 1986). On the term racial ethnics, used here instead of the more pejorative "minorities," see Elizabeth Higginbotham, "Laid Bare by the System: Work and Survival for Black and Hispanic Women," in A. Swerdlow and H. Lessinger, eds., *Class, Race, and Sex: The Dynamics of Control* (Boston, 1983), pp. 200-15. "Racial ethnic," a term not altogether satisfying either, is defined as an ethnic group that is phenotypically divergent from the dominant group in a society.

19. James Midgley et al., *Community Participation, Social Development, and the State* (New York, 1986), p. 4.

20. See Frances Fox Piven and Richard Cloward, *Regulating the Poor: The Functions of Public Welfare* (New York, 1971); Midgely et al., *Community Participation*, p. 4.

21. Piven and Cloward, for example, moved from one position to another, as reflected in their changed perceptions in *Regulating the Poor* and *The New Class War*.

22. Manuel Castells, *The City and the Grassroots* (Berkeley, 1983); Robert Fisher and Joseph Kling, "Community Mobilization: Prospects for the Future," *Urban Affairs Quarterly* 25 (Dec., 1989): 200-11.

23. Pierre Clavel, *The Progressive City*, cited in Feagin, *Free Enterprise City*, p. 287. Also see Fisher, *Let the People Decide*.

24. See Piven and Cloward, *New Class War;* Castells, *The City and the Grassroots;* Fisher, *Let The People Decide.* Feagin, *Free Enterprise City*, argues that more attention needs to be devoted to the local level of state activity.

25. Ian Gough, The *Political Economy of the Welfare State* (London, 1979), p. 65.

26. On the shift in organizing, see Fisher and Kling, "Community Mobilization"; and Joseph Kling, "Social Movements in the Era of the Corporate Urban Complex: Building an Explanatory Framework" (Paper delivered before Urban Affairs Association, Baltimore, Mar., 1989).

27. See Fisher, "The Urban Sunbelt in Comparative Perspective," pp. 33-58.

28. On the difficulty of grass-roots organizing in Houston, see Don Carleton, *Red Scare: Right-Wing Hysteria, Fifties Fanaticism, and Their Legacy in Texas* (Austin, 1985); Robert Fisher, "Community Organizing in Historical Perspective: A Typology," in Fred Cox et al., eds., *Strategies of Community Organization* (Itasca, Ill., 1987), pp. 387-97.

29. For additional obstacles, see Fisher, "Where Seldom Is Heard a Discouraging Word."

30. Of course, the situation cannot be simplified to say that racial ethnics love the state. Historically in Houston they have opposed zoning, feared the police, and opposed additional taxation, among other things. In general, however, they see the state as their best hope—as employer, as arena, as ombudsman, and as target.

31. Louie Welch cited in Joe R. Feagin, "Tallying the Social Costs of Urban Growth under Capitalism: The Case of Houston," in Scott Cummings, ed., *State, Class, and Urban Revolution* (Albany, N.Y., 1987).

32. Barry J. Kaplan, "Urban Development, Economic Growth, and Personal Liberty: The Rhetoric of the Houston Anti-Zoning Movements, 1947-1962," *Southwestern Historical Quarterly* 84 (Oct., 1980): 133-68; Barry Kaplan and Charles Orson Cook, "Civic Elites and Urban Planning: Houston's River Oaks," *East Texas Historical Journal* 15 (1977): 29-37; Bruce J. Weber, "Will Hogg and the Business of Reform," (Ph.D. diss., University of Houston, 1979); Bruce Weber and Charles Orson Cook, "Will Hogg and Civic Consciousness: Houston Style," *Houston Review* 2 (Winter, 1980): 21-38; Peter C. Papademetriou, "Urban Development and Public Policy in the Progressive Era, 1890-1940," *Houston Review* 5 (Fall, 1983): 115-32; Archie Henderson, "City Planning in Houston, 1920-1930," *Houston Review* 4 (1987): 107-36.

33. Holcombe quoted in Amy Bridges, "Boss Tweed and V. O. Key Head West" (Paper presented at the American Political Science Association, Chicago, 1984), p. 20.

34. Feagin, *Free Enterprise City*.

35. Kenneth E. Gray, "A Report on the Politics of Houston," unpublished report by Joint Center for Urban Studies of M.I.T. and Harvard University (1960), IV-12.

36. W. Gail Reeves, president of the Property Owners Association of Houston, to members, July 6,[?] 1950, Paul Roemer Collection, Box 1, Folder 5, Houston Metropolitan Research Center.

37. Barry J. Kaplan, "Urban Development, Economic Growth, and Personal Liberty: The Rhetoric of the Houston Anti-Zoning Movements, 1947-1962," *Southwestern Historical Quarterly* 84 (Oct., 1980): 133-68.

38. Thomas Wright, "Oldtime Black Houston Freedom Fighters Left Proud Legacy," *Forward Times*, Mar. 17, 1973. John J. Herrera, a leading Mexican-American activist in Houston, noted that "in 1929 when the Texas Rangers were still prevalent and they were lynching Mexican Americans regardless of their citizenship, we felt like if we were too militant, we would be kept from organizing. So we started the League of United Latin American Citizens as a civic, patriotic organization singing 'My Country Tis of Thee,' and reciting Washington's Prayer,

and having the Flag there and saluting it in order to show them we were not communists or agitators." See John J. Herrera interview, Houston Metropolitan Research Center, Nov. 13, 1980.

39. Charles Alexander, "Crusade for Conformity: The Ku Klux Klan in Texas, 1920-1930," *Texas Gulf Coast Historical Association* 6 (Aug., 1962): 17.

40. Wright, "Oldtime Black Houston Freedom Fighters Left Proud Legacy," *Forward Times,* Mar. 17, 1973.

41. John Mollenkopf, *The Contested City* (Princeton, N.J., 1983).

42. Feagin, *Free Enterprise City,* pp. 274-75.

43. Bullard, *Invisible Houston,* p. 121.

44. Richard Murray, "Houston: Politics of a Boomtown," *Dissent* 27 (1980): 503.

45. John Gilderbloom and Stella Capek, *Community versus Commodity: Tenants and the American City* (Albany, N.Y., 1992).

46. These are the arguments developed in Roger Friedland, *Power and Crisis in the City* (New York, 1982) and Mollenkopf, *Contested City.* For a comparative perspective that includes Western Europe, see Fisher, "Urban Sunbelt in Comparative Perspective."

47. Bullard, *Invisible Houston,* p. 23.

48. Robert V. Haynes, "Black Houstonians and the White Democratic Party, 1920-1945," in Francisco A. Rosales and Barry Kaplan, eds., *Houston: A Twentieth Century Urban Frontier* (Port Washington, N.Y., 1983), reprinted in this volume; Merline Pitre, "Lulu White and the Civil Rights Movement in Texas, 1943-1949" (Paper presented at the American Historical Association meeting, San Francisco, 1989). See also James SoRelle, "The Darker Side of Heaven: The Black Community in Houston, Texas, 1917-1945," (Ph.D. diss., Kent State University, 1980).

49. Moses Leroy says the Wallace rally was the "first integrated political rally in the South" and opened up southern politics to black participation. See Thomas Wright, "Oldtime Black Houston Freedom Fighters Left Proud Legacy," *Forward Times,* Mar. 17, 1973. That the Wallace campaign through the South had this impact is supported by Richard J. Walton, *Henry Wallace, Harry Truman, and The Cold War* (New York, 1976), p. 170. Moreover, emphasizing continued militance after the war, in 1946 Anne Pittmann of the Houston NAACP advised Moses Leroy, newly reelected to the executive board, to "be thinking of what can be done to make our Branch more militant." See letter, Anne Pittmann to Moses Leroy, Nov. 26, 1946, Moses Leroy MSS, Box 1, Folder 1, Houston Metropolitan Research Center.

50. Carleton, *Red Scare,* is the best account available on the cold war in Houston.

51. Alwyn Barr, *Black Texans: A History of the Negro in Texas, 1528-1971* (Austin, 1973), pp. 182-85.

52. Among other sources, see Barr, *Black Texans,* pp. 173-84, and Davidson, *Biracial Politics: Conflict and Coalition in the Metropolitan South* (Baton Rouge, 1972).

53. David McComb, *Houston: A History* (Austin, 1981), pp. 164-69.

54. See F. Kenneth Jensen, "The Houston Sit-Ins of 1960-1961," this volume.

55. Student papers in my social movements course at the University of Houston, Downtown, based primarily on local newspapers and student newspapers at local universities, studied in detail both the rebellion and the police response.

56. William McCord et al., *Life Styles in the Black Ghetto* (New York, 1969), p. 80.

57. "Texas: The Stocky Generation," *Newsweek* 49, no. 22 (May 29, 1967), p. 24.

58. "Houston on the Verge of a Black Explosion," *Voice of Hope* 18 (Apr., 1970), p. 2.

59. F. Kenneth Jensen, "Houston Sit-Ins," p. 19. It is often remarked that despite Houston's large black population, the Southern Christian Leadership Conference (SCLC) never came to Houston.

60. Saul Friedman, "Houston, A Backwater of the Revolt," *Texas Observer* (Nov. 15, 1963), p. 8.

61. Ralph Cooper, "Comments: Black Problems in Houston," *Voice of Hope* (June, 1970), p. 5.

62. Welch quoted in *Houston Chronicle,* May 28, 1964.

63. Susan S. Fainstein and Norman I. Fainstein, "Economic Restructuring and the Rise of Urban Social Movements," *Urban Affairs Quarterly* 21 (Dec., 1985): 192.

64. Sidney Tarrow, *Struggling to Reform: Social Movements and Policy Change during Cycles of Protest* (Ithaca, N.Y.: Cornell Studies in International Affairs, Occasional Paper no. 15), p. 3, suggests that "political opportunity structure," a term adapted from Peter Eisinger, includes three elements: "(1) the openness or closure of formal political institutions; (2) the stability or instability of political alignments within the political system; and (3) the availability and strategic posture of support groups."

65. Fainstein and Fainstein, "Economic Restructuring," p. 192.

66. Piven and Cloward, *New Class War.*

67. Editorial, *Voice of Hope,* Apr. 25, 1970.

68. "Some Houston Firms Quietly Desegregate," the *Informer,* Sept. 3, 1960; Bob Dundas, interview with Russell Simmons, Spring, 1989, transcript in author's possession. The notice in the black newspaper, the *Informer,* was a very small item, appearing two days after the event and not on page one.

69. Of course, the moderation thesis has some serious limitations. As black militancy escalated in the late 1960s and into 1970, Houston's public response, in the form of Police Chief Herman Short, was anything but moderate. And even earlier—for example, when elite-backed mayor Roy Hofheinz decided to try to increase the telephone company's taxes to help pay for needed city services—Houston's business leaders turned their backs on him and "called upon their old allies, Oscar Holcombe and the press, to defeat him." Kenneth Gray, *A Report on the Politics of Houston* (Cambridge, Mass., 1960) V-11 [page numbers from original manuscript].

70. Barry Kaplan, "Houston: The Golden Buckle of the Sunbelt," in Richard Bernard and Bradley Rice, eds., *Sunbelt Cities* (Austin, 1983).

71. See Feagin, *Free Enterprise City,* for additional sources and discussion on Houston power structure.

72. Joe Feagin and Beth Ann Shelton, "Community Organizing in Houston: Social Problems and Community Response," *Community Development Journal* 20 (1985): 99–105; Robert Fisher, "Urban Policy in Houston," *Urban Studies* 26 (1989): 144–54; Fisher, "A Typology of Community Organizing Practice."

73. See, for example, Carleton, *Red Scare.*
74. Ibid; Fisher, "Where Seldom Is Heard a Discouraging Word."
75. For a beginning examination of social contestation that compares Houston and sunbelt cities to more "liberal" and West European cities, see Fisher, "Urban Sunbelt in Comparative Perspective."
76. Gray, "A Report on the Politics of Houston," p. V-10.
77. Davidson, *Biracial Politics,* p. 138.
78. Davidson, *Biracial Politics,* p. 141.
79. The relationship between laissez-faire ideology and social movement challenges is discussed best in Piven and Cloward, *The New Class War.*
80. Davidson, *Biracial Politics,* p. 141.
81. James W. Button, *Blacks and Social Change: Impact of the Civil Rights Movement in Southern Communities* (Princeton, N.J., 1989), pp. 24, 215, 222–23.
82. The focus here is on blacks, but the process described herein vis-a-vis the public sector and community mobilization is appropriate as well for Hispanics, though to a lesser extent, given their smaller population in the city. See Arnoldo DeLeon, *Ethnicity in the Sunbelt: A History of Mexican Americans in Houston* (Houston, 1989).
83. Davidson, *Biracial Politics,* p. 121, notes that in 1960 there were 39 black police officers out of more than 1,000 officers working for the Houston Police Department. By 1970 the actual percentage had declined from 3.9 percent to 3.2 percent (53 black officers out of 1,654).
84. Bullard, *Invisible Houston,* pp. 124–25.
85. Davidson, *Biracial Politics,* p. 122, notes that in 1968 some 30 percent of teachers in HISD were black, owing to the heavy reliance on black teachers in black schools.
86. Button, *Blacks and Social Change,* p. 226.
87. Button, *Blacks and Social Change,* pp. 233–34.
88. Bullard, *Invisible Houston,* p. 136.
89. Increasingly, however, as more black and Hispanic candidates and factions emerge, unity is harder to achieve.
90. Feagin, *Free Enterprise City;* Albert Schaffer, "The Houston Growth Coalition in 'Boom' and 'Bust,'" *Journal of Urban Affairs* 11 (1989): 21–38.
91. Susan MacManus, *Federal Aid to Houston* (Washington, D.C., 1983), p. 6.
92. For critiques of problems other than those quality-of-life concerns raised by the business community, see Duncan Cormie, "We in Texas Ought to Be Putting People First," *Houston Chronicle,* Apr. 19, 1989; Robert Fisher, "Houston Is Moving to the Left," *Houston Chronicle,* Jan. 24, 1988; Robert Fisher and William Buffum, "Houston Should Bring Its Ills to a 'Social Roundtable,'" *Houston Chronicle,* Apr. 30, 1989.
93. Stephen Klineberg quoted in Robert Fisher and William Buffum, "Houston Should Bring Its Ills to a 'Social Roundtable,'" *Houston Chronicle,* Apr. 30, 1989.
94. Robert Warren, "National Urban Policy and the Local State: Paradoxes of Meaning, Action, and Consequences," *Urban Affairs Quarterly,* forthcoming.
95. Fisher, "Where Seldom Is Heard a Discouraging Word."
96. On neo-Alinskyite efforts, see Fisher, *Let the People Decide,* pp. 142–53.

97. Geoffrey Rips, "Privatization: The Next Big Lucha," *Texas Observer* (Feb. 21, 1986), p. 13.

98. See, for example, "Hearings before the Subcommittee on Housing and Community Development of the Committee on Banking, Finance, and Urban Affairs, October 14, 1985," in *Public Housing Needs and Conditions in Houston* (Washington, D.C., 1986).

99. Lenwood Johnson lecture, University of Houston, Downtown, Apr. 22, 1986.

100. Susan Fainstein and Norman Fainstein, "The Racial Dimension in Urban Political Economy," *Urban Affairs Quarterly* 25 (Dec., 1989). Students in my U.S. history survey course conducted interviews on how Houston's neighborhoods have changed since the 1950s. While many affluent areas remained the same, bemoaning the absence of community and "small-town atmosphere" that disappeared with the economic boom of the 1960s and 1970s, the poor and racial ethnic communities seem to have been ravaged in the past fifteen years by mounting problems and fewer resources to address them.

About the Contributors

Howard Beeth, whose work is centered on southern history, is a member of the history department of Texas Southern University. His most recent research has appeared in *Southern Studies* and *Quaker History.*

Robert D. Bullard is a member of the department of sociology at the University of California, Riverside. A specialist in the politics of urban environmentalism, he is the author of several books, including *Dumping in Dixie: Race, Class, and Environmental Quality* (1990).

Barry A. Crouch, is professor of History at Gallaudet University in Washington, D.C. He is coauthor of *A Place of Their Own: Creating the Deaf Community in America* (1989) and author of *The Freedmen's Bureau and Black Texans* (1992).

Frances Dressman, a graduate student in the Public History Program at the University of Houston, is at work on a thesis about Gus Wortham, a twentieth-century businessman, philanthropist, and civic leader in the Bayou City.

Robert Fisher, on the faculty of the Graduate School of Social Work at the University of Houston, is the author of *Let the People Decide: Neighborhood Organizing in America* (1984; 2nd ed. forthcoming) and, with Joseph Kling, coeditor of *Mobilizing the Community: Local Politics in a Global Era* (forthcoming).

Lorenzo J. Greene (1899–1988), a lifelong member of the Association for the Study of Afro-American Life and History, earned his doctorate at Columbia University and taught for many years at Lincoln University in Missouri. He "retired" as head of his department there in 1971. His study, *The*

Negro in Colonial New England, 1620-1776, has gone through several editions since it originally appeared as a revised dissertation in 1942.

Cecile E. Harrison, who received her doctorate from the University of Texas, is a member of the Department of Sociology and Social Work at Texas Southern University. Her principal interests are urban and political sociology.

Tamara Miner Haygood received her Ph.D. in U.S. history from Rice University in 1983 and an M.D. in 1988 from the University of Texas in Houston. She currently is in residency in diagnostic radiology at the University of New Mexico in Albuquerque.

Robert V. Haynes, author of *A Night of Violence: The Houston Riot of 1917* (1976), as well as many other works, served as a professor of history and also in administrative posts at the University of Houston. He is presently vice president of academic affairs at Western Kentucky University in Bowling Green.

F. Kenneth Jensen (1943-88) received his doctorate in history from Notre Dame University. He spent most of his career in Houston as a member of the history department at Texas Southern University.

Alice K. Laine is a member of the Department of Social Sciences at the University of Houston-Downtown. Her chief interests are the sociology of inequality and the study of the future.

Merline Pitre is a member of the history department and dean of the College of Arts and Sciences at Texas Southern University. She is the author of several articles concerning the history of African Americans as well as *Through Many Dangers, Toils, and Snares: Black Leadership in Texas, 1868-1900* (1985).

Clifton F. Richardson, Sr., moved to Houston in 1911 after graduating from Bishop College in Marshall, Texas, where he majored in journalism. In Houston he founded two newspapers, the Houston *Informer* in 1919 and the Houston *Defender* in 1930. Both of these newspapers have survived, sustained by a black readership for decades. Prior to his sudden, unexpected death in 1939, Richardson was a leading activist in black Houston.

James M. SoRelle, who has written about African-American urban history in the twentieth century, received his doctorate from Kent State University and is a member of the department of history at Baylor University.

Cary D. Wintz has written several articles about urban Texas and is also the author of *Black Culture and the Harlem Renaissance* (1988). He is a member of the history department at Texas Southern University.

Index

(Italicized page numbers refer to illustrations)

A&P grocery stores, boycotts of, 226–27
Abernathy, Ralph, 232
ACORN, 269
Acres Homes, 237
Adams, Henry, 79
Adam Smith Institute, 254
Adkins, John, 157
Affirmative Action Division, Houston, 247
African Americans. *See* blacks
African Methodist Episcopal Church, 94
African Myths, 144, 148
Alamo, 4
Alexander, Charles, 260
Alexandra, Agnes, 64
Alfred, Barbara, 57
Alinsky, Saul, 269
Allen, Anna, 59
Allen, Augustus, 32
Allen, Earl, 224
Allen, John Kirby, 32
Allen, Martha, 57
Allen, Peter, 18
Allen, Richard: and biracial politics, 76–79; and black dock workers, 92; early career of, 74–75; and Gregory Institute, 25–26; and James G. Tracy, 76–79, 81; later career of, 79–81; legislative career of, 29, 77–78; personality of, 29, 81; and Republican party, 80, 157
Allen Parkway Village, 243–45, 269
Allred, James V., 200
Allwright, S. E., 206
American Baptist Missionary Association, 80
American Federation of Labor, 92

American Indians, 80
American Missionary Society, 25–26
American Mutual Benefit Association, 109
American Red Cross, 188
Ancient Free and Accepted Masons, 131
Ancient Order of Pilgrims, 131
Anderson, Allie, 123
Anderson, Emeline, 60
Andrews, R. L., 108
Andrue, J. D., 35, 41
"Antar of Araby" (Maude Cuney-Hare), 148, 152
Anthony, Harriet, 64
Antioch Baptist Church, 24–25, 27, 94, 129
apprenticeship laws, 56–57
Asian immigrants, 243–45
Association for the Study of Negro Life and History, 134, 136
associations, civic, 94–95, 131–32
Atkins, J. Alston, 197–99, 201, 202, 203, 204, 208
Atkins, Miriam, 139
Atkins, Mr., 140
Atlanta: black discontent in, 262; black education in, 97–98; black-owned businesses in, 94; black population of, 261; civil rights movement in, 157; protest movements in, 218, 262
auctions, slave, 43–44
Aury, Louis de, 14
Austin, Dean, 136
Austin, Moses, 14
Austin, Stephen F., 34
Austin, Tex., 14, 46, 220

281

Bagby Street, 24
Baker, William R., 47
Ballinger, William, 16
Banks, Mr. and Mrs. T. R., 136-37
Bannister, Calvin, 27
Baptist church, 94. *See also specific churches*
Barnes, Lucy, 40
Barnes, Milly, 59
Bayou City Bank, 76
Beaumont, Tex., 151
Bebee Tabernacle Colored Methodist Episcopal Church, 129
Beeth, Howard, 278
Bell, W. H., 200
Bell v. Hill, 200, 203
Bergin, J. W., 44
Bethel Baptist Church, 129
Bethlehem Negro Day Nursery, 133
Bexar County, Tex., 194, 200
Birmingham, Ala., 261, 262
Bishop College, 25, 96
Blackburn, John H., 205
Black History and the Historical Profession, 1915-1980 (Meier and Rudwick), 3
blacks: and beginning of free community in Houston, 19-27; businesses owned by, 92-94, 103-12, 125, 149, 165; and children, 56-59, 63, 65; and civil rights movement, 157-63, 172-73, 211-20, 223-24, 260-66; and community, 98-100, 135, 163-72; and crime, 20, 66, 168, 169-70; culture of, 131-32, 150, 165-66, 227-28; death rate of, 102, 130; demographics of, 13-14, 19-20, 21, 22-24, 88-89, 129, 164, 166-69; as dock workers in Houston, 93; and economic consciousness during segregation, 107-11; and the economy, 92-93, 103-12, 119-20, 138-39, 143, 147, 148, 149, 164-65, 168-69, 226-31, 233; employment of, 20-21, 24, 29, 75, 77, 91-92, 129, 133, 138, 139, 143, 147, 148, 151, 168-69; and families, 55-59, 65-66, 168; during the Great Depression, 107; historiography of, 3, 7-8, 67; history of, 5, 7, 145, 148; and labor unions, 16, 91-92; racial consciousness of, 107; and religion, 18, 24-25, 94, 129; social organizations of, 94-95; in Spanish Texas, 13-14; wages for, 75; and white-

blacks (*cont.*)
owned businesses, 93. *See also* education, black; women, black
Blacks Organized for Leadership Development, 171
Bledsoe, Harold, 145
B'nai B'rith, 214
Boozer, Miss, 146
Bordersville, 237-38
Boyce, J. H. M., 129
boycotts: of A&P grocery stores, 226-27; against Burger King, 227; and Houston's sit-in movement, 215-16; of streetcars, 118
Boynton Chapel Methodist Episcopal Church, 129
Breed, Henry C., 15
Bright, M. H., 130
Brisco, Andrew, 44
Britton, W. R., 123
Brooks, B. T., 176
Brooks, Dolores, 163
Brown, Julia, 65
Brown, Lee, 170
Brown, Mollie, 97
Brown, Mrs. R. V., 177
Brown, Washington, 58
Brownell, Blaine, 104
Brown's Chapel African Methodist Church, 129
Brown v. Board of Education, 212
Broyles, M. H., 157
Bryant, Ira B., 176
Bryant, Theodore E., 106
Buffalo Bayou, 32
Bullard, Robert D., 172, 261, 266, 278
Burdette, J. R., 129
Bureau of Refugees, Freedmen, and Abandoned Lands. *See* Freedmen's Bureau
Burger King, boycotts of, 227
Burlington, Edward, 57-58
Burr, J. M., 131
Busby, Mary, 56
businesses, black-owned, 92-94, 103-12, 125, 149, 165
Business Men's Luncheon Club, 109
Butler, J. B., 129
Butler, Stuart, 255
Button, James W., 266

Cabeza de Vaca expedition, 13
Cain, J. J., 74

Calloway, Cab, 187
Campbell, I. S., 25
Capshaw, Mrs. M. L., 19
Cardozo, Benjamin, 196
Caribbean: and slave trade, 33, 36
Carnegie, Andrew, 187
Carnegie-Myrdal study, 176
Carson, Harriet, 57-58
Carter, H. P., 130
Carvercrest, 237
Catholic church, 94. *See also* St. Nicholas Catholic Church
Central High School, 153-54
Chicago, 13, 226-27, 262
child labor, 63
children, black, 56-59, 63, 65. *See also* blacks; families, black; women, black
Chong, Wing, 107-108
Christian Methodist Episcopal Church, 94
"Cimbee's Ramblings" (Simeon B. Williams), 106, 107, 109, 122, 179, 184
Citizens' Relations Committee, 217-18
City Auditorium, 187
City Democratic Executive Committee of Houston, 158
City Directory of Houston, 120
City Railway Company, 76
civic associations, 94-95, 131-32
Civics for Houston, 128
Civil Rights Act of 1964, 224
civil rights movement, 157-63, 172-73, 211-20, 223-24, 260-66. *See also* desegregation
Civil War, 4, 19-20
Clark, Colonel, 19-20
Clark, William, 78
Clay Street, 24
Cleveland, Ohio, 13
Cloward, Richard, 264
Cockrell, J. L., 178
Coffee, Aaron, 16
Coleridge-Taylor Choral Club, 131-32
Collins, Freddie, 112
Colonel Mayfield's Weekly, 178
Colored Carnegie Library, 187-88
Colored Citizens Club, 124
Colored Citizens' Committee, 182
Colored Democratic Club, 27
Combs, W. A., 203
community: black, 98-100, 135, 163-72;

community (*cont.*)
empowerment of, 254-55; mobilization of, 257-59, 260-65, 266-70
Community Chest funds, 188
Conally, Ben C., 163
Condon, James, 196
Continental Bus Terminal, 217
Cooper, George, 63
Corpus Christi, Tex., 151, 220
Corsicana, Tex., 200
Cortes, Ernesto, 269
Cotton Screwmen's Association of Galveston, 152
Covington, B. J., 143-44
Covington, Ernestine Jessie, 132
Covington, Jesse, 143-44
Covington, Mr., 146
Crane, William C., 24-25
Creuzot, Percy, 169
crime, 20, 66, 168, 169-70. *See also* violence
Crouch, Barry, 29, 278
Cuba: and slave trade, 33
Cullinan, J. S., 130
Cullinan, John Halm, 131
culture, black, 131-32, 150, 165-66, 227-28
Cuney, Mr., 148, 152
Cuney, Norris Wright, 80, 92
Cuney-Hare, Maude, 148, 152
Cuney Homes, 90
Cut Rate Auto Line, 120
Cutrer, Lewis, 213, 216, 217

Dallas, Tex., 142, 200, 220
"Dallas," 4
Dallas *Express,* 197
Darden, William J., 38
Davidson, ———, 265, 266
Davis, Dr., 137
Davis, Edmund, 76, 79
Davis, Gladys, 146
Davis, Henry S., Jr., 205
Davis, Mr., 148
Davis, W. L., 194-95
Davis Hospital, 187
deaths, black, 102, 130
Defender, 100, 128, 197, 204
Delaney, Ida, 269
Democratic Harris County Rump Convention, 207
Democratic Party: and black politics, 27,

Democratic Party (*cont.*)
  192, 193-208; integration of, 212; in Texas during segregation, 87
demographics: and black deaths, 102, 130; of black communities, 13-14, 19-20, 21, 22-24, 88-89, 129, 164, 166-69; of Harris County, 38-41, 45; of Houston, 4, 38, 55, 135, 149, 236; of Methodists, 18; of slavery, 38-41, 45
Department of Housing and Urban Development, U.S., 238-39, 241, 242
Depression, Great, 107
De-Ro-Loc, 98, *99*
desegregation: of education, 213, 224; of employment, 218; in Houston, 157-63; and Operation Breadbasket, 226-31, 233; of public facilities, 213-18; residential, 164-65. *See also* civil rights movement; segregation
Detroit, 13, 96-98
DeWalt, Mr., 145, 147, 149, 150
DeWalt, O. P., 131, 178, 196
Dibble, Elias, 25-26
discrimination: in education, 160, 180-83; gender-based, 249-50; in housing, 245-51; life-style-based, 250; in the postal service, 141-42; and public transportation, 184-85. *See also* racism; segregation
Dorcas Home, 188
Douglass, Frederick, 193
Drake, William M., 110-11, 200, 203, 204
Dresel, Gustav, 34
Dressman, Frances, 278
Drucker, Peter, 253
drug abuse, 168
Du Bois, W. E. B., 54, 100, 106
Duer, C. T., 47
Dunbar High School, 149-50
Dunjee, Roscoe, 202
Durham, W. J., 205, 206

economy: black, 92-93, 103-12, 119-20, 138-39, 143, 147, 148, 149, 164-65, 168-69, 226-31, 233; of Galveston, 151; of Harris County, 34-36, 42, 43-44, 45, 48-49; of Houston, 3-4, 32, 43-44, 48-49; and racism, 226; of San Antonio, 139
education, black: desegregation of, 213, 224; Freedmen's Bureau and, 25-26; in Houston, 18-19, 25-27, 75, 94-98, 137,

education, black (*cont.*)
  143, 149-50, 153-54, 180-83; segregation of, 88, 94-98, 133, 160, 180-83
1840 Census of the Republic of Texas (White), 35
Eighth Annual Houston Area Survey, 268
elections: white primary in, 157-60, 172, 193-208, 211
Ellington, Duke, 187
emancipation, 19-27
Emancipation Day, 25
Emancipation Park, 25, 130, 187
Emancipation Park Association, 80-81
Emancipation Proclamation, 54
employment: of blacks, 20-21, 24, 29, 61-64, 75, 77, 91-92, 129, 133, 138, 139, 143, 147, 148, 151, 168-69; and desegregation, 218
Erma Hughes Business College, 216, 218
Europe, Eastern and Central, 253
Evans, R. D., 195, 202, 203
Ewing, J. R., 4
Exodus, 79-81

facilities, public, 133, 150, 186-88, 213-18
Fairchild, Thornton, 104
Fair Housing Act of 1968, 245
Fair Housing Division, 246-47, 248
Fair Housing Ordinance, 246
families, black, 55-59, 65-66, 168. *See also* blacks; children, black; women, black
Farnstein, Norman, 255, 263-65
Farnstein, Susan, 255, 263-65
Faubus, Orval, 212
Feagin, Joe R., 260
Fifteenth Amendment, 192-93, 195-97, 205
Fifth Ward: black Catholics in, 94; blacks in, 88, 164, 165, 237, 239; demographics of, 23; flight of money from, 164; Frenchtown in, 89; Kelly Courts in, 90; parks in, 133; schools in, 181, 182, 183; St. Elizabeth's Hospital in, 170; St. Nicholas Catholic Church in, 94
First Baptist Church, 25
First Ward, 23
Fisher, Robert, 172, 278
Fitch's Photography Studio, 108
Flash, Caroline, 57
Flowers, Maria, 59
Foley's department store, 163-64, 216, 217, 218, 264

Forde, Dr., 144, 146
Fornell, Wesley, 43
Fortson, Richard, 120, 121–22
Fort Worth, Tex., 142, 200
Forward Times, 219-20
Fourteenth Amendment, 27, 192–93, 195–97
Fourth Ward: blacks in, 22, 88, 164, 236–37, 239; Colored High School in, *132;* condition of, *246;* demographics of, 23; as economic center, 165; Emancipation Day celebrations in, 25; First Baptist Church in, 25; flight of money from, 164; Gregory Institute in, 25; jitney service in, 184; library facilities in, 88; parks in, 133; police brutality in, 161; public housing in, 242; racial violence in, 107–108; San Felipe Courts in, 90; segregation of, 24; Trinity Methodist Episcopal Church in, 18
Fox, Professor, 143
Franklin, N. A., 105
fraternal organizations, 94-95, 131
Frazier, E. Franklin, 103, 202
Freedmantown, 22, 91, 236
Freedmen's Aid Society, 22
Freedmen's Bureau: and black women, 59–64; and child labor, 63; and education, 25–26; and emancipation, 21, 29; and employment, 24, 61–64; and Gregory Institute, 75; protects black families, 55–59; and Richard Allen, 75; and rights, 67; role of, 54–55; and violence, 64–66
free market ideology, 259-60
Free School Bill, 75
Frenchtown, 89-90
Friedman, Saul, 262
Friends of SNCC, 224
Frierson, John M., 104
Frierson and Company, 120
Frosttown, 22

Galveston, Tex.: black economy of, 151; black education in, 153-54; black enclaves in, 152; desegregation of, 220; historiography of, 6; slaves in, 46
Gandhi, Mahatma, 212
Garner, John Nance, 204
Garvey, Marcus, 100
Gates, James, 214
Gathings, Joe, 137

Gentry, George, 60
George Street, 143
German Baptist Church, 25
Germany, 253
Gibson, G. W., 151–52, 153–54
Gibson, J. W., 153
Gonzales, Henry, 269
Good Hope Baptist Church, 204
Goodson, George S., 120
Gough, Ian, 258
Graham, Milly, 65
Grand United Order of Odd Fellows, 94, 131
Granger, Gordon, 19
Grant, John, 80
Grant's department store, 216, 217
Graves, Curtis, 159, 224
Graves, Lucinda, 61
Gray, Kenneth, 265
Gray, William F., 33
Grayson County, Tex., 200
Great Britain, 253, 254
Great Depression, 107
Gree, Will, 203
Greenback Party, 79
Greene, Lorenzo J.: on Association for the Study of Negro Life and History, 137–38; biographical information on, 134-35, 278; on black culture, 138–39, 150; on black economy, 138–39, 143, 147, 148, 149; on black education, 143, 149–50, 153; on black enclaves, 143, 152; on black history, 145, 147; on black mail carriers, 141–42; on black politics, 151; on business in Houston, 140; on Galveston, 151, 152; on Howard University, 143, 146–47; on Prairie View State College for Negroes, 136–37; on racism, 144, 145; on religion, 153; on Tennessee State University, 146
Greene, Thomasina, 136
Greensboro, N.C., 213
Gregg Street Presbyterian Church, 129
Gregory Elementary School, 180–81
Gregory Institute, 25–26, 75, 96
Griffith, G. W., 194–95
Grigsby, J. B., 196
Grigsby, James B., 109
Gross, Jerry, 57
Grovey, Richard Randolph, 112, 183, 198–99, 201, 204, 205

Grovey v. Townshend, 202, 203
Gulf Coast historiography, 6

HACH. *See* Housing Authority of the City of Houston
Hadley, T. B. J., 39, 44
Hamblin, Dony, 57
Hamblin, J. P., 217
Hampton, Carl, 262
Harlan, John Marshall, 193
Harmon, J. H., 92
Harmon, John, 138, 147
Harmon, Mrs. John, 138-39, 146
Harper Junior High School, 183
Harris, Va., 57-58
Harrisburg, Tex., 32
Harris County: black children in, 58-59; black education in, 75; black voters in, 200; demographics of, 38-41, 45; economy of, 34-36, 42, 43-44, 45, 48-49; foundation of, 32; free blacks in, 37; geography of, 32; landholding in, 40; railways in, 44-45; slavery in, 32-33, 34-49; and Texas independence, 34. *See also* Houston
Harris County Commissioners' Court, 37
Harris County Community Action Association, 225
Harris County Council of Organizations (HCCO), 160, 171, 217, 223-24
Harris County Democratic Executive Committee, 194-95
Harris County Hospital District, 170
Harris County Negro Democratic Club, 198-99
Harris County Republican Club, 25-27
Harrison, Cecile E., 172, 279
Harrison, E. L., 129, 130
Harrison, Stafford, *150*
Harroll, Alfred, 59
Hartridge, Dr., 65
Harvey, David, 256
Hasgett, Sidney, 204, 205
Hayes, Rutherford B., 192
Haygood, Tamara Miner, 29, 279
Haynes, Robert V., 172, 279
HCCO (Harris County Council of Organizations), 160, 171, 217, 223-24
health, black, 102, 130-31, 168, 170
Heard, Julia, 63
Henderson, James Pinckney, 37

Henig, Jeffrey R., 255
Henke and Pillot supermarket, 215
Herndon, C. C., 195
Hester, Rachel, 61
Hickman, Cynthia Ann, 57
Hicks, C. W., *110*
Hill, David, 64
Hill, Melissa, 66
Hill, Miss, 145
HISD. *See* Houston Independent School District
Hispanic Austin High School, 269
historiography: of blacks, 3, 67; of black women, 54-55; of Houston, 3-7; of Reconstruction, 74; of the South, 28-29
history, black, 5, 7, 145, 148
Hitler, Adolf, 203
Hofheinz, Roy, Sr., 212
Hogrobrooks, Holly, 214, 215
Holcombe, Oscar, 121, 179, 259
Holmes, George Washington, 59
Hope Development, 224
Hotel d'Afrique, 21-22
housing: in contemporary Houston, 236-51; desegregation of, 164-65; public, 238-45, 250-51, 259; segregation of, 20, 21-22, 88, 90-91, 129-30, 133, 143, 176
Housing Act of 1937, 239
Housing and Community Development Act of 1974, 238
Housing Authority of the City of Houston (HACH): and Allen Parkway Village, 243-45, 269; and black housing, 90; formation of, 239; and public housing, 239, 240, 241, 242
Houston, Charles, 202, 203
Houston: black economy of, 103-12, 138-39, 143, 149, 164-65, 168-69; black education in, 18-19, 25-27, 75, 94-98, 137, 143, 149-50, 153-54, 160, 180-83; black enclaves in, 88-90, 164-68, 225, 236-38; black experience in, 171-72; black leadership of, 171; community mobilization in, 255, 258-59, 260-65; condition of streets in 1930, 143; crime in, 20, 66, 168, 169-70; culture in, 6; demographics of, 4, 38, 55, 135, 149, 229, 236; desegregation of, 163-64, 212, 218, 220; dock workers in, *93*; economy of, 3-4, 32, 43-44, 48-49; foundation of, 32; free black community in, 19-27; historical over-

Houston (cont.)
  view, 13-14; historiography of, 3, 28-29; history of, 3-6; jitneys in, 116-25, 184-85; Ku Klux Klan in, 178; market solutions to problems of, 259-60; Operation Breadbasket in, 223; police brutality in, 160-61, 169-70, 177-78; protest movements in, 218-19, 224; public sector of, 266-70; race relations in, 151, 175-88; racial violence in, 160-63, 164, 172, 177-80, 184, 185, 194, 214, 215-16, 219, 224; record keeping in, 5-6; research in, 6-7; segregation in, 87-100, 118-19, 125, 135, 184-85, 186-88; sex discrimination in, 249-50; sit-ins in, 214-15, 216, 217-18; slavery in, 15-16, 29, 43-44, 45-49; zoning in, 260. *See also* Harris County; *specific wards*
Houston Baptist Academy (Houston College), 25
Houston Chamber of Commerce, 105, 180, 267-68
Houston Chronicle, 240
Houston Citizens Chamber of Commerce, 165
Houston City Attorney, 247-48
Houston City Council: and abolition of jitneys, 116; and free blacks, 17; and Riceville, 237; and San Felipe Line, 120-22, 123, 184; and segregation in transportation, 125, 185
Houston City Hall, 216-17
Houston College (Houston Baptist Academy), 25
Houston College for Negroes, 183
Houston Colored Commercial Club, 108-109
Houston Colored High School, 96, *132,* 181
Houston Colored Junior College, 96, 135, 183
Houston Electric Company, 117, 120-24
Houston Independent School District (HISD): black teachers in, 266; and desegregation, 163, 213, 224; and Hispanic Austin High School, 269; and Houston Colored Junior College, 183; and segregation, 94-98, 180, 181-82
Houston Junior College, 96
Houston Metropolitan Research Center, 6
Houston Negro Chamber of Commerce, 93, 109-11, 128

Houston Negro Chamber of Congress, 160
Houston Negro Hospital, 131
Houston Police Department, 169-70, 177-78, 225
Houston Post, 121, 124, 176, 239
Houston Public Library, 6, 187, 212
Houston Review, 6-7
Houston Sentinel, 131
Houston Social Service Bureau, 188
Houston Telegraph, 57
Houston: The Bayou City (McComb), 5
Howard University, 143, 146-47
HT Taxi Company, 119
Hubbard, A., 129
Hubbard, O. L., 178
Hubert, J. W., 130
Huggins, W. O., 199, 200
Hurst, Bishop, 147
Hutcheson, Joseph C., Jr., 196, 198

illiteracy, 96, 168
Independence Heights, 89, 133
Indian-Anglo wars, 4
Indians, American, 80
Informer: on black economic consciousness, 108; on black education, 182-83; on black jitneymen, 120; as black newspaper, 131; on black-owned businesses, 105, 106; and black suffrage, 198, 199, 203, 206; and black teachers, 160; on Colored Carnegie Library, 188; on Colored High School, 181; establishment of, 100; foundation of, 128; on Gregory Elementary School, 180-81; on *Grovey v. Townshend,* 202; on Houston Colored Commercial Club, 109; and Ku Klux Klan, 178; on "Negro Trade Week," 109; on race, 107, 175, 176, 180; on racial violence, 160-61, 163, 185, 216; and Robert Powell lynching, 179-80; on San Felipe Line, 184; on segregation, 119, 185, 186; selling of, 177; struggle for control of, 197
Institute for Economic Affairs, 254
Institute of Public History (University of Houston), 6

Jackson, Elvidge, 104
Jackson, Jesse, 226, 227, 232
Jackson, Newman, 63
Jackson, T. M., 129

Jack Yates High School, 133
James, Alice, 66
Jaworski, Leon, 217
Jefferson, Miss, 145, 146
Jefferson Davis County-City Hospital, 133
Jensen, F. Kenneth, 172, 262, 279
Jensen Drive, 165
Jim Crow. *See* segregation
jitneys, 116-25, 184-85
Johns, Mrs., 139, 143, 145
Johns, Vernon, 139
Johnson, A. J., 130
Johnson, Charles S., 185, 186
Johnson, Jack, 153
Johnson, Lenwood, 269
Johnson, Lyndon Baines, 213
Johnson, Rosa, 57
Johnson, W. L., D., 146
Johnson, Wash, 65-66
Johnson, Willis, 176
Johnson, Zenobia, 65-66
Jones, Bill, 145-46
Jones, E. L., 200
Jones, J. B., 213-14
Jones, Jesse, 259
Jones, Martha Yates, 99
Jordan, Barbara, 159, 224
Joske's department store, 218
Journal of Urban History, 5
Juneteenth, 98, 99
juvenile delinquency, 168

Kansas City, 116
Keene, Nellie, 61
Kelly Courts, 90
Kelly's Cafe, 186
Kennedy, John, 63
Kennerly, Judge, 203, 205, 206
Kiamata, 14-15
King, Coretta Scott, 232
King, Langston, 179
King, Lucy Ann, 66
King, Martin Luther, Jr., 212, 223, 226, 227, 232
King, Otis, 214, 215
King, Wesley, 66
Knights and Daughters of Tabor, 131
Knights of Labor, 91-92
Koch, Edward, 253
Kohl, Helmut, 253
Kress department store, 216, 217

Ku Klux Klan: activities of, 161, 177, 178, 260; and Felton Turner, 216; and Houston Police Department, 225
Kyle, W. J., 45

Lafitte, Jean, 14
Lagrone, Oliver, 136
Laine, Alice K., 172, 279
Lampkin, Daisy, 204
landholding and status, 40
Landy, Miss, 146
Lash, John, 219
Lawson, William, 224, 227, 229
Lebsock, Suzanne, 54
Lee, Bishop, 152
Lee, H. E., 130
Leroy, Moses, 260
Lewis, John, 56
Lincoln Theatre, 131
Linney, Michael, 64-65
Little Rock, Ark., 46, 212
Loew's State Theatre, 187
Long, James, 14-15
Long, Jane, 14-15
Longcope, Charles S., 22
Lord, America, 63
Louisiana, 194, 205-206
Love, Charles Norvell, 131, 158, 194-95, 197, 198, 204
Love, Henry, 27
Lovelady, Manilla, 112
Lovell, J. H., 129
Loyal Union League of America, 78
Loyal Union League of Texas, 78
Lubbock, Francis Richard, 40, 42
Lubbock, T. S., 45, 47
Lucas, Albert A., 204
Luizza, James E., 206
Lundy, Benjamin, 14
lynching, 179-80
Lyons, Ben, 63
Lyons Avenue, 165

McAskill, D. A., 194
McCall, H. C., 260
McComb, David G., 5, 44
McCoy, Homer E., 109
McDonald, Gladys, 139
McGruder, C. H., 130
McGruder, Mr., 147-48
McKinney Street, 24

MacManus, Susan, 267
Mading's drugstore, 214-15
Majestic Theatre, 187
Manning, O. K., 111
Mapie, J. C., 47
Marshall, Pluria, 227-29, 232, 233
Marshall, Thurgood, 158, 204, 205, 206
Martin, Dr., 146
Matthews, Emily, 65
Matthews, Emma, 65
Meier, August, 3
Memphis, Tenn., 261
Merrit, Ailsie, 58
Methodist church, 18-19, 94. *See also* specific churches
Metropolitan Organization (TMO), 269
Metropolitan Theatre, 187
Mexican Americans, 7-8, 139, 151
Midgley, James, 257
Midwest Journal, 134
migration. *See* demographics
Milam Street, 24, *150,* 177
Miller, W. E., 130
Mississippi, 193-94
Mitchel, Rachel, 107
Mollenkopf, John, 260
Montgomery, Ala., 157, 218, 262
Moody, A. S., 123-24
Moody, Dan, 179
Moon, Henry Lee, 145, 146, 147, 148, 152
Moore, Joe, 61
Morgan, James, 41-42
Morning Star, 36, 37, 44
Mosely, Dr. and Mrs., 151
Moton, Robert R., 129, 147
Mount Corinth Baptist Church, 129
Mullinax, Otto, 203
Murray, Richard, 261
Music Hall, 187
mutual aid societies, 94-95
Myrdal, Gunnar, 112

NAACP. *See* National Association for the Advancement of Colored People
Nabrit, Atkins, and Wesley (law firm), 197, 198, 200
Nabrit, James, 146, 197-99, 201, 204
Nabrit, S. M., 219
National Association for the Advancement of Colored People (NAACP): and black suffrage, 158, 159, 195-97, 199, 201; and

National Association for the Advancement of Colored People (NAACP) (*cont.*) black teachers, 160; and civil rights in Houston, 211-12, 223-24; and Clifton F. Richardson, 203-204; and *Grovey v. Townshend,* 202; growth of, 204, 207-208; and *Hasgett v. Werner,* 205-206; Houston chapter of, 128; membership drive by, 202-203; and Robert Powell lynching, 179; and school desegregation, 163, 212; use of black lawyers by, 202
National Black Media Coalition, 231, 233
National Business League, 129
National Labor Union (Colored), 91
National Negro Business League, 92, 108-109, 128
National Newspaper Publisher's Association, 197
National Urban League, 175-76
Native Americans, 80
Neal, Rachel, 60
Negro Democratic Club, 151
Negro Plays and Pageants, 152
"Negro Trade Week," 108-109
New Deal, 188
New Orleans, La., 94, 97-98
newspapers, black-owned, 131. *See also Defender; Informer; Texas Freeman*
Newton, Johnny Mae, 137, 140, 146
New York, N.Y., 94, 97-98, 253
Nixon, Lawrence A., 195-97
Nixon, Richard, 217
Nixon v. Condon, 199
Nolan, W. G., 63
No-Tsu-Oh, 98
"Nu Way" Cafe, 138

Oats, James W., 42
Oberholtzer, E. E., 182
Oberholtzer, Mr., 150
Odd Fellows, 138
Oklahoma, 195
Olmsted, Frederick Law, 43
Omaha, Neb., 116
Omni International Hospital, 170
Operation Breadbasket: assessment of, 233; confrontational activities of, 228-31; in Houston, 226-28; operation of, 226-27, 231-33
Operation PUSH (People United to Save Humanity), 232

Orange, Tex., 151
Orgen Barber Shop, 105
Orphan Society, 59
Our Mother of Mercy Catholic Church, 94
Our Mother of Mercy School, 183

Page, Lavinia, 56
Palace Theatre, 187
Palmerston, Lord, 36
Parker, Clara, 57
Parker, H. C., 39
Parker, Selina, 64-65
Pasadena, Tex., 242
Payne, Sam, *110*
Peach Point Plantation, 15
Peacock, Dr., 137
Pease, W. B., 60
Pease Street, 24
People's Party II, 164
Perry, James, 15
Philadelphia, 226
Phillips, Earl, 269
Phillips, Wendell, 151-52
Phyllis Wheatley High School, 149-50
Pickens, William, 202
picketing, 216
Pierce, Alexander, 57
Pilgrim's Life Insurance Company, 138
Pilgrim Temple, 141
Pitre, Merline, 29, 279
Piven, Frances Fox, 264
plantations, 15
Pleasant, S. A., 129, 139, 143
Plessy v. *Ferguson*, 193, 212
Poe, John, 136, 137, 138, 143, 145, 146, 147, 148, 154
police brutality, 169-70
politics, black: and desegregation, 158-60; in the 1960s, *225;* since the 1960s, 267; in 1930, 151; during Reconstruction, 27, 29, 74-81; during segregation, 87, 193-208; since World War II, 170-71, 172, 212, 267
poll tax, 211. *See also* suffrage; white primary
Pope, Ned, 139
Porras, Charles, 195
Port Arthur, Tex., 151
Porter, L. G., 129
Postal Employees Alliance, 141-42
Postal Service, U.S., 141-42

Potter, David M., 28
poverty, 60-61, 250-51
Powell, Robert, 161, 163, 178-80
Prairie Street, 24, 177
Prairie View State College for Negroes, 136-37
pregnancy, 60, 168
primary, white, 157-60, 172, 193-208, 211
The Private City (Warner), 253-54
privatization, 253-65
Progressive Party, 261
Progressive Youth Association (P.Y.A.), 216, 218, 224
Property Owners Association of Houston, 259-60
prostitution, 64
public facilities, 133, 150, 186-88, 213-18
public housing, 238-45, 250-51, 259
public transportation, 88, 116-25, 184-85
Pullum, N. P., 92
P.Y.A. *See* Progressive Youth Association

race relations, 151, 175-88
racial discrimination. *See* discrimination; racism; segregation
racial violence: during civil rights movement, 261-62, *263;* Friends of SNCC and, 224; in Houston, 160-63, 164, 172, 177-80, 184, 185, 194, 214, 215-16, 219, 224; during Reconstruction, 64-65; during segregation, 107-108, 117-19, 160-63; during sit-ins, 214, 215-16. *See also* violence
racism, 3, 7, 144, 145, 171-72, 176-77, 226. *See also* discrimination; segregation
railroads, 44-45
ranching, 37-38, 47-48
rape, 66
Reconstruction, 4, 74, 77
Red Book of Houston, 98-99
Red Star Line, 120
Reed, Stanley, 207
Reese, Johnny, 120
Reeves, Mr., 136
religion, 18, 24-25, 94, 129
Republican Country Club, 76
Republican Party, 27, 77-79, 192
Retail Merchants Association, 217
Reynolds, Joseph J., 76
Rice, C. W., 148, 151
Rice, William Marsh, 216

290   INDEX

Rice Institute, 216
Rice University, 5–6, 216
Riceville, 237
Richardson, Clifton F.: biographical information on, 100, 128, 279; and black economy, 92–93, 105–106, 109; on black education, 182; and black-owned businesses, 106–107, 111; and black suffrage, 122, 198, 203; death of, 204; as editor of *Informer,* 131; and Houston Colored Commercial Club, 108, 109; and Houston Negro Hospital, 130; on jitneys, 119, 122–23, 124; and Ku Klux Klan, 161, 178; and the NAACP, 203–204; and the Safety Loan and Brokerage Company, 197; and segregation in transportation, 185; and white primary, 158
Richardson, Clifton F., Jr., 204, 205
Riordan, Edward, 43
rioting, 161, *162,* 172, 194, 261–62
River Oaks, 125, 185
Riverside, 164
Riverside General Hospital, 170
Riverside National Bank, 165, 168–69
Roberts, Owen, 201–202
Robey, Ella, 140
Robinson, Judson, *95,* 160, 267
Robinson, Martha Sneed, *95*
Robinson, Mr., 148
Roemer, Ferdinand, 43
Roett, Dr., 144–45, 146, 148
Rogers, Mary, 60
Rose, Pleasant W., 33, 35
Rose, Willie Lee, 55, 67
Rosenberg, Harry, 153
Rosenwald, Julius, 147
Rudwick, Elliott M., 3
Runaway Scrape, 34
Runnels, O. A., 58
The Rural Negro, 137
Russell, Elenora, 217
Russell, Frank, 217
Ryan, Professor, 141

Safety Loan and Brokerage Company, 197
St. Elizabeth's Hospital, 170
St. John Baptist Church, 94, 129
St. Nicholas Catholic Church, 94, 129
St. Nicholas School, 183
Sam Houston Coliseum, 187
San Antonio, Tex.: blacks in, 13, 139, 142,

San Antonio, Tex. *(cont.)*
200; desegregation of, 220; jitneys in, 116
San Antonio *Express,* 197
Sanders, L. J., 129
San Felipe Auto Repair, 120
San Felipe Courts, 90–91
San Felipe Jitney Association, 120
San Felipe Line, 116, 120–22, 123, 125, 184
San Felipe Street, 24, 25, 88, 161, 165
Santa Anna, Antonio López de, 32, 34
Santa Monica, 261
Sante Fe, N. Mex., 143
Scanlan, Thomas H., 27, 76
Schappert, Carl, 129
SCLC. *See* Southern Christian Leadership Conference
Scott, Emmett J., 187
Scott, J. S., 130
Scott, James, 35, 41
Scott, Mrs., 137
Scott, W. E., 142
Second Ward, 22, 23
Section 8 Rental Assistance Program, 238–39
segregation: black response to, 103; and economic benefits for blacks, 104; in education, 88, 94–98, 133, 160, 180–83; in Galveston, 152; of housing, 20, 21–22, 88, 90–91, 129–30, 133, 143, 176; patterns of, 175–76; of public facilities, 186–88; of public transportation, 88, 118–19, 125; violence during, 107–108, 117–19, 160–63. *See also* discrimination; racism
Sellers, Mary, 63
Sentinel, 179
Sessuns, Wash, 59
Shadoner, Dr., 148, 149
Shea, Mary E., 63
Sheridan, Francis, 36
Shreveport, La., 46
Simpson, L. H., 212
sit-ins, 211, 213–20, 224. *See also* civil rights movement
Sixth Ward, 24
slavery: in Austin, 14; demographics of, 38–41, 45; in Harris County, 32–33, 34–49; in Houston, 14–19, 29; in Mexican Texas, 14, 33–34; in Spanish Texas, 13–14; outside Texas, 46–47; in Virginia, 144
Small Business Administration, 233
Smith, ———, 138

Smith, Ashbel, 41
Smith, Julius, 205
Smith, Lonnie E., 158, 204, 205, 206, 223
Smith, Mrs. P. O., 132
Smith, Peter, 66
Smith v. Allwright, 158–59, 207, 211–12
Snowball, James, 27
social clubs, 94–95
Social Service Bureau, 133
Sojourner, C. B., 62–63
SoRelle, James, 172, 279
the South, 7, 28, 77, 143
Southern, Mr., 136–37
Southern Christian Leadership Conference (SCLC): Houston branch of, 224; Houston chapter of, 227; and Operation Breadbasket, 223, 226, 228, 232, 233
Southern Pacific Railroad, 89
Soviet Union, 260
Spears, Charles, 44
Spivey, L. H., *110*
Spring Branch, 242
Standard Bank and Trust Company, 147
Standard Life Insurance Company, 147
Standard Savings Association, 165
Stanley, L. C., 41, 45–46
Starr, Paul, 253, 255
Stearnes, Eldrewey, 216, 217, 218
Stevens, Julianna, 60
Stiles, W. W., 38
Stocks, Gilbert T., 131
Straight-Out ticket, 79
streetcars, 116–18
Strickland, Arvarh E., 136
students, protest by, 213–20
suffrage, black: Clifton F. Richardson and, 122, 198, 203; *Informer* on, 198, 199, 203, 206; and jitneys, 122–23; NAACP and, 158, 159, 195–97, 199, 201; struggle over, 192–208; Supreme Court and, 193, 195–97, 201–202, 206–207. *See also* white primary
Sullivan, Leon, 226
Supreme Court, U.S.: and black suffrage, 193, 195–97, 201–202, 206–207; and *Brown v. Board of Education*, 212; and *Grovey v. Townshend*, 203; and school desegregation, 224; and *Smith v. Allwright*, 211–12; and *Sweatt v. Painter*, 212; and *United States v. Classic*, 205–206; and white primary, 211–12, 223

Sweatt, Erma, 95
Sweatt, Heman, 95, 224
Sweatt v. Painter, 212

Talbot, Hannah, 55–56
Tanks, Adeline, 65
Tanks, Levi, 65
Tarrow, Sidney, 264–65
Taylor, Hobart, Sr., 104, 109
teachers, black, 147, 266
Teal, A. C., 177–78
Telegraph, 76, 78
Telegraph and Texas Register, 39
Tennessee State University, 146
Terrell election laws, 194, 211
Terry, Frank, 45
Texarkana, Tex., 200
Texas Freeman, 131, 179, 197
Texas Independent Veteran Bill, 75
Texas Observer, 262
Texas People's Coalition, 231
Texas Rangers, 4
Texas Southern University (TSU): and black culture, 165–66; demonstration at, 263; foundation of, 96, 102, 183; and Houston historiography, 6; and Operation Breadbasket, 233; and Progressive Youth Association, 216; racial violence at, 164; and sit-ins, 163, 213, 218, 219, 224; and student movements, 227, 261–62
Texas State University for Negroes, 102
Texas Supreme Court, 200, 203
Texas Welfare Rights Organization, 231
Thatcher, Margaret, 253
Third Ward: blacks in, 22, 88, 164, 183, 237, 239; as business and cultural center, 165–66; Cuney Homes in, 90; demographics of, 23; education in, 183; Emancipation Park in, 25, 130, 187; Houston College in, 25; Houston Colored Junior College in, 96; Houston Negro Hospital in, 131; Operation Breadbasket headquarters in, 228; racial violence in, 164; Riverside General Hospital in, 170; St. John Baptist Church in, 94
Third Ward Civic Club, 198
Thomas, Jesse O., 175, 176
Thompson, Senfronia, 101
Tijerina, Felix, 217
TMO (Metropolitan Organization), 269
Touraine, Alain, 256–57

Townshend, Albert, 201
Tracy, James G., 76-79, 81
transportation, public, 88, 116-25, 184-85
Traveler's Aid, 188
Travis Street, 24
Trinity Methodist Episcopal Church, 18, 24, 25, 94, 129, *150*
Tri-Weekly Telegraph, 19, 20
trolleys, 116-18
TSU. *See* Texas Southern University
Tucker, C. B., 39
Turner, Felton, 215-16, 219
Turner, G. B. M., 120
Tyler, Tex., 200

Union, 74, 76
unions, 16, 91-92
Union Station, 218
Union Station Auto Transfer Company, 120
United Brothers of Friendship and Sisters of the Mysterious Ten, 131
United Farm Workers, 229
United States v. *Classic,* 205-206
United States v. *Reese,* 193
Unity Bank, 169
University of Houston, 5-6, 261
University of Texas, 5, *95,* 212, 224
Urban League, 111
U.S. Postal Service, 141-42
U.S. Supreme Court. *See* Supreme Court, U.S.

Vick, Mary, 63
Vinegar Hill, 22, 24
violence: against women and children, 64-66; in workplace, 64-65. *See also* racial violence
Virginia, 144
Voice of Hope, 224, 262, 264

Waco, 142
Wade, Richard, 29
wages, 75
Walgreen's drugstore, 215, 216, 217
Walker, W. B., 39
Wallace, Henry, 261
Waller, Fats, 187
Walls, Mr., 140, 141-43
Ward, R. H., 178
Warner, Sam Bass, Jr., 253-54
Warren, Robert, 268

Washington, Booker T., 100, 187
Washington, Tina, 61
Washington Avenue, 161
Washington High School, 133
Watergate, 217
Waugh, T. L., 121
Webster, George H., 197
Webster, Mr., 140
Webster, Mrs., 149
Webster-Richardson Publishing Company, 131, 197
Weingarten, Jack, 214
Weingarten, Joseph, 213
Weingarten's grocery, 163, 213-15
Welch, Louie, *225, 259, 263*
Werner, Theodore, 205
Wesley, Carter: on black doctors, 112; and Clifton F. Richardson, 204; and *Grovey* v. *Townshend,* 201, 202, 203; and Houston Negro Chamber of Commerce, 110-11; and *Informer,* 106, 128, 197-99, 205; and Lorenzo Greene, 139, 140, 143, 146, 149; and NAACP, 208; and *Smith* v. *Allwright,* 206-207
Wesley Memorial African Methodist Episcopal Church, 129
West, Rachelle, 63
Westbury, 242
West Dallas Street, 165
West End Transfer Company, 120
Wheeler, Malinda, 60
White, Gifford, 35
White, Hattie Mae, 158
White, Julius, 178, 197, 198, 199, 200, 203, 206
White, Lulu, 204
White, Mr., 139
White, Mrs. Charles, 224
White, Walter, 202, 204, 206
white primary, 157-60, 172, 193-208, 211. *See also* suffrage
White Swan Barber Shop, 105
Whiting, Louisa, 59
Whitmire, Kathy, 171, 269
Wickliff, A. M., 217
Wiley College, 96
Wilkey, ———, 136
Williams, Adeline, 65
Williams, Albert, 66
Williams, Andrew Johnson, 65
Williams, Beneva, 163

Williams, Dollina, 65
Williams, Octavia, 59
Williams, Simeon B., 106, 122, 179, 197
Wintz, Cary D., 280
women, black: and black men, 59-60; employment of, 61-64; and Freedmen's Bureau, 60-61; historiography of, 54-55; and pregnancy, 60, 168; and prostitution, 64; and racism, 144; and rape, 66; during Reconstruction, 29, 66-67; violence against, 64-66. *See also* blacks; families, black; slavery
Wood, W. E., 121
Woodall, Durke, 60
Woodson, Carter G., 134, 136, 137, 139-40, 145, 154
Woodson, Mrs., 141
Woolworth, 215, 216, 217
Wooster, Ralph, 38
Wooten, Doris B., 131
Workman, Mrs., 149
workplace violence, 64-65
Wren, Dinah, 65
Wren, Rebecca, 65

Yates, Jack, 25, *26,* 96
Yates, Pinkie, *99, 132*
Yellow Cabs, 104
Young Men's Christian Association (YMCA), 100, 131
Young Women's Christian Association (YWCA), 131, 139, 188

Black Dixie was composed into type on a Compugraphic digital phototypesetter in ten point Times Roman with two points of spacing between the lines. Permanent was selected for display. The book was designed by Jim Billingsley, typeset by Metricomp, Inc., printed offset by Thomson-Shore, Inc., and bound by John H. Dekker & Sons, Inc. The paper on which this book is printed carries acid-free characteristics for an effective life of at least three hundred years.

TEXAS A&M UNIVERSITY PRESS : COLLEGE STATION

www.ingramcontent.com/pod-product-compliance
Lightning Source LLC
Chambersburg PA
CBHW031234290426
44109CB00012B/294